FOO

A JAPANESE-AMERICAN PRISONER

OF THE RISING SUN

War and the Southwest Series

Number 1

FOREWORD AND NOTES

BY STANLEY L. FAULK

INTRODUCTION BY ROBERT WEAR

University of North Texas Press

Denton, Texas

A Japanese-American Prisoner

of the Rising Sun

The Secret Prison Diary of Frank "Foo" Fujita

Grateful acknowledgment is made
to the following news sources for
permission to reprint previously
published material:
Abilene Reporter-News, Abilene, Texas
The Associated Press
Electra Star-News Publishing Company,
    Electra, Texas
Fort Worth Star-Telegram,
    Fort Worth, Texas
The New York Times Company.
    © 1955. Reprinted by permission.

General Series Editors for
War and the Southwest
    Richard G. Lowe
    Gustav L. Seligmann
    Calvin Christman

The paper in this book meets the
minimum requirements of the American
National Standard for Permanence of
paper for Printed Library Materials,
z39.48-1984.

Library of Congress
Cataloging-in-Publication Data
Fujita, Frank, 1921–
FOO, A Japanese-American prisoner
of the rising sun : the secret prison diary
of Frank "Foo" Fujita / foreword by
Stanley L. Falk ; introduction by
Robert Wear.
p. cm.—(No. 1 in the War and the
Southwest series)
Includes bibliographical references
and index.
ISBN 0-929398-46-7
1. Fujita, Frank, 1921–   2. World
War, 1939–1945—Prisoners and prisons,
Japanese.   3. World War, 1939–1945—
Personal narratives, American.
4. World War, 1939–1945—
Participation, Japanese-American.
5. Prisoners of war—Japan—Biography.
6. Prisoners of war—United States—
Biography. I. Title.   II. Series: War
and the Southwest series ; no. 1.
D805.J3F85 1993
940.54'7652'092—dc20
[B] 92-36893
CIP

10 9 8 7 6 5 4 3 2 1

CONTENTS

Foreword by Stanley L. Falk ix

Chronology xiii

Introduction xv

CHAPTER ONE

Foo Joins the Texas National Guard : 1938–1941 1

CHAPTER TWO

The 2d Battalion Sails for "The Plum":

1941–1942 33

CHAPTER THREE

Java Falls to the Japanese: January 1942–

March 1942 57

CHAPTER FOUR

Foo Becomes a POW: Jaarmarkt and

"Bicycle Camp": March 1942–October 1942 85

CHAPTER FIVE

Singapore and Fukuoka Camp in Nagasaki, Japan:

October 1942–February 1943 113

CHAPTER SIX

Labor in the Shipyards: February 1943–May 1943 137

CHAPTER SEVEN

Guard Discovers Foo's Japanese Heritage:

June 1943–July 1943 155

CHAPTER EIGHT

Foo Beaten, Dutchmen Tortured: July 1943–

October 1943   169

CHAPTER NINE

Camp Routines at Omori and Bunker Hill:

October 1943–December 1943   187

CHAPTER TEN

Bunker Hill Boys Broadcast: December 1943–

June 1944   209

CHAPTER ELEVEN

Bombing Raids, *Benjo Honcho* Plans Escape:

June 1944–January 1945   231

CHAPTER TWELVE

Fire Bombings of Tokyo: February 1945–

May 1945   257

CHAPTER THIRTEEN

Night of Ethyl/Methyl Alcohol: May 1945–

July 1945   277

CHAPTER FOURTEEN

Japan Surrenders: August 1945   297

CHAPTER FIFTEEN

Okinawa, Alabang, Reunions with Old Friends,

Home: September 1945   317

CHAPTER SIXTEEN

Tacoma to Texas: September 1945–February 1946   335

CHAPTER SEVENTEEN

Epilogue   351

Index   361

LOST BATTALION

Drawn by Frank "Foo" Fujita in Jaarmarkt POW Camp, Soerabaja, Java, May 1942

• FOREWORD

When Japanese planes attacked Pearl Harbor on December 7, 1941, an American convoy of seven ships escorted by the heavy cruiser *Pensacola* and the sub-chaser *Niagara* was at sea in the mid-Pacific with ground and air reinforcements for the Philippines. To escape Japanese interception, the convoy was diverted to Australia and reached Brisbane three days before Christmas. Among its passengers was Sgt. Frank Fujita, Jr., son of a Japanese father and an American mother, and a member of a recently mobilized Texas National Guard field artillery battalion. In mid-January 1942, Fujita's battalion was sent to Java, in the Netherlands' East Indies, as part of a hastily organized Allied force preparing to meet an expected Japanese invasion. Sadly, however, the Java defenders were overwhelmed by superior Japanese army units and forced to surrender on March 8. Three months after the start of the war, twenty-year-old Frank Fujita, Jr., and his fellow Texans became prisoners of the Japanese, doomed to nearly three and one-half years of cruel incarceration.

Of the nearly 550 members of Fujita's battalion, only 300 survived their wartime captivity. Their experience matched that of other Allied soldiers and sailors captured by the Japanese during WW II and held in prison camps throughout Japanese-occupied territories and in Japan itself. Locked in a barbarous purgatory that callously defied the normal rules and customs of war, prisoners of the Japanese were subject to brutality, starvation, mental and physical abuse, and cold-blooded murder. They suffered on appalling "death marches" and "death ships," were forced to perform heavy labor under harrowing conditions, were denied food, water, and medical care, underwent systematic beatings, torture, and other forms of gross physical punishment, and fell victim to arbitrary execution by bullet, bayonet, sword, or medical experimentation. Of the nearly twenty-six thousand Americans captured by the Japanese, almost eleven thousand died before they could be rescued by liberating Allied forces. Those who survived would bear forever the physical and mental scars of their excruciating incarceration.

A good number of these former prisoners of war have written about their experiences with varying degrees of skill and perception. In general, they project a pattern of captivity with which students of WW II have come to be familiar. Occasionally, however, a memoir offers a fresh perspective, a unique circumstance, or a facet of POW existence absent from other personal accounts. Frank Fujita's memoir is a welcome addition to this literature because it describes an unusual type of POW experience. Fujita's wartime incarceration was as cruel and agonizing as that of any other Japanese prisoner, and he suffered no less than others in the brutal hands of his captors. Yet his memoir—based on a carefully maintained and hidden diary—is unique on several accounts.

First of all, while roughly six thousand Japanese-Americans saw military service in the war against Japan—primarily as interpreters and translators, but frequently in duties involving great danger—only two were captured by the Japanese: Fujita on Java and Richard Sakakida in the Philippines. For Japanese-Americans capture always involved the implicit threat of torture and execution as alleged traitors to Japan, and both Fujita and Sakakida suffered for their ancestry. The latter was an army linguist, whereas Fujita, who did not speak Japanese, was an artilleryman, the only Japanese-American combat soldier taken prisoner by the Japanese. Sakakida was in particular danger because of his work in army intelligence, but Fujita was also subject to special attention, not the least because he had killed Japanese soldiers in battle. In the end, both men managed to outwit their captors and defeat them in their purposes. Each displayed a rare blend of courage and imagination and a fierce loyalty to a United States government that, unfortunately, viewed all Japanese-Americans with suspicion and distrust.

Most Japanese-Americans serving in the Pacific bore with them the depressing knowledge that their families in the mainland United States had been torn from their homes and thrust into so-called "relocation centers" in a gross and baseless miscarriage of justice. Many of them also had relatives in Japan, some even serving in the Japanese military, who might be subject to punishing retaliation were their kinship discovered. But Fujita's family was fortunate to escape the indignity of a "relocation center" and his relatives in Japan were careful to conceal their relationship to him even while apparently acknowledging secretly his presence in a nearby POW camp.

Japanese-Americans in the Pacific also faced the ironic possibility that they could be killed by other American troops who in the heat of battle might mistake them for enemy soldiers. Fujita managed to escape this danger since, because of his Caucasian mother, his features did not readily manifest his Japanese origins—as even the Japanese themselves would discover.

Another unique aspect of Frank Fujita's wartime experience is the fact that he was one of the fewer than nine hundred Americans taken prisoner on the island of Java. The bulk of American POWs in Japanese hands surrendered in the Philippines—some twenty-two thousand, or more than 85 percent of all Americans held by Japan—and most of the published American POW memoirs reflect their experience. Fujita's account of the defense of Java and of the fate of the "Lost Battalion" of Texas artillerymen thus serves to distinguish his memoir from all the others and to enhance our knowledge of these little-known events.

Fujita also had the unusual experience of being forced to participate in a major Japanese radio propaganda project, a fate he shared with only a handful of other Allied prisoners and about which the published literature is relatively scarce. Fujita managed to resist efforts to force him to contribute worthwhile information to the propaganda broadcasts, limiting himself to innocuous announcements that he was well, had received mail, and wished his family the best. He also contrived to write such useless radio scripts that the Japanese either rejected them out of hand or completely redid them for broadcasting. A few of his fellow prisoners were less able to resist Japanese pressure and in some cases appear to have gone along willingly with their captors' desires. Fujita had little use for them and would later be called to testify in these matters.

Finally, Fujita's descriptions of the American B-29 raids on Tokyo offer an interesting perspective on the rain of fire and explosives that destroyed the Japanese capital. Held prisoner barely eight blocks from the Imperial Palace, he was well situated to observe Japanese reactions and to note them in his secret diary.

Fujita writes about his wartime experiences in a calm, dispassionate manner with occasional touches of humor. At times his deeper feelings emerge, such as when he describes the brutality of certain guards or the collaboration with the Japanese of some of his fellow prisoners. His memoir is at once a combination of facts and emotions, an unintended tribute to courage and grace under adversity, and a unique narrative of circumstances and events rarely touched upon by other writers and historians.

Stanley L. Falk
Former Chief Historian of U. S. Air Force
Author of *Bataan: The March of Death*
Alexandria, Virginia
1992

CHRONOLOGY

SEPTEMBER 28, 1892

Tsuneji Fujita is born near Nagasaki, Japan.

JUNE 14, 1914

Fujita arrives in the United States, changes his first name to Frank.

JULY 3, 1919

Fujita marries Ida Pearl Elliott.

OCTOBER 20, 1921

Frank Fujita, Jr., born in Lawton, Oklahoma.

FALL 1937

Fujita family moves to Abilene, Texas. Frank Fujita, Jr., adopts nickname "Foo."

1938

Frank Fujita, Jr., enlists in Texas National Guard: Headquarters and Headquarters Battery, 1st Battalion, 131st Field Artillery Regiment, 61st Field Artillery Brigade, 36th Division.

AUGUST 1940

36th Division on maneuvers in Louisiana.

NOVEMBER 1940

36th Division mobilized.

AUGUST–SEPTEMBER 1941

36th Division participates in major U.S. Army maneuvers in Louisiana.

OCTOBER 1941

Fujita transfers to E Battery, 2d Battalion, 131st Field Artillery.

NOVEMBER 21, 1941

2d Battalion sails in convoy for the Philippines.

DECEMBER 22, 1941

Convoy arrives at Brisbane, Australia.

JANUARY 11, 1942

2d Battalion, 131st Field Artillery arrives Soerabaja, Java.

FEBRUARY 3, 1942

2d Battalion comes under first air raid.

FEBRUARY 27, 1942

E Battery detached from 2d Battalion.

MARCH 1, 1942

Japanese forces land on Java.

MARCH 8, 1942

Java surrenders.

MARCH 10, 1942

Frank Fujita, Jr., becomes a prisoner of war.

OCTOBER 1942

Fujita is moved to Singapore.

NOVEMBER–DECEMBER 1942

Fujita is moved to Nagasaki, Japan, and placed in
Fukuoka POW Camp #2 to work in the shipyards.

JUNE 1943

The Japanese discover Fujita is half-Japanese.

OCTOBER 1943

Fujita is transferred to the Omori POW camp,
near Tokyo.

DECEMBER 1943

Fujita is transferred to Tokyo's *Bunka Gakuin Kanda*,
assigned to Japanese radio propaganda project.

NOVEMBER 24, 1944

First B-29 raid on Tokyo.

MARCH 9–10, 1945

Major fire-bombing of Tokyo.

AUGUST 15, 1945

Japan surrenders.

AUGUST 23, 1945

Fujita is moved back to Omori POW Camp.

AUGUST 29, 1945

Fujita is liberated by U.S. naval forces.

INTRODUCTION

O ut of all the far-flung, world-wide deployment of American armed forces in WW II, one of the strangest mysteries throughout the war was the fate of the "Lost Battalion" of the 36th Infantry Division. That unit was the Second Battalion of the 131st Field Artillery Regiment. It had been detached from the 36th Division late in 1941 and was sent to the Pacific Theater.

Not until the Japanese surrendered in Tokyo Bay on September 2, 1945, and prisoners of war were rescued did the true story of the "Lost Battalion" come to light—a saga of brutality, torture, starvation and suffering.

One of the most vivid and poignant versions of what happened is that related by Sergeant Frank Fujita, Jr., a native-born American from Abilene, Texas. Frank's father had remained a Japanese citizen although living in the United States since 1914, because immigration restrictions had prevented his naturalization. Young Frank's mother, Ida Pearl Elliott, was an Oklahoman of English-Scottish and American Indian descent.

Frank, Jr., just out of high school in Abilene, enlisted in the Texas National Guard's 36th Division in 1938, at the urging of a high school buddy. After mobilization in November 1940 and "war games" training in Louisiana, in 1941 Frank transferred from Headquarters Battery, 1st Battalion, 131st Field Artillery, to E Battery, 2d Battalion, which was being shipped overseas.

The main elements of the Texas 36th or "T Patch" Division were committed to Europe. They wrote a chapter of heroic history in their own blood in the landings at Salerno and Anzio and at the Rapido River in Italy.

The 131st Field Artillery's Second Battalion, to which

Frank had transferred, was made up mostly of Texans. This detachment shipped out of San Francisco aboard a troop transport in November, 1941. The ship stopped briefly in Honolulu on November 28. From there, the vessel headed toward the Philippines—until December 7. It was in mid-Pacific on that date when the Japanese surprise attack on Pearl Harbor stunned the United States and the rest of the world. The small troop convoy altered course, zig-zagging to the Fiji Islands, then to Australia. To meet the swift pace of the Japanese overrunning Southwest Asia, the Americans were rushed to Java to bolster Dutch defense of that colonial outpost.

Young Fujita's narrative, based on the secret diary he kept during the next three and one-half years, presents a sordid picture of Dutch colonials anxious to surrender Americans to the Japanese in a futile effort to escape execution, to salvage their properties and to maintain the luxury life they had been leading.

Shifted to Singapore by the Japanese, part of Frank's battalion was detached to work on a railroad the conquerors were building in Burma. One Japanese transport was sunk by an American submarine without knowledge that American POWs were aboard. Fujita was among those who drew red strings in Java's bicycle camp. His group went to Japan to work in a shipyard—ironically, in Nagasaki, the birthplace of Frank's father.

A natural artist since childhood, Fujita had planned to go to art school after he finished high school. War cancelled that idea. In prison, he found an artist's ready-made school of anatomy in sketching the bone structure and muscles of the emaciated prisoners around him. In one prison camp in Tokyo, he had access to books and music "liberated" by a Japanese in the conquest of the Philippines. Frank educated himself reading those books and playing classical records which he says he might never have encountered in normal, civilian life at home.

Throughout the Fujita narrative is the maturing philosophy of a man who underwent and witnessed the extremes of arrogance, brutality, senseless cruelty, selfishness, treason, endurance, suffering, kindness and sharing of men thrown together in the ultimate debasement of forced labor, starvation and illness in a POW camp. Betrayed at last by his Japanese name, Fujita steadfastly refused efforts by his captors to force him to denounce the United States. His punishment, after brutal beating, was demotion to keeper or *"honcho"* of the latrine—the *benjo*.

Fujita recorded carefully in his diary, much of it in a coded Javanese script of his own devising, the crescendo of American bombing raids on Tokyo with fleets of B-29s in 1944–45. He described the anger and terror of the Japanese, the awe and apprehension after atomic bombs obliterated Hiroshima and Nagasaki. He had to leave that diary boarded up in a wall of his prison cell, for fear of execution if it were discovered. One year after his liberation, he diagrammed for American military searchers the building and room where that diary would be found. After it was recovered, prosecutors made use of it in the post-war War Crimes trials held in Tokyo. It took five more years for Fujita to get his diary back from the United States Government.

This writer was one of the war correspondents who accompanied Navy rescue teams led by Comdr. Joel Boone* when American and other Allied prisoners were liberated from camps around and in Tokyo. A yellowed clipping in a scrap book records how Fujita and other starved POWs swam hysterically from Omori Prison, on an island in Tokyo Bay, to meet the PT boats coming to free them.

Now past middle age and married, Fujita is still buoyed by the sense of humor and the stubborn, unyielding independence that sustained him during captivity. He will carry throughout his life permanent injuries suffered at the hands of his captors; but Fujita is relaxed, finding expression in his unusual style of painting and in the traveling he does with his wife, indulging in his favorite sport of fishing.

Fujita is uneasy, though, at the thought of the United States being caught again as it was in 1941—with "tripods, but no machine guns and ammunition; antique artillery and no shells; too few planes and those out-dated; air fields without anti-aircraft guns or missiles to defend them."

---

* Official accounts of the rescue operation identify this officer as Comdr. Roger W. Simpson. Samuel Eliot Morison, *History of United States Naval Operations in World War II: Victory in the Pacific, 1945* (Boston: Little, Brown, 1960), pp. 358, 361; Benis M. Frank and Henry I. Shaw, Jr., *History of U.S. Marine Corps Operations in World War II: Victory and Occupation* (Washington: Hqs, U.S. Marine Corps, 1968), pp. 781–82.

Throughout his ordeal, Fujita was unswerving in one thing: faced with a choice between his Japanese ancestry and his American birthright, with the danger of execution if he chose the latter, he remained loyally American to the core.

> Robert Wear, War Correspondent,
> *Fort Worth Star-Telegram*, Fort Worth, Texas
> Summer 1980

(Robert Wear accompanied the initial landing party in Tokyo Bay that went in to reclaim Allied prisoners of war in WW II.)

1

FOO JOINS THE TEXAS

NATIONAL GUARD

1938–1941

Omori Prison Island, Tokyo Bay, Japan,[1] 29 August 1945

It seems like I have been swimming to freedom for miles, but it really has been only about forty or fifty yards from shore. My final act of defiance is this gross stupidity. There is no energy in my body. I am drowning. Other emaciated men are thrashing in the water near me. But I cannot help them. I am not able to help myself. I have lost the ability to move one arm just one more stroke. God! I have been so foolish. The salt water is in my eyes, my mouth, my lungs. The sharks will feast upon my remains. The green water now covers me. Vaguely the hull of a landing craft launched from the USS *Gosselin* moves closer in the fuzzy, final annihilation of my skull. My head is about to be crushed by my rescuers.[2]

1. The city of Omori, on the western shore of Tokyo Bay, lies just south of the Japanese capital. The Omori prisoner-of-war camp was on a small island about fifty yards offshore, linked to the mainland by a wooden footbridge. Alfred A. Weinstein, *Barbed-Wire Surgeon* (New York: Macmillan, 1948), p. 218.

2. The *Gosselin*, a large high-speed transport, was part of a special U. S. Naval task group evacuating Allied prisoners of war in the Tokyo Bay area. Benis M. Frank and Henry I. Shaw, Jr., *History of U.S. Marine*

年 月 日	品　名	数量	替	買入金額	支払金額	借或貸	差引残高

November 5, 1941

Camp Bowie, Texas – I transfer from 1ST Bn. Hq. Bty. of the 131ST Field Artillery to the 2ND Battalion, "E" Battery, of the same regiment which was ordered on foreign Service. I transfered in grade, becoming "Machine Gun" Sergeant for "E" Battery.

November 10, 1941

We are leaving Camp Bowie. The Battalion is going to "Frisco" on two trains. I am in the first train and the other will follow in the morning. It was sure hard to say good-bye to Charlie, Ed, Joe and the rest. We got under way at 10:00 P.M.

November 14, 1941

We arrived in San Francisco, de train at Fort Mason and go by tug out in

It was only moments ago that I, Frank "Foo" Fujita, started over the fence. For days I have been guarding two prisoners within our prisoners of war camp—Americans who had betrayed their flag without cause or reason—the lowest form of men I have ever known. My only weapon has been a club. They will not speak to me, nor do I bash in their skulls. Once, I waited for each of them in secret, ready to kill them with a knife that I had stashed for my own ultimate escape to freedom. But I have not touched these two, for I knew that we would eventually be able to testify to their betrayal, and what better punishment than public justice?

So I have not harmed them. It was only moments ago that Smitty offered to guard these two traitors for me. He said "Foo, grab a ditty bag full of goodies from the air drops and go into town like the rest of us and trade for whatever suits your fancy."

I am an American Army sergeant with the distinguishing characteristic that my father is Japanese, born in Nagasaki[3] and wed to my Oklahoma mother. I have been a prisoner of war of the Japanese for almost three and a half years. It has not been easy. Yet, as weak as I am, the idea of a short excursion into town had its appeal. I was atop the fence when someone yelled, "Torpedos coming!" I looked over the other fence on the bay side of Omori, and saw several sprays being kicked up and heading straight for us.

I jumped down, discarded my ditty bag and went over the opposite fence with some other POWs. The sprays were not torpedos but landing barges coming for us. Some of us started wading out towards them and then began to swim. At first I swam like a champion but after a few yards I began to slow and about forty or fifty yards out there was nothing left. The water is green, gray, the boat hull over my head. I die now. I . . .

The two largest hands ever created on earth slip over my head. They are strong hands. The boat hull thumps the hands and not my skull. I

Corps Operations in World War II: Victory and Occupation (Washington: Hqs., U.S. Marine Corps, 1968), pp. 781–82.

3. Tsuneji Fujita was born on September 28, 1892, in the tiny village of Ozeki, Saga prefecture, near the port of Nagasaki on the southern Japanese island of Kyushu.

Frank "Foo" Fujita, 1940, Hq. Bty. 1st Bn. 131 F.A.

am not dead. The hands lift my head to the air above the water. They grasp my ears. Arms grapple for me. There is great strength in the arms, in the bodies, in the faces of these men of the United States Navy who lift my frail 110 pounds into the air and set me gently on the deck of this landing craft.

These are the first free Americans that I have seen in almost four years. I am so grateful not to have drowned for my own foolishness that I cannot even cry. They are indeed the toughest men I have ever seen. We arrive briefly back at Omori. There is absolute jubilation. We are about to be the first POWs liberated from Japan. The Commandant of Omori comes storming down to the dock. He shouts, "What are you doing here? The war is not over, officially. You must not do this!"

I look up from the dock where these big husky sailors have put me down as gently as a robin's egg. Each of them carries a submachine gun. One of them raises his hand peacefully to the Jap commandant, who is quite frustrated with the event. "We are taking these prisoners of war out of here, starting right now! What's more, you are to have every Allied prisoner in the Tokyo area right here by tomorrow morning so that we can take them, too!" I am fully aware that I have not drowned. My final foolishness has not killed me. I am alive! I am free! And how this has come about is a long series of events and miracles.

• • •

My dad was born the second son to a well-to-do family in a village just outside of Nagasaki, Japan. His mother was a social climber and could not be bothered with nursing a baby so a wet nurse was hired for him until he was two years old. He was raised by a grandmother, and he loved her deeply. He was always fearful, as she grew older, that she would be taken to the mountain and left to die—a practice that was evidently not uncommon in those days. He was sent to a boy's school for education and learned to speak English there. His father owned and operated a nursery, and when my dad had finished his education at the boy's school, he was sent to the United States to study American methods of agriculture. He

Abilene, Texas, 1938. Back row, L to R: Ella Elliott (grandmother), Frank Fujita, Jr., Ida Pearl Elliott Fujita, Frank Fujita, Sr., Herbert Fujita. Front row, L to R: Patricia, Rita, and Naomi Fujita.

arrived in America on the 14th of June 1914.[4] Evidently my dad had no intention of going back to Japan or of going to school either, for that matter. Upon arriving in the U.S. he assumed a Christian name, Frank. Instead of going to school he took to gambling. He did not remain in San Francisco

4. Japanese immigration to the United States had begun in the late nineteenth century, reaching its peak in the early years of the twentieth. In 1908, in accordance with a U.S.-Japanese "Gentlemen's Agreement," the Japanese government stopped issuing passports to laborers intending to come to the continental United States. As a student, Fujita presumably was not affected. Roger Daniels, *Asian America: Chinese and Japanese in the United States since 1850* (Seattle: University of Washington Press, 1988), chap 4.

where he disembarked but went to Los Angeles and stayed with a relative by marriage who was already established there. During this time he got involved with the Salvation Army and would carry their flag or banner as their band would play and parade down the street. Somehow a well-to-do lady hired him as a houseboy and later sent him to chef's school.

This new qualification landed him a job as the private chef for officials of the Rock Island Rail Road and he traveled the country in their private car. El Reno, Oklahoma was more or less a company town. The railroad was its biggest employer, with extensive switching and freight yards, offices and a large "round house" that was one of their major repair and maintenance facilities. The company's main offices were in Rock Island, Illinois. During a layover here, my dad went to the dining room of the Southern Hotel and there met my mother, Ida Pearl Elliott, who was a hash slinger or waitress there. He fell for her and met her parents, who were typical uneducated sharecroppers from the mountains of eastern Oklahoma. They were greatly impressed with him and the way he lavished gifts on them. They were only too glad to have him marry their daughter. Frank and Ida were married 3 July, 1919, and to this union were born two boys and three girls, in that order. I was number two son.

Dad quit the railroad and started cooking short orders and sandwiches in various oil fields around Oklahoma. He evidently had developed "itchy feet" while traveling with the Rock Island and so he moved around quite a bit. Each of us children was born in a different town. In 1925, Dad took a job as cook in a restaurant in Fort Worth, Texas. One pay day Dad went into one of the back rooms and found the restaurant owner and some other men playing poker. He asked them what they were playing and his boss said that it was an American game called poker. Dad feigned ignorance of the game while at the same time showing great interest. His boss must have thought that he would be an easy make and that here was a chance to get the wages back that he had just paid Dad. He invited Dad to play. When the game was over, Dad owned the restaurant. While operating it, he would paint the daily menu on the window two and three times a day. When he became proficient in painting letters, he sold the restaurant and started painting signs. This manner of earning a living afforded him the opportunity to continue his nomadic life style. His family was growing, however, so he took to leaving my mother and us kids behind while he hit the trail gambling and painting signs.

He would paint signs and take it out in trade for clothing or food. Consequently, we never knew what he would bring home. Once he brought home some brogan shoes, which were fine for farm work, but since we were not farmers we were not too happy to wear these shoes, especially on Sunday with our knicker britches and billed caps. Even these shoes, however, were for Sunday and school only. In the summer we were required to go barefooted. To this day I have a terrible aversion to goat head stickers and hot sidewalks.

Even though he was gone a lot, he provided us with an adequate subsistence. When he was home he insisted on having meat at every meal, a commodity that none of my schoolmates experienced during the depression years of the 1930s. Dad always made sure that he left his family in a town where there were no Japanese or Japanese influences. He wanted his children to be one hundred percent American. His greatest desire was to become an American citizen, but the law of the land was that naturalization was not open to Japanese. When he first applied for naturalization, he found out that not only could he not become an American but, upon marrying him, my mother became an alien and had to be naturalized. She, having been born an American citizen, was permitted to do this.[5]

---

5. The naturalization law passed by the first United States Congress restricted naturalization to "white persons" and (as amended after the Civil War) aliens of African descent. Although these restrictions were sometimes ignored (particularly in Hawaii, with its large Asian population), they were strictly applied to Japanese in the continental United States and their application was upheld by the Supreme Court. Mrs. Fujita's loss of her American citizenship was the result of a 1907 law requiring any American woman marrying a foreigner to take the nationality of her husband (even as a foreign woman marrying an American citizen automatically became a citizen herself). The Supreme Court upheld this law as reasonably required under the norms of international relations. Not until 1934 did Congress change the law and allow American women marrying foreigners to retain their citizenship. Daniels, *Asian America*, chap. 4; Edward S. Corwin, *The Constitution and What It Means Today* (New York:

My mother was born Ida Pearl Elliott on 11 August 1903 in the small town of Scullyville, just west of Fort Smith, Arkansas in the Choctaw Nation, Indian Territory. Her father was a big man of Scottish, German and Catawba American Indian descent, and her mother was a Cromwell of English descent. She was an only girl growing up in a house full of men—three brothers and two half brothers. She had a half sister, but she was already married and living away from home.

I was born October 20, 1921 in Lawton, Oklahoma. Lawton was a rough-and-ready town—drunken and brawling soldiers from nearby Fort Sill were not an uncommon sight. Geronimo, the notorious Apache war leader, had once been imprisoned there. There was an Indian reservation and school nearby. On weekends Indian families would come to town and spread their blankets down on the sidewalks and streets and spend the weekend there—squaws, papooses, dogs and all. If people wanted to pass by them, they would just have to go around.

My schooling began in the first grade at the age of five and one-half years old. I learned right off the bat about the "board of education." My mother and I had a Persian cat each, and we kept a sandbox in the house for the cats' use. On my first day in school I had to empty my bladder. Up in front of the room was a large sandbox. I must have reasoned that if a small sandbox was for cats then this large sandbox must be for the kids. So I went up in front of the class and proceeded to relieve myself. Well, out came the "board of education," and I was sent home with a blistered rear end. Needless to say, when I got home more of the same awaited me.

Dad had built himself a gambling stand and was traveling some with a carnival. We moved from Chickasha to Cement, Oklahoma, and then on to El Reno, Oklahoma, where once again I started to school in the first grade. We lived in this town for ten years. When my brother and I were old enough, we joined the local Boy Scout troop. There was a Cheyenne and Arapaho Indian reservation across the river north of town and they also had a Boy Scout troop, but in order to do so they had to be affiliated

Atheneum, 1963), p. 58; Frederic A. Ogg and P. Orman Ray, *Introduction to American Government* (New York: D. Appleton-Century, 1942), pp. 132–39.

with a white troop. Our troop and the Indian troop would get together and play games. Many times the games would take place on their reservation. It seemed that the Indian elders would root for my brother and me. They thought, "those poor little Indian boys over there with all those white boys."

Our growing-up years in Oklahoma were during the depression of the 1930s, and hunting rabbits was an almost daily necessity. Rabbits were eaten three times a day. Many a family of that day would have been considerably worse off than they were had it not been for rabbits. There were near tragic consequences in the mid-30s when the cottontail population was smitten with "rabbit fever," making the animals inedible. Money was hard to come by. The average daily wage for a grown man was one dollar per day. This made it very hard on those who had families, and belt tightening was the norm. Model T Fords could be bought for five dollars but no one had five dollars. Since the greatest percentage of families were in the same boat, as it were, the situation was not psychologically depressing—at least to us kids. We would forage up and down the back alleys and vacant lots and gather wild greens, such as lamb's quarter, dandelions and wild mustard greens. We ate lots and lots of eggs, for we knew a farm family who raised chickens and sold us a three-gallon water pail full of eggs for twenty-five cents. We had a number of other farm friends. We would help them when butchering time came about, and they would share the meat with us along with cracklins and hog lard. City folk who did not have farm friends never experienced such fine eating. Almost all these friends went to the Church of the Nazarene where Mom took us.

In the summertime, several families would gather at one of the farms and have a great time of eating, visiting and playing games. Our family was always popular at these outings. Dad would bring Kewpie dolls from his carnival gambling supplies to give away as gifts, and he would bring sweet syrup in many flavors and the ice shaver from his snow cone stand. All this coupled with the watermelons, cantaloups, fresh roasting ears of corn, other fresh garden vegetables and homemade ice cream made for a feast and outing that memories are made of.

The hardships and deprivations of the depression years went a long ways in toughening us up, both physically and psychologically, to cope with the trials of prisoner of war camps in later years. I say "we" because most of the guys who went overseas with me were about my age and had parallel experiences.

As I said before, we lived in El Reno ten years and for the first time Mom was able to cultivate close friends in the church and neighborhood. This was very important to her. Dad had opened a sign shop and had taught himself the new art of making neon signs. After a few years, in 1936, he got itchy feet again and went to Abilene, Texas, where he became a salesman for a neon sign company there. When he told Mom to pack up the children and move there she was very upset. She put her foot down and said this would be the very last time that she would change towns. We moved to Abilene in the fall of 1937. This was the sixteenth move Mom had made since marrying my dad eighteen years earlier. My older brother, Herbert, was in his senior year of high school and wanted to stay behind and finish his schooling in El Reno. He was granted permission to do so and delivered papers and worked at the bus station to provide for himself. He even slept at the bus station.

At this time Oklahoma schools went to the twelfth grade and Texas schools only went to the eleventh. I was elated because I felt sure that I would wind up in the senior class. This was not the case, however, and I was unhappily put in the ninth grade. I was born with a natural talent for art and copied every kind of art work that I could. This gave me some basics in various techniques. There was a cartoon strip in the Sunday funnies back in El Reno that I liked very much. It was a slapstick cartoon about a fireman by the name of Smoky Stover. All through this strip there was a cat that had its tail injured and it always wore a bandage tied in a bow knot on it. The cat always said "Foo." I liked this cat so much that I started drawing it on my school papers instead of signing my name, and before we left El Reno I was being called "Foo."

In Abilene High School I immediately became known as "Foo." My drawings drew attention to me. My art teacher told the local newspaper about me, and consequently I had my picture and a write-up in the *Abilene Reporter News*. Boy! This was heady stuff for the new kid in town.

Foo's drawing of the cat which inspired his nickname.

The Abilene Reporter News
Abilene, Texas
[Winter 1937]

East is East, but West is West and the best place to live after all, says Frank Fujita, Jr., sixteen-year-old Abilene high school junior.

Born of a Japanese father and an American mother, Mr. and Mrs. Frank Fujita, 1649 Beech, the bright-eyed youth feels no desire whatever to visit his father's country, especially with a war in progress.

"I'd rather draw cartoons," he said in all seriousness. Frank, Sr., is a sign painter for Taggart Sign Company and the boy naturally follows in his father's footsteps. Ever since he can remember he has been drawing. He has tried his hand at all phases, but always ends up drawing cartoons.

Called "FOO" by his classmates—"they just dropped the L," he says—the little Japanese-American has made a name for himself in high school for his drawings. Anywhere, anytime that he gets his hands on a pencil or pen and ink he starts drawing. More than likely it will be a cartoon—and a "scary" one at that.

"I just like to draw scary things," he said. "I have never seen the moving picture 'Frankenstein,' but I bet I'd like it."

While a cameraman was taking his picture, he displayed some of his work. Grotesque cartoons of the God of War, skeletons gathered around a tombstone and horrible caricatures of movie stars.

Many of his cartoons bear a close resemblance to political cartoons in the daily newspapers—distorted but well proportioned and with a definite idea behind them.

Frank has never had a lesson from an art teacher except in regular public school art classes. At present he is taking art from Beth Coombs at the high school. He and his family moved to Abilene in October from El Reno, Oklahoma.

He has no plans as to college education. It does not make any particular difference to him where he goes for advanced learning. "Just someplace where I can take four years of art," he said. "That is all I want out of college."

For his material, "FOO" likes a crow quill pen—a short, slender pen used by draftsmen for lettering—and ink. He has tried pencil, oil painting and other methods, but always comes back to pen and ink.

His drawings show the intricate thoroughness and detail that characterizes Oriental artists. There is just one thing that makes "FOO" unhappy. He cannot draw women. He can draw men in any shape or position, but time and time again he has tried women for models and failed utterly. "Guess I just wasn't made that way," he says.

• • •

I was assigned as Staff Cartoonist to the school paper called *The Battery*. Also I was in a class or group called the Thespians. I wasn't an actor nor did I have any aspirations in that direction, but I was on the stage crew. The teacher in charge of this class was forever talking as fast as he could about the play we were about to put on, or some related subject, and I found that if I needed an excuse to miss a study hall period that he would sign the paper without even looking at it. I decided to see if he would sign a blank sheet of paper. When I caught him enthusiastically talking to someone, I handed him the paper and said, "Mr. Ford, I need your signature on this," and he signed it and never stopped talking. Many times after that I used him for excuses that I would write myself in order to miss class. Along with other school chums, we would go downtown to a pool hall and goof off.

At times someone in the group would have a dollar or two and we would buy a half pint of grain alcohol and mix it with Nehi chocolate soda and get pretty high. Abilene was a dry town in a dry county, but liquor was not only available from the local bootleggers, but some of the drug stores also had a liquor room in the back. Of course, the alcoholic beverages were for medicinal purposes only. At each store there would be an old retired doctor who would write prescriptions for whatever amount you thought would make you "well," and they would charge five cents for each prescription.

A few of my best friends and I were forever pulling some sort of prank at school that was designed to disrupt classes. Once or twice we set fire to a trash container in the hallway. The steel containers had swinging lids on them and so the flames were contained inside and quickly went out for lack of oxygen, but they did create enough smoke to cause some excitement. Then one of the guys' dads had a photography studio and he had a lot of flash powder left over from the days before flash bulbs were invented. Well, it was found that if one took a small amount of this flash powder and added a small amount of sulfuric acid to it that it would create a heavy white vapor that would soon spread all up and down the hall and would have a very foul odor like that of rotten eggs. We would separate and set these stink bombs off at the same time on each of the three floors and soon the whole school stunk like rotten eggs. Needless to say, this was not conducive to the pursuit of higher learning.

Our school football games were played at the local stadium at Fair Park. Once a friend and I crawled over the fence to see the game without paying. Mr. England, one of the school staff, saw us and chased us all around the stadium until we were finally caught. He turned us over to one of the city policemen and had him drive us out to the city limits on the other side of town and leave us. This he did but we quickly flagged down an approaching motorist who was driving rather fast. When he stopped, he asked if we were going to the game and we said we were. He said that he was, too, and that the game was about to start so we would have to hurry. We were back at the stadium and inside of it before the policeman got back. We were expelled from school for this and our parents had to get us reinstated.

Dad was a strict disciplinarian. A good education was a must for us kids, and when I was expelled I thought he was going to beat me to death. I had always dreaded to see my father come home, for without fail, it meant a whipping or beating for me and it had been this way since early childhood. All of us kids were whipped on occasion and this was not limited to just us but Mom came in for some of the same. Dad retained his old country ways in this respect, and he was lord and master of his household and held absolute power over same. My brother, being number one son, received a little more leniency when he would err but not so with me. I was whipped with anything from his bare knuckles to an iron rod. I had no love or respect, only fear, for my dad until I was captured by the Japanese army in WW II. Only then did I begin to have some understanding of my dad.

My friend Roy McCullough had been in the Texas National Guard for some time and was a corporal. He painted a picture of adventure, excitement and good times in the Guard, so I decided that I just had to belong also.

When I joined, I was underage and had to have my parents sign for me. This suited Dad fine for he wanted his children to be one hundred percent American, and what better way than to be in the service of your country?

When I tried to enlist I was told that I had to be an American citizen. It seemed that there was a question as to whether I was or not and so the question was turned over to the civics teacher at the high school. Well, there were a lot of pros and cons and a lot more of ignorance but it was finally decided that I was indeed a natural-born citizen. As I said, I was underage. I was seventeen and a half and was supposed to be eighteen. The clerk signing me up asked how tall I was. I was just a hair under the minimum, but he put it down as it was supposed to be. He then asked me how much I weighed and I said 105 pounds. The minimum was 135 pounds so he said to go outside the door. Then he said "Come here! How much do you weigh?" I said, "105 pounds." He very irately said, "Git outside that door! Come here! How much do you weigh?" I said "135 pounds," and he said "That's what I thought you said," and went ahead and finished signing me up.

I enlisted in Headquarters and Headquarters Battery and Combat Train, 1st Battalion, 131st Regiment, 61st Field Artillery Brigade of the 36th Infantry Division, Texas National Guard.[6] The 36th Division was one of the last of the army's square divisions which was made up of brigades, regiments, battalions, batteries or companies and squads. A squad was eight men and a corporal. When we had close order drill we would "dress right" at elbow length from the next guy and would "count off" by fours. Later the division was streamlined or "triangularized," as it was called, and "close order drill" was replaced with "dressing right" at arm's length, and among other things, the squad formation was eliminated from the drill.[7]

• • •

Hand-written letter, Frank Fujita, Sr., to Immigration and Naturalization Service

873 Sycamore Street
Abilene, Texas
October 13, 1941:
I want to take this opportunity to express my great appreciation for

6. The combat train of an artillery battalion included the ammunition, fuel, maintenance, and equipment required for the immediate support of its combat elements.

7. In an effort to increase combat flexibility and mobility, the large and unwieldy WW I "square" divisions (four infantry regiments in two brigades) were "triangularized" (dropping the brigade structure and reducing the number of infantry regiments to three). Among other changes, the size of the squad was increased from eight to twelve men. Kent Roberts Greenfield, Robert L. Palmer, and Bell I. Wiley, *The Organization of Ground Combat Troops* (Washington: Historical Division, Dept. of the Army, 1947), pp. 11–12.

this great country of America and how I love and honor its democracy even though I have not had the wonderful privilege of becoming a naturalized citizen.

I am a native born Japanese of Japanese parents. I came over to this country in 1914 and have enjoyed the wonderful freedom and privileges, all these years. All the time, [I have been] hungry to be a citizen of this country that had given me so much.

When leaving my country, I left all behind, breaking every tie that would bind me to it, or any of its traditions, breaking all family ties and have never written or had any communication from them since. I wanted to become a full fledged American by naturalization but to my sad disappointment I found that the law had been passed in 1917 barring a Japanese from becoming a citizen of this country. I was disappointed over this fact but was determined to be one in my heart and life, even though I could not be in name. So I began to hunt work where there were no other Japanese that I may break completely away from my mother tongue and any Japanese influence, so I might better qualify myself to be worthy of living in America.

In 1917 when this country went to war I wanted to help it by showing my love for the stars and stripes, by enlisting as a soldier for Uncle Sam but was rejected on account of physical conditions.

In 1919 I was living in El Reno, Oklahoma, employed by Rock Island R.R. as cook. There I met and married an American girl, to us was born five children, two oldest which are boys 19 and 20 years of age, both in Government service, one in regular army at Fort Sam Houston, San Antonio, the other in the National Guard here at home but will leave soon for [a] year's training.

In 1926 I changed my occupation from cooking to sign writer of which I followed several years, always trying in whatever work I was in to be honest and upright, hoping someday I might have the opportunity to become a real citizen. So in this same year, [1926], I tried once more to be naturalized so I applied for my citizenship, under the same court clerk as I had ten years before. He remembered the time and said he would do all he could, so I filled out my papers and he sent them to Kansas City immigration office. After several weeks they were returned and I still could not be naturalized myself, but found out that an American girl marrying Japanese citizen forfeited her birthright, so I, wanting to do everything I could to make my family complete[ly] American, urged my wife to apply, so she did, which she received in 1937.[8] Of course, all my children were natural born citizens, so all my family were citizens of this great country, but myself and I was a Japanese without a country, for I was here living, working and supporting my family yet in a sense not part of either.

I have tried to raise my children, three girls, ages 9, 15, and 16, and two boys, 19 and 20, to be good citizens. I have tried to stay away from all Japanese influence that I might become more like American and better help my family and this country, which I would like to call mine.

I have tried to express my feelings about my desire to become a citizen and I am wondering whether or not I can ever have that privilege. Would it make any difference if this country and Japan should ever have trouble? Would I be allowed to stay in America with my family or will I be forced to leave for old country? Please, for my sake and sake of family, give this due consideration, even to as high officials as it can go, and let me know soon as can.

Thanking you for all consideration,
Mr. Frank Fujita

• • •

Upon enlisting I was assigned as a chauffeur with a private first class—fifth class specialist rating. I was to drive the battery and battalion officers around in a Chevrolet station wagon. I was later assigned to drive one of the brand new Dodge 6 × 6 trucks that were coming in to replace the old 1934 2 × 4 trucks that we had had prior to that time. As truck drivers, we could get extra duty by hauling new recruits in the "tree army," as we called the Civilian Conservation Corps, from Abilene to the CCC regional camp at Brownwood, Texas.[9]

---

8. Probably 1931 or 1932.

9. The Civilian Conservation Corps was established by Congress in March 1933 to

The Guard was required to conduct training exercises and mini-maneuvers on farm and ranch lands all over the central part of the state. Also we were required to go to a large ranch in northwest Texas and have what was called a battalion shoot. That is, we would take our old WW I French 75-mm fieldpieces there so that the officers and the gun crews could gain needed practice in firing artillery problems. In order to save money we had some 37-mm guns that were mounted to the barrels of the 75s, and this is what was actually fired.

Each battery had its own mess facilities, mess sergeant and cooks, headed up by the battery mess officer. Whether you ate good or not depended entirely upon how good your mess officer and sergeant were. They had so much money allotted each month for food, and they would have to shop around and get the best buys. This money could not be used for anything but food or drink. Our mess crew was tops and we ate very good and still had money left over at the end of the month. Since the allotment had to be spent during that month or turned back in, our captain would have a beer bust to use up the balance. Even later, after we had mobilized, he had a large ice-cooler trailer built, and maintained a battery canteen for us. He would issue us chits against our next paycheck, and that way we could have beer all month long—until top brass put a stop to it.

My study habits and my grades were not the best, and, after a bad report card, Dad told me that from that date forward I would leave the house and go straight to school and then return home with no stops along the way. I would then study until bedtime with time out for meals. I could not deviate from this routine for the duration of the school year. I could either abide by these rules or get out of his house. I chose to get out. I sold my only possession, a single shot .22-caliber rifle, for five dollars and went to the north edge of town and started hitchhiking back to Oklahoma. The

provide jobs for unemployed young men aged 18–25. Enrollees lived in work camps and were assigned to reforestation, road construction, flood and fire control, and other reclamation projects. The program and the camps were administered by the War Department and run by the army. Arthur M. Schlessinger, Jr., *The Coming of the New Deal* (Boston: Houghton Mifflin, 1959), pp. 337–41; Forrest C. Pogue, *George C. Marshall: Education of a General, 1880–1939* (New York: The Viking Press, 1963), pp. 274–80, 303, 308–11.

weather was bitter cold and the north wind cut right through you. A big new Chrysler pulled up to me and stopped, and the man asked me where I was going. I told him to El Reno, Oklahoma, and he said that he was going to Oklahoma City and asked me if I could drive. I told him yes, and he slid over in the seat and said, "Fine—you can drive! I have driven all the way from California without rest and I have got to get some sleep. My wife is asleep in the back seat and I will just sleep here. If you need gas or anything, wake me up." I drove straight into El Reno and woke them up. We thanked each other for a mutual blessing and they went on their way. El Reno was 35 miles west of Oklahoma City.

I went to stay with my best friend there. We had been friends since the first grade and grew up like brothers. I helped his dad painting houses, doing repair work and hanging paper in return for board and room. I then got a job on a farm for five dollars a month plus board, room and laundry. I then got a job as a display artist and relief projectionist for the local theaters for nine dollars a week. My parents came to try and get me to return home but I told Dad that I intended to stay. Dad said that the rules had not changed so I refused to go back with them.

At this time Hitler had started the war in Europe and the situation in the Pacific between Japan and the U.S. was rapidly deteriorating. The newspapers were full of the status quo and there was increasing talk of mobilizing the National Guards. The 36th Infantry Division stood a good chance of being one of the divisions called up. I felt sure that they would be called up, so I returned to Abilene to be near my National Guard unit.

Upon returning home I was re-established in the National Guards and began hanging around the armory, "gobbling up" all the rumors of possible mobilization. Most of our speculations were wild and fanciful. I realized, however, that mobilization could be a long way off, and to keep down the friction with my dad I would have to find a job. Here again, my friend Roy was working in a cake shop near the high school, and he had me see his boss. I did, and landed a job working fourteen hours a day, six days a week for $5 per week. My duties were to fry doughnuts and fry or bake sweet rolls for the morning cafe trade. Our day began at three o'clock in the morning. Roy was "bench man," and he would mix up the batter for the different things, roll it out and cut out the doughnuts. I would pick them out, place them on a board, put them in a proof box and from there into the fry pot and icing pot. The rest of the day was spent in making and baking cookies and cakes.

The owner of the building lived upstairs, and we did not get along with him. I decided one morning that I would disturb his night's sleep. I removed my big fry pot from the four burner stove, lit one burner and placed an empty flit fly spray can about one fourth full of water over the flame. The can swelled with steam until it burst with a terribly loud explosion. All the grates were blown from the stove and two windows in that room were blown out. Not only did it wake the landlord but the neighborhood as well.

This routine was maintained until August of that year, 1940, and then I took leave from my job to go to the first Louisiana maneuvers which lasted for three weeks.[10] We artillerymen were called "Red Legs" by the other guard units, because of the knee high reddish brown lace-up boots that we wore. The rest of our uniform consisted of a safari type sun helmet, wool O.D. shirts, and khaki knee britches or boot britches, all left over from horse-drawn artillery days. I had been reassigned from the station wagon to drive one of the new 6 × 6, 2½ ton Dodge trucks. These trucks had so much spring in the seats that every time I had to drive across country, I would spend as much time on the ceiling as in the seat.

The maneuvers were a make-believe war and we fought with the zeal of the real McCoy. The war with the ticks and mosquitoes and poison ivy were real enough, however, and they, along with the heat and high humidity, really made life miserable. Constipation was a major problem on these maneuvers. The cooks would make us sandwiches out of big slabs of GI bread baked specially for field use, thick slices of Spam and equally thick slices of cheese. By the time you ate two of these and bounced up

10. In August 1940, to prepare for the anticipated expansion of the army, more than 200,000 National Guardsmen began a three-week period of training, starting at the lowest levels and culminating in major maneuvers with large units. The shocking deficiencies revealed in these exercises demonstrated that the National Guard was woefully unprepared to go to war and increased pressure to bring it under federal control. Christopher R. Gabel, *The U.S. Army GHQ Maneuvers of 1941* (Washington: U.S. Army Center of Military History, 1991), pp. 12–14.

and down hard on the wooden seats of the trucks for hours, it seemed at times as if we would have to use "blasting caps" to have a BM.

Fresh recruits were always fair game for many types of pranks. On summer encampments you could tell the recruits by the big greasy circle in the seat of their britches. They were told that the summer camps would be the most enjoyable of their lives except for "muster." When they would ask just what muster was, they were told that at the end of camp every one would be required to drop their pants and drawers and bend over and the medicos would put mustard up their rears and their reactions to the mustard would tell them if they had caught a venereal disease while at camp. They were told that the pain of this mustard was almost unbearable and that the only way that they could stand it was to keep their rear end well greased with vasoline for the two weeks prior to muster. Long before time for muster, the recruits were already becoming obvious by the oily seats of their britches.

There was one recruit who had a full head of pretty wavy hair. Several of us who were always pulling these shenanigans told him that he had to have a regulation hair cut as long as he was at National Guard Camp. He said that he wasn't going to have his hair cut. We held him down and took a pair of clippers and cut a two inch strip from his forehead, over his pate and down to the nape of his neck, and left him like that. When we got back to Abilene from camp, his dad, who owned a candy kitchen there, was infuriated and tried to have us arrested for ruining his boy's looks. That didn't work so he tried to get our officers to court-martial us. And that didn't work either.

If any one acted like he was better than the rest of us and did not want to "belong," he was singled out to be the recipient of some hazing. There was one corporal who always stayed to himself, would have nothing to do with the rest of us. He would get drunk every evening after retreat, stagger into the tent before lights out, undress and flop down on his cot and pass out. We took a piece of string and tied it around the foreskin of his penis, ran the string down and around the end of his GI steel cot and then took it back and tied it to one of his big toes. We would then tickle the bottom of his foot and when he would react by jerking his foot back he would almost decapitate his foreskin. Of course, no one knew who did it.

Another time we killed a harmless bull snake that had gotten into the tent. We coiled it up and put it under his blanket. He came back from the canteen after the lights were out, crawled into bed and when he came into contact with the snake, he came up screaming to high heaven. Our final prank on him was a lulu. We told him that being a corporal he should have known that everyone had to be circumcised according to regulations and that he had to go to the medics immediately and have it done. He bellowed and roared and said that he wasn't a Jew and wasn't just about to get circumcised.

We told him that in that case we would do it for him. He was a big man and it took six of us to tie him to the bed and gag him. We told him that there was nothing to it if he did not fight us. We held his penis up by the foreskin, wrapped a string around it just back of the head of it. As the string was pulled by one end I am sure that it must have felt like he was being cut on; at the same time we dribbled some warm water on him which ran down his penis and over his scrotum which he must have thought was blood. We taped the end of his foreskin shut and then wrapped his penis up in a lot of gauze and poured lots of Mercurochrome over it and his testicles. We told him that the bandage had to stay on for two days. He had to urinate the next morning and removed the bandages only to find that there was nothing done to him. Boy! Was he ever mad.

As the end of maneuvers was drawing nigh, the "First Shirt" or First Sergeant would fall the battery in and tell them that no good soldier would think of returning to home base minus any item that had been issued him and that any such item would be withheld from their pay. Word was then passed around that a "Moonlight Requisition" was in order. That meant that you would have to sneak over to the enemy lines and "borrow" from them any item that you were missing.

Back in Abilene, construction of Camp Barkeley, just west of town, was going full steam ahead and many of the men got jobs of one kind or another at this base as well as at the new camp that was being built at Brownwood, Texas—Camp Bowie. Camp Bowie was being built for the 36th Infantry Division, a one hundred percent Texan National Guard unit, and Camp Barkeley was being built for the 45th Infantry Division, from Colorado, Oklahoma, New Mexico and Arizona.

I did not return to my job, for now it was certain that the guard would mobilize, but just when was as yet undetermined. The division was ordered to bring its troop strength up to full wartime levels, and so I was issued one of the new O.D. uniforms, complete with garrison cap,[11] given the use of the battery station wagon and given the temporary title of recruiting sergeant. I made the rounds of the school, saw all my school chums, and got many of them to join up. My friend Roy had gone to San Antonio, Texas, and joined the Army Air Corps at Brooks Field.

In the latter part of November, 1940, the long awaited word to mobilize came through,[12] and the Armory was a hubbub. My battery (Headquarters Battery) of the 1st Battalion, 131st Field Artillery, was bivouacked at the local American Legion Hut; E Battery of the 2d Bn. was bedded down at the city's Fair Park. The local cavalry troop went to Camp Wolters at Mineral Wells, Texas, and I don't recall where the local company of the 141st Infantry went. Physicals were given, shots were given, and blood was typed. I was typed as AB, the rarest type, only to find out years later after WW II was over, that my type was really B Rh+.

At the American Legion Hut, we set up pyramidal tents left over from WW I. Each tent held eight men. I was made charge of quarters and moved into one of the tents. The units would drill through the day, and at night, the men who lived in town were allowed to return home. Draftees were beginning to be assigned to us. I don't know what some of them lived on before being drafted, but they acted as if they had never had a full stomach in their lives. I was in charge of all the men who stayed in the tents, and I was responsible for seeing that each man bathed twice a week.

---

11. The O.D. uniform was the wool, olive drab winter uniform adopted in 1939. The garrison cap was the visored hat worn with it. Erna Risch, *The Quartermaster Corps: Organization, Supply, and Services,* Volume I (Washington: Office, Chief of Military History, 1953), chap. 3, passim.

12. Induction of National Guard units into federal service began on September 16, 1940, and, as housing and equipment became available, continued through late 1941. The 131st Field Artillery Regiment was inducted on November 25, 1940. Greenfield, et al., *The Organization of Ground Combat Troops,* p. 10; Department of the Army, "Lineage and Honors: 131st Field Artillery (The Lost Battalion)," Jan. 26, 1978, in U. S. Army Center of Military History, Washington, D.C.

A

B

C

E

D

Camp Bowie 1941:
    A. *6 × 6 trucks*   D. *B.C. Scope*
    B. *Sgt. Frank "Foo" Fujita*   E. *Range Finder*
    C. *Bty. Street*

The American Legion Hut had no shower facilities, and so arrangements were made with a motel next door for our men to use their showers. One of the new draftees from Buffalo Gap refused to bathe, and from his looks he had never bathed before. After his second refusal to bathe, I told him that if he did not bathe voluntarily that I would see that he got bathed. He reckoned that I was not man enough to do this. That night I got three other sergeants to help me bathe him. The weather was freezing cold. Just across the fence from our tents was a cow lot with a small frozen-over pond of water. We all grabbed this guy, pulled his clothes off, took him over the fence, threw him into the pond and jumped in with him and proceeded to give him a good scrubbing. We scrubbed him with a GI brush of split bamboo or palm fronds and GI lye soap. This not only took off the dirt but the skin too must have felt as if it were coming off. This man enjoyed his baths from that time forward.

The men were ordered to wear their uniforms at all times, even while off base at night. Sergeants of both E Battery and Headquarters were rotated to pull MP duty in and around town. During the day, many hours were spent at close-order drill and it took some men quite a while to learn the difference between their right foot and their left foot.

In January of 1941, Camp Bowie and Camp Barkeley both were completed enough to be occupied, so we bundled up and moved to Brownwood on January 14. Pyramidal tents had been set up with wooden walls and floors with a small funnel-shaped iron woodburning stove called a Sivly stove. The streets were solid mud in the battery areas, and the main streets were yellow caliche that got onto everything. Each battery had its own showers, motor pool and mess hall. We stayed on garrison rations while at this camp, and food was plentiful and good.

I joined the guards at $21 per month, made corporal at $42 per month, and now I had made sergeant after being transferred from the drivers section to the survey and instrument section, and was making the fabulous sum of $54 a month. Boy! That was "tall cotton." Our mess sergeant was an old WW I vet, and could outcuss any sailor that ever lived. He was a fine old boy and an excellent cook. One day he decided that he would start bootlegging whiskey in competition with a bootlegger next door in B Battery. One night I was in a bull session with the wire chief, a staff sergeant and the regimental commanding officer's driver. We decided to go over to the cook's tent and buy some of the mess sergeant's whiskey. When we went in and ordered some whiskey, he let out with a lot of swearing and then said that the first drink would be on him so we sat down. He pulled a pint from his footlocker, opened it and handed it to the driver, then to the wire sergeant and me. When I handed it back, there was barely enough left for him to have a drink, and he went off on a cussing binge. Finally I got him calmed down and told him that I would pay for the next bottle. That bottle went the same way as the first and we each took turns at paying for the bottle.

Some GI came in and wanted to buy a bottle, and we threw him out and told him that there wasn't enough to sell. The mess sergeant was fit to be tied, but we kept drinking and throwing his customers out until one of the cooks, a huge guy, decided that he needed to get some sleep and demanded that we leave. This did not go over too big and we told him to be quiet. The cook decided that since he was in his own tent that he had a right to evict us, and so he started to throw us out. It wound up that we threw him out, but it took all of us to do it, and what's more we had to throw him out two more times before he decided that perhaps he could get more rest elsewhere.

In my new assignment in the survey and instrument section, I was not only to learn to operate the Aiming Circle, B.C. Scope and Range Finder,[13] but had to learn to set all the instruments and field glasses to the requirements of each officer in my battery, battalion staff and regimental staff. When I was out on the range for firing problems and any one of these officers came to the forward observation post, he would tell me which instrument he wished to look through and I would have to set the instrument to fit his eyes.

In the summer of 1941, the army put on its biggest maneuver in history and the Second Army was to fight against the Third Army. Each army consisted of two or more corps, each with a combination of national guard and regular army divisions plus attached troops such as cavalry, armored

13. The Aiming Circle, Battery Commander's Scope, and Range Finder were used to set and aim the weapons.

engineers, etc. The 36th Division was in the VIII Corps of the Third Army, along with the Oklahoma National Guard 45th Division, the regular army 2d Division, and a cavalry regiment. Our participation in the maneuvers began on August 5th and lasted until the 30th of September.[14]

There were well over 150,000 troops that converged on Louisiana and it really disrupted everything there. Ice was almost impossible to get by civilians or military, and one had to drink hot beer or do without. The military was paid off in two dollar bills, so that a determination could be made of the impact that was made on the local economy by the input of military payroll.

The country was covered with long leaf Louisiana pine, and they grew so thick that the wind could barely penetrate, and the heat along with the high humidity was almost unbearable. There were so many trees trying to reach sunlight that a large percentage of them were saplings of two or three inches in diameter. We found that they were quite flexible, and we would climb them until they began to bend, and then we would swing down and hand-walk them further out towards the top and then ride them down to the ground. This was a lot of fun.

The army was going to try out the concept of an anti-tank platoon on these maneuvers, and so a provisional anti-tank unit was formed, and I was designated scout sergeant in charge of locating the best sites to set up anti-tank guns. We were supposed to have 37-mm anti-tank guns, but what

---

14. The 1941 maneuvers involved four phases: two major operational maneuvers in Louisiana in late September and two more in the Carolinas two months later, both preceded by preliminary training exercises in August and October. The participating forces included a total of 27 regular and national guard divisions plus non-divisional and air corps units—altogether about three-quarters of a million men. Not all units participated in all aspects of these maneuvers and the composition and organization of the opposing forces shifted markedly between each phase.

The 36th Division (which included the 131st Field Artillery) was commanded by Brig. Gen. Fred L. Walker, one of a number of regular army officers who replaced national guard commanders that summer. The division was in the VIII Corps of Lt. Gen. Walter Krueger's Third Army (called the "Blue" army) in both of the Louisiana phases, but did not participate in the Carolina maneuvers. Gabel, *The U.S. Army GHQ Maneuvers of 1941*.

we had was old drive shaft cowlings mounted on the rear wheels and differentials from old autos with plywood shields on them; from a distance they looked like real guns. We would set these dummy guns up at a strategic location, and when a tank or armored enemy vehicle would approach, we would yell BOOM! and a referee would determine whether or not we got the tank or were wiped out ourselves. I would take my crew out in a weapons carrier and we would go scouting for good locations. The action was moving at such a fast clip that at times we could not find our unit which had moved out just ahead of an enemy push. Once, I took my crew out to do our laundry and while out I heard from some 2d Division men that they were bivouacked about ten miles from the laundry. My brother was in the 2d so I decided to go and look him up. It was in the wee hours of the morning before we returned to our bivouac area only to find that our unit had moved. Three days later we finally caught up with them.

These mock battles were carried out in some cases with bloody realism. The two armies were designated the Red Army and the Blue Army. One day my crew and I came up on a squad of Blue Army infantry that had captured some Red Army troops and were marching them back to their lines. The reds were dragging their feet and one of the blues began to prod them with his fixed bayonet. The reds turned and jumped their captors and in a flash the darndest fight broke out with no holds barred. In a few minutes there were men fighting almost as far as you could see. This was very close to the front lines and there were red troops and blue troops fighting on both sides of a road and they covered the road for several hundred yards. A column of tanks came down the road but couldn't get through so they piled out and joined the fight. Someone said that it was Patton and his tanks.[15] There must have been a thousand men or more in the fight, and when it was over the casualty list was pretty high, and we heard later that there were a couple of deaths resulting from this encounter.

Later, I was checking out a spot for a gun location when one of my men said, "Look at that!" and he pointed to a horse and what was left of

15. Maj. Gen. George S. Patton commanded the 2d Armored Division in both Louisiana and the Carolinas and distinguished himself by his daring and unorthodox tactics. Ibid., passim.

a man slumped over in the saddle. I went over to check this out. It turned out to be a cavalry trooper, and someone had beaten him to a pulp, stolen his pistol and everything else he was supposed to have. When we heard some troops approaching we presumed they were the enemy, and we did not relish the idea of getting some of what that trooper got, so we lit out of there.

We were bivouacked near Lake Charles, Louisiana, when a three-day rest period from the maneuvers was declared and passes were to be issued to all who wanted them. Everyone, it seemed, wanted to go to fabulous New Orleans. I just did not want to be there when 150,000 other troops were there bent on the same thing, so two of us decided we would go in the opposite direction to Port Arthur, Texas. The other guy managed for a car, so we headed back to Texas.

Just as we neared Orange, Texas, we saw what to us was the world's tallest bridge. It was a bridge that was built from sea level high enough to clear the tallest ships as they went up the Sabine River. That night, Port Arthur seemed like a ghost town, for a hurricane warning was in effect and most of the businesses had boarded up their windows and left for higher ground. We both managed to get a date with some carhops that didn't have any cars to hop. The hurricane hit, and we were down on the embankment of the Intracoastal Canal. The rain came down in unbelievable amounts. The wind was howling like some banshee from hell, and boats and ships riggings were sailing through the air. We decided that it might be a little safer in town, so we went down on the main drag. The streets were flooded and the water level was up into the shops. One could not determine just exactly where the street was. We thought that if we stayed in the middle we would be okay, but it happened that main drag was a boulevard and we got stuck in the mud in the center of town.

We could not lower the windows for the fierce wind-driven rain, and as my date and I got down to some serious petting, the sweat and temperature in the car rose dramatically. As we completed our tryst, the olfactory evidence of love play in action was overwhelming in the hot steamy car. My gal said that if we did not leave the car the other girl would not give in to my friend. We got out into the raging storm, grabbed hold of an oleander bush for protection from the stinging rain, lay down in the water and had another go in the hurricane.

The next morning we started back to Lake Charles and when we topped the Orange Bridge we wondered how fast we would be going when we hit the bottom if we gave it the gun and then coasted down the rest of the way. The speedometer quit working, so we never knew for sure, but it was plenty fast. When we got back, what used to be the bivouac area had disappeared. The hurricane had cleared things out. The trucks were scattered about, but the tents and personal belongings were strewn all the way from Calcasieu Parish to Nachitoches.

As the maneuvers came to a close we were reminded that a good soldier never returned to camp short of any equipment. The troops were old hands at moonlight requisitioning by now, that is, crossing over into the enemy lines, going through their gear and tents and taking anything, especially alcohol and tobacco, that might be useful or that could be traded off. Both armies practiced this, but woe unto the man that was caught in enemy territory stealing. The cavalry trooper back in the woods had an easy time of it compared to what was meted out to raiders.

The army had plans for starting some sort of a new combat group, and the highest scoring field artillery battalion out of the two armies was to receive overseas assignment to a place called "Plum," the code name of our destination, to form the nucleus of this new group. It was learned that the 2d. battalion of my regiment, the 131st Field Artillery, won the honors.[16]

16. "Plum" was the Philippines, to which large numbers of reinforcements were being sent in the fall of 1941. The 2d Battalion would be part of the newly formed 26th Field Artillery Brigade. Louis Morton, *The Fall of the Philippines* (Washington: Office, Chief of Military History, 1953), pp. 37, 145–46; Edwin W. Hundertmark, "Uncertain Destiny: The Story of the 2d Battalion, 131st Field Artillery," typescript in 131st Field Artillery file, U.S. Army Center of Military History.

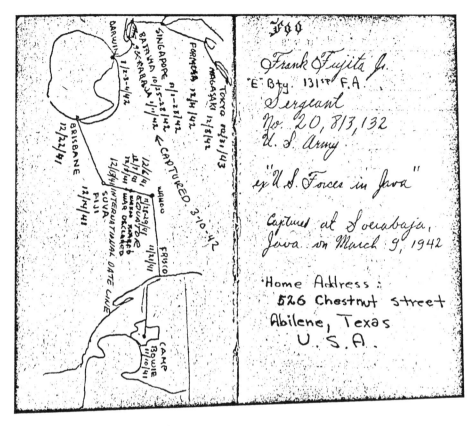

Page from Frank Fujita's first diary showing his journey.

2

THE 2D BATTALION

SAILS FOR "THE PLUM"

1941–1942

The big maneuver now being over and all the various units of the Second and Third Armies having returned to their home bases everyone was eager for passes to go home. Going back home to Abilene could prove to be quite hazardous since the 45th Infantry Division occupied Camp Barkeley. Everywhere we tried to go, there would be the 45th. They were lined up at the theaters, cafes, the bowling alley and just lolling about the streets. We would go around looking for dates at the homes of girls that we knew, and the 45th would be there too. They would give us "T Patchers" (the shoulder patch worn by the 36th Division was a capital "T" inside of a light blue arrowhead) a hard time, and we in turn would refer to them as "Humming Birds" (their shoulder patch was a red diamond with an Indian symbol of a bird that was called a thunderbird). This would invariably start a fight, and each time that we went home it would be to a series of fights.

One weekend, I rode back home with a couple of other fellows and a lone tanker was hitchhiking. We stopped and picked him up. He was from up north and wanted to know what in hell there was to do out here in the Wild West and wasn't there any whiskey to be had? I told him that if he craved a little action and something to drink just to go home with me and I believed that I could fill both orders. When we got to Abilene, we went to a drug store that had a liquor room in the back for medicinal purposes only. There was an elderly doctor sitting at a table just outside the liquor room, and he would ask you how sick you were and write you a prescription for whatever amount and whatever type you wanted and charge a nickle per prescription. Well, we got "sick" several times over the weekend and had to return for some more healing water.

We managed to get into five different fights, and were beginning to show considerable wear and decided that we had better go to my house and bed down for the night. As we passed a small hotel, there were two T Patchers that stopped us when they saw my T Patch and told us that they had just been "took" in a crap game upstairs with loaded dice and would we help them get their money back. We said yes and went upstairs and demanded to see the dice and of course they were not loaded so the tanker and I started to leave when six "Humming Birds" in the hallway decided we couldn't go past them. Well, we managed to get past them after the dust settled, but we did not fare too well on that go-around. When we got home, our uniforms were torn to shreds, and we were bleeding from head to foot. The next morning we were all but incapable of moving, so we stayed home until our ride came to take us back to Camp Bowie.

There was a lot of excitement in the 131st area since the 2d Battalion of the regiment was awarded the trip to "Plum." There was a lot of jockeying for position. Some were trying to get out of going, and some were trying to hop aboard. I was in 1st Bn. Headquarters, but had made up my mind that no one was going anywhere without me. I tried to transfer to 2d Bn. Hq. in the same job that I had in 1st. Bn. All sergeant positions in the battalion were filled, except Machine Gun Sergeant in E Battery, so I jumped on that while I still had the chance. I knew a lot of these guys since E Battery also came from Abilene.

The month of October was spent in drawing new gear and equipment, and the shifting of men from the 132d and 133d Field Artillery regiments, the other two units of the 61st F.A. Brigade, in order to bring the 2d Bn. up to full wartime strength. Each of these three regiments took this opportunity to rid themselves of the drunks, the troublemakers and anyone else that might have fallen into disfavor with the officers or the First Sergeant. Consequently, our group that headed for "Plum" was a motley crew indeed.[1] During all the hubbub I had my twentieth birthday. It seemed that most of the men felt that we were going on some long extended vacation in some exciting land of constant pleasure. I would try to shoot down their wild dreams by telling them we were a fighting outfit and because of the shape the world was in at the time, we wouldn't be back in a few months. But, I told them, we would get into a war and see action before we did come back. They all thought I was crazy and a killjoy.

At last, on the tenth of November, 1941, we had loaded our last piece of equipment onto two separate trains. I was on the first, which pulled out at 10 P.M., and the second train left several hours later on the eleventh. We were on the train for the next four days, and most of the men kept occupied by playing poker or black jack or shooting craps. Some, like me, kept their eyes glued to the windows. This big wonderful land of ours was indeed a sight to behold. I loved every foot of it and felt cheated that the train would travel at night and I would be unable to view the sights. I would lie in my bunk and try to visualize what the pioneers had to cope with in their trek westward, and how the cowboys lived on the trail rides, and how the Indians lived and hunted, and how they must have felt as ever increasing hordes of Bright Eyes forced them from their ancestral grounds and on to the eventual reservations.

On the fourteenth of November, 1941, our trains arrived at Fort Mason, California. We detrained and loaded onto tug boats and were taken out into the San Francisco Bay, out past Alcatraz to Fort McDowell on the next Island—Angel Island—the San Francisco Port Of Embarkation. What a thrill to see the Golden Gate Bridge and the long Oakland Bay Bridge. Frisco looked beautiful whenever the fog lifted enough to enable us to see it. I was fascinated by the harbor activities, with the constant comings and goings of boats and ships of all sizes.

1. The 541 officers and men of the 2d Battalion, 131st Field Artillery, came from a number of Texas cities, including Abilene, Amarillo, Decatur, Fort Worth, Jacksboro, Lubbock, and Wichita Falls. Edwin W. Hundertmark, "Uncertain Destiny: The Story of the 2d Battalion, 131st Field Artillery," typescript in 131st Field Artillery file, U.S. Army Center of Military History.

The ship which carried the "Lost Battalion" to Australia in 1941; shown here without armaments.

• • •

Letter to Mother, 1941, Fort McDowell, Angel Island, California:

November 20
11:A.M.
Dear Mom:

When you get this I'll be well on my way across the Pacific. We are leaving sometime before midnight, I think, on the USS *Republic*.

There are over three thousand men going on this same boat, I think.

It is rumored that we will not stop at the Philippine Islands but go on to Singapore, close to the Burma Road.[2]

2. Destined for the Philippines, the U.S. Army Transport *Republic* carried the 2,600-man 26th Field Artillery Brigade, of which the 2d Battalion, 131st Field Artillery, was a part, and several hundred air corps ground troops. Lida Mayo, *The Ordnance Department: On Beachhead and Battlefront* (Washington: Office, Chief of Military History, 1968), pp. 34–35; Louis Morton, *The Fall of the Philippines* (Washington: Office, Chief of Military History, 1953), pp. 145–46.

I sure hope so because we may get to see some action real soon.

Tell the girls goodbye for me and tell Herb I'll see him in a shell hole somewhere, sometime.

I'll send you some souvenirs from wherever we go.

Don't worry about me because I'll be back with a load of trinkets, a gun full of notches, and a belly full of lead Ha! Ha!

With lots of love
Your son FOO Fujita

P. S. Here's a big kiss for you—SMACK

* * *

At Fort McDowell, we got our first introduction to Consolidated Mess. That is where everyone on base ate at the same facility. They were still on garrison rations at this time, and we spent Thanksgiving there. I will never forget that dinner. We ate on either side of long tables and the meal was unbelievable. For each ten men or so, there would be a carved turkey flanked by all the traditional trimmings. Then there would be several different pies and several different cakes, a bowl of fruits, a bowl of nuts, and then a baked ham flanked by all its usual trimmings, followed with water, tea, coffee or milk to drink. When you were finished eating, you were faced with barrels of candies and barrels of assorted cigarettes as you went out.

Our time here on Angel Island was spent getting more shots for Asian maladies, last minute check of gear and indoctrination. Passes were issued, and the sights of San Francisco were taken in by most of the men. My touring and sampling of the many, many treats that were offered in the area was limited by the fact that I only had five dollars left from my last payday. I made good use of it by having a meal of fried oysters and a Tom Collins, riding the famous trolley, and getting a folding post card depicting all the interesting sights of the area to send to my mother.

On the twenty-first of November, we went back across the bay by tug-boat to the army pier number five. Excitement was running very high, for the day of embarkation had finally arrived and speculation was wild as to where our "Plum" would be. My mind would conjure up all the strange, exotic and exciting places that I had ever read about, heard about, or seen

A page from Fujita's first diary with an illustration of the "Sky Watch" on the sundeck of the Republic.

in the movies, and wonder which would be our ultimate destination. As we stood on the dock awaiting our turn to board, we had our first cases of sea sickness. The closed building part of the pier was to our backs, and the vast side of the thirteen-thousand-ton United States Army Transport *Republic* was in front of us, and this caused us to feel as if we were in a canyon, except that the ship would rise and fall with the wave action of the bay. It made one feel as though the ship was still, but the dock on which we were standing was going up and down, and this sensation was so real that some seasickness resulted.

We boarded the *Republic* carrying our ditty bags and duffle bags with us. We would be told to settle on a certain deck, and before we could get situated, we were told to move to a different deck or section of the deck.

After several such moves, E Battery wound up on F deck, two decks below the main deck. The quarters were close and dank and were dimly lit. The bunks were canvas laced between iron pipe frames and were placed three high, one above the other. I grabbed a top bunk because I felt that it would be the best place in case there was a lot of seasickness. This proved to be a good move as far as the seasickness was concerned, but it was very hot. Fortunately, at the end of my bunk was an air scoop from topside that scooped fresh air to the decks below, and this made it a little more bearable.

At 12:15 P.M. we embarked and all hands were on deck to watch the proceedings and to bid farewell to the Good Old U.S.A. It was a thrilling sight to see all the hustle and bustle of the harbor with what seemed like hundreds of sailboats and speedboats darting in and out of the trawlers and tugs, liners and tankers, cargo ships and naval vessels. The Golden Gate Bridge that loomed ahead and above us made me tingle all over. The thrills and pleasures of the moment were short-lived, however, for as we neared the bridge and pulled out into the entrance of the bay, we had a devastating introduction to land swells—huge, gently rolling swells that lifted the ship beginning at the bow and, as it began to fall, the fantail would come up and this was constant for what seemed to be forever. The deck would feel as if it was dropping out from under you, and as you would plunge to follow it, your stomach would seem to remain back up where you started from. This sensation was coupled with the visual effects of seeing men unsteady on their feet, grabbing hold of one another for support or comfort or onto anything that was solid that would offer some semblance of security. All of a sudden, someone became seasick and began to vomit, and as if by signal it seemed that the entire ship began to vomit. Men would try to reach the rails to upchuck over the sides, but the rails filled quickly, and being unable to hold it, they spewed all over the deck or anyone or thing that happened to be in front of them. Before the Golden Gate was completely out of sight, a full eighty to ninety percent of the three thousand men on board were seasick, including the captain of the ship and most of the crew, who were on their first cruise to learn seamanship.

To say that the ship was a mess was to put it lightly. The ship became instantly hazardous; as the ship would react to the land swells, men would go sliding across the deck and then back again. The vomit covered everything. Just imagine five decks of vomit with its accompanying odors. I was lucky to be among the percentage that did not actually become sick, although I almost did. During the height of the seasickness, I suddenly had the urge to pay my respects to nature, so I slipped and slid my way down to the "head," as the sailors called the latrine, and found an empty stall. It was covered with vomit also, so I had to use the commode while standing on my feet; the lock on the door had been broken, and just as I began to take care of my needs, a sick sailor jerked the door open and threw up all over me, and it took all that I had to keep from getting sick.

As the ship sailed off into the west, the seasickness subsided and we went about familiarizing ourselves with our new environment and developing our "sea legs." The ship had a very good canteen on board, which the navy calls a store or ship's store, and the wares were very cheap compared to prices ashore—like six cents for a package of cigarettes for instance. The line to the ship's store was always long, and sometimes they would close before you could work your way up to the window. As is always the case, there would be those enterprising souls at the head of the line who would buy a lot of cigarettes and candy, and then go back and sell it to those still standing in line at double or triple the price, and, too, as always, there were those who would rather pay the jacked-up price than sweat the line.

Food in the mess was unusual to us in some respects, as they would serve pinto beans and pickled cow's tongue loaf and other cold cuts for breakfast several days a week. We would eat standing up at long tables, and in rough seas, your tray would slide down the table and back again if you did not have hold of it. At times it was difficult to hold on to the table and your plate or tray while eating at the same time. The saltwater showers were exasperating because you could not work up a lather, and what dirt you had on you would just slide around on your skin and you would have to rub hard with a towel to get it off. Movies were shown on deck after dark, and the usual card games and crap games would take place in out-of-the-way places.

We were gradually building up a new vocabulary with words and phrases such as: bulkhead, deck, port and starboard, "the smoking lamp is lit," and "lay aft to the fantail." We thought it odd indeed that the marines did not have to man the brooms and mops and only had to stand guard duty, and since they didn't have to pull KP either, we thought they really had it made.

In addition to the ship's complement of sailors and marines, there was our outfit, the 2d Bn. 131st field artillery, which numbered 558 men;[3] another artillery unit, the 26th Brigade Headquarters battery from the east garrison, Camp Roberts, California; and three units from the Army Air Corps, two bomb groups and a material or fighter squadron. All total, there were over three thousand troops on board. We did not get along too well with the fly boys.

On deck, the crew set up a boxing ring, and we began to have daily boxing matches. There were some really good boxers on board, and some topnotch bouts were staged. The 26th outfit had a very good boxer by the name of Ben Dunn, who became known as Dynamite Dunn for his comparison to the comic strip character. E Battery had some good boxers, Ronald Moses and Hugh Garland, the latter of whom we promptly nicknamed "Judy." The other units also had some good boxers, as did the navy, marines and fly boys. Espirit de corps was fanned to a feverish pitch, and this made the bouts all the more interesting.

I would spend every possible minute on deck watching the sea. I was almost stunned to see how really blue the water was. Back home, when Mom would do the family wash she would pour some bluing from a bottle into one of the rinse tubs, and that is what this very deep blue sea reminded me of. I loved to watch the porpoises race the prow of the ship. They were such beautiful and graceful creatures. I marveled at two albatrosses that were our constant companions, and how they would skim the water mere inches away and never touch a wing tip, no matter the wave condition. Then too, I was fascinated by the large schools of flying fish that would suddenly burst from the water, give a few waggles of their tails for extra propulsion, and then go sailing off for maybe up to a hundred yards before dropping back into the water. The galley crew would go on deck in the early morning and gather the flying fish that had fallen on

3. Probably 541 men. Hundertmark, "Uncertain Destiny."

deck, and I suppose that they would prepare them for the officer's mess, since I do not recall ever having been served any.

We had passed only one other ship on our journey before we pulled into the harbor at Honolulu, Hawaii on the 28th. As we passed the Aloha Tower, there were some GIs standing around who shouted to us that we could now write home and tell our mothers that we had seen some real soldiers. We had a good view of Pearl Harbor from where we docked. We remained here overnight, and four-hour passes were issued to go ashore. It being so late in the month almost everyone was broke, and so we were limited to walking around town or down to Waikiki Beach. I managed to borrow five dollars, so the trip into town wasn't a complete dud. The polyglot of nationalities seemed strange, and women barbers were something that we had never heard of. I spent part of my five dollars on a haircut and a manicure. I was disappointed with Waikiki Beach, perhaps because it was at night and I couldn't really appreciate the waves and the view.

The *Republic* took on fresh water, fruits and other supplies, and then on the morning of the 29th we sailed once again toward our "Plum," which we all felt by now would be the Philippine Islands.

We headed once again toward our unknown destination, but this time we were in convoy with seven other ships and were being escorted by the heavy cruiser USS *Pensacola*. There was another very small naval vessel, which looked like a private yacht, that had been converted into a subchaser and was called the USS *Niagara*. The other ships in the convoy, besides our ship the *Republic,* were a naval transport, the *Chaumont,* two small cargo ships, the SS *Admiral Halstead* and the SS *Meigs,* another transport that I think was called the SS *Coast Farmer* and a Dutch ship, the HMS *Bloemfontein,* a very sleek diesel liner. The next day another transport loaded with artillerymen caught up with us bringing our convoy to nine ships. The name of this ship was the SS *Holbrook* or *General Holbrook.* The pace of the convoy was rather slow, and we learned that the speed of any convoy is no faster than its slowest ship.[4]

4. The *Pensacola* convoy, as it is usually referred to, carried 4,600 artillery and air corps troops as well as crated planes, bombs, ammunition, vehicles, and other equipment. To avoid the Japanese mandated islands on the normal route to the Philippines,

Pencil self-portrait by Frank Fujita in 1941.

Upon leaving Honolulu, we underwent some vigorous training to learn what to do in case we were ever faced with hostilities. The *Republic* had four, 3-inch anti-aircraft guns located one each, in each quadrant of the ship, and had a 5-inch naval rifle located on the stern. Up on the sun deck there were four water-cooled .50-caliber machine guns for additional anti-aircraft protection. The army gun crews had to take turns with the navy in manning the 3-inch guns, but only the navy manned the 5-inch gun. The machine gun sections of each battery also rotated with the navy and air force in manning the sun deck guns. General quarters would be sounded, and every man was to instantly report to his battle station. To avoid mass confusion and collisions, all troops going forward or up would use the stairs or ladders on the starboard or right side of the ship, while those men going aft, or down, were to use the ladders on the port side.

The usual daily activities went on, such as boxing matches, night movies, and the news information programs and the question and answer programs on the public address system. Poker games and crap games would take place in secluded areas of the ship, such as down in the holds or in the life boats. One day one of the medicos, we called him Medico Jones, met me in the sleeping quarters, and when no one was near, he asked me to give him my canteen and motioned for me to be quiet. He disappeared, and shortly he reappeared and handed me back my canteen and suggested that I taste it. I did, and it was 190-proof medical alcohol. He told me not to let anyone know about it and that he would refill it whenever I ran out. He kept me supplied with alcohol the rest of the way across the Pacific.

Another thing that some of us enjoyed on the trip was hot bread. We learned what days of the week the bakers would come out of the bakery with huge trays loaded with hot bread on their shoulders, and we would just happen to be in the corridor that led to the room where they would store the bread. As they would carry the bread past us, we would be on their blind side and snatch off a loaf or two and really have a feast on hot bread. Once one of the bakers saw us do this, and he motioned for us to

---

the convoy followed an unusual southwest course. Mayo, *On Beachhead and Battlefield*, p. 35; Morton, *Fall of the Philippines*, pp. 145–46.

come to the door of the bakery. We did and he split several loaves of hot bread open and swabbed melted butter on each half with a paint brush and gave them to us. Boy! Was that ever good.

We crossed the equator on the 6th of December, and were converted from "polywogs" to "shellbacks," and issued cards to that effect after we had been initiated. For a week or more previous to this, many of the sailors had been behaving rather strangely. They had each made themselves a canvas tube about three inches in diameter and about three feet long. They would stuff these socks full of kapok, a material used for filling in the life-jackets, and go around banging them on the decks or bulkheads and packing them down until they were very hard clubs. As they would do this they would cast evil glances at us, and they would always have a sardonic smirk on their faces. We were completely in the dark as to what was going on, but to our dismay, we were soon to find out as we crossed the Equator.

It seems that it has always been a navy tradition to properly initiate a polywog, a person who has never been south of the Equator, into the sacred domain of King Neptune. The old salts who were already shellbacks had a free reign to devise any sort of contraption or procedure to put the polywogs through that would inflict great humiliation or pain, short of death or permanent injury. The "biggie" for the shellbacks was a thirty-foot long canvas tube big enough for a man to crawl through. The tube would lie flat until a man was in it. The shellbacks would line up on either side of the chute, and as a helpless polywog would crawl through, they would take their kapok clubs and beat him until he emerged out the other end. If you faltered, they would beat you unmercifully until you moved on, or until an officer would put a stop to it, and have you pulled from the chute.

Another procedure involved a large barber chair erected over a tank of sea water. The barber and his assistants would hold you down in the chair, and one of the aides would slap you in the face with a large paint brush dipped into a mixture of slop from the galley—oil and paint—and then the barber would take a very big straight razor that was connected to electricity, and rake it across your face while the assistants would tilt the chair over backwards. As you were getting the full charge of electricity you were dumped into the big vat of water, which was ringed with shellbacks who would push you back into and under the water until you were almost drowned.

There were many other tortures, and not everybody had to go through all of them. Every polywog that had already been through the mill and was duly made a shellback also joined the ranks of the tormentors, and took his revenge out on the others that were still being processed. Occasionally one of the polywogs would be painted up more than the rest and would have a big "S" painted on his chest and back to denote that this victim was to receive extra special treatment. Some of the ones marked like this wound up in the hospital with serious injuries.

Every polywog on board was to receive the initiation regardless of rank. I was one that had been marked as a special case and was so gaudied up that King Neptune thought that I had already been put through the paces, and so he gave me a handful of subpoenas for officers that had not reported for the festivities. He told me to go and get them out of their cabins and not to take "no" for an answer, and that I was to call upon the marshalls, if need be, who roamed the ship to escort the unwilling. He said, "Get them down to the action no matter what it takes!" and that no charge of insubordination could be lodged against me by any officer that had to be forcefully escorted. Most took it as an undesirable inevitability and accepted their subpoenas and reported for their initiation, but a few had to be dragged down by the marshalls. Needless to say, I was completely overjoyed to be lucky enough to miss out on the special treatment that I had been lined up for.

About this time, I was called into the "headshed" and asked to design a shoulder patch, or emblem, for the "Taskforce South Pacific," which our convoy was a part of. I drew up a shield with the Southern Cross star constellation on it, since it could only be seen from below the equator. I don't remember what else I had on it, nor do I know if it was accepted or not.

I never seemed to get enough of watching the sea and the other ships. For the whole trip I spent most of my waking hours on deck, riding the very prow of the ship, and once was even permitted to go up into the crow's-nest. I never tired of watching the albatross or the flying fish, and now we would occasionally see sea snakes. The lumps of phosphorescence, both large and small, that would show up in the water at night were always fascinating.

As the days passed and we became accustomed to the battle drills, there were still those who were convinced that this trip was some sort of glorified sightseeing trip with the tab being picked up by the Army. On December 7, 1941, this illusion was shattered forever when the loud speakers began blaring out that Japan had just bombed Pearl Harbor,[5] and pandemonium broke out aboard ship. It was almost unbelievable that such a thing could happen and that Japan would dare to attack the mighty and invincible United States. The shock was compounded by the knowledge that we had just left there a mere eight days before, and here we were out in the middle of the ocean not too far away and most of our fleet had been sunk in the raid at Pearl!

Battle drills were stepped up, and we began having life boat drills with Mae West life jackets, and we became proficient in all that we were supposed to do. The initial shock of disbelief and rage at the surprise attack on Pearl Harbor subsided. It was replaced by different feelings and emotions by different people. Most were determined that if and when we were called upon to do our bit, we would give it our best shot, while others were so fearful they practically became mental cases. Our movies were cut out, and no smoking was allowed on deck after dark, nor lights of any kind.

One day someone asked on the information program if "there was a Jap on board this ship?" I wrote a short reply to this and gave it to the MC of the program and he read it on the next day's program. It read: "I do

5. An initial radio message to this effect, picked up at 11 A.M., was confirmed shortly thereafter by an official alert from the U.S. Asiatic Fleet. The announcement over the *Republic*'s loudspeakers stated: "Attention all hands. A state of war exists between Japan and the United States. Pearl Harbor has been attacked. Good luck." The next day, the convoy was ordered to head to Suva, in the Fiji Islands, until Washington could decide whether to allow it to proceed. Not until December 12 was a decision reached to order the convoy to Australia, from which point its passengers and cargo would somehow be sent to the Philippines. After a brief stop at Suva, the ships reached Brisbane on December 22. Mayo, *On Beachhead and Battlefield*, p. 35; Morton, *Fall of the Philippines*, pp. 145–48.

not know if there is a Jap on board or not, but there is an American army sergeant who happens to be half Japanese—I know, for I am that person, Sgt. Frank Fujita." I never heard more of this, but was very apprehensive for awhile. We crossed the International Date Line on the 13th and were issued cards to show that we had been duly initiated into the mysteries of the orient.

On the 14th we saw land for the first time in almost two weeks. We had come to the Fiji Islands, and we docked at Suva, the capital city, to take on fresh water and other supplies. A small group of white dignitaries came down to dockside to greet us while the native king was being rowed around our ship so that he could look us over. A band played the national anthems of the U.S. and Britain. On the dock were several native policemen. They wore dark blue tunics trimmed in red and white sarongs that were pinked at the bottom. They were barefoot and wore their hair in large, flat, thick pancake-like masses, which not only served as hair, but functioned as sunshades also. I threw down a pack of Lucky Strike cigarettes to one of them, and he threw me back a Fijian penny, which I still have.

A day or so out of Fiji, we were alarmed when we came upon some naval vessels. The *Pensacola* put on full speed ahead and went to check them out. She was an impressive sight as she plowed through the water, flexing or limbering up her four 8-inch gun turrets as she went. We all watched her go with a high degree of excitement and apprehension as we manned our battle stations. Soon the *Pensacola* flashed back a message that the ships were the Australian cruiser HMAS *Perth* and the French cruiserette *Le Triumphant*. They escorted us to Brisbane in Queensland, Australia.

When we started our convoy in Honolulu, the *Pensacola* was painted white, but now she had been painted battle ship grey as had all the white on our ship. The signal lights were used for all communications, except at times semaphore flags and other flags strung from the masts were used. A radio black out had been maintained since Pearl Harbor.

We arrived at Brisbane on the 22d of December. The *Republic* was too big to navigate the river leading up to the dock, so the USNT *Chaumont* and a Norwegian tanker pulled alongside and drained most of our fuel oil off. Even so, all passengers on board were ordered on deck, and orders were given over the PA system for all hands to move forward, or aft, as the need arose to keep the prow or fantail out of the mud. The river was as white as snow, and looked for all the world like a river of milk. When we got into the middle of it, we found that the white appearance was caused by hundreds of thousands of jelly fish. They were literally jammed together, and were of all sizes from two or three inches across to over a foot in diameter.

We were the first American troops to land in Australia in WW II.[6] It seems that the locals had expected us a couple of days earlier, and thought that we had been sunk, and so there was no fanfare or gala greeting upon our arrival. It was decided that we should march from the dock area to the Ascot Race Track at the edge of town so that the Aussies could get a good look at us. We set up our tents at the race track, and this was to be our base camp while in Brisbane.

The troops were given ample leave to visit town, as there wasn't much to be done until the decision was reached as to what to do with us. It was decided that vast quantities of ammunition and torpedoes would be off-loaded and stored here. It was my misfortune to catch ammunition guard duty, and this is where and how I spent Christmas in 1941. The Australian army went all out to fix up a sumptuous meal for the occasion and there was a near riot when mutton was served as the main course along with hot tea. They found out right quick that Texans did not eat mutton and did not "cotton" to tea. When I got off guard duty, all there was left to eat was link sausage, foul-tasting coffee and very bitter marmalade. Many of the men had met Australians by this time, and had been invited to their homes to share the holidays with them.

Buses, trams the locals called them, ran from the racetrack to town and were free to the Yank GIs. I managed to get to town along with my buddy. We decided to get off the tram and go bar hopping since there

6. They constituted the beginning of an American base in Australia, aimed initially at supplying the Philippines and transformed in a few short months into the Allied Southwest Pacific Area command under Gen. Douglas MacArthur. Louis Morton, *Strategy and Command: The First Two Years* (Washington: Office, Chief of Military History, 1962), pp. 151–53 et passim.

were numerous pubs along the way. The Aussies were most hospitable and would not let us pay for our own drinks. Before long we were getting pretty "loop legged" and came across the local zoo, called the botanical gardens, so we decided to have a look-see at the native flora and fauna. In a large fenced pen in the center of the park were lots of kangaroos, wallabys, kiwis and birds of many colorful and raucous varieties. There was a small kangaroo next to the fence, and so I reached through the fence and petted it. It became interested in my finger and before I knew it the "roo" chomped down on it. I let out a squall and vaulted over the fence and began to chase the roo, bent upon revenge. The next thing I knew, one of the caretakers was chasing me, and when he caught me he explained that the kangaroos could be very dangerous. If caught or cornered, they would grab a man around the neck with their short front legs or arms, sit back on their massive tails while at the same time it would bring its powerful hind legs up and with a sudden downward thrust, they could and have disemboweled men. I was convinced that my best bet was to remain on the outside of the pen.

We received a partial pay while in Brisbane, and this sure did help matters a bunch. I had seen a real pith helmet in one of the stores and decided that I just had to have it. One night a bunch of us were all "drunked up" and went in to one of the local dance halls on the second floor of a downtown building. As the night progressed, we were all having a good time when a private suddenly stood up to a group of Aussies and announced that he would "whip any son-of-a-bitch in the house." This soldier would always go out with us and party but would never get loud or say anything, for that matter, until just before "passing out." That is what happened this night. We found that if there was anything the Aussies liked better than beer it was fighting, so before you could say Waxahachie, all hell broke loose, and when the going started to get a little tough, the soldier went over to the nearest window and stepped out. He had forgotten that we were on the second floor, and he wound up with a broken leg and was put in the local hospital.

On December 28, the 2d Battalion, 131st Field Artillery, and Headquarters Battery, 26th Field Artillery Brigade, were ordered to board the

Dutch liner *Bloemfontein.*[7] The departure was held up because some of the men were not aboard. While the "wheels" were trying to find out about them, a loud commotion was coming down the street. The commotion turned out to be the three missing men, and they were pushing a rollaway hospital bed with the injured soldier in it. They had a bottle of booze that they would pass around, and then up to the patient. They did not intend to leave him behind.

It was a good try, but the soldier was left behind after all, and did not know at that time just how lucky he really was. After things quieted down, we sailed off again to our "Plum," and once more we were alone. There was an Australian pilot that stayed on board, and he was to do all the navigating, since our route around Australia was to take us inside the Great Barrier Reef. It was still dark and I was on watch. There seemed to be one scare after another as the ship was going at a pretty good clip. Suddenly a massive reef would jump out of the darkness at us and just as it appeared that we would crash into it, the pilot would swerve to miss it, only to be faced with another, and another and another. We were not allowed the use of the ship and had to bed down on the deck. The officers were given state rooms. Lt. Col. Searle was the C.O. of the 26th, and as senior to our Lt. Col. Tharp, was in command.[8]

On the 30th, as we rounded Cape York, the northernmost point of Australia, we could see Australia on one side of us and New Guinea on the other side. Also, what we could see right here in the middle of the Torres Strait was what appeared to be the entire Jap navy between us and Thursday Island. Sure enough, we were in luck again, for the ships turned out to be American. In the group were the cruisers *Houston, Marblehead* and *Boise,* five destroyers and two or three cargo ships. After some chit-chat between ships, we were on our way again. We passed on through the

7. In an effort to speed the badly needed artillery units to the Philippines, the entire 26th Field Artillery Brigade sailed north that afternoon on board the *Bloemfontein* and *Holbrook,* the two fastest ships in the convoy. Morton, *Fall of the Philippines,* p. 154.

8. Lt. Col. Albert C. Searle, commanding 26th Field Artillery Brigade, and Lt. Col. Blucher S. Tharp, in command of the 2d Battalion, 131st Field Artillery.

Torres Strait into the Gulf of Carpenteria, on through the Arafura Sea, and then turned south past Melville Island and into Port Darwin. Port Darwin was a miserable looking frontier outpost. It had no facilities for troops and for the four days that we remained here we were not allowed ashore.[9]

While awaiting the decision from higher ups as to what we were to do next, we unloaded our 75-mm guns from the holds and lashed them to the decks along with some 37-mm anti-tank guns. The *Bloemfontein* had no armaments. The machine gun crews of each battery broke out their Browning Automatic Rifles (BARs) for protection against aircraft.

We had spent New Year's Day 1942 plowing through the Gulf of Carpenteria, and after four days of sitting idle here in Darwin we were glad to be on the move again on the 5th.[10] The *Boise* and *Marblehead* were with us. We sailed west out of Darwin into the Timor Sea, past the islands of Timor, Flores, Sumba and Sumbawa, and then turned north through the Lombok Strait between the islands of Bali and Lombok. We were alerted that a Jap submarine was lying in wait for any ship that dared to come through the strait. We spent the whole night on full alert, and we were ordered to wear our life jackets at all times.

We made it through the strait without mishap, but a ship ahead of us, a Norwegian tanker, and the SS *Liberty* behind us, were sunk. Our luck was holding out. It was as we were coming through the Timor Sea that we saw several whales that would come up and blow, and this in a setting of placid seas with a number of water spouts way off in the distance. The sun was coming up as we rounded Bali, and its rays would cast dancing silhouettes of the palm trees onto the gyrating screen of swirling mists that covered the island. It was easy to become oblivious to the imminent dangers of

9. Japanese advances into the Netherlands East Indies seriously threatened any effort to reach the Philippines. Accordingly, Maj. Gen. George H. Brett, the new American commander in Australia, ordered the *Bloemfontein* and *Holbrook* to put in at Darwin. Morton, *Fall of the Philippines,* p. 154.

10. The troops on the *Holbrook* debarked at Darwin but a portion of the 26th Field Artillery Brigade headquarters and the 2d Battalion, 131st Field Artillery, remained aboard the *Bloemfontein* and sailed for Soerabaja to reinforce the defenses of Java, now endangered by the onrushing Japanese. Hundertmark, "Uncertain Destiny."

being torpedoed in the midst of such beauty. After rounding Bali, we proceeded westward between the islands of Madoera and Java and to the port city of Soerabaja, the largest city and port on eastern Java, an island about eight hundred miles long and close to three hundred miles wide.

The port of Soerabaja was a hive of activity, and boats and ships of every size and description filled the harbor. I was especially impressed with the native boats called Sam-Pans, on which whole families of Javanese were born, lived their entire lives, and when their times came, died, never knowing another home but the Sam-Pan. Each family would have its own style of painting and decorating its boat, and always in very brilliant colors. There were also large ocean-going Chinese Junks, very picturesque with their bamboo ribbed sails. We docked about 3:00 P.M. on January 11th. Smoke was billowing up a short distance away, and we heard that a lone Japanese plane had come over shortly before we arrived, dropped a single bomb, and that is where the smoke was coming from.

I was somewhat disappointed with this port, for it seemed as though I had been here before. Of course I hadn't, but this feeling was with me every place we went from then on out. This was a weird and uncanny feeling.

Upon arriving, we immediately debarked and loaded onto a narrow-gage train and headed south into the mountains of east Java. The railroad followed a river, and we all watched with great fascination the vistas and scenes that unfolded before us as we proceeded inland. The train had a wood-burning engine, and we would go "hell bent for election" for a good ways and then it seemed that the train would slow down considerably, and then we would go again at break-neck speeds.

It seemed to us that life itself revolved around and upon the river. The river was used for everything. Here would be someone fishing, and then someone would be washing down some carabao. There would be native women doing their laundry next to someone taking a bath, next to a person squatting on the end of a plank held out over the water on stilts, relieving himself.

From downtown, the buildings changed from modern stucco buildings to the thatched-roof dwellings of the natives, and then on into the countryside with the fascinating terraced rice paddies. As I was looking out my window there was what seemed to be two haystacks, side by side, moving along the roadway. Suddenly they stopped, and a native man stepped out from between these huge piles of straw to stare at us as we passed. The man had been carrying the hay on what we came to call a yo-yo pole, a pole that would be placed over one shoulder and equal loads would be suspended from either end. It was unbelievable what heavy loads these natives could carry in this manner. Also along the road there was a never ending procession of two-wheeled bull carts, gas burning vehicles of every sort and a constant stream of natives going in both directions. Taxis were numerous also. There were the two-wheeled horse drawn types, and the three-wheeled motorcycle and tricycle types.

Soon, it became too dark to view the countryside, so we would just speculate on where we would wind up and what we would be faced with once we got to where we were going. We were climbing higher and higher into the mountains and several hours later the train stopped near the town of Malang.[11] Some Dutch army officers ushered us onto army buses which took us about eight miles from town to an army airfield and camp. We detrained in the dark, and some Dutch army personnel served us sandwiches, hot tea and bananas. The soldiers wore dark green uniforms with wrap leggings and hobnailed shoes and wide-brimmed straw hats that had one side turned up and pinned to the crown.

• • •

Letter from Sgt. Frank Fujita to Mrs. Pearl Fujita

Singosari Airfield
Malang, Java
January 13, 1942

Dear Mom:

Perhaps this letter will ease your mind a little because I can now tell you where I'm at.

11. About 50 miles south of Soerabaja.

I'm in top shape and sure love this side of the world. We made our trip O.K. and are now in Java.

So far I haven't seen any action but may at any time. I sure wish you could see this side of the world. It is sure a beautiful place indeed. However, it is rather uncomfortably hot down here sometimes.

We spent many a day on the high seas and saw a lot of things and will probably see many more before it is over.

Well, tell everybody hello and write to me. (All my friends.)

Well, goodbye until next time.

Love,

FOO

P. S. I haven't had a letter since we left.

年 月 日	品　　　名	数　量	巷	買入金額	支拂金額	倍 或 袋	差引殘高

January 11, 1942

About 3:00 P.M. we docked at "Soerabaja, Java" after having come through the "Madoera Strait" ← *just bombed still smoking* unmolested. We immediately dis- embarked, got on to a train and *BATHER'S HAY STACKS ← TYPE OF TRAIN* started south (inland). After riding for several hours we stopped some where near "Malang" and it was very dark. We then loaded onto busses and went to an Aerodrome about eight miles from "Malang". This place is called "Singosari" and is located in the mountains of East Java. Dutch soldiers in green uniforms met us at the camp and had hot tea, sandwiches and bananas waiting for us. We slept on straw on a cement floor. Next day we got beds and organized. I guess this will be our "PLUM".

reload tape at 137'

3

JAVA FALLS TO

THE JAPANESE

January 1942–March 1942

After eating, we were shown to some stucco buildings and told that this is where we would bunk down for the night. These buildings were very open and were more like horse stalls than sleeping quarters. The floors were bare, and all we had to sleep on was straw over a concrete floor. When we were told where the showers were, everyone made a mad dash for them, for a freshwater shower was absolute heaven after all the saltwater showers aboard ship. The island of Java is only seven or eight degrees below the equator and quite warm, but up there in the mountains it was cool and the showers were icy cold.

The next day we were issued cots and mosquito netting to replace the straw with. Work details and all the truck drivers were taken back to the docks in Soerabaja to get our vehicles and all the battalion equipment and supplies. It looked as if this was going to be our "Plum." It was called Singosari and consisted of an army camp adjoining a grass airfield. What was left of the U.S. Army's 19th Bomb Squadron, under the command of a Col. Eubank from Clark Field in the Philippines, was here and trying to fly from this field. Most of the 19th's planes were lost on the ground when the Japanese attacked them. The planes were B-17 Flying Fortresses.[1]

1. The 19th Bombardment Group, commanded by Lt. Col. Eugene L. Eubank, lost roughly half of its B-17s in the Japanese attack on

The reason that the 19th was trying to fly from this base was that flight crews were all they had. They were trying to service the few planes they had, as well as load the bombs, belt the ammunition for the machine guns and do everything that was necessary to keep bombers performing. They were desperate for help, and even needed men to fill out their flight crews, so Col. Eubank asked our C.O. to furnish the necessary men and assistance.

Of course our colonel agreed to this, and these extra duties added to our own multitudinous tasks of trying to get all of our equipment up from the docks, establish our new camp and outpost guards, plus all of the usual duties that are connected with the normal operation of a military unit, made life tedious indeed. We took our rest if and when we could, and duty hours stretched around the clock. If you had a little time in between shifts, there was a small village near our camp that we called Monkey Village. Beer and sex could be had for next to nothing. Sex here was known as "mac-mac," and was the most plentiful commodity that was available to us. The jungle came right up to our camp and airstrip, and native drums seemed to be constantly sending messages back and forth all through the mountains. With all our modern communications, the drums were usually first to get any new information to the camp.

There were huge obstacles made from trees and resembling jacks, like my sisters used to play with back home, and these were to be moved out onto the runways in case the Japanese attempted to land aircraft, gliders or paratroopers here. We had to furnish the guards for our camp and the airfield too. One of the guard posts was set up on the road leading into the air strip. Once, when I was Sergeant of the Guard and was making my rounds, the guard at this post said "Sarge, what am I supposed to do? These Air Force officers won't stop when I order 'Halt.'" I asked him if

---

Clark Field on the first day of war. A few more were lost in action during the week that followed and the surviving heavy bombers were then evacuated to Australia. By January 1, 1942, they had moved to Singosari airfield, where they were subsequently joined by a few other B-17s newly arrived from the United States. Wesley Frank Craven and James Lea Cate (eds.), *The Army Air Forces in World War II*, 7 vols. (Chicago: University of Chicago Press, 1948–58), I, pp. 213, 220–22, 372–78.

he knew his general orders for guard duty and he said that he did, and so I asked him what the orders said to do and he said, "Holler 'Halt' three times and if they don't stop then shoot." I said, "Then why are you asking me what to do when you know what to do?" I drove off back to the main camp and a jeep full of fly boys whizzed past me going towards the guard post. Sure enough a shot rang out. I whipped my jeep around and went back, and the guard had three badly shaken pilots standing at attention. We had no further problems with them not stopping to be identified.

Another amusing incident about a guard was one involving a private from a town near Abilene who was assigned to Headquarters Battery. This soldier had a speech impediment and when we mobilized in Abilene he could not be understood. Our medical officer, Lt. Lumpkin, operated on his tongue, and now with a great deal of effort one could understand him. He was known in Abilene as "Corky," but the guys in headquarters called him "Bo." Anyhow, he was on guard duty one night and the Sergeant of the Guard had put him on post number one, which was just outside the guard house, so that he could keep an eye on him. Late that night a command car came toward the gate and Bo said "Halt!" The car kept coming and Bo, not remembering what to say next, raised his rifle, cocked it and said "Dod dammit, I taid Haut!" The car squealed to a halt and Bo said "Git out!" They all piled out, and it was the medical officer. As Bo said nothing else, the doctor said rather sneeringly—"What's the matter soldier—you forgot what to say next?" and Bo, while never lowering his rifle, said "Yes, and Dod dammit, ou better not moof, til I tink of it!"

When we left the USA, we were supposed to be the best equipped field artillery unit in the whole army. We were supposed to have the new split trail 105-mm howitzers. At that time, I understand there were only six in the entire army[2] and they were not in our outfit. Instead we had WW I French 75-mm guns with the split trail American modification. We were supposed to have the new .30-caliber carbines but we had WW I 1903 A-3,

2. This is something of an understatement, but the new howitzers were nonetheless in short supply. Constance McLaughlin Green, Harry C. Thomson, and Peter C. Roots, *The Ordnance Department: Planning Munitions for War* (Washington: Office, Chief of Military History, 1955), pp. 186–87.

"You take a city bred boy and put him out in the jungle by himself where there are known tigers, bear and snakes of all kinds, and his imagination will run away with him." Jungle Outpost, pen and ink drawn by Frank "Foo" Fujita, "Bunker Hill" POW Camp, Tokyo, Japan, 1944.

.30-caliber Springfield rifles with 5 rounds of ammunition per man. We should have had thirteen air cooled, tri-pod mounted .50-caliber machine guns for the battalion. We had thirteen tri-pods. No guns and no ammo. We had WW I steel helmets and training gas masks that were good for one hour in tear gas. We were a formidable force indeed.

We had established outpost guard stations around the perimeter of our camp and the air strip, and they were connected to a switchboard in the guard house. One night an E Battery corporal was very drunk and some-one told him that his mother was wanting to talk to him on the switch-board. He said that his mother did not know that he drank and would someone talk to her for him. Every one laughed and refused, and he had to be physically restrained from shooting someone.

These outposts were in the jungle or tall grass, and out of sight of the camp itself. Now, you take a city bred boy, and put him out in the jungle by himself where there are known tigers, bears and snakes of all kinds, and his imagination will run away with him. The ever-booming native drums kept one on edge, for we were told that the Fifth Column was very active in the area, spying on our every move. It was easy to think that the drums were telling some hidden sniper that you were out here all alone and ripe to be shot. A troop of wild monkeys at times would come into our camp and would pass through the tall grass. On several occasions this caused a nervous sentry to fire away at the unseen enemy.

The only canteen at the air strip was for officers only, but since there were no other facilities of this sort for the enlisted men, they did allow non-commissioned officers to use it also. Once, several of us sergeants got to a point in our work loads that we had enough free time to indulge in a few rounds of elbow bending. Some Royal Air Force (RAF) had moved into our camp, and when we entered the canteen there were a number of the RAF officers sitting around with some Dutch officers. With great pomp and ceremony, they would sip their little thimble-like drinks. When the Texans came in, each one ordered his own bottle and we sat down and began drinking from the bottles. The Dutch and the Limeys, after their original disdain of such actions, were later impressed and vowed that they had never seen such drinking before.

One day in the latter part of January we were ordered to stay in from work details and get spruced up, for we were to put on a show of our capabilities for the commander-in-chief of the ABDA (American, British, Dutch and Australian) Powers in the far east. This was a one-eyed British general who wore a patch over his bad eye—Gen. Archibald Wavell.[3] We exhibited sufficient skill in the performance of our military duties that the

3. The ABDA Command was established on January 10, 1942. Gen. Sir Archibald P. Wavell had previously commanded British forces in the Middle East and India. Louis Morton, *Strategy and Command: The First Two Years* (Washington: Office, Chief of Military History, 1962), p. 161.

general was duly impressed. We heard that he said that he had never seen such big men. I must not have been in his line of sight. E Battery was assigned to take care of the air units and the rest of the battalion was relieved from this chore.

Some of our men were transferring into the Army Air Forces to become a permanent part of the 19th Bomb Group. My buddy Ben Keith and I tried to transfer as tail gunners, but our captain said that we were indispensable. One day I was called into the head shed and was told that Lt. Col. Searle had been promoted to full Bird Colonel, and since there were no military stores on Java that sold US Army insignias, I was asked if I would draw up a set of eagles so that a native craftsman in Malang could embroider some for the colonel to wear. Of course I did, and the colonel was very proud of them.

Upon arriving in the Dutch East Indies, we were placed under Dutch command—a move, I presume, designed to placate the Dutch command and assure them that not only were American troops on hand to help defend Java, but we were the tip of the iceberg, so to speak, of more troops to come.[4]

On the 3d of February 1942, we got our first bombing raid at Singosari. I had set up my gun position in a field about 200 yards from our main camp and had the crew dig a foxhole next to it. When the first wave of bombers came over, I was standing next to my jeep with Cpl. Ben Keith. Ben was not in my machine-gun section, but he and I were fast buddies, and he spent as much time with me at my gun position as he could. As I said, this was our first raid and we were fascinated by the ghostly formations of planes. Their white undersides made them hard to see distinctly, and they looked like ghosts. We watched as they opened

4. The 2d Battalion was initially attached to the 19th Bombardment Group. Not until the dissolution of ABDA at the end of the month did it, along with all other Allied forces on Java, come under Dutch command. Edwin W. Hundertmark, "Uncertain Destiny: The Story of the 2d Battalion, 131st Field Artillery," typescript in 131st Field Artillery file, U.S. Army Center of Military History; Maj. Gen. S. Woodburn Kirby, *The War Against Japan*, 5 vols. (London: Her Majesty's Stationery Office, 1957–69), I, p. 429; Lionel Wigmore, *The Japanese Thrust* (Canberra: Australian War Memorial, 1957), p. 495.

their bombbays and saw the bombs leave the planes in long strings. It all seemed fairylike and unreal. The whole scene did not seem threatening. War and bombing raids were something that we had read about that happened to other people in other times and places and had nothing to do with us.

Suddenly, we heard the swish—swish—swish of the falling bombs, and it dawned on us that this was the real McCoy. It was too late to get to the fox-hole, so we just flattened right where we were. The noise was terrible, and the concussion from the bursting bombs and flying shrapnel and earth brought home the deadly reality of it all. Dirt was splattered on my jeep, and when everything had calmed down and the planes had gone, we found that the edge of the nearest bomb crater was a mere twenty-five feet from us. The ground was very moist down to six or seven feet, and this caused the bombs to go deep before detonating. The main force of the blast was consequently directed more vertically than laterally, thus sparing us the full force of the explosion, the bursted ear drums and possible brain concussions. We never were caught in the open again.

There were a total of twenty-seven bombers that took part in this raid, and, fortunately, we had no casualties or damage to the camp. The 19th had been flying B-17s that had no tail guns. The Japanese pilots knew this to be a blind spot and would attack the planes from the rear. Earlier in the day, the fly boys had been very excited about a new version of the flying fortress that had twin .50-caliber machine-guns and a gunner's seat in the tail that was coming in from North Africa. Another B-17 was ordered up for a test flight after having been repaired from being shot up. Two of our artillerymen were aboard, and while out on this run they were attacked by Zeros and shot down. All on board were lost, and these were our first casualties of the war. Our men were: Pvt. Don H. Barnes (one of a pair of twins), F Battery from Lubbock, Texas; and Pvt. Jack E. Bingham, Headquarters Battery, Christoval, Texas, (who had transferred when I did from 1st. Bn. Hq. Bty. back in Camp Bowie, Texas.)[5]

5. The attacking Japanese planes, from the naval 21st Air Flotilla, also destroyed four B-17s on the ground and damaged the Singosari runway. Despite heavy fire from the 2d Battalion's 75-mm guns, the low-flying enemy aircraft escaped without damage.

Everything seemed to be going the Japanese's way. They had taken the American islands of Guam and Wake, did as they pleased in China, and on Christmas day of 1941, had taken the British Crown Colony of Hong Kong and the American detachment of marines, and at this very moment were breathing down the throat of the British Empire's impregnable fortress of Singapore. The native drums would talk back and forth day and night, and they would give you an eerie feeling to say the least. As the air raids went on we learned to pay attention to the drums, for in spite of our modern communications systems, the drums seemed to always have the news of an impending raid before the radio or telephones got the message to us. We could tell by the frenzied activity of the drums when raids were about to take place.

In addition to all the work details we had to perform for both ourselves and the air force, each battery had to rotate pulling MP duty in town. It does not take a GI very long in a new place to find just where to locate the things he fancies. This little mountain town of Malang had everything we wanted. The Toko Oen Restaurant quickly became one of the favorite eating and drinking places; they served a very good steak—probably carabao—and the dark Heineken beer was absolutely delicious. The whole country was under black-out conditions at night, and this made our surroundings seem very eerie, with the many, many shadowy figures that would suddenly loom out of the dark, and then just as suddenly disappear. The weird strains of the native music and the unforgettable smell of native cigarettes; the ghostly tricycle taxis with their barely visible blue, black-out lights; and all the other strange smells and sounds would cast an exotic spell over me.

There were other types of taxis, too. Some were three-wheeled motor-cycles with a canopied seat for two people that was fastened to the motor-cycle where the front wheel should be; and the horse drawn taxis, two-wheeled carts that would hold up to four people, two on each side, with the driver on a seat mounted in front, and pulled by a diminutive native horse. All of the taxis were highly decorated in brilliant colors, with

Walter D. Edmonds, *They Fought With What They Had* (Boston: Little, Brown, 1951), pp. 312–13; Craven & Cate, *Army Air Forces*, I, p. 383.

bangles and bells too. When we arrived in Malang, the taxi fare around town was thirty-five cents in their money, but this did not last for long. As is usually the case when a bunch of GIs go out and get drunked-up, they also get sort of free-hearted, and they would give the drivers maybe two or three gulden (like our dollars). Well, this was as much as they could make all day carrying the Dutch around. It got to where they were reluctant to pick up a Dutchman and would rather take a chance on picking up an American soldier. The Dutch didn't take too kindly to this.

Native vendors would go up and down the streets pushing their two-wheeled carts with their wares in them. What they were vending determined how the carts were built. Some of them had charcoal braziers or ovens on them, and others that sold ice cream had freezer compartments in them. Some vendors were selling Dutch pastries. I have never tasted any pastries that were any richer or flakier than those made by the Dutch. They were out of this world.

Another snack that was sold from the carts was a sort of pig-in-the-blanket-like thing. It was a sausage link wrapped in very flaky pie crust and baked. It was delicious. Another that I had been eyeing ever since we were in Java was what appeared to be barbequed chicken halves. They were golden brown and always looked so tantalizing. They displayed these out in the open, and I had noticed that there were never any flies around them. One day I was full of good Dutch beer and came to a vendor selling these chickens; I decided that I would try one. The vendor handed the chicken half on a piece of banana leaf as a napkin. I tore off a leg, bit into it and liked to have gone into orbit. The chicken had been marinated in hot pepper juice and was just slightly cooler than a blow-torch.

The banana leaf was a universal tool on the island. It was used as an umbrella during the rain, and as wrapping and packaging material for all sorts of products and foods. When the native vendor gave me the chicken on the leaf, it was intended to be used as a plate.

All kinds of pets were offered for sale, and quite a few monkeys were bought by men of the outfit. The cats that were native to the island were without tails. When I first saw them I thought that was a man-made fashion for them.

On my trips into town, I was fascinated with the fancy, wavy bladed knives made by the natives, called kris. They had very porous steel blades that were sometimes filled with a poisonous substance. I bought two of these knives, one of which I wore stuck into my pistol holster, and the other kris stuck through my belt in back. Sergeants and above wore the .45-caliber automatic pistol for sidearms, and corporals and below were issued the 1903 A-3 Springfield .30-caliber rifle. Another item that caught my fancy was the highly ornate, hand carved Balinese dancer head; and I bought three of these.

On February 9, the Japanese bombed us again,[6] and this time they had more success—both our supply houses were hit. The canteen, the mess hall, the water main, two trucks and a command car were also hit. A bomb hit near where Sgt. Leon Sparkman of F Battery was located, and completely covered him up with dirt. I was told that before his buddy could dig him out, a second wave of bombers made their run and another bomb burst uncovered him.

Earlier that morning I had a frightening experience. We had been issued smoke pots to set off in case of a threatened paratroop drop, to obscure the airport runways. Ben was with me as well as a couple of my regular machine-gunners with their BARs, and we were wondering just what these pots did and how much smoke they put out. I told one of the men to put one down into the fox-hole and set it off and we would see. We were startled at the huge cloud of smoke that issued forth from the fox hole. It climbed high into the sky, and there was no wind to disperse it. I became fearful of not only rousing the ire of the officers, which would result in reprimand for myself, but also for sending up a signal that would pin-point our location to any enemy plane that might be in the area. I yelled for the men to pour water from our GI cans on the pot, and put it out. This only made it burn more. We emptied the rest of our water cans on it until it was submerged in water, but it kept on smoking fiercely. We then took the sand bags that were piled up around the jeep and covered the thing up completely, but it just kept on sending up this cloud of smoke

6. During this period, Japanese airstrikes on Java's ports and airfields continued almost daily, but this was apparently the first attack on Singosari since February 3. Kirby, *The War Against Japan*, I, p. 433.

until it burned itself out, with me expecting at any minute to see the whole battalion staff come riding up to throw the book at me.

Money had been a very scarce item with us until Valentine's Day, when we received what proved to be our very last pay day of the entire war. We were paid up to, and including, January 1942. We were paid in the currency of the East Indies, called gulden, but we called them gliders or gilders.

On the 18th of February, we knew a raid was coming by the frantic activity of the drums. Sure enough the air raid sirens soon went off and we were told that six Jap Zeros were coming in. Then shortly after the all clear was sounded, and we were told to go about our usual business because the planes were American P-40s and not Zeros. Well, it happened that the first report was more correct. Nine Zeros destroyed five B-17s on the ground, strafed the airdrome and camp, and wounded several men, including Pvt. Joe Holder of E Battery.[7]

We usually got our raids at noon, and on this day I decided to go into camp and eat early so that I might be back on my guns when the raid came. I had recently moved my twin 50s to a new location out on the edge of the East-West runway, and they were about a quarter of a mile away from the main camp. Today the planes came early. I was in the canteen having a beer with a sandwich that I had picked up at the mess hall, when suddenly I heard machine-gun fire. I jumped up and started running across the very green grass in my very bright Khakis, toward my gun pit. I was about halfway across this field when three Zeros that had made a strafing pass at the hangars and main camp, circled around and were coming in for a run at the officers' quarters that flanked the runway across from my gun position. Evidently they saw me out in that dark field, standing out like a new dime. I was between them and the camp, and all three peeled off and strafed at me on their way to the camp. The rattle of their machine-guns sounded like a handful of dried beans being shaken in a tin can, and the 20-mm canon they carried would explode upon impact and throw dirt

7. The Japanese flew air sweeps over eastern Java for several days to cover their invasion of Bali. The attack described here may well have actually occurred on February 20. Edmonds, *They Fought With What They Had*, pp. 363, 399–400.

all over me. My heart pounded so hard that I thought my blood vessels would burst. I felt as if I was literally bouncing up and down, I was shaking so much. To this day, I would swear that I crawled completely under my WW I steel helmet. After the planes passed on, the ground around me looked as if someone had taken a table fork and dug up the whole area. I jumped up and finished the rest of the distance to my guns in what must have been some sort of a world record. Pvts. Hugh Garland and Eddie Donaho had been watching from the gun pit, and when I came up and dived into the pit, they said, almost in unison, "My God! Are you what they were firing at?"

By the time the planes were again coming around to make another run, I was ready for them and cut loose on them with my twin 50s as they made a pass over camp. They circled and came right down the runway. I kept my guns loaded in such a manner that I could always see just where I was shooting. I had loaded my ammo belts with one tracer round, an armor-piercing round and two rounds of ball ammunition. By staggering the two guns' ammo belts, I could see where I was shooting. After the raid was over one of the pilots, who had been watching the whole thing from the front porch of his quarters, came over to my gun pits and asked if I was the one that had been firing the guns on that last pass, and I said I was. He said, "That was the best shooting I have ever seen; you and another gun over in the Army camp poured lead into that one plane right on the money. That plane fell in the jungle over near the foot of that mountain." He told me that if I needed verification for shooting it down, that he would furnish the necessary facts, and then he gave me his name and rank, which I did not write down.

After my experience of being caught away from my guns, I decided to have my gun pit extended into a three room complex where I could live and even sleep there without having to leave. A group of natives passed by and I motioned for them to come over to me. They must have been on their way to Monkey Village to sell their produce, for they had bananas, chickens and vegetables with them.

There was a Dutch soldier not far away and I yelled for him to come over and interpret for me. He told me that the natives understood what I wanted and would be back the next morning to begin work. He said that it would cost me ten cents a day for each worker and not to pay them more than that. He said that the average cost per meal for the natives was three cents and if I paid them more than that they would only lay off work until what I paid them was used up at that rate.

I bought one of the stalks of bananas and offered them one each. I sort of thought that, having been born and reared around bananas and coconuts and the likes, they would be burned out on them. Not so. They went after the bananas as if they had never had one before. I then figured out that they were so poor they had to sell what they grew in order to purchase the other staples they needed to subsist on.

They came the next morning to work—five of them, and one was acting as the head man. They dug me out an adjoining room to my gun pit the first day, and I just could not bring myself to only giving them ten cents and so I gave them twenty-five cents each. They all beamed with joy and bowed and thanked me profusely. The Dutchman was right, for I had given them more than two days wages and they did not come back until the second day later. They obviously were accustomed to living meal to meal or day by day and never looked beyond that.

Although the loss of the B-17s was a blow, it was a boon to the machine-gun crews of the battalion, for now we had plenty of .50-calibers, which were taken from the destroyed B-17s to augment our Browning Automatic Rifles with. This had been one of the most eventful days I had experienced so far. Surviving the three Zeros convinced me that my time was not up yet and that someone was watching over me, so that night I went into Malang, had a steak and a few beers, and then went to the telephone office and placed a call back home to my mom. The operator said that she did not know how long it would take for the call to go through and that I would just have to wait. I went out into the darkness and sat on a bench in the yard to wait. A very dim blue lightbulb lit up the doorway to the building and after a few minutes I could see pretty good for several feet in all directions. A young native girl was lingering about, and every few minutes she would come over and ask, "Mac Mac? Lima poela sen!" An hour went by and when I checked with the operator she again said that she did not know when the call would come through. Back outside, I was accosted by the young girl again, and decided that since the night was very dark, and the grass was thick and soft, this would not be a bad way to pass a little time.

Later, the call came through and it was as clear as if my mom was right there in the phone room with me. I was so excited that I looked at the clock wrong, and hung up at the end of two minutes instead of the three minutes that I had paid for. The call to home cost me thirty-five gliders, the mac-mac fifty cents, and I returned to camp a very happy man to still be alive.

The navy began to send some of their submariners to Singosari for R&R. One day some of these sailors were sitting next to Corky in the mess hall during the noon meal. As I said before our bombing raids usually came around noon, and consequently everyone would eat his meal in complete silence. No banging of silverware or plates, and any talking was in very muted tones—everyone had one ear cocked, listening for the air raid siren to go off, or for the sound of planes.

One of the sailors asked Corky what the sirens sounded like so that they would know to take cover. Corky couldn't think of words to describe the sirens and decided that he could demonstrate the sound better. He cupped his hand around his mouth and began to sound like a siren and the whole mess hall, as one man, took off en masse. When Corky saw everyone else run, he took off also. We always made jokes that when the siren went off everyone would run so fast and so far in one minute, that it would take them an hour to walk back.

On the 19th of February two Zekes, this is what we called Zeros, came over and strafed hangar number one, and then on the 22nd of February we had another bombing raid, and again, they completely missed us or were bombing something out of our sight.

Singapore and Sumatra had fallen to the Japanese, and now they were poised to land on Java, which was not only the main island of the Dutch East Indies, but the base for the Allied Far Eastern Command, and a source of vast quantities of oil.[8] Col. Eubank of the 19th Bomb received orders to

8. By now the Japanese controlled not only Singapore and Sumatra, but also Borneo, Celebes, Amboina, Bali, and Timor—leaving Java as the only major island in the Indies still in Allied hands. A devastating raid on Darwin, Australia, by Japanese

evacuate Java and take his group to Australia. The colonel offered to take all of the artillerymen along, with one ditty bag per man. We were under Dutch command and they would not allow this, but instead, ordered the battalion to Batavia, on the west end of the island, to meet the threat of Japanese landings in that area.[9] In F Battery there was a young Chinese-American who had been drafted in Texas where he had gone to become a real cowboy. Eddie Fung was his name. He knew that I was half Japanese, and when we were told of the impending Japanese landings, he came up to me and asked "Sergeant, what are we going to do? They are going to kill me and you!" I told him that they had to get us first and that we could take a bunch of them with us, if and when that happened.

It was decided that the battalion would saddle up and head west, except for one battery, which would be left behind to help ready Col. Eubank's planes for their trip to Australia, and store the battalion gear and equipment that was not taken with them. On the 27th they moved out, and we of E Battery were the ones left behind for the cleanup and storage work. After completion of this task, we were to rejoin the battalion. We had finished the job by the next day, and moved from Singosari into Soerabaja and stopped at a "waroe," rubber or sugar factory, just six miles outside of the city. I set up my machine-guns at a nearby road junction leading to the factory and on into town. I had made myself a personal uniform that I put on at this position. It consisted of the India-type pith helmet with my garrison cap insignia on it that I had purchased in Australia, and a Khaki uniform that I had made into shorts with a short-sleeved shirt, onto which I had sewn my sergeant stripes and my 36th Infantry Division "T" Arrow

---

carrier-based planes on February 19 had also neutralized that city as a base for Allied efforts to support Java. By the end of the month, the Japanese would have wiped out or forced the evacuation of practically all Allied air units on Java and, in the Battle of the Java Sea (February 27), destroyed the last Allied naval force blocking their way. Craven & Cate, *Army Air Forces*, I, pp. 388–402; Kirby, *The War Against Japan*, I, pp. 431–43.

9. The 2d Battalion became part of a mixed Australian-British unit know as Blackforce (for its commander, Brig. A. S. Blackburn) which was then ordered to western Java. Kirby, *The War Against Japan*, I, p. 436; Wigmore, *The Japanese Thrust*, pp. 496–97.

Foo's homemade uniform, worn in the front trenches at the machine gun position east of Soerabaja, Java

shoulder patch, and had affixed my enlisted men's brass to the collars. I had taken the straps off a .30-caliber cloth bandoleer, and sewed it to my pistol belt to hold .45-caliber ammo in cowboy style. I had added an extra double .45-caliber ammo clip holder to my belt as well as an extra first-aid pouch full of .45-caliber ammo and crossed bandoleers, one over each shoulder. I carried the two native krises in the manner that I described earlier. I thought that this was not only a keen get-up, but a functional and practical rig as well. My steel helmet I carried over my shoulder. Probably my captain or other officers would not share my appraisal of this uniform.

Shortly after midnight, February 28-March 1, the Japanese landed at three different places in western Java—at Merak, Bantam Bay, and Ereten-wetan—and at Kragan in eastern Java.[10] It was now impossible for us to join up again with the battalion, so we were ordered to move into town on 5 March and to take up positions at the city zoo. We arrived just past midnight on the 6th. The zoo was by a river crossing on the southwest edge of the city, and we were to be prepared not only to fight, if need be, but to shoot any dangerous beast or reptile that might be set free by shell fire. The Java Sea battle had taken place, and the USS *Houston*—"The Galloping Ghost of the Java Coast," and the HMAS *Perth,* an Australian cruiser, had both been sunk in the Sunda Straits at the west end of Java, while attempting to escape the Java Sea and get to the south side of the island. They had run smak-dab into a whole bunch of Japanese naval ships protecting the Imperial Army landings. The ensuing engagement was one of the great sea battles of the war, and the two cruisers made a very good showing for themselves.

The Japs, after having been stalled for three days by the rest of my battalion fighting with some Australians, were walking right through the islands at will.[11] As I said earlier, the Dutch ordered E Battery to take up

10. The 2d Division plus a regiment of the 38th landed in western Java; the 48th Division plus a regiment of the 56th came ashore at Kragan. Wigmore, *The Japanese Thrust,* pp. 498–99; Kirby, *The War Against Japan,* I, pp. 443–45.

11. Although most of the defending Dutch forces were in western Java, the Japanese advanced rapidly there. Blackforce, including the bulk of the 2d Battalion, 131st Field Artillery, was involved in a number of actions in that area and fought effectively but in vain. Wigmore, *The Japanese Thrust,* pp. 495–503.

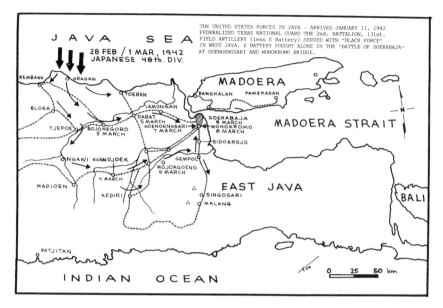

A map of Java drawn by "Foo."

position at the city zoo. Our captain was trying to determine where to put who, and several of the officers and I were standing by for our orders. The captain told one of our first lieutenants to take me up to the front trenches and show me where to set up my machine guns. The lieutenant cleared his throat and reckoned as how since he was second in command he should stay at the zoo in case anything should happen to the captain, and he told 2d Lt. Straughn to show me the place. I assigned zoo locations to my other crews then took one machine gun crew with me and followed the lieutenant to the front trench. He stopped short of the trench and pointed to the general area to be guarded and told me to choose my own location. The trench here was at the southwest edge of the city, flanked by the Goenoengsari Golf Club, and it had a very nice concrete pill box with a small .30-caliber air-cooled Browning machine-gun inside of it. This position commanded an excellent view of the main western entrance to the city. The good highway was flanked on the north side with a fast flowing creek, and on the south side with a river. Our trench and pill box were at the top of a small hill or embankment, looking down the road.

I had my men dig a pit for our guns about fifteen yards down the slope. About another 175 yards the creek passed under a bridge and became one with the river on the other side. Lt. Hollis Allen took two of our 75-mm gun crews with him to a place about 250 yards behind me and to my left. Here they could cover almost all the same stretch of road that I could. Sgts. Roger White and Warren Robertson were the ones with their crews, and Sgt. Henry Spalding had a telephone there also.

The front trench was filled with Dutch and native soldiers, with their green uniforms on, steel helmets, American hand grenades and what appeared to be .30-caliber ammo. There were army, navy and marine officers milling around the trenches in their whites. When I saw these soldiers with their steel helmets, I could not help but recall an amusing incident with some Dutch soldiers back at Singosari. One day we were commenting about the simplistic design of their helmets, and they all bragged on them and said they were the safest military helmets yet designed and could not be penetrated with a bullet. I had some 1903 A-3 .30-caliber armor-piercing bullets for my BARs, and I got up a bet with them that I could shoot through a helmet. There was excitement while the bets were being placed and speculation was rampant, both pro and con. The Dutch hung the helmet on the side of one of their armored cars. Everyone watched with bated breath as I drew a bead with one of my men's rifles, and then I fired. The armor-piercing round not only went through the helmet, but went through the armored car as well. We had left behind some mighty shook up Dutch that day.

The weather here was highly humid. During the rainy season, you could just about set your watch by when it started raining—4:00 P.M. Our .50-caliber ammo was belted with metal links, and they would corrode so much overnight that they had to be torn down, cleaned, oiled and rebelted every day to prevent a malfunction. There were explosions everywhere, it seemed, and huge billowing clouds of black smoke were climbing skyward from all parts of the city. There was a lone Jap seaplane that kept circling around town with no opposition whatever. One of the gun crews had dug a hole and dropped the trails of their 75s in it, in order to gain more elevation, and fired off a round at the plane. They missed, but the round came close enough that the plane was not seen again.

We could see vehicles and men milling around in the trees across the river, but did not know who or what they were. The battery, back at the zoo, experienced some action on the night of the 6th and then were

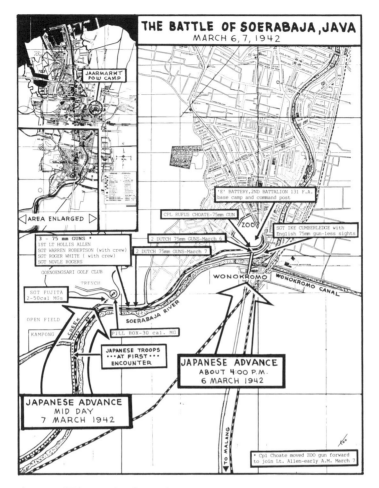

A map of The Battle of Soerabaja, Java, with detail by Frank "Foo" Fujita.

ordered into the city.[12] Sgt. Novle Rogers had come up to the front guns to relieve one of the sergeants. I had one of my 50s torn down for its daily cleaning. I had three men up front with me—Pvts. Hugh "Judy" Garland, Eddie Donaho, and Mickie Perez. There was a Dutch marine sergeant at the pill box with me. Perez and Garland were lounging about the trench and Donaho was cleaning the .50-caliber in the pit.

12. The Japanese involved in this action were advance elements of the 48th Division, which would reach Soerabaja in force the next day. Kirby, *The War Against Japan*, I, p. 448.

Around midday 7 March 1942, I was stretched out in the cool pill box having a cool beer that the marine sergeant had just given me a few minutes before. The sergeant came back into the pill box and said, "There are some American soldiers coming down the road." We had been getting rumors that 20,000 American GIs were about to land, and re-enforce us. I jumped up, and ran out to see them and welcome them; they were coming down the road towards us in three different groups, waving and yelling, "Don't shoot! We are American soldiers!" They were Japanese troops. "Americans Hell! Open fire!" I yelled. The first group had five men with bicycles and were about two hundred yards from us, approaching the bridge. The second group of fifteen or twenty men was about thirty yards behind the first, and the last group looked as if it must have been the entire Jap army, and they disappeared around a bend in the road.

When I yelled to fire, Donaho got off five rounds with the .50-caliber before it jammed, and then he wanted to know what to do. I told him to make a run for the trench where we were and I would cover him. I looked around and one of my men sat with a frozen stare on his face and did not respond to my orders. I realized his condition and took his rifle and began to fire. Sergeants were allowed only .45-caliber automatic pistols, and when the enemy was close enough to use them they were entirely too close. When the forward gun crews heard our open fire, they cut loose with their 75s and were bore-sighting their guns.

When the firing started, the first two groups of Jap soldiers split. Some dropped down on the creek side of the road in plain view of us and others went on the river side of the road where we could not see them. I took the idle rifle and shot at one of the first group. My heart was pounding so hard I thought it would burst. I was hyperventilating, and I fired off two more wild shots without hitting anything. Shrapnel was bursting and whizzing all over the place. I thought to myself if I didn't pull myself together, I would be a goner. I took a more steady aim and pulled the trigger, and this time my target rolled off into the water. These guys were close enough to see their facial features. As he did not come back up, I unintentionally waited to see what sort of reaction I would have to killing a man. To my surprise, there was no immediate reaction, so I put another one in the creek. Then I shot at the second group and rolled another soldier off into the creek, but this time he came back up. He had his head and shoulders out of the water and was slumped over. I shot at him again, and splashed the water up just in front of him, and then on my next shot he went under and never came up again. I got one more at this location, and then we had no more close targets except for some of the first group that had gone under the bridge. In order to get a shot at them, we had to move through the trench to a different vantage point, and so I called to Donaho and Garland to come with me and we stepped out into the main trench. What a disgusting sight! The trench was filled with Dutch and native troops huddled down in the bottom of the trench, and not one was looking over the top towards the enemy. Not one had fired a shot or intended to. There was not a Dutch officer of any rank in sight. I was the highest ranking man in the front trench—a buck sergeant. A Dutch corporal ordered us to quit fighting because we would only infuriate the Japanese and they would come in and kill us all. Donaho and Garland were fit to be tied and wanted me to let them shoot every son-of-a-bitch in the trench. I was so mad, I almost said go ahead, but told the Dutchman, "I may yet give them the O.K.," and he took off.

We moved around to where we could see under the bridge and I got one more, and Donaho or Garland got one too. This brought my score to five at this point. Donaho asked me what I would do if I looked down my rifle and saw one of my kinfolk? I told him that he had better shoot before I did. We went back to our original positions and began to shoot at targets of opportunity in the native village at the far end of the road where the bulk of the Japanese troops had gone. The 75s were systematically destroying it.

While this was going on, the thought struck me that the Church of the Nazarene that Mom took us to had missionaries in Japan and that their converts believed in the same God that we did, and just as surely believed that God was on their side. Here I was, convinced that God was on our side. One of us was going to die, obviously. Then God could not be on both our sides, so our way at looking at him must be at fault. This realization suddenly altered a belief that had always been there. It seems to me now that as one grows and learns from childhood forward, each new experience becomes a "bubble" containing the knowledge and truth of this experience as it is assimilated into our consciousness to help fill the outer shell of what will ultimately become Us, a composition of all our past learning and experiences. That day, the realization that God could not be protecting both my enemy and me caused one of the main bubbles of my being to burst, leaving a void within my outer shell that would not be replaced until many, many years later.

My crew and I ran out of .30-caliber ammo and started back to the forward guns to get more from them. Then I noticed that the guns were not firing; there was only silence from their direction. As we came out of the trees into their area, Sgt. Cumberlidge was at the wheel of a British Bren-Gun carrier, and his gun crew were loading onto it. I yelled out to Ike, "What the hell's going on?" He said "Come on Foo, and you guys get aboard. The captain has got a boat and is about to run off and leave us." It turned out that the captain had commandeered a small ship and hoped to take the battery to Australia and said that the men could go or stay as they chose. Sgt. Killian shed his uniform and commandeered a Ford car and came hightailing it back to the forward guns to tell what the captain was about to do. Lt. Allen had gone back to the battery area to ask the captain for some relief up front. He was told that the captain had taken the men that were with him and gone to the docks to catch a ship to Australia. Lt. Allen made his way to the docks, only to find that the battery was already loaded aboard ship. He managed to see the captain before they shoved off and ask him if he had notified Sgt. Fujita and his crew and the forward gun crews that they were leaving. The captain said he was leaving orders that every man was on his own and that the Dutch had told him that everyone at the front trench had been killed. He didn't bother to send someone up there to verify this or even to call on the telephone to see if someone at the gun positions would answer.

The Abilene Reporter News
Abilene, Texas
March 8, 1942

Round-cheeked Naomi Fujita isn't behind the novelty counter at Woolworth's anymore.

Naomi has a brother with the presumably hardpressed American

Forces on Java, and another in training at Sheppard Field.

But she isn't working at the five-and-ten any longer because their father is a Japanese, making them children of a mixed marriage.

Naomi used to stand there and sell jewelry, cards, phonograph records and assorted other merchandise.

For customers benefit she often played the semi-hit tune, "Let's Slap the Jap Off the Map."

"And she got just as much kick out of the piece as anyone else," says L. W. Davis, manager of F. W. Woolworth Co. store.

Naomi was not discharged, as both she and Davis hastened to give assurance.

They agree she is a victim of racial prejudice grown bitter with the war.

She still has a job at Woolworth's—if she wants it. Because of repeated complaint heard by Davis, however, it would be in the stock room.

Manager Davis, expressing regret, said he proposed a transfer to spare both Naomi and the store criticism from persons he described as "Fanatics."

"The story was going around that we had a Jap girl working in the store," he said, "and I even heard of people inquiring if I myself was a Nazi Agent."

"It had reached the point that some fanatic was bound to write a letter of protest to my head office, and by that time the story would have been so exaggerated I would have been unable to explain."

Naomi refused the stockroom job.

"That would be hiding," she said. She added that Davis had been completely fair and that she regarded him as her friend.

The store manager, reporting "the girls in the store are for Miss Fujita 100 percent," said her work was above reproach.

Her mother, Mrs. Frank Fujita, said that neither she nor Naomi felt bitter toward individuals who had registered complaints with Davis.

"I am sorry that some people don't understand," observed the mother. "Only those persons who have children can realize how deeply wounded Naomi has been."

At least two other Woolworth girls are of German blood, but Manager Davis said there has been no complaints regarding them.

Naomi Fujita is a pretty, dark eyed girl of 18. She enrolled in Abilene High School last fall as a senior. She would have been graduated this spring if she hadn't quit school to go to work. The position of salesgirl was her first job. She worked there part time before Christmas and became a regular employee soon afterward.

She has a sister, Freda Mae, 16, who also found it necessary to abandon her studies and help earn a living. Freda Mae and her mother are employed in a dry cleaning shop here.

A third daughter is 10 year old Patricia Ruth.

"She comes home crying part of the time," said the mother, "because some of the other children at school call her a 'Jap.'"

Mrs. Fujita was awaiting news from Java anxiously Saturday afternoon. Her younger son is Sgt. Frank Fujita, 20, who departed Camp Bowie last fall with West Texas Battery "E" and whose whereabouts for tense weeks were a matter of speculation.

Sgt. Fujita called her from Java on February 14, and she since has received two letters, both of course written prior to the telephone conversation.

The other son is Cpl. Herbert Lee Fujita, 21, in the Air Corps ground school at Sheppard Field, Wichita Falls.

"He tried to enlist as an aviation cadet for pilot training," Mrs. Fujita said, "But they told him he was a Jap and so far they haven't let him transfer."

With only the women folk at home, the family lives in a modest duplex at 1241 Oak Street.

Mrs. Fujita admitted simply that their circumstances are somewhat straitened because of the war and intolerance it has inspired.

Her husband is a neon sign salesman who travels, and his business has required that he maintain headquarters at Electra.

"When the war started, he reported promptly to the Federal authorities," she said. "He was proud to tell them again he is loyal to the United States."

Fujita has since been issued the credentials required of Aliens and permitted to go about his business in a normal fashion.

"But people don't buy much from him anymore because he is Japanese," said Mrs. Fujita. "He can't always be sure he will be able to help us at home."

Mrs. Fujita is a youngish Occidental woman, married when she was 15. She has never lived anywhere except in the Southwest. Her husband was a cook aboard a railroad official's train and she a waitress when they met at El Reno, Oklahoma.

•   •   •

The firing pins and breech blocks had been removed from the 75s and thrown into the river, so we took off in the Bren-Gun carrier for the docks at top speed. As we were passing some shops, there was a man with several cases of whiskey out on the sidewalk, and he was breaking the bottles and letting the contents pour down the gutter. I told Ike to stop so that we could get us a bottle or two. He stopped, and I jumped out and told the man that we wanted several bottles and he refused to let us have any, and I told him that we were intending to pay for the stuff, but he still would not let us have any. So I pulled out my .45 and pointed it at him, and told him, that in that case, we would just help ourselves. We did and drove off and left him standing there staring at us.

Sure enough, when we got to the docks, there was no boat to be seen. The captain and the battery had left. They did not go far, just across the narrow body of water that separated Java from the next very small island of Madoera.

There was talk around that the Japanese were taking no prisoners. I have wondered many times since, what would have been the fate of me and my crew had we not run out of ammunition when we did. We came very near being left behind as it was. We would have had no way of knowing what had happened to the forward guns or the battery either. It frightens me to think of it.

Back at the Soerabaja docks Lt. Allen was told that a truck containing 75mm detonators or fuses had been left behind at the forward gun positions and he asked me to ride "shotgun" while he drove a jeep back to get the truck. Cpl. Howard Plant went along to drive the truck of detonators back. The road ran along the river's edge, and we could see a lot of activity on the other side among the trees and bushes. We pulled out into the field where the truck was parked and Cpl. Plant started the truck up and headed back towards the docks with us right behind him. As we got into town, there was a Dutch man wearing white shorts, a shirt, and a pistol holster. Just as Cpl. Plant came alongside of him, he whipped out his pistol and ordered Plant to stop. I aimed my rifle at him and had a very nervous trigger finger. Had he pointed his pistol at Plant, he would have been a dead man—he came mighty close to being one anyhow.

Back at the docks the truck was driven off into the water, and then one of the men told Lt. Allen of a house called "The Christian Marine House" where all of those that were left or stayed on the docks when the battery left were staying, and that there was plenty of food. We went to this house, which was not very far from the docks. There we found a number of our men, and they told us that the Dutch had ordered us to destroy our uniforms and all our identification and get into civilian clothes. The group that was there had already changed and was eating sandwiches made from several canned whole hams that were sitting around the kitchen area. These hams were taken from a warehouse at the docks, and there were all kinds of other goodies as well.

We spent the night here in heated discussions as to what our best course of action would be. While these discussions were going on my good buddy Cpl. Ben Keith and I found some civilian shorts, socks and shirts to wear, but I could not find any 6½ shoes. I had to cut the U.S. out of the soles and the tops off of my GI shoes. Destroying all our identification was really a very stupid thing to do. Ben was already at the Christian Marine House when I got there, but we immediately buddied up again. We decided that we would prefer to take our chances with the invading Japanese army in the mountains of east Java. Lt. Allen wanted us all to stay together as a group, and when we told him that we were going to the mountains and that any one else that wanted to could go along, Allen said that since the captain's orders were "every man was on his own," he could not order us to do otherwise. No one else wanted to go with us.

Ben and I decided to spend the night there and go to the mountains the next day. I had time to think over the events of the day, and it had been quite a day for sure. When we picked up the truck full of detonators, we had no sooner started to move out of the field when the spot where the truck had been went up in smoke. Evidently, the Japs had had a mortar zeroed in on the truck and had just waited too long to fire. If we had known that the troops we could see on the other side of the river comprised a full Japanese army division, we would have had to change our "skivvies" in short order. When I discarded my uniform, I kept my .45 stuck under my belt and under my shirt.

4

Foo Becomes a

POW: Jaarmarkt and

"Bicycle Camp"

March 1942–October 1942

8 March. The Dutch capitulated all of their East Indies to the Japanese, a mere eight days after invasion forces first landed along the Sunda Strait on the west end of Java as well as on east Java.[1]

1. At 9 A.M. on March 8, 1942, Lt. Gen. Hein ter Poorten, the Dutch commander, broadcast a statement that resistance had ceased and that all Allied forces on Java should lay down their arms. British, Australian, and American units complied at about 2:30 that afternoon, even as ter Poorten and the Dutch governor general were surrendering to the Japanese 2d Division. On the 12th, Maj. Gen. H. D. W. Sitwell, Brig. Blackburn, and Col. Searle, the ranking British, Australian, and American officers, signed a formal surrender document at Bandoeng. At their request, Lt. Gen. Masao Muruyama, the 2d Division commander and senior Japanese army officer on Java, agreed to insert a passage promising to adhere to the Geneva Convention rules for proper treatment of prisoners of war. Maj. Gen. S. Woodburn Kirby, *The War Against Japan*, 5 vols. (London: Her Majesty's Stationery Office, 1957–69), I, pp. 448–49.

Japan had signed and ratified the 1907 Hague Convention with Respect to the Laws and Customs of War on Land, which included provisions for the humane treatment of POWs, and had signed but

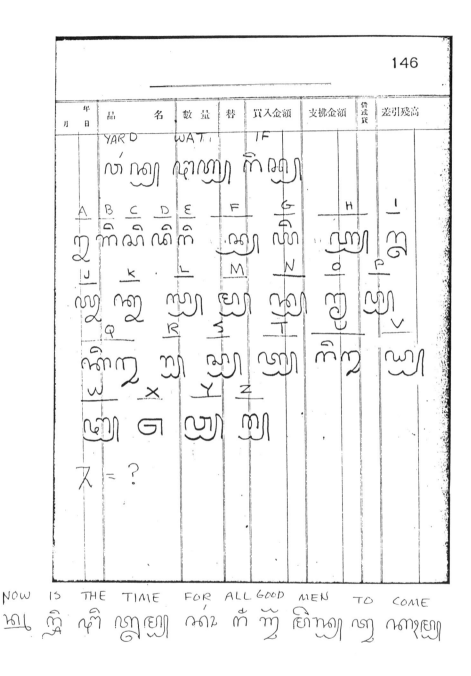

The code Frank "Foo" Fujita developed for his diary using the Javanese alphabet.

Having spent the morning at the Christian Marine House trying to determine the best way to the mountains and what part of the mountains would be our best bet for our purposes, Ben and I took off on our own. Some of the men were fearful for our success and several wanted to go with us but were more afraid of what we would face than they were of what they would face by remaining in town—a handful of American soldiers in a strange land, surrounded by an unfriendly population. There were 31 of us that had been left on the island to fight off the invading Japanese army.[2] Some, however, had the option of going with the captain or staying on Java. Others were more fearful of being on the water than on land, so they opted to stay in Soerabaja. Lt. Allen had the choice but refused to leave until my crew and I had been notified of the pullout.

It was early in the afternoon when Ben and I left the others and headed for the southern part of the city as this was the direction of the nearest mountains. Activity in the streets was like a red ant bed that had been stirred up. People were going every which way and no one knew which way to turn. There were no boats or ships at the docks to escape on, there

---

never ratified the more detailed 1929 Geneva Convention Relative to the Treatment of Prisoners of War. Nevertheless, in early 1942 Japan announced that she would observe the Geneva Convention *mutatis mutandis* and would also take into consideration national and racial customs when feeding and clothing prisoners. E. Bartlett Kerr, *Surrender and Survival: The Experience of American POWs in the Pacific, 1941–1945* (New York: William Morrow and Company, 1985), pp. 25–27, 43; Kirby, *the War Against Japan*, V, p. 532. The Hague and Geneva Conventions are reproduced with annotations in Howard S. Levie (ed.), *Documents on Prisoners of War* (Newport: U.S. Naval War College, 1979), pp. 76–80, 178–200.

2. This refers to the members of E Battery still in Soerabaya. The nearly 500 other men of the 2d Battalion, 131st Field Artillery, were with Blackforce in western Java. Another 350 Americans, survivors of the cruiser *Houston,* sunk in the aftermath of the Battle of the Java Sea, also fell into Japanese hands on Java. British and Australian forces surrendered on Java totalled about 12,000. Dutch forces on the island had numbered about 25,000 regular troops, plus perhaps about 40,000 Home Guard troops, but it is not clear how many of the latter actually became prisoners of war. Kerr, *Surrender and Survival*, p. 44; Kirby, *The War Against Japan*, I, p. 432, V, p. 536; Lionel Wigmore, *The Japanese Thrust* (Canberra: Australian War Memorial, 1957), p. 495.

was no air traffic and nothing on further in east Java offered anymore safety than did the city, so there was quite a bit of confusion.

We strolled through the city working our way to the south and were fascinated by all this activity, but our anxious feelings were not exactly helped by the terror written in almost every face that we saw. It was now getting rather late in the evening and we decided that it would not be too wise to reach the jungles in the dark so we went up to a two-storied, stucco house and knocked. A Dutch woman came to the door, and after saying hello to her, we asked if we might spend the night there. She asked if we were English, and I said, "no we are American soldiers." She said for us to enter and told us that they were just sitting down to their evening meal and that they would be happy for us to join them.

There were two women and two young girls at the table. They had a good meal but had no bread. I asked if they had bread and the lady at the head of the table said that we were having potatoes tonight and that when potatoes were served, rice and bread were not.

We finished our meal and then they took us outside and showed us their garden. They had a very lush garden with a number of different trees and a multitude of flowers. Ever since we had been in Java, I had been impressed with the lush vegetation; the kapok trees were something that we had never seen before and were easily recognizable by their straight trunks and the opposing limbs at equal intervals and originating at the same level. There were beautiful big fan palms, many varieties of lush ferns, mangos, papayas, breadfruit and the ever present banana palms.

Our hostesses were very interested in us and wanted to know everything possible about America. When they asked where our uniforms were, we told them the story of that and about our fight with the Japs at the west edge of the city and of our plans to hide out in the mountains. They were quite concerned as to what sort of treatment could be expected from the Japanese when they came in. The reports of their atrocities committed every place they had taken were not reassuring. They showed us to a room on the ground floor and said that we could spend the night. We thanked them for their hospitality and went to bed. Sleep did not come easily. As I lay there, I began to realize just what a dangerous predicament I was really in. I had heard that the Japanese considered anyone with Japanese blood, regardless of where their citizenship was, as also a citizen of Japan.[3] If this were indeed the case and they found I was—in their eyes—a Japanese fighting against the Japanese, their reaction against me could be quite gruesome. I finally dropped off to sleep, only to spend a very restless night. Early the next morning, the women knocked on our door and told us frantically that we must leave immediately because the Japanese were here. I ran over to the window and looked out and my heart did a flip-flop and liked to have jumped right out of my mouth. We had not noticed the night before that this house was directly across from the train station. There were two trains pulled into the station that were loaded with Japanese soldiers. There were convoys of trucks that were also loaded with troops. There were hundreds of troops on bicycles and troops all over the yard.

The women were fast becoming hysterical and insisted that we leave. I decided that I had better not be caught with my .45 automatic, so I got a piece of oil cloth from them, wrapped my pistol in it and then buried it in the garden. I felt so helpless and naked as I did this. We went back inside and to the front door. I pulled the shade aside and peeked out and Ben peeked out over me. We gasped for breath, for we were almost literally scared to death. There sitting on the porch and lounging in the yard and in the street were Japanese soldiers as thick as fleas. The women were all but pushing us out the door and I knew that we had no alternative but to leave. I told Ben that we had to act very calm when we walked out and by all means we shouldn't run.

I am sure that Ben was going through the same trauma that I was. Like in the front trench when I first shot a man, I was hyperventilating; my heart felt as if it would surely burst, and I felt like I was about to pass out. I said to Ben, "let's go," and I just knew that the moment we stepped

3. Japanese law allowed dual citizenship, even for those Japanese-Americans who were U.S. citizens by birth. Japanese living abroad, however, were required to register their children with the Japanese government as Japanese citizens, a requirement which Frank Fujita, Sr., ignored. P. Scott Corbett, *Quiet Passages: The Exchange of Civilians between the United Sates and Japan During the Second World War* (Kent, Ohio: Kent State University Press, 1987), p. 86; Donald E. Collins, *Native American Aliens: Disloyalty and the Renunciation of Citizenship by Japanese Americans during World War II* (Westport, Conn.: Greenwood Press, 1985), p. 72.

"FOO PHONICS"

I developed this phonetic alphabet using the Javanese script.

ROOT SYMBOLS

(all roots carry <u>AH</u> sound unless altered)

AH. BAH {CAH / KAH} DAH FAH GAH HAH JAH LAH MAH NAH PAH RAH SAH

TAH VAH WAH X YAH ZAH

VOWELS

A   E   I   O   U

[symbol] = CHAH
[symbol] = SHAH
[symbol] = THAH

SOUND ALTERANTS

(SYMBOLS + SOUNDS)   [symbol] = ROOT

[symbol] = DROP <u>AH</u> SOUND   EX: [symbol] = NAH   [symbol] = N

[symbol] = WHEN ONE ROOT IS PLACED BELOW ANOTHER IT TAKES ON THE FIRST LETTER OF TOP ROOT. EX: [symbol] = TAH, [symbol] = RAH [symbol] = TRAH AND ANY ALTERANTS WILL APPLY TO THE LOWER.

[symbol] = LONG E   o = —   [symbol] = LONG A

[symbol] = LONG I   φ = !

[symbol] = O or OH   ʒ = ?

[symbol] = OO or OOH   [symbol] = .

[symbol] = UH   [symbol] = ,

[symbol] = OW   [symbol] = ;

[symbol] = EH   ε3 = " "

[symbol] = +D at end   [symbol] = apostrophe

[symbol] = + NG " "

[symbol] = + L " "

[symbol] = + S " "

[symbol] = + R " "

[symbol] = + R before vowel

[symbol] = + T after starting letter

[symbol] = + D   ←?

NOTE | when an alterant is used with a root it replaces the AH sound with indicated sound OR: ADDS sounds to the root. Several combinations may be used to acquire desired sound

EXAMPLES:

{[symbol]} = TWANG ~ [symbol] = FEAR

{[symbol]} = THAT ~ [symbol] = CAMEL

{[symbol]} = TAUGHT ~ [symbol] = SING

VOWELLS

A   E   I   O   U

(formed with ROOT AH)

ROOT SYMBOLS (ALL CARRY **AH** SOUND)

AH   BAH   {CAH / KAH}   DAH   FAH   GAH   HAH   JAH   LAH   MAH   NAH

PAH   Q   RAH   SAH   TAH   U   VAH   WAH   X   YAH   ZAH

CHAH   SHAH   THAH

SOUND ALTERANTS: ▨ = ROOT

= long A

= long E

= long I

= O or OH

= OO or OOH

= UH

= OW or OU

= EH

= + D - Past Tense

= + NG

= + L

= + S

= R after Vowel

= R before Vowel

= + T after starting letter

= — vowel   **NOTE:** when a root appears below another it eliminates the vowel sound of the above AND any alterants will apply to the lower.

o = —

= ;

φ = !

乙 = ?

= Period

= Comma

ε▨3 = " "

= apostrophe

= ?

NOTE: When an alterant is used with a root it replaces the AH with the indicated sound

Several combinations may be used to acquire desired sound.

EXAMPLE: = TWANG   = FEAR

through the door we were dead men. I was almost literally sweating blood. That was the hardest thing that I have ever had to do—step through that door. As we passed through the soldiers sitting on the porch and in the yard, all of them with fixed bayonets, I felt as if my feet were disconnected from the rest of me, for they wanted to run in spite of my efforts not to do so.

We calmly strolled off down the street, or at least we thought we calmly strolled, until we were clear of the massed troops at the train station. The soldiers only glanced at us with curiosity and not one appeared hostile or said anything to us. We decided that we had better head for the mountains—"Post Haste!"

As we came closer to the city limits, we could hear gun fire ahead, so we asked a Dutchman what the firing was all about. He told us that the Japs were offering the natives five gulden a head, to point out any native or Dutch military men that were trying to leave town as civilians. Five gulden was an enormous sum to the natives and evidently they were pointing out most everyone that was leaving town, and the Japanese were shooting them as soon as they were pointed out. It was immediately obvious to us that if a native soldier dressed in a sarong could not get out of town, we stood no chance at all.

We turned and headed back towards the heart of the city. We walked rather aimlessly, for we had no plan of action now. We saw a building with the Red Cross emblem on it, so we headed there and went in. There was a man hastily throwing some things into a valise, and I asked him if he could tell us the best and safest route out of the city and on to the mountains. He asked "Are you English?" and I said, "No, we are Americans." With that bit of news he turned as pale as a sheet and began to yell for us to get out of there. I said, "You are supposed to help us. You are International Red Cross." He said that he would not help and that the Japanese would kill him if he so much as talked to Americans. I told him "Then the least that you can do is take a message from us, and when you have the opportunity you can mail it so that our folks might know that we were alive on this date." He kept raving for us to leave and said that he would not help us in any fashion. I told him, "You son-of-a-bitch, if I hadn't buried my

.45, I'd blow your damn head off!" He closed his valise and took off in a high lope.

We started walking again towards downtown; there were Jap trucks and cars whizzing around and soldiers on bicycles roaming the streets. We avoided any Jap that we saw. Before the capitulation, there were Dutch military men everywhere you turned and now that the Japanese were here, there were none in sight. About the middle of the afternoon we came upon a large, well manicured lawn with a white building in the center of it. Around the building were several hundred Dutch and native soldiers in their green uniforms standing around; all were facing a doorway in the building. We walked over to the crowd and stood around to see if we could determine what was going on. Occasionally a very pompous, fat, Dutchman in a white officers' uniform would come out and make an announcement. Once when he did this, I asked one of the Dutchmen standing there what the guy had said. Instead of answering he asked, "Are you English?" I said "No, we are Americans." His face flushed and he yelled out something in Dutch and the whole bunch of soldiers scattered. When we tried to approach any of them, they would move away from us. We felt bad enough as it was, and this sort of treatment didn't exactly calm us down.

It turned out that this was a police station and the fat officer was relaying orders from the Japanese. He came out again, made an announcement, and then every one started to leave. A Dutchman came over to us and said that he heard that we were Americans and we told him that we were. He said, "I am sorry for the way my fellow Dutchmen treated you. They are afraid of their own shadows. We were just told to go home and that all military men were to report back here in the morning at 8 o'clock." And then he asked if we had any place to go, and when we said that we did not, he said, "You can go home with me. I will feed you, give you American whiskey and cigarettes and a Dutch wife a piece to sleep with." I told Ben, "By golly, we can't beat that for openers."

This man's name was Ernest Wolf. He was an artist, and when I told him that I was, too, we hit it right off. He had a very nice home. It was of stucco, like all the other buildings and houses were. The walls did not go all the way to the ceiling, but had elongated slots between the ceiling and the top of the walls to let cross ventilation cool the house. He kept his cigarettes in a small round oven built into the hallway wall. It seems that unless this was done the cigarettes would mildew. We had a couple of drinks and then a good meal. I felt the need to relieve myself, and I was shown to a little building in the back yard that was the Dutch version of a toilet. When I had finished with my urgent call to nature I could see no tissue, so I yelled out for Ernest. He came up outside and asked what the problem was. I told him that there was no toilet tissue in here, and he told me to take one of the bottles of water that were in a rack on the wall beside me and with one hand tilt the bottle and pour the water into the top of the crease in my rear end, and as the water runs down your crack and over your rectum, you then take your other hand and by using the middle finger you wash until you are clean. There is a lavatory there to wash your hands when you have finished. The toilets that they use are porcelain troughs in the floor and one must drop their drawers and squat down over the trough. There's one thing about this method, you sure can get squeaky clean.

The maid fixed a double bed for us while we sat around visiting. After a little while, he arose and wished us a good night. I asked if he was not forgetting something, and when he asked what, I reminded him that he had promised us a Dutch wife a piece. He laughed and pointed to two long pillows on the bed that were about eight inches in diameter and said that those were called Dutch wives. You were supposed to wrap yourself around them as you slept to prevent being galled in this hot tropical climate. The emotional strain that we had been through during the day and the long walk through the city had sapped our energies to the point where we did not wake up once during our last night as free men.

The next morning after breakfast, Ernest led us back down to the police station, where hundreds of military men were gathering. There were native soldiers as well as Dutch and English. All branches of the military were represented. The curious thing about the Dutch is that they thought that since they did not fight the Japs that the Japs would allow them to continue their normal lives as civilians. Boy! Were they ever fooled.

There were ten of our men already here and it seemed that neither they nor anyone else knew what lay ahead for us. The Dutch and English left a wide area between us and them, and this only added to the jitters we were already experiencing. Finally, around noon we were marched a few blocks away to the local fair grounds, a fenced-in area that was called Jaarmarkt. This was quite a large compound that would cover about six square blocks. There was a large two-storied building towards one end and on either side, along the outer walls, were exhibit sheds and rooms.

We were put into the big building and told to bed down there. This was on the 10th of March 1942. The next day Lt. Allen and fourteen more of our men from the 131st were brought into camp as well as a couple of thousand other Allied troops. Japanese guards were all over the place with fixed bayonets, and I was quite fearful that they would find me out whenever one would come near me. I asked Lt. Allen where they were yesterday and the following story came out. In scouting the town, Cpl. Rufus Choate had found the American Embassy. When he told Lt. Allen about it, the Lieutenant decided to take Choate and go there and seek help in getting out to the mountains. When they arrived there, the Americans were gone and the place was full of Dutchmen. When Allen asked to be helped out of town, the Dutch told them that not only could they not leave town but that they could not even leave the building, and then and there placed them under house arrest. They kept them there overnight and then took them down to the police station and turned them over to the Japs the next day.

There were three thousand or more military men that were herded into Jaarmarkt, and around the middle of the afternoon on the 11th of March we were ordered to assemble by nationalities out in the very large open area in the center of what had now become a prisoner-of-war camp. There were many Japanese army personnel of all ranks, some obviously in command and others with clip boards and abacuses in hand. We were introduced to the first of many thousands of *tenkos,* or roll calls. After many counts and recounts we were given an oral list of what we were expected to do and not to do from this day forward. Having finished with this, we were told to fall out, or break ranks, and each man was to find himself a place to bed down—a place that was to become his permanent quarters. When the signal was given to fall out, there was a mad rush for the sheds and rooms along the camp walls. The Americans were up front and near the closest row of buildings. Lt. Allen, Sgts. Spalding and O. B. Williams, Robertson and myself, Cpl. Keith and Pvt. Pete Evans, along with about twenty Dutchmen, all piled into a room that would accommodate 15 men lying down. There was one hell of a row as to who was going to get to stay in the room, and for a while it looked as if blood was going to be shed. When the dust finally cleared, the ones I have just mentioned remained in the room with ten Dutchmen.

We really were lucky, for the room was of stucco construction and had a shower and a toilet and lavatory in it. The outside latrines were very near and so the other prisoners used them, which in effect gave our room its own private facilities. Pvts. Frank Ceplinski, Hugh Garland and Eddie Donaho fixed themselves a living space along the wall outside our room. All of the E Battery men in the room with me, especially my buddy Ben and the lieutenant, pleaded with me to change my name to a Spanish or Filipino name, for they were certain that when the Japs found out about my Japanese ancestry I would be summarily shot. I was really in anguish, for I thought the same thing and the temptation to change my name was almost overwhelming. However, I felt that if I changed my name and I should die for any reason during the war then, if my death were reported at all, it would be reported under my assumed name and my parents would never know what happened to me. So I kept my own name. The decision was not an easy one since I felt that my longevity would certainly be brief, under the circumstances, with a name like Fujita.

Soerabaja is right on the water's edge and its proximity to the equator caused the humidity to be almost unbearable. Our room was hot and humid, but I am sure that it was more comfortable than other areas of the camp. We had a very thin woven reed mat that was the only padding between our bodies and the concrete floor. I suffered greatly with my right shoulder. I had contracted rheumatism sleeping in the rain and mud on the Louisiana maneuvers, and the concrete floor did not help it any. I was complaining loudly about it when one of the Dutchmen said: "You Americans are not very smart in some ways. You suffer ailments that you do not need to." He brought out a small tin container—like Mentholatum comes in back home—about the size of a quarter and it was filled with a very pungent Chinese salve called Tiger Balm. He rubbed my shoulder with it and then told me to sleep in a long sleeved sweater that I had and the next day I would be cured. It is still hard to believe but to this day I have not been bothered with rheumatism in that shoulder.

One day Pvt. Pete Evans and I managed to get some boards and gunny sacking (burlap bags) and we proceeded to build us a double deck bunk bed. When it was finished, Pete grabbed the bottom bunk and I informed him that rank had its privilege and I would take the bottom bunk. That night I was awakened by a downpour of urine. It seems that Pete at times could not control his bladder, so he got the bottom bunk after all. At times ghecko lizards would come into our room in search of mosquitos and other insects and would call out their only cry. The Americans named these lizards for what they said—fuck you! lizards. The natives said that if they stayed in your house and gave their cry seven times that it meant good luck, and they said that the lizards said "ghec-ko!" That may be so in Javanese, but in English we had them properly named.

The main requirement laid down by the Japanese was that all POWs were to come to attention and bow to any Japanese that passed if you were bareheaded, and to salute if you had any sort of head gear on.

On the very next day a Dutchman refused to bow to a Jap guard and so the guard bashed him in the face. The Dutchman hauled off and knocked the guard for a loop. He let out a yell and about six more guards came running from the guard house and began to beat and kick the Dutchman and hit him with their rifle butts. The guy turned and ran but the guard caught him, knocked him to the ground and stomped him unmercifully and then stoned him with large stones that were piled nearby. They then took him to a pole that stood alone on the parade ground, tied him to it, each took a turn at beating him and then left. He was beaten by each guard shift as they came on duty and then again as they went off duty. The next day the Japs shaved his head, and the beating routine plus the hot sun on his bare head was driving him mad. His cries would fill our ears, day and night, and during the afternoon of the third day, the man died. I am only thankful that I was not the first man made to bow, for that would have been me out there on the pole instead of the Dutchman. It eliminated once and for all any thought of not bowing or saluting from the rest of us. We did start wearing hats or caps for it seemed somehow to go less against the grain to salute than to bow.

The cook shack was very near our quarters and the smells that came from it were, for the most part, strange to us. We were served a generous portion of white rice topped with a big gob of fresh ground, red hot peppers, and a bowl of vegetable soup. We went through the chow line and got our portion and went back to our quarters to eat it. When we started to eat, we noticed small black balls all through the rice. Upon closer inspection, they turned out to be worm heads. When we tried to pick them out of the rice, there would be this long white bag attached to the black head, and this was what was left of the worm's body. If we managed to pick all of them out, there would be considerable less rice in our bowls. The worms' insides were already cooked out into the rice, in any case, so the effort was fruitless. We would hide our eyes or find a dark place to eat. There was a lot of bitching at first from the Americans for having to eat heathen chow. As time went on and it became evident that we would probably be there for a while, we went ahead and ate it—rice, worms and all.

We were able to supplement our camp meals with black market items brought in by the volunteer work parties. If you had any money, that is. One day I heard some native yelling through our drain opening in our shower, a hole through the wall at floor level, about two inches in diameter, which allowed the bath water to drain into the ditch just outside the camp. I could not understand the "Lingo" so I called one of the Dutchmen over to see what the native wanted. The Dutchman got excited and said that it was a native street vendor and he wanted to sell us "Eskimo pies" for ten cents. The pies were small enough to go through the drain pipe. We bought all the man had and he promised to return the next day with more. Boy! Were they ever good. They were made with real rich cream and very tasty chocolate. We purchased many things through our drain.

Ever since we had been in this room the Dutchmen seemed to be somewhat leery of me. After finding out that I was half Japanese, they thought that I might be a Japanese "plant" to spy on the POWs. After a while, since the Americans all seemed to hold me in high respect, they relaxed. One of them even started teaching me Javanese at my request. I was very fascinated with the Javanese script or alphabet. It was beautiful to behold, and

A watercolor by Frank Fujita. "This was not commonplace. This was specialized punishment for various infractions of the rules. This took place in the Dutch East Indies and also in Nagasaki. In some instances bayonets were used instead of bamboo."

I felt that I had to find a way of putting it to my own personal use. I never learned the language, but I did formulate a personal phonetic alphabet that no one except me could read.[4] I utilized it all through the war to enter important items in my diary. About this time and frequently thereafter, we were told that if anyone was caught keeping a diary they would be shot.[5]

We were learning to adapt to the food that was issued and we ate the rice, worms and all, as if it were indeed a delicacy. However, we did not want to eat rice even if it was clean, and we petitioned to be issued bread. After a while, the galley began giving a choice of rice or a small bread bun. We all chose the bread, but found that it was invariably soured or moldy

4. See pages 86, 90–91 for examples from Frank Fujita's diary.
5. See footnote No. 1, p. 85.

and left us feeling still hungry. We all went back to eating the wormy rice. We could get red palm oil, kachung oil or peanut oil, and all the little tabasco chilies we wanted on the black market. We had some steel helmets that we used for cooking utensils, and we recooked our rice in oil with the chili peppers and made it a little more palatable. We thought that this food was awful and inadequate. We were to find that we would look back upon these meals as veritable feasts.

The men that went out on work parties always had much better food to eat. The guards would allow them to buy food when out on these parties but would not let them take any of it back into camp. There always seemed to be some who would get past the inspection that the work parties had to submit to upon returning to camp. Soon, more and more men would volunteer for work party and finally even I went out on some. One day as we were marched to a work site we saw four of our E Battery men standing on a corner with some Dutch and native pedestrians. We could only gesture with our eyes that we recognized them, for we did not want to jeopardize them or their freedom. We would speculate on how they managed to remain free and what they did to survive. We would see them almost every time that we went out on work party.

The work that we did was rebuilding all the things that the Dutch had blown up prior to capitulation. The work parties were all volunteer in the beginning, but as time went on participation became required. The Japanese had not been too harsh on us to start with, even though to us, having just lost our freedom, anything that restricted our activities or exercise of our free will was reprehensible. After it became obvious to the Japanese that they were not going to be able to take Australia, they became quite mean. Beatings and searches for forbidden items became more frequent. The work parties became harder with fewer and fewer rest periods and fewer opportunities to purchase food. The guards roamed through the camp at all hours to make everyone bow or salute. They got a great pleasure out of this, particularly when someone did not perform to their satisfaction and they would beat the hapless victim unmercifully. Some of the torture they would use could and would leave a victim scarred physically and emotionally for life. They would make a victim kneel down with his shins atop the sharp edge of a triangular piece of wood, or have the same piece of wood inserted behind his knees and make him sit back on his heels. This treatment would seriously damage the bone or muscles. They would make someone stand at attention and remove his shirt and then they would jam lighted cigarettes into his flesh. Hanging victims by their thumbs was also practiced, and the usual beatings with fists and rifle butts was more or less constant. If someone happened to fall to the ground during a beating, then they would add kicking and stomping to the action.

Food became much poorer in quality and less in quantity as well. Diseases caused by vitamin deficiency were becoming widespread. I became a victim of pellagra; my skin would crack open around and under my nose, under my ears and at the corners of my mouth. All the coating came off of my tongue, leaving a painful, purplish raw blob. All the skin came off of my scrotum, leaving it a raw, bloody and weeping mess. When my legs would brush against my testicle, the pain was almost unbearable. I took to wearing only my shirt or G-string hanging loose, for I could not stand pants at all. I would tie a string around my penis, pull it up and then tie the string around my waist like a belt. I decided to make a sack in which to carry my testicles that would at the same time leave my penis free so that I could urinate. The pain was intense when I first put the sack on. The cotton cloth felt as if it were made of sandpaper when it came in contact with my raw scrotum. Soon I was able to walk around and it did not hurt. I took a walk around camp for the first time in a good while and visited with the other men from E Battery. That night I slept good and really enjoyed moving around without all that pain. The next morning when I awoke my testicles were solidly cemented to the cloth. The raw bag had weeped through the night and the juice came through the cloth and turned into a solid scab when it air dried. I could not even begin to remove the sack because of the pain, so I went into the shower and stood under the running water until the sack loosened. Even then, I suffered all the tortures of Hell trying to get it off.

Ben lucked out and got a job in the sick bay. This kept him off of the other work details and he even managed to get a little better food there.

There were no medicines, only "rice polishings." This was a residue from processing rice and this is what you were given as a curative, no matter what the complaint.

On April 29th we were allowed a visitors' day in honor of the Japanese Emperor's Birthday. There was quite a mob of people who came bearing food and gifts for their loved ones, and the reunions were very touching. We Americans even had visitors; local members of the Salvation Army came and brought us food and sweets.

I was surprised to see this organization in this part of the world. I had thought that they were a Texas welfare outfit. My family lived across the street from their chapel and dormitory back in Abilene. They asked if there was anything they could do for us and we asked if they could get us some American uniforms. They took our measurements and said that they would have us uniforms "tailor made." I also asked if they could get me some art materials, like drawing paper and pen and ink. They brought me the art supplies on a later visit but the Japanese would never allow them to give us the uniforms after they had had them made.

I learned to have great respect for the Dutch women. Daily some of them would come to the camp gates and try to deliver food or clothes to their men inside the camp. The Jap guards would beat them and drive them off, but they would just keep trying—day after day. If the Dutch men had had the spunk that their women had and used it when the Japs were first entering the city, perhaps we could have still been at the front fighting. As I watched these brave women get beaten up for trying to help their men, I could not help but think of how mad I got at the yellow-bellied Dutch soldiers in the front trenches. They had not fired a shot at the oncoming Japanese troops, and when I had tried to get them to fight they refused and said that we would only make the Japs mad and they would kill us all. I asked them just what in the hell they thought war was all about? I told them that they had their homes and families and property to protect and all we Americans had to lose was our asses, but that we would put up one hell of a fight before we would lose those.

Early in May the four E Battery men that had been living on the outside were brought into our camp—making thirty-one of us that had been left on Java by our captain. We had a joyous reunion with them and were happy to see that they were well and good. They were Sgts. Ike Cumberlidge and George Killian and Pvts. Luz Ortiz and Willie Robinson.

I had begun to utilize the art materials that the Salvation Army had brought me. I did some very detailed pen and ink drawing and had started a book about our outfit and called it the "Lost Battalion." I never got to finish it and later when I was separated from the battery, Sgt. Dave Williams kept it for me and gave it back to me when we met on Okinawa after having been liberated. The book is now in the Lost Battalion Museum located in the Wise County Museum in Decatur, Texas. Some of the pen and ink drawings were taken from me by a Jap officer, but some I still have.

About this same time back home:

• • •

Letter from Adjutant General, War Department, to Frank Fujita, Sr.

War Department
Washington, D. C .
1942
Dear Mr. Fujita:

According to War Department records, you have been designated as the emergency addressee of Sergeant Frank Fujita, Jr., 20813132, who, according to the latest information available, was serving in Java at the time of the final capitulation.

I deeply regret that it is impossible for me to give you more information than is contained in this letter. In the last days before the capitulation of Java there were casualties which were not reported to the War Department. The Japanese Government has indicated its intention of conforming to the terms of the Geneva Convention with respect to the interchange of information regarding prisoners of war. At some future date this government will receive through Geneva a list of persons who have been taken prisoners of war. Until that time the War Department cannot give you positive information.

The War Department will consider the persons serving in Java as "missing in action" until definite information to the contrary is received.

It is to be hoped that the Japanese Government will communicate a list of prisoners of war at an early date. At that time you will be notified by this office in the event his name is contained in the list of prisoners of war. In the case of persons known to have been present in Java who are not reported to be prisoners of war by the Japanese Government, the War Department will continue to carry them as "missing in action," in absence of information to the contrary, until twelve months have expired.

At the expiration of twelve months and in the absence of other information, the War Department is authorized to make a final determination.

I am enclosing for your information a memorandum regarding benefits to certain dependents of missing, captured or interned personnel. Yours very truly,

The Adjutant General

Fort Worth Star-Telegram
Fort Worth, Texas
June 19, 1943

Somewhere in the rugged terrain of Java there is a bunch of Texas men who are members of the Second Battalion, 131st Field Artillery which until last November was a unit of the Lone Star State's own 36th Division.

The fate of these men, who comprised one of the first American contingents to face the overpowering odds of the Japanese in the Pacific, is unknown. The War Department has simply said that the soldiers are considered "missing in action." There have been rumors that the Texans may still be fighting in the mountain vastness of the Netherlands East Indies island but the general assumption is that they are prisoners of war.

But wherever they are and whatever they are doing, Texas is certain that they will uphold all the glorious traditions of America. Just as certain of this are the hundreds of bereaved fathers and mothers of the boys of the "Lost Battalion."

The spirit of these parents is exemplified in letters that have been received by this writer after the recent publication of an article on the activities of the 131st during the Louisiana war maneuvers of 1940 and 1941. The reporter covered those maneuvers and was closely associated with the soldiers of the battalion.

There has been no authentic news concerning the West Texans who comprised the personnel of the unit. But that doesn't keep the parents from thinking of their boys every minute of the day. It doesn't keep them from scanning every newspaper and listening to every news broadcast in hopes of seeing or hearing some mention of the battalion. . . . Let's keep talking about the boys of the "Lost Battalion," who deserve more than can ever be given them.

by: Jim McMullen

• • •

Up to this time there had been several attempts at escape. One native soldier had escaped but was recaptured, or more likely was turned in by other natives in the city. He was very severely beaten. The next escapee was recaptured after about a week and then shot. The Japanese then issued the statement that in the future if anyone escaped they would not try to find them but instead would shoot ten of his fellow countrymen or tribesmen. We had pondered escape before this announcement but had vetoed the idea. Escaping would be no problem, but where we would go and what we would do afterwards was. The native population was very anti-white at this time and looked upon the Japanese as their liberators from the white man's yoke. Even if we could escape and manage to evade the natives (a very unlikely scenario on an island that had the world's highest population density) there was always the sea to block further progress. There was an incident of escape by a native Javanese soldier, and word went around camp that the Japs did indeed shoot other Javanese.

There were now about four thousand prisoners of war in this camp— Dutch, Native, Australian, English, Chinese and American. Work parties were now mandatory, and all who were able had to go out on detail every other day. Work was everything that was against the Geneva Convention, as were our treatment, our quarters and our food. We rebuilt airport runways, oil storage facilities, railroads and dock facilities.[6]

On the eighth of July we were allowed another visitor's day and the Salvation Army people showed up with all sorts of goodies and more art materials for me, but the Japanese still would not allow them to give us the tailor-made uniforms. Ernest Wolf, the exceptional Dutchman who befriended Ben and me, had his quarters not far from me and I took him some of the art materials for his use. He was overjoyed. His health was failing, and he was deeply depressed and worried constantly about his wife. My sharing the supplies with him obviously cheered him up, and he seemed to perk up in the days ahead.

The Japanese decided to pay everyone for the work that they performed. Officers received 25 sen per day, non-commissioned officers received 15 sen per day and the privates received 10 sen per day. One day Lt. Allen came to me and he was visibly shaken. His face was ashen. He said that one of the men, outside our room had just told him that he was going to kill him. He did not say why but asked me to keep careful record of the event and watch over him and to report his murder and the murderer to the U.S. Military after the war if the threat was carried out. Fortunately, it never came to pass.

One day one of the men outside our room piled his sleeping mat and most of his clothes into a heap and set fire to them. I asked why he was doing this since clothing would be almost impossible to replace, and he said that they were covered with crabs. He was a big hairy guy and his body was covered with body crabs. He was very nearly bald, so was lucky there, but his eyebrows, neck and every place else had to be shaved.

Rumors began to float around that the Americans were going to be moved out of this camp and put into another camp in that city, where we

6. The Geneva Convention allowed captor nations to require enlisted prisoners of war to work (officers and others of equivalent status were exempt), but only on projects that had no direct relation to military operations. Dangerous or unhealthful work was prohibited, physically unfit prisoners were to be exempt, and working conditions were to be reasonable. Prisoners were also to be paid at rates comparable to those in force for soldiers of the captor nation. Levie, *Documents,* pp. 183–85.

would rejoin our captain and the rest of E Battery. This rumor worried me deeply for I could not help recalling how mad the men were who had been left at the front by the captain. I feared that when we were put back together blood would be shed, and I was especially fearful of what I might do. I was particularly bitter at the captain for not sending me word at the front trenches that they were leaving the island, and I went into a rage at the mere thought of coming in contact with one of our lieutenants. Lt. Allen had told me a month or so ago that while we were at Singosari, this officer and the first sergeant, who had been cronies for many years in the National Guard, had sought to have Cpl. Ben Keith and myself busted or reduced in rank, for they wanted our ranks to go to two friends of theirs. Boy! Did this bit of information blow my stack. It was night when Allen told me this and I lay in my bunk until very late thinking how I was going to get revenge on these two. In any case, here we were about to be reunited with the Madoera bunch, some of who had bad feelings towards those that willingly stayed behind on Java and donned civilian clothes.

On September 5, we thirty-one Americans were moved to a big tin building down on the water front and sure enough, the rest of the battery was there. Many men had grown beards and we did not recognize them at first. There were some scowls and growls but this gave way to good-natured reunions. I was surprised at myself for not reacting in a more violent way. I kept away from the captain and the first lieutenant until I had plenty of time to get my emotions in order.

We remained in this tin building overnight and then were moved to HBS, a school building, still in the same city. This wasn't a bad location. There were a lot of native soldiers in this camp and at least one of them was highly skilled at chip carving. Ben and I were watching a native do this. He had a helper who was holding the piece of wood that he was carving on. The natives kept whispering to each other and casting furtive glances at me. Suddenly one of them pointed to me and then to a Japanese guard that was standing where we could all see him, and said "Somma-somma," which meant that the soldier and I were the same or alike.

I didn't like the looks on his face nor his insinuation and I made a grab for him, but he jumped back and then took off running with me right behind him. He ran into the native quarters and I lost sight of him so I went back to my own quarters. All the natives were watching me, and Ben told me that I had better play it cool and to always stay with our boys for my own safety. I was in a new camp, surrounded by a new set of POWs, and word had gotten around that I was Japanese, so I was greeted on all sides with varying reactions. Some were openly hostile, some were incredulous and some were just curious. Here again, after a while it was obvious to all that the other Americans thought I was okay so the camp relaxed and I was able to breathe a little easier.

Since our reunion with the rest of E Battery, I found that there were some men from other batteries who had been left behind when the battalion moved to Batavia, as well as an Army Air Corps T/Sgt. I have no recollection of having to work at this camp, but the food was bad and inadequate. Wet beriberi was showing up in many of the prisoners including myself. There was no pain to this type of beriberi. The feet, ankles and calves would swell, sometimes to enormous size, giving us an "Alley Oop" appearance. If you pushed a finger into the swollen area and then withdrew it, a hole would remain for several minutes where you punched before the spot returned to normal. Dry beriberi was also showing up more and more. We called it the "electric foot." It seemed to effect you the most at night when severe pains, like electric shocks, would shoot through your lower legs and feet. Men would jump up from bed screaming with pain. There was no swelling with this type of beriberi.

I came down with dysentery and was suffering with the terrible cramps that accompany this malady. On October 24, E Battery was loaded onto a train and we headed west. We travelled all night and the next day we arrived in Batavia, where we were taken to a POW camp called Bicycle Camp.[7] In this camp were some of our men from the battalion, headed

7. The Bicycle Camp (the origin of the name is unknown), a former Dutch barracks, held about three thousand prisoners, primarily Australians and Americans, at this time. The most senior British and Dutch commanders were also there, but they were held separately in a small compound. Brig. Blackburn was camp commander for the prisoners, with Col. Searle as second-in-command. Kirby, *The War Against Japan*, V, p. 536. Wigmore, *The Japanese Thrust*, pp. 533–34; Rohan D. Rivett, *Behind Bamboo: An Inside Story of the Japanese Prison Camps* (Sydney: Angus & Robertson, 1946), pp. 111–12; Kerr, *Surrender and Survival*, pp. 65–66.

by Col. Searle. We were told that the Dutch had not fought here either. The battalion had come under the command of an Australian outfit and was able to get in some good licks at the Japs before being ordered to surrender. We were told that a private out of D Battery had died earlier this month from dysentery.

The colonel gave us some money from the battalion pay that he had possession of and some canned food products that he had purchased. These were a godsend, but very nearly came too late for me. My dysentery had progressed to the point that I was very near death. I had to go to the latrine so often that soon I became too weak to go back to our quarters and so I just laid down outside the latrine door and then I could just roll over to the slit trench to relieve myself. The cramps were so horrendous that I felt I just could not withstand another one. They hurt so bad that I also thought that I would surely go stark raving mad with sheer pain. When I managed to get over the trench I could only pass a very small dab of mucous. The slit trench was a concrete trough about ten inches across and eighteen inches deep, with about eight inches of water in it. Every thirty seconds, some sort of mechanism would shoot a fresh gush of water through the trench and thereby flush out the urine and offal. I became terrified of the trench; I thought that in my weakened condition I might slip into it and be drowned. The cramps were the worse pain I have ever experienced.

The good food that Col. Searle was able to buy at this camp began to have a healing effect on me. I became a little stronger and the cramps became a little less severe. We had been told that the rest of the battalion, along with the survivors off the USS *Houston* and the Australian cruiser *Perth,* had been sent to Singapore or Thailand to build a railroad.[8]

We had only been in this camp three days when the Japs had all able-

8. At the beginning of October, the Japanese began to move prisoners out of the Bicycle Camp, sending them to Singapore, Borneo, Sumatra, and Japan. Many of those going to Singapore were then moved north to Burma to work on the infamous Burma-Thailand railway. Lt. Col. Tharp and most of the 2d Battalion left on October 11 for Singapore. Wigmore, *The Japanese Thrust,* pp. 535–36, 557–58; Kirby, *The War Against Japan,* V, p. 536; Rivett, *Behind Bamboo,* pp. 117, 128, 141; Kerr, *Surrender and Survival,* p. 114.

bodied men assemble in the courtyard, or parade ground. I was very, very weak, but I insisted that Ben help me stand up so that I would not be left out on whatever was about to happen. The Japanese guards split the group in two and had each half move away from the other half. Soon some guards came with a handful of red ribbons and gave each man in my group one. We were told to tie them around our arms. We wondered what this would signify and we were not long in finding out. The red-ribbon group were going to be sent to Japan and the other group were going to Thailand or Burma. Two sailors off the USS *Houston* wound up in E Battery's group. We were taken to the dock and put aboard a small rusty cargo ship, the *Dai Nichi Maru,* which looked as if it would sink at any moment. There were one thousand men in our group, and we were all ordered to board ship and to go down into the holds. We were split into two groups of five hundred men each, and one group was put into the forward hatch and the other into the aft hatch. The holds were about sixty feet square and all 500 men were packed into each hold. There was no room to lie down, so we had to sit between each other's legs. The boiler room was next to us and the heat coming through the bulkheads or walls, coupled with the body heat of 500 men, quickly raised the temperature to well over 100 degrees. The floor was covered with residue from previous trips, mostly grain, and it was alive with all sorts of vermin. As if things weren't bad enough these crawling creatures made things even more of a nightmare.

The first deck in the hold was occupied by a Japanese cavalry unit, along with their horses. The opening to the bottom half of the hold was boarded over with heavy planks with one- or two-inch cracks between planks. When the horses relieved themselves, the liquids poured right through the cracks down on the hapless POWs below. Ben and I were next to the engine room wall and the heat must have been 120 degrees. I had a face towel and I sweated it full twice, and then I got out a bath towel and sweated it full twice, and then I just quit sweating. I was so weak and the dysentery pain hit me again. Ben explained to the guard that I had dysentery and he let me go up the ladder and out on the upper deck, but not before I had thoroughly messed up my clothes. Evidently, the Japanese did not want people with dysentery to be in the same hold with the cavalry unit and required all men thus infected to stay top side. They made me remove my pants and throw them overboard and stay close to the latrine.

The latrine was a rickety wooden affair that hung out over the side of the ship, crude but effective. This staying topside and the fresh air is the only thing that saved my life. One hour more in the hellhole below, and I am certain I would have died. The ship's galley was near to where we were and it too was set up on the outside deck. The cooks were preparing food and the most wonderful aroma wafted from them to us. I thought that this strange and tantalizing smell was truly the most wonderful that I had ever smelled. It was Indian curry and when we got our meager portion of food, I thought that it tasted just as wonderful as it smelled.

We were lucky insofar as we only remained on this ship five days. Later, I met a sailor who had been on an identical ship (it may have been the same one), and they were kept on board for near thirty days. Of the one thousand POWs who had started the trip, only 31 survived.

●　　●　　●

Letter written by Mrs. Frank Fujita to a Texas newspaper

The Abilene Reporter News
Abilene, Texas
October, 1942

I am proud of my two boys and their volunteer service for our wonderful USA. I am not regretting their enlistment, and since it has come to war, and of course that means fighting, I only wish I had two more to go. I have three girls, Naomi, Freda and Patricia, and myself—all to give freely in whatever way we can serve. And also Mr. Fujita, who is an alien, but through no fault of his own. He has tried several times to be naturalized, but the law, of course, [says] no. But he is 100% American at heart, and has been so ever since coming to this country in 1914. He is willing to be used in whatever way Uncle Sam can use him. He renounced all relations to Japan when coming to this country—even to writing to his mother. He would not teach his children the Japanese language, as he wanted them to always speak American.

We are both proud to have two boys to give in defense of our country; and if they should lose their lives, it would be for a glorious cause. We would gladly do the same.

5

SINGAPORE AND

FUKUOKA CAMP IN

NAGASAKI, JAPAN

October 1942–February 1943

We had a Japanese sergeant in charge of the POWs and he had about fifteen soldiers under his command. After all were loaded, the ship pulled out and we headed north for a couple of days and then turned westward. In so doing, we skirted Sumatra and a couple of islands off its coast and then as we neared Borneo, we crossed back over the equator and entered the South China Sea. Our westward movement brought us to the tip of the Malay Peninsula, to the capitol of Malaya, the island city of Singapore. We debarked and were loaded onto trucks and taken to Changi military base and were off-loaded in Area XIV, on the outside of the main camp, and were put into some very ragged pyramidal tents. These tents were located in a coconut grove that also had sweet potatoes planted among them, which belonged to the British.[1]

1. The Changi area, at the northeast tip of Singapore Island and the site of a pre-war British military barracks and prison, contained the main Japanese POW camp in Malaya. In October 1942 it held about fifteen thousand British and Australian prisoners. Lionel Wigmore,

1942

年 月 日	品 名	数 量	替	買入金額	支拂金額	俵 入 袋	差引殘高

December 7, 1942
1 Canteen of tea in 10 days, no other water

We arrive at Nagasaki, Japan — This
deck passage is O.K. on the equator
but it is about 21° here in Japan,
the wind is blowing — about to
freeze. We go to a P.O.W. camp
(about ~~400~~ 300 Limies and we
100 yanks) We make about
1,300 men in this camp which is
Camp Fukuoka N°2 — Work is
Ship Building. About 40 Yanks
gobs are here (from Java Sea
Battle)

    Food is Rice + Barley mixed,
(Radish)
daicon and fish. 60 men in
a room — 5 Blankets, no doors,
no cieling — By God! it's cold.
and no fires.

    We don't stop shivering until
Spring.

I was taken to a hospital, along with the other dysentery victims. The curry-flavored food that we were fed on the tramp steamer must have had a healing effect on my dysentery, for I did not have one single bowel movement for five days, after which they put me back with E Battery in the coconut grove. We had experienced some pretty bad food in camps before this one, but this was absolutely the worse possible. There was no salt to be had in any of the POW camps and here, a detail was sent down the cliff to the sea each day to bring back a fifty-five gallon drum of seawater. The leaves from one sweet potato vine were plucked, chopped up and put into the boiling seawater. If you were lucky, you got some leaf in your boiled seawater and that is what we were fed.

The British ran things here and their orders were that we were not to dig any sweet potatoes or eat any of the coconuts. If anyone was caught doing either, he would be arrested and placed in jail. It was rather ridiculous, but a jail was actually built of lumber about three feet by three feet and Cpl. Monroe Woodall was appointed jailer. Of course, no one was ever jailed even though we did eat some of the forbidden foods. We had the usual rice and worms, like in Java, except that here the rice seemed a lot dirtier and the worms more plentiful. Everyone soon became a walking skeleton, and the vitamin deficiency diseases became more prevalent and more pronounced. To top this off, some of the men caught malaria from mosquito bites, some experienced fevers that were caused by hook worms that would enter the body through the feet, and some had tropical ulcers that would eat to the bone.

After a week or so on seawater and sweet potato leaves, we were issued about half a teacupful of dried minnows that Lt. Allen managed to buy. We dubbed them "white bait." They stunk to high heaven and were hard to eat while they were looking you in the eye. They did not taste bad, though, and were our only source of protein. My weight fell to eighty-nine pounds and each and every bone of my body could be seen. I had weighed 145 when we left the states. I was still weak from my bout with

The Japanese Thrust (Canberra: Australian War Memorial, 1957), pp. 512–32; Maj. Gen. S. Woodburn Kirby, *The War Against Japan*, 5 vols. (London: Her Majesty's Stationery Office, 1957–69), V, pp. 534–35.

dysentery and the present conditions were about to get the best of me. One night I sat out on a log under a bright moon and decided to try and send my mother a message by ESP. I managed to alter my state of awareness to some degree, and then I endeavored to tell her that when I left Texas I had told her not to worry about me for I would go through a war before I came back, but that I would come back and all in one piece, and that I would still do so. When I did get back Mom said that she very definitely received my message and felt a deep sense of relief.

There were no Japanese guards here at Changi. Sikh Indians who had been in the British army guarded all areas of this huge and sprawling military complex. They also were the guards at the Changi Prison, used by the British to house violent and dangerous criminals. It made me angry to see these guards in the employ of the Japanese. The starving conditions under which E Battery was forced to exist were made even more irritating by the fact that just across the fence from our area was a large palatial manor that a bunch of British officers occupied. They lived here in splendor and had their "dog robbers," or soldier servants, to do their bidding. They were well-dressed, well-fed and swaggered about with their little riding crops as if they were royalty and answered to no one. Their lawn was immaculate, the hedges were neatly trimmed, and in their front yard were two big trees that were literally full of some sort of yellow fruit that turned out to be mangos. To us starving men, that sight was more than we could cope with, and several of us went over the fence and began to knock fruit from the trees and stuff our shirts full. The British officers came running out ordering us to stop stealing "Her Majesty's fruit!" We knew damn well that the Queen was not eating this fruit, but that these well-fed, pompous, stuffed shirts were.

We observed a supply cart one day pull up in front of the manor and the Tommys that were handling the cart unloaded all sorts of foodstuff, including a whole sheep carcass. We learned that there were almost daily trips into Singapore to purchase food for the officers and that they used a trail that passed through the jungle very near our area. We took to raiding the supply carts in the middle of the jungle and absconding with various items like peanuts, red palm oil, sugar, tea and any other food except the mutton, which "would stink a dog off of a gut wagon," as we would have

Aerial photograph of POW Camp Fukuoka #2, Nagasaki, Japan

said back in Texas. This did not happen but two or three times before the British doubled or tripled their guards on these supply carts.

It did not take us long to develop a genuine dislike for the Englishmen. They would very begrudgingly issue the sorry rice that we did receive. Some Red Cross food parcels came in from South Africa and the damn English would not share them with us. They said the Red Cross parcels were sent from the British Empire and were intended for British troops only. Later, however, they did condescend to allow us some bulk Red Cross food sent in by the American Red Cross.

We were required to go out on work parties even though we were barely able to walk. The work, to our surprise, was grubbing up rubber trees. It seemed that the Japanese army needed vegetables badly and that there were plenty of rubber trees in Malaya. We were working near one of the monstrous 15-inch cannons anchored in concrete that had given the British the feeling that Singapore was impregnable. These huge guns were all pointed out to sea to repel invaders. They were never put to use because the invaders came down the peninsula behind them, a maneuver that the British had thought to be impossible.[2] Here we were allowed to purchase food from the natives, at least those that had money could.

Even though we were on starvation rations, the different foods that we were issued and the outside food that we were able to get had allowed the skin to start growing back on my testicles so it was no longer a torture to walk or wear clothes. However, I, as well as many of the other guys, wore mainly the G-string. This was a piece of cotton cloth about eight inches by thirty-six inches, and on one end a three- or three-and-a-half foot string was attached. To wear this you let the cloth hang down behind you and then bring the string around your waist and tie it in front. You then pulled the cloth up between your legs, over your privates and up through the string, allowing the excess to hang down loosely in front. This was a one-size-fits-all garment. Most all the pants and socks worn by the Japanese military were made on the same order, one size fits all. The socks were what we now call tube socks and the britches were made with flaps, both at the waist and at the ankles. These flaps also had strings on them so that all you had to do to obtain a fit was to wrap the flaps around your ankles and middle until a comfortable fit was had, and then merely tie the strings to make them secure.

Due to the starvation conditions, we ate anything that we felt might stop the gnawing hunger pangs in our stomachs. We sometimes were able to find jungle snails as big as your fist, and these we would turn upside

2. This is a common myth. In fact, the 15-inch guns all had 360° traverse and many of the other fixed artillery pieces on Singapore also had arcs of fire covering the landward approaches to the island. Most saw action during the fighting. Stanley L. Falk, *Seventy Days to Singapore* (New York: Putnam, 1975), pp. 202–204 et passim.

down in a bed of hot coals and cook them in their own juices. Boy! Did they ever stink, and they tasted almost as bad as they smelled, but they would calm the hunger pangs for awhile. Our latrine was an open slit trench that smelled even worse than the jungle snails. Flies would blow the contents (lay eggs in it) and when they would hatch the maggots would swarm out in all directions from the pit. They were white and made the ground surrounding the pit look as if it were covered with snow. Sparrows would come down and feast on the maggots. Some of us managed to get an old auto inner tube and we fashioned bean flips or catapults out of it. By using small pebbles for projectiles we would shoot the sparrows. Sparrows fried up in red palm oil until they were crisp were really good eating. The amusing thought struck me that this procedure very nearly equated the theory of perpetual motion. We would defecate into the pit, the flies would eat it and lay their eggs in it, their maggots would crawl out to be eaten by the sparrows, we would eat the sparrows and in turn pass them back into the trench to begin the whole process over again.

Cpl. Howard Plant was "Dead Eye Dick" with his sling shot and one day he brought down one of the flying foxes (fruit bats), that were quite numerous in the area. There were those that reckoned the critter wasn't fit to eat and there was some hesitancy for awhile, but hunger won out and the bat was eaten. We were never issued salt, sugar, soap, toilet tissue or tobacco. Growing up, we had taken for granted the simplest things, like salt. It had always been there in the food our mothers prepared, in the bread we ate and in the food that you purchased at the store. We had never given it a thought, and there was no reason to think that it would not always be thus. When salt disappeared from our lives, it became another one of those bubbles of experience that suddenly burst, leaving one more void within the outer shell of our total being. Life without salt was a whole new experience. It altered our sense of taste and turned all foods into strange and, for the most part unpleasant, taste sensations. It changed our awareness of food from something that produced great pleasure and satisfaction into something that was only valued to fill the void of an empty stomach. Liking food without salt was something that had to be learned.

We tried roasting every kind of seed that we could find in an attempt to find something that would approximate the taste of coffee. We tried smoking every kind of leaf and grass in an effort to find a satisfying substitute for tobacco, but we were never successful in either category. Grass and leaves were, however, an effective substitute for toilet tissue. We rinsed our clothes in plain water as well as our bodies. We never found a substitute for soap.

November 21 marked one year since leaving the USA, and in a way it turned out to be a memorable day here in Changi. We were required to stand *tenko,* or roll call both morning and evening and all POWs had long since learned to count in Japanese. Today when we had to assemble for the evening *tenko,* a sailor from the USS *Houston* that was stranded with us, Danny Rafalovitch, and I were the last two to leave the tent for *tenko* and—lo and behold there was a dog trying to catch the sparrows around the slit trench. Danny and I both thought that here was meat on the hoof and we didn't intend to let it get away. We got into a hurried debate as to which one of us would hold the dog until after *tenko.* We tossed a coin and I lost, so he took off at top speed and would answer for me when my turn came up. We had just completed digging a new garbage pit that day and it was about four feet deep. I grabbed the dog and jumped down in the pit with it and began to pet it and hoped that it would not start yelping or whining. It was one of these dogs that was a dog-and-a-half long and a half-a-dog high. It turned out to be real friendly and so I had no problem with him. All I had to worry about was whether or not Rafalovitch would botch the *tenko* bit. I crouched low in the pit, expecting at any moment to hear all hell break loose. Luck was with us and soon Danny came back, relieved to see that I did indeed have the dog.

Word got around real quick that we had a dog and were fixing to butcher it, and most of the battery was looking on to see if we would actually go through with it. I told Danny that since I stayed behind with the dog that he would have to kill it. He said OK and jumped down into the pit with an iron rod and I climbed out. I kept waiting and waiting but nothing happened so I looked down in the pit and he was just standing there. I wanted to know what he was waiting for and he said that he just couldn't hit the dog with him looking at him. I told him to get out and that I would do the job. The dog wagged his tail and looked up at me and I couldn't

Nov 21, 1942

The following two men have permission to see the American Doctor in the Southern Area – for treatment.

Pvt. R.N. Moses

Sgt. F.F. Fujita, Jr.

Hollis K. Allen

1st.Lt. Cmding Sect.XIV

The pass written for Pvt. Moses and Sgt. Fujita to visit the doctor after eating the RAF mascot.

hit him either. It was getting dark by this time and I had to wait until it was good and dark before I could deliver the "coup de grace" to the dog.

Back in Oklahoma and Texas when I would skin rabbits, I could cut the skin around the neck and then just pull the skin off in one easy movement. A dog turned out to be like a cow. You had to cut every bit of the skin away from the carcass. While I was cutting up the meat, Danny got a fire going and had red palm oil getting hot in a steel helmet. Most of the other guys were still hanging about to see if we would really eat the meat. By fire light, I cut the dog up into small pieces, and then popped them into the hot oil. I didn't have any type of seasoning except hot chilies and raw peanuts so I put some of both into the pot.

When the meat was done, I offered to share it with any one who wanted to. No one wanted to, so Danny and I jockeyed back and forth to see which one would take the first bite. We decided that we would both take a bite at the same time at the count of three. We counted and bit off a little bit of meat and cautiously began to chew it up. To our surprise it tasted very good and when it became obvious to the others that we were really enjoying it, some of them decided that they wanted to try it also. I offered some to Lt. Allen, but he refused. I did not cook all the meat and kept some in water over night and intended to make some stew the next day, but the meat spoiled without refrigeration and so had to be buried.

I had several fried pieces left over and decided to take some over to the main camp and ask our doctor, Lt. Lumpkin, if it was OK to eat dog meat. Lt. Allen was the commander of our area, which was area XIV, and he wrote a pass for Pvt. Moses and me to visit the American doctor in the southern area for treatment. The doctor said that of course the meat was good to eat and he proceeded to eat a piece I had given him. A corpsman off the USS *Houston,* Griff Douglass, who was the doctor's assistant, ate the other piece.

Col. Tharp, our original battalion CO, was at this camp with most of the battalion and a lot of sailors and marines off the *Houston.* We were told that one group had been sent on to Burma and another smaller group had been sent to Japan. The Americans here in the main camp were obviously doing a great deal better than we were down in the coconut grove. The colonel seemed to have plenty of money to purchase food from the British black market in camp, at double the price that the English could buy it for. There was one American corporal that had quite a lively black market of his own going. Long after the war was over, I was told that this corporal was the subject of a novel by James Clavell called *King Rat*.[3]

Back in our own area a day later, an English army sergeant major came swashbuckling into our area. His demeanor was haughty; his movements were very precise. He stopped at a group of our men, and he flipped his swagger stick with one hand and twitched his waxed mustache with the other before he then asked if any one had seen a small dog, which he then described. One of the men pointed to me and said, "You see that little sergeant over there? Go over and ask him." He came up to me and said "I say, mate!" except when he said it, it sounded like "I sigh mite! 'ave ye seen a small dog about?" I told him that I had and he wanted to know where the dog was and I told him that we ate it. His face was red to start with but it really turned red now and he said, "Blinkin 'ell mite, 'e sure was a good little dog." I said, "I just gotta agree with you, Sarge, he sure was a good little dog." It seemed that the dog was the RAF mascot and had been in Dunkirk and Crete with them and had over two hundred hours flying

3. Clavell was a young British officer captured at Singapore and held at the Changi POW camp. His novel, about life in Changi, has as its protagonist an American corporal who by a number of devices manages to acquire large quantities of scarce possessions and live much better than the other prisoners. James Clavell, *King Rat* (New York: Delacort Press, 1962).

time. The sergeant called me a cannibal and that he would return with some of his men and do us in. He did return with his men, but nothing but a lot of bluster occurred.

On the 27th Ben took sick and had a high fever. He was put into the hospital and was diagnosed as having pneumonia. The next day the Americans were issued British wool battle dress and hobnailed shoes that Lt. Allen was able to purchase with some of the money he received for E Battery's payroll. We no sooner had these clothes than we were ordered to load onto trucks and were taken back to the harbor area and loaded aboard the Japanese luxury liner, the *Kamakura Maru*. The ship had previously been utilized in the repatriation and exchange of Japanese and British civilians. We were not permitted inside the ship, but had to bed down on the open deck, just like we had done on the Dutch liner *Bloemfontein* when we left Australia. Ben had to be left behind, for he was too ill to travel, and this made me feel sad. However, Sgt. Don Heleman and I had become fast friends and his companionship helped ease the pangs of regret that I felt for having to abandon Ben.

Our relationship was close, that is, one POW to another, and we would help and encourage each other in our bleak and dismal existence, but it seemed that each held a certain something back that prevented us from being really, really close. This was more or less a self-preservation measure, for the closer one felt towards his buddy, the more he would be tempted to come to his aid when he fell victim to some atrocious act by our captors. We had already found that if anyone tried to help another, he would receive far worse treatment than the first victim and would in all likelihood be killed in the process.

We sailed out from Singapore on November 28, out into the South China Sea, and pursued a northeastward course which took us east of French Indo-China and west of the Philippine Islands. The same one thousand men who had started the trip from Java together were still together on this trip.[4] The same Japanese sergeant and his fifteen-man detail were

4. According to one source, the *Kamakura Maru* carried some 2,200 prisoners: about 500 Americans, 560 Australians, 200 British, and 950 Dutch. Wigmore, *The Japanese Thrust*, p. 613.

still our escorts. I was amazed at the authority that the Japanese army placed in its sergeants, because if one thousand prisoners were being escorted by the U.S. Army there would be at least a major in charge. We called this sergeant "The Bull." He was a short but massively built man, and he hulked around like a gorilla. He was a very strict commander to both his troops and to the POWs. If you stepped out of line in any way, you knew that he would beat you unmercifully, but he was the same with the guards under him. Several times during the next ten days, one of his guards would do something that displeased him and he would line up the entire guard detail, in plain sight of the POWs, and beat the living daylight out of each one of them.

About a week later, we pulled into the harbor at Taipei, Formosa and let off some POW officers. The trip thus far had really been very pleasant. The deck passage was very enjoyable, for the constant breezes kept us cool and comfortable. We even enjoyed "The Bull" when he would daily try to converse with us, and was rather comical in the process. The one unforgettable thing about this trip was that we were issued one canteen of tea per man and this had to last us seven days and we were given no explanation why, for there was obviously plenty of water on board. After we left Formosa, we were given tea almost whenever we wanted it, a direct reversal of policy. We were never able to fathom Japanese reasoning.

We sailed into the northeast and entered the East China Sea, which took us between the mainland of China and the Ryukyu islands. The weather was now turning rather cool and we started wearing the wool battle dress. The farther we travelled, the colder and foggier the weather became.

• • •

Associated Press Dispatch

Washington AP Offices
Washington, D.C.
March 18, 1942
President Roosevelt today signed Executive Order No. 9102, creating the War Relocation Authority to help care for an estimated 110,000

Japanese-Americans now being moved by the U.S. Military into ten isolated "camps" guarded by the army. Milton S. Eisenhower was named
as director of the new agency.[5]

• • •

The first anniversary of the bombing of Pearl Harbor found us coming
into the southernmost main islands of Japan proper. The waterway was
clouded in a swirling mist and a cold wind was blowing down from Korea,
and to us in our weakened condition and having just come off of the equator, it was bitter cold. Rocks and small islands would suddenly loom out
of the mist and with their grotesque pine trees it made me feel as if I was
in some eerie fantasyland, and I half expected to see elves and gnomes
dancing about.

As we came nearer to land, the harbor traffic increased, and it became
evident that this was a fair-sized city. I was experiencing strange feelings
as I gazed about, and as had happened so many times in our travels, I
had this strange feeling that I had been here before. A wave of excitement
came over me when someone announced that this was Nagasaki, Japan.
My mind was awhirl with the incredible odds of my having arrived at the
very place from which Dad had left back in 1914. I wondered if any of
those on shore watching our arrival might be distant relatives. We docked
and debarked and were transferred to a tug-like harbor craft and taken
across the bay to Fukuoka POW Camp #2 on Koyagi Shima, a small
island a few miles from the city.[6]

---

5. Eisenhower resigned three months later and was replaced by Dillon S. Meyer.
The forcible removal of the Japanese-Americans, most of whom were U.S. citizens,
from the West Coast to isolated "relocation" centers was an unnecessary product of
wartime hysteria, racism, and political indifference. See footnote #1, page 159. Roger
Daniels, *Concentration Camps USA: Japanese Americans and World War II* (New York:
Holt, Rinehart and Winston, 1972); Commission on Wartime Relocation and Internment of Civilians, *Personal Justice Denied: Report of the Commission on Wartime Relocation
and Internment of Civilians* (Washington: U.S. Government Printing Office, 1982).

6. This was one of about two dozen camps in the Fukuoka complex of POW
camps in western Kyushu. Thousands of Allied prisoners were held in these camps to

Fukuoka camp was built on some land that was being reclaimed from the mountains. The mountains were being blasted away and the resulting rock was dumped into the bay and thus the usable land area was being gradually extended out into the bay. It was so new that it was not completed when we arrived. The camp was built in a rectangular shape with an open area in the center that was used for the wash-up area. There were several rows of wash troughs and each had cold water taps running from one end to the other. In front of the camp was the administration building, which housed the office complex, guard billets, the guards' dining room, and the camp commander's quarters upstairs. Just outside the main entrance to the camp sat the guard house. Out behind these buildings were the parade grounds where we would form work parties every morning and, after being counted, would disperse each night. The *benjo,* or latrine, was located outside the main building and to the rear.[7]

There were about twelve hundred POWs here consisting of English, Dutch, a smattering of other nationalities, and we one hundred Americans. We performed work here as slave laborers that the Japanese military had leased out to the huge shipyards about a mile from the camp. Our living quarters were about 20′ × 45′ with sixty men housed in each room. Two shelves ran down each side of the room. The bottom shelf was eighteen inches from the floor and the top shelf was 4 feet above that, with the rafters another four feet above that. These shelves were covered with *tatamis,* straw mats two inches thick by thirty inches wide and six feet long. Each man had his own *tatami* and four very thin cotton blankets that provided very little warmth. The concrete floors were always wet or damp, and stayed that way until the following summer. There were openings for windows but no glass on them, and the cold Siberian winds blew right through the room, for there were no doors hung either. Heaters of any kind were unheard of.

Food, as in all the camps was "Shoo-shoo,"[8] and consisted of a cup of

work in nearby mines, factories, and shipyards. *Reports of General MacArthur,* 2 vols. (Washington: U.S. Government Printing Office, 1966), I Supplement, pp. 102–103.

7. *Benjo* ("convenient place") is the common Japanese word for bathroom.

8. "Shoo-shoo," meaning "scarce" or "a small amount," is apparently one of many

*Photograph of Fujita taken by the Japanese at POW Camp "Fukuoka #2"
to be used for identification purposes.*

rice and barley mixture and a vegetable soup made from pumpkin, squash and large white radishes called Daikon. Most of the time the soup would have fish bones, entrails and heads, complete with the eyeballs. The Japanese cooks would cut the meat from the fish that was brought in and put it in the food that went to the Japanese staff and guards and what was left went into our rations. On rare occasions we would get a whole smelt per man and this was delicious. Sometimes someone would be too sick to eat their ration and attempt to save it until the next day. This did not work out too well for rats would get into it and devour it. In desperation, one fellow suspended his leftovers from a wire, hanging from a rafter, which worked well for two or three nights and then the rats figured out how to shinny down the wire and get the food.

Soon after we arrived at this camp, the Japanese took pictures of each one of us, individually, and kept them for identification purposes. We were also assigned new numbers. Each room had a room chief that was responsible for the room and everyone in it. I was in Room 20 and we had several sergeants in it, one of which was an army/air force technical sergeant. Since he was the ranking man in the room he was supposed to be the room chief. He pleaded with me to take the job, since I had experience in handling men and he had not. His experience was clerical. Much to my regret I allowed him to persuade me to take the job. If anything went wrong in the room, or if the room did not pass inspection, then the room chief received a beating. If anyone in the room goofed up in any way that would bring on a disciplinary beating, then the guilty culprit would

---

POW slang words invented by the prisoners (and apparently also used by some of the guards), derived from words or expressions in the various languages they spoke or had been exposed to, from Japanese words as the prisoners thought they heard them, from pidgin English used by the guards, or from some combination of these sources. Some words were used with a completely different meaning than they had held in their original language, while others were fairly close to their original meanings. Sometimes they were combined with grunts and sign language and they often were the only means of communicating between prisoners and guards or between prisoners of different nationalities who did not understand each others' languages. See, for example, the "P.O.W. Glossary" in Rohan D. Rivett, *Behind Bamboo: An Inside Story of the Japanese Prison Camps* (Sydney: Angus & Robertson, 1946), pp. 394–400.

get bashed around and the room chief would be bashed also for having permitted the act to happen in the first place. If the guilty person was not found out, then the room chief would get a beating any how. It was a no-win situation for the room chiefs, for we caught hell no matter what happened.

Unfortunately for me, two privates in my room were always getting out of line and causing me to get beat up. They had presented a disciplinary problem ever since they had been in the military. The height of one's ambition was to be another Al Capone; you could call him a crook or a thug and he would beam with pride. One day after they had caused me to get a rather severe beating, I told them that if their behavior continued as it had been, I might just have to kill them for self-protection. They bellowed and snarled around and flexed their muscles a bit, but they did clean up their act.

We had twenty-two Americans in Room 20 and the rest were Englishmen and one Canadian. Our officers had Room 21 to themselves, and the rest of E Battery was in Room 19. We had *tenko* morning and night in the barracks and the same thing out in the courtyard when we formed work parties.

The prisoners were formed into work groups to work on some aspect of ship construction, such as caulkers, pipe fitters, welders, torch cutters, electricians, and riveters. My crewmen were called stage builders. We had to erect the staging or scaffolding inside and outside the ship as it was being constructed so that the other workers would have something to work from. We had to memorize a Japanese character and whenever we saw two rivet holes in the steel plates that had a circle chalked around them and had this character written by them, then we knew to install a steel "A frame" at that location. These A frames were spaced about sixteen feet apart and onto these we would lay two wooden planks to form the catwalk or stage. I was put in charge of the stage builders, and I had one Irishman and six Englishmen in the crew.

The dockyards [shipyards] were located about one mile from our camp and we were marched to and from there daily. The road ran through a shanty town where Korean and Japanese laborers lived. The foot traffic on this road was made to stand aside while the POWs marched past. If

Watercolor by Fujita of Room 20, Fukuoka POW Camp #2,
Nagasaki, Japan

any of them would try to cut through the column, the Jap guards would beat them and scold them. These laborers were not much better off than we were. We began work at the dockyards on the 12 of December 1942. If you had anything to say or if the work bosses had any instructions for the day, they had to be given or said before work started, for once the riveters started you could not hear a thing.

There were several ships under construction at the same time and the POWs would head for the ship they were working on once they were inside the dockyards. All of these ships required staging and so my crew moved about from one ship to another, installing stages inside and out. We had to carry the steel angle iron A frames from ship to ship, and sometimes we had to carry the planks. If the next ship we were to work on was at the other end of the yard, then the planks were bundled up and floated to the location.

On the 23rd of January, some men were taken to a radio station and allowed to make a broadcast home. H. T. Shaw, Howard Plant, Roger White and Pete Evans were the lucky ones. I was amazed that I was still alive and I knew that my family would be highly fearful that the Japs would have killed me by now. I asked Pete if he would mention me in his message so that my parents would know that I was still alive and this he did. The work at the dockyards was so hard, the weather so cold, and the food rations so inadequate, it was surprising we were able to withstand the demands made upon us. We would return to camp in the evening bone weary and barely able to walk. The effects were accumulative, and as time went on we became weaker and even more susceptible to the ravages of disease and malnutrition. All through the night, men would scream out from the effects of dry beriberi. Every cell of our bodies was crying out for rest, but this was not to be had. Before retiring, we had to perform the gray-back ritual—that is where we had to remove all our clothing and meticulously search every seam and wrinkle and remove the big gray-back lice that infested our clothes. We would nearly freeze in the process. This completed, we had to make our last call to the *benjo* before trying to sleep. This was a terrifying trauma each and every time, for there would always be guards between the barracks and the latrine. They would always amuse themselves by making the POWs bow and then bashing them around. If one had to go during the night, the guards were particularly brutal and at times would keep you standing at attention in the freezing wind until he tired of it. If you had dysentery and were unable to control your bowels, then you would really get a beating.

This *benjo* ordeal caused some of the English and Dutch to use their mess tins for toilets during the night and then empty them the next day. I am proud to say that no American stooped to this action that I was aware of. We had no soap or disinfectants of any kind, no boiling water in which these mess tins could be sterilized, and so these men just compounded the effects of their illnesses.

If you managed to get the gray-backs without freezing and go to the *benjo* without being killed, you then crawled into your thin blankets desperate for sleep and rest. But Alas! This, too, was to be denied us, for when we were in our blankets the bedbugs and fleas would attack us. Oh how viciously they would bite and then retreat before you could catch them. Just as you were about to get the trapped air in your blankets warm enough that you might stop shivering, the demon bedbug would bite and when you threw the covers back to catch it, you lost all the accumulated warmth. The hours would pass rapidly as you became more frantic to get some sleep before the next work shift

The call to wake up for *tenko* would come, it seemed, before you could get to sleep. Your body was aching and spent from the previous days' work, and you just felt that it was impossible to go on. Some men were to the point of self-mutilation to keep from going to work. When a POW felt that the end of the road was near, he would ask a buddy to break his arm or leg so that he could get out of the work gangs, and his buddy would, out of compassion or pity, grant the request. The little Irishman of my crew reached this point and asked me to break his arm. I told him that I would, so I placed two 4″ × 4″ pieces of wood on a table, about twelve inches apart and told him to lay his arm across the gap that was formed. I picked up one of the steel angle iron "A frames" and raised it above my head and told him not to look while I broke his arm. He peeked and jerked his arm away just as I brought the iron crashing down. He said "Blinkin 'ell, I didn't want me arm crushed—just broken!" I tried two more times with the same result, and then he decided that he did not want his arm broken after all.

• • •

A *bilene Reporter News*
Abilene, Texas
Wednesday morning
February 17, 1943
First news since fall of Java—
ABILENIAN, JAP CAPTIVE, HEARD ON AIR

First news of their sons since the fall of Java, almost a year ago, came Tuesday night to Abilene mothers by shortwave transcriptions from Tokyo. Several listeners to the Tokyo broadcast heard Robert L. Stubbs, son of Mrs. S. S. Stubbs, 1642 Victoria, say he is a prisoner on Java, and is "well and being well taken care of, and have not been sick a day."

Private Stubbs, previously unreported, referred to two friends, Sgt. Frank Fujita and Cpl. Ben C. Keith, Jr.

The message was the first word to come to Sergeant Fujita's mother, Mrs. Frank T. Fujita, Sr., 1241 Oak. Frank was previously unheard from. Both fathers, S. S. Stubbs and Frank Fujita, Sr., are away on defense jobs.

Mr. and Mrs. Ben C. Keith, Sr., of Caps, had been notified by the War Department a few weeks ago their son was a prisoner of war.

Also heard on the broadcasts was Joe Fender, Roby attorney, whose parents live in Dallas, and other references were to Thomas Watson, Grapevine, and Jack Turner, Slaton.

Robert Stubbs said all members of the 131st Field Artillery organization in Japanese hands are receiving good care, medical attention when needed, and food on which they are gaining weight, with "no hard work to do."

The broadcast was heard clearly by Golda Slone, 717 Poplar, whose brother, First Lt. Reuben Slone, is an officer in Battery E of the 2nd Battalion of the 131st.

It was heard too, by Mr. and Mrs. Earl Johnson, of Baird, who hear the Tokyo broadcasts regularly, and keep a scrapbook of the transcription conversations.

The Japanese short wave station is heard each day at 1:15 and 6:15 in the afternoon, and 1:15 and 7:15 each morning, Mrs. Johnson said.

The initial word from the Stubbs and Fujita boys increases to 34 the total of Abilene area artillerymen who have been heard from as Japanese prisoners. A total of at least 11 are still unheard from.

• • •

War Department Telegram

Provost Marshall General
Washington, D.C.
February 9, 1943
Mrs. Frank Fujita:
A shortwave broadcast from Japan has been intercepted from Sergeant Donald Heleman. He stated that Frank Fujita is well and in good health. "He and I have been buddies ever since we left Brownwood, Texas." Unquote. This broadcast supplements previous official report received from International Red Cross.

• • •

Letter from Adjutant General, War Department, to Frank Fujita, Sr.

War Department
Washington, D.C.
February 24, 1943
Dear Mr. Fujita:
The records of the War Department show your son, Sergeant Frank Fujita, Junior, 20, 813, 132, Field Artillery, missing in Java since February 24, 1942.
Every effort has been made through the American Red Cross with the Japanese Government to obtain information regarding the names of men taken as prisoners, but to date few reports have been received.
The case has been carefully reviewed and as there was no evidence warranting contrary action, the War Department has, under the provisions of Public Law 490, 77th Congress, as amended, made an official determination continuing him on the records in a missing status. The law cited provides that pay, allowances, and allotments are to be continued while in such status.

Please be assured that the War Department will continue its efforts to determine his status and you will be notified promptly if additional information is received, or when circumstances warrant a change in the present determination.

Yours very truly,
The Adjutant General

1943

年月日	品 名	数量	替	買入金額	支拂金額	貸借	差引殘高

February ?¹² , 1943

Victor Syrett , a Canadian Pvt.
of my room died of Phnewmonia .
fleas, lice, Bed bugs, , Rats, land crabs
March 1, 1943

Two Yank Naval M.D.'s One Aussie
M.D. and 8 U.S. Navy Corpsmen
came in from Zentsuji — A Godsend —
the Yanks came from Guam.
sick, kill flies
March 3, 1943

Hatheral an English Pvt. of the
R.A.F. of my room died of
Phnewmonia.
Coffins + Barrels   one for Plant
March 15, 1943

First cigarette issue — 3 packs

6

Labor in the Shipyards

February 1943–May 1943

We had begun shivering with the cold when we reached Japan and had not stopped since. Every muscle and bone was sore and ached from the shaking. I was lucky to have my bed in between Sgt. Donald Heleman and Sgt. Herb Lucas. Lucas was from F Battery and got left behind with us in Java. Lucas had a knee length, leather sheep skin flight jacket and he let me sleep under it with him. This was the only time that I was able to get warm.

In the shantytown that we had to pass through each day, there was a large community bath, and after much complaining to the Japanese camp officials, we were finally allowed to use the community bath every other week. The Japanese method of bathing is that both men and women bathe together, soaping and scrubbing down outside the main tub, rinsing off, and then entering the piping hot bath for some socializing and steaming. No one bothered to tell us POWs the procedure and so when we got into the bath house, everyone peeled off their clothes and jumped in. There was a lot of hollering and dancing on water trying to get back out onto the deck surrounding the tub. It seems that a fire is kept going continuously under the bathwater and the ideal temperature is just short of being hot enough to par-boil you. It was indeed a shock the first time we tried it, but we soon learned to enter with caution. That first time, we were literally black with coal dust and soot from the dockyards, and we had no soap, so we jumped in dirt and all. This brought a loud protest from the shantytown residents who were ganged up all around the bath waiting until after the POWs finished bathing. We had no soap and we always left a sizable ring around the tub.

It seemed that everyone in town, as well as some from the surrounding area, came down to the bath house on POW night to view these naked men from so many different countries. The men would stare with unbelieving eyes, and the women would giggle and both sexes would say "*Okii! Okii!*(Big! Big!)" We POWs made no attempt to conceal ourselves and there were some that displayed truly monumental organs. For instance, an Englishman in my room would at times place both his hands on his penis as if he were grasping a baseball bat, and still would have more left over than the usual man. He would start whirling the excess around and around and then walk up behind an unsuspecting roommate and pop him on the rear with it. This would bring a roar of laughter and comments such as: "A tool such as that is only good for extra-large women or small cattle, or barroom betting." "He could rake the chips off the table with it."

Cigarettes or tobacco had never been issued to us by the Japanese, but there always seemed to be tobacco around. It would be traded for at the dockyards and re-traded again back in camp. It was never plentiful but it came in several forms—cigars that had worms in them, a very finely shredded tobacco that resembled hair and was called WOG Tobacco or just WOG,[1] and a still finer shredded tobacco that we called Monkey Fur. The cigars could be crushed in the hands and, after the worms were removed, rolled into cigarettes. The WOG was also rolled, so paper that was thin enough to use for cigarette paper was at a premium. Every American GI was issued a pocket sized New Testament, and because the paper used in it was the thinnest that could be found around a POW camp it was much

---

1. WOG is a British euphemism for a native of India and, by extension, of any Far Eastern country. The acronym is sometimes said to stand for "Wily Oriental Gentleman" or "Westernized Oriental Gentleman," but the term was more probably a pejorative derived from "golliwog," a grotesque black doll with fuzzy hair and staring eyes in a late 19th century children's story and a popular British nursery toy—as well as a DeBussy piano solo, "The Golliwog's Cakewalk." Robert L. Chapman (ed.), *New Dictionary of American Slang* (New York: Harper & Row, 1986), p. 471.

in demand. The Monkey Fur tobacco was smoked in a very special way in a very special pipe. The pipe was about twelve inches long, usually bamboo about the diameter of a lead pencil, but had a small, metallic bowl on one end that would just hold a small pea into which the Monkey Fur was rolled. The smoker then lit the pipe and took one pull of smoke and then knocked the remaining ball of fire into the palm of his hand and quickly rolled another ball of Monkey Fur, put it in to the pipe and relit it with the ball of fire from the hand. This procedure continued, one puff at a time, until the smoker had been satisfied.

Each time that a guard came into the room or near me, I was always afraid that he had found out that I was half Japanese, and I almost always imagined the worse possible scenario of ensuing events once that happened. Sometimes, though, I felt like telling the Japanese camp officials that this is where my father had come from and that more than likely I still had kinsmen living in or near Nagasaki. I wondered how they would react when they found out that they had had a Japanese-American soldier under their command all the while and did not know it. I wondered, too, how they never realized that I was half Japanese, because I never allowed my buddies to talk me into changing my name, so it had been on the roster for almost a year. My buddies and I had speculated on what they would do and in one way or another we would convince ourselves that they would kill me. We had *nisei* interpreters (they had been caught in Japan when hostilities broke out and were put into the Japanese army)[2] and it is a mystery why they did not recognize my name. As if the fleas and bedbugs, rats and lice, shivering cold and constant hunger, overwork and disease, mean guards and frequent beating were not enough to make life miserable, I also had this nagging fear to contend with. All my hair came

2. *Nisei* are second-generation Japanese-Americans. At the outbreak of World War II, about ten thousand *nisei* were in Japan, as students, tourists, or visiting relatives. Many were coerced, or driven by circumstance, to work for the Japanese, and some were forced to join the army or navy. Masayo Duus, *Tokyo Rose: Orphan of the Pacific* (Tokyo and New York: Kodansha International, 1979), pp. 55–56; Joseph D. Harrington, *Yankee Samurai (The Secret Role of Nisei in America's Pacific Victory)* (Detroit: Pettigrew Enterprises, 1979), pp. 175, 222, 257.

out from the front to past midway back on my scalp. There was not even any fuzz left. Later, when I was relieved of the room chief job, the hair grew back in.

The Japanese were mortally afraid of fire, and anyone caught with matches would be beaten almost to death. There were many things that were forbidden—pencils, radios, knives or any sharp pointed instrument. The guards were always pulling sneak raids to try and catch someone with any of these items. The guards were getting meaner and more brutal. Most of them were soldiers that were too shot up or crippled up to perform fighting duties and so were put into POW camps as guards. The meanest and cruelest of the guards were Koreans. The Japanese looked upon them as subhuman and almost any soldier of any rank could beat them up. They had no recourse until they were placed as guards over POWs, and here for the first time in their lives they could beat someone up—and they sure did.

Work at the dockyards was miserable to say the least, and the cold winds and rain would make it even more so. I was always glad when we had to hang staging inside the new ships, because at least we were out of the wind there. One day I was working at ground level when Wham! I was hit in the head with one of the big steel rivets that were used to rivet the ship's steel plates together with. They probably weigh a half to three-quarters of a pound each and are capable of raising quite a large lump on one's head and "smarting like all get-out!" I looked up and saw a coolie grinning from directly above me, as if he thought that was real funny. I got a good look at him, and I knew that sooner or later my turn would come. Sure enough, two or three days later I saw this same riveter working some side plates. I worked myself into position about three stages above him. Huge bolts were used to temporarily hold steel plates together until they could be permanently riveted. These bolts weigh about a pound and a half each. I took one of these bolts and loaded it down with washers and nuts until it must have weighed twelve pounds or more. I took good aim at the riveter below me, and "Bombs Away!" My aim was good, and I hit him square in the head. He fell to the ground and never so much as wiggled. I made it to the other side of the dockyard in record time.

In our normal work routine, we would go from one ship to another, building scaffolding higher as new plates were added. Two of us would

LABOR IN THE SHIPYARDS

carry one of the planks that we used to the new location. In doing so we would have to cross over steel ribs for the new ships that were laid out neatly next to one another to facilitate their use when needed. Just as our stage builders crew had a Japanese character that told us where to install an "A frame" for staging, the POW torch cutters also had their symbol yellow chalk, and a line always accompanied it to show where their Japanese foreman wanted the steel cut. I learned to write their symbol and on several occasions, as we would carry our planks over these ships ribs, I would stoop down and write the cutting symbol in yellow chalk that I found and with a piece tied to the end of a stick I would draw a yellow line across all the ribs as we crossed over them. Sooner or later here would come a POW torch-cutting crew, pushing their two-wheeled carbide tanks and torches and when they spotted the yellow symbol and line they would fire up their torches and cut all the ribs in two. Of course when their foreman would catch them doing this, they would be beaten.

For every job that was required to build a ship, the Japanese put a POW crew on with a Japanese foreman, and sometimes they would work with the regular Japanese crew. We had been issued a green suit, pants, coat and cap similar to that worn by just about everyone of the working class. The POW coats had red bands sewed across the shoulders that identified them from other dock workers. When our clothes wore out they were hard to replace, particularly the shoes. I knew that there was a special work crew called *Kutsu Nashi* or "No Shoe" crew, and they had a special job. I had always thought that perhaps their job was easier than ours until one day my shoes fell apart and I was put on the *Kutsu Nashi* crew. I was sorry to find out that their job was to feed coke to the blast furnaces. The coke was in big heaps inside a metal building that housed the furnaces, and was piled on two floors. The furnaces were made of fire brick about ten feet in diameter and extended through the roof in the form of very tall smokestacks.

Scrap metal would be tossed into one of the open doorways, and then we would have to toss in chunks of coke through another doorway. I found that the blast furnace was aptly named. The molten metal was poured into ingots on the lower level. Why this job was chosen for those who had no shoes, is beyond me. Coke is the residue from coal after it as been subjected to destructive distillation, and it looks and feels like lava rock with razor-sharp edges that were pure hell on bare feet. At day's end, our feet looked like big chunks of raw, bloody meat. After a day or two on the *Kutsu Nashi* crew, I was issued a pair of Japanese tennis-type shoes. They were made of canvas and rubber and opened at the back with tabs to close them with, and they had a separate compartment for the big toe. Surprisingly they were quite comfortable. Other foot gear included straw sandals that did not last long, and wooden clogs that we called "go aheads" because they were hard to back up in.

Almost every man was physically unfit to perform manual labor, and sickness and physical exhaustion was taking a heavy toll. The death rate in this camp was now at five per day. We had a hospital in camp but in order to be put into it, you had to be virtually gasping your last breath, and not many survived the hospital alive. There were two other categories in which one could be sick enough to miss work and one was "sick in quarters." In this category you could not lie down, but had to sit or stand up all day and were required to catch and turn in to the Jap guardhouse one hundred flies per day. The third category was "sick in bed." In America we would classify these people as critical. They were allowed to get into bed, but had to catch fifty flies per day. In either category, if the flies were not turned in then that person had to go back to work. There were quite a number that died on the job. Most of us would catch flies after or before work, and put them into the kitty for the sick to turn in.

There was a Dutch doctor that we called "Fish Paste" in charge of the hospital. He was big and plump and wore his white military uniform at all times. One day I was visiting Donaho in the hospital, who had something wrong with his feet as well as being deathly ill. His bed was near the desk of the Dutch doctor, who was not in at the time. Two beds down from Donaho, a POW was obviously dying, and his food ration was sitting at the head of his bed. In a little bit, the Doctor came in, looked over to the dying man and said to his orderly, "Isn't he dead yet? Bring me his ration." The orderly did, and the doctor sat down and devoured the man's ration. This just added to my hatred for the Dutch men.

Of all times to cut a wisdom tooth, I cut my first and only wisdom tooth in the POW camp. My jaw was swelled and there was a big bag of pus covering the tooth. It was giving me so much pain that I went to the sick bay, which was the hospital, and this doctor took a look and said that he would simply lance the bag of pus. He cut and sliced several times, and then asked if that did not feel better, and I told him that not only did it not feel better, it hurt like hell. He let out a grunt and said that it would be better in a while. I went back to my room and took out a small piece of mirror and looked to see what he had done, and damned if he did not chop up the wrong tooth. I took out a piece of double-edged razor blade (the Japs did allow us to have razor blades, but they never issued any) and I lanced it myself.

There was one guard who was becoming more and more suspicious that there was something about me that needed looking into. He would come up to me at the wash troughs and look me over from head to foot. One day, he put his arm up next to mine and pointed to his skin and then to mine and said "*Somma, Somma, Ne?*"—in other words, "they are just the same, aren't they?"[3] I tried to let on like I did not understand what he was trying to say, but he wasn't buying any of that and began to get highly agitated and kept on insisting "*Somma, somma, Ne?*" Finally, as he swung his rifle with fixed bayonet from his shoulder and got it into a position for a thrust, I shook my head yes and said "*Somma, Somma!*" He grinned and then turned and grinned at other POWs standing there, and acted as if he had really extracted some big military secret from me. He then turned back to me and said "*Rosoberuto, Joto nai, Ne!*"[4] Here again I put him off as long as I felt safe and finally had to agree with him that Roosevelt was no good. This pleased him no end and this ritual took place quite often from then on out. I was always afraid that he would ask my name, put two and two together and then sure enough I *would* be in hot water.

For Christmas in 1942, the Japanese softened up a bit and issued us an apple apiece and a small amount of sweetened coffee in addition to our

3. The words "somma, somma" appear to be one of those POW slang expressions. It is not a Japanese term (a Japanese pronouncing the English word "same" would probably say "sēmu" or "sēmo") and Fujita first heard the expression used by a native Indonesian (see p. 107).

4. Literally, "Roosevelt is not first class, right?!"

normal rations. We were all taken by surprise and started wishing each other Merry Christmas as we sipped our sweet coffee and ate the apple. When you have nothing, a little can be a lot.

On the 19th day of January, 1943, a Limey in my room (R. A. Malkin) died from locked bowels, or twisted intestines. He had complained to me the day before that he had not had a bowel movement in over a week. I took him to the sickbay and told the doctor his problem and after talking with the Jap medico, it was decided that they should operate on him. They did and found the problem. He never recovered from the operation. The Japanese had a good sickbay for their troops and their medicos were very good at everything, including surgery. The only problem was that they were very reluctant to share their medicines with the POW sickbay.

The starvation rations and the resulting malnutrition had our bodies in such poor condition that if any other sickness overtook us we were unable to overcome it. The Canadian private in my room, Victor Syrett, came down with a very nasty cold, which turned into pneumonia and he died on the 12th of February.

On the 1st of March our spirits were raised, for one Australian medico and ten American medicos from Guam were brought into camp.[5] Not only were we glad for their medical expertise, but it was good to see new faces and hear news from other camps. The winter was bitter cold, or at least in our weakened condition it seemed bitter cold, and the wind would howl through the window and door spaces and we would shiver and shake as if we housed some sort of big vibrators within our bodies. The medicos' presence did not help another Englishman in my room A. M. Hatheral, for he died on March the 3rd of pneumonia. On this same day, the Japanese decided to give us an opportunity to spend some of the yen that we were amassing at ten, fifteen and twenty-five sen per day. They brought in

5. The Americans were naval medical officers, captured with about 400 Marines, naval personnel, and civilians on December 10, 1941 and brought to Japan a month later. Samuel Eliot Morison, *History of United States Naval Operations in World War II: The Rising Sun in the Pacific, 1931-April 1942* (Boston: Little, Brown, 1968), pp. 184–86; Benis M. Frank and Henry I. Shaw, Jr., *History of U.S. Marine Corps Operations in World War II: Victory and Occupation* (Washington: Hqs, U.S. Marine Corps, 1968), pp. 734–36.

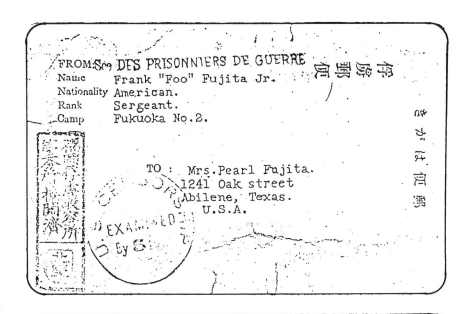

FROM 9 DES PRISONNIERS DE GUERRE 俘虜郵便

Name   Frank "Foo" Fujita Jr.
Nationality American.
Rank   Sergeant.
Camp   Fukuoka No.2.

TO : Mrs.Pearl Fujita.
       1241 Oak street
       Abilene, Texas.
       U.S.A.

EXAMINED
By 5

福岡俘虜収容所俘虜郵便   IMPERIAL JAPANESE ARMY

Dear Mother,
       I am a prisoner of war in Japan. I am
in good health, am working six days a week for pay.
How is the family? Any serious sickness? Tell all
my friends hello and to write. I haven't had a letter
since I left home so each of the family write.
         All My Love.

Frank (FOO) Fujita Jr.

3-10-43
FUKUOKA No 2
NAGASAKI, JAPAN

*Front and back of the post card sent by Frank Fujita to his mother. The date and
place shown in the lower left-hand corner were not on the card originally.*

THIS UNFINISHED DRAWING BY "FOO" WAS STARTED IN POW CAMP "BUNKA" IN TOKYO 1944

Unfinished drawing by Fujita of Crew #8 "Stage Builders." Nagasaki Ship yards.
Fujita (section chief) is third from the left. All other crew members are English.
POW Camp "Fukuoka No. 2."

cigarettes, ten to a pack, and let us buy three packs per man at forty-five sen per pack and also packets of semi-sweet cookies for eighteen sen per packet which had twelve count in each.

About this time, one of the British POWs came around and was selling what he said was oleo margarine for five yen for about a quarter of a pound. Sgts. Lucas and Heleman and I went in together and bought a piece of it and spread some of it onto one of the cookies and began to eat it. We chewed and chewed and the cookie dissolved and disappeared, but we kept on chewing the oleo. We never could chew it up. Later at the dockyards, when a new ship was about to be launched, I was down under the ship and noticed the skid and ramps were covered with the same "oleo." It was launching wax.

On the 10th of March, each man was given a postcard that he could fill out and it was supposed to be mailed for us. This date was the first anniversary of my becoming a POW.

We were required to have our clothes in good repair at all times, holes or tears patched, buttons on and all buttons had to be fastened. We were never issued needles or thread, buttons or cloth for patches, but somehow there always seemed to be some on hand when needed. We were also required to shave, but here again we were never issued razor blades or shaving soap. I shaved with the same double edged razor blade for almost three years. I would take the blade and place it inside a water glass, place my index finger down on it long ways, so that it would bend and conform to the inside curve of the glass. I would then swish it back and forth and the glass would act as a hone. To put the finishing touch to the blade I then took it by one edge and whisked it back and forth over the heel of my hand. This procedure kept the blade to where I could, with much pain and difficulty, rake off the whiskers. I do not have a very heavy beard and I was always thankful that I was not as hirsute as many of the other guys. Haircuts were also mandatory.

On Easter Sunday another small ship, about six thousand tons, was launched; that made two of these ships that had been launched since we had been working there, as well as two eight thousand or nine thousand ton ships and a small subchaser. I was always amazed at what the Japanese could accomplish with the absolute minimum of crude tools and equipment. They took chances that no one except desperate people would take. One day, I was carrying an A frame to a new location, and there was a very large bulkhead that had been preformed on the ground and the Japanese workers were in the process of raising it, intending to place it into position on a new keel that had been laid for a new ship. They were using one of these fixed cranes and were lifting it with one single cable. There were many workers engaged in this effort, both Japanese and POWs. One man was standing on the top edge of the bulkhead where the cable was attached, and he was directing the crane operator. As they slowly maneuvered the bulkhead into an upright position, I noticed that the cable had a bad frayed spot in it as well being very, very rusty. I hurriedly got out of the danger area, in case the cable broke. Sure enough, when the bulkhead was lifted, one or two strands of the cable snapped and began to unwind, probably cutting in two the man on the top; the rest of the cable then snapped and the bulkhead came crashing down, trapping and crushing some of the workers below. I noticed that the POWs had moved clear. They had probably seen the bad spot in the cable too.

Finally, doors and windows were installed in our rooms and it seemed like a little bit of heaven not to have the wind blowing through the room. It may have been our imaginations, but the rooms even seemed to warm up.

The work at the shipyards continued without letup or rest, and the death toll had risen to six per day. Each day when we came in from work we had to pass by the room where the carpenters built the new coffins. As they were completed they were stacked against a wall, and we could see the ends of the coffins that had the numbers belonging to the POWs that had died that day painted on them. Only hope and hatred were keeping us alive, and it was evident every day that once a person gave up hope it would only be a matter of hours until he was dead.

Cpl. Howard Plant had become increasingly despondent and no matter what we did we could not perk him up. Cpl. Cecil Powers was one of the carpenters and we arranged with him to paint Plant's number on the end of a coffin and have it placed next to the open door of the carpenter's room where every one could see it as we passed by. That evening Plant was moping along as usual, staring off, glassy eyed, and as we passed the coffins someone said rather loudly that Plant must have died that day for there was his coffin. There were a lot of oohs and ahs and they began talking about Plant in the past tense and reckoned what a good old boy he was, and how they were going to miss him. Plant then perked up and said that he had not died but everyone ignored him and kept on talking about him in the past tense as if they could not hear him. He insisted louder and louder that he was still here. This little episode did wonders for Plant, for he took a renewed interest in life and lived to return home at war's end, only to be killed in a car wreck shortly after his return.

As the war progressed and supplies diminished, the carpenters were not permitted to build coffins anymore. Instead *miso* barrels were used. *Miso* is a reddish brown paste made from soy beans and has a very good flavor. The barrels were about thirty inches in diameter and twenty-four inches tall. A dead body would not fit into a barrel that size, so the bones of the corpse were broken in order to cram the body into the barrel. What was used for a coffin really did not matter, for the dead were taken away and cremated. A ceramic urn, about a gallon in capacity, was used to put some of the ashes in and then a label with the person's name, rank and nationality was pasted on to it. Once the Japanese decided to move the urns to a larger room, and I was on the detail to do this. Most all the labels had fallen off, so they were gathered up and would be replaced later when they had been moved. If a correct label ended up on the correct urn, it was purely accidental, but the families back home would never know otherwise.

On May 9, 1943, some new POWs came in. When they found out that there were Americans here from the 2d Battalion 131st F. A., one of the Dutchmen told us that he had left Java from the "Bicycle Camp" and that Col. Searle and some of the men were still there. He also stated that a lot of the battalion were still at camp Changi, in Singapore. At least they were as of January of this year.

Now that the weather was warmer, we had two more pests to plague us, in addition to all the others—land crabs! These little devils, about two to three inches long, ran sideways and carried one huge claw in front, like the fiddler crab. These crabs were very fast and they seemed to be everywhere. They would climb the stucco walls of the camp and could be seen on the roof, on the walls, on the rafters and in the rooms. They would run from you if you approached and so did not present a problem from being attacked, but they would get into your bedding and sleeping area and if you happened to put your hand down on one or sit on one, he could deliver a nasty pinch.

Mosquitos were the second new pest to plague us, and plague us they did. Even though we now had windows and doors, there were still plenty of openings for them to get in to us. They were even worse than the fleas and bed bugs, because their bites would itch for much longer periods of time. Everyone complained so much that the Japanese decided to let us cover the large cracks between the planks of the walls and the ceiling. They gave us stacks of old Japanese newspapers to be torn into strips. We enjoyed looking at the papers and the pictures that were in them. The galley made up a lot of rice or wheat paste, and each room was issued two soy sauce buckets full of paste to stick the newspaper strips up with.

When the paste was brought into the room, someone immediately tasted it and declared that it sure was good. The paste was divided and every one lapped it up as if it was ice cream. When it was gone, there was still not a single piece of paper covering a crack. The buckets were taken back to the galley for more paste. When all the rooms started doing this, the Japanese couldn't figure out how they had miscalculated the amount of paste that would be needed. When it finally dawned upon them what was happening to the paste, they cut it off. There were a few bashes, but not what we expected, and we still had to live with the mosquitos and cracks. Back in the shipyards, another ship was being readied to launch. When the ships reached this stage, a fantastic amount of debris, hoses, electrical cables, planks and scrap steel lay everywhere. I was topside gathering some of our equipment when I noticed a coolie type laborer clearing the deck. He would gather an armload of wood, trash or scrap metal and run over to the side rail and throw it over and then he would look down to see if anyone was under him. An Englishman unfortunate enough to be under an armload of steel was hit in the head and killed.

On one of these ships that was nearing the launching stage, my crew was on the deck and the overhead crane was jockeying one of the final steel plates into position which would form the very top edge of the ship. This ship was being built in a dry dock and the distance from where we were must have been about 100 feet or more. The plate would be positioned and the big bolts would be inserted to hold it in place for the riveters. To make the plate more stable, a pole made from two pine trees bolted together was set up on the floor of the dock and the top of the pole had a steel eyelet fastened to its end. We were supposed to insert a bolt through the eyelet and match it to a rivet hole in the plate, secure it and thereby helping hold the plate in place. We were having a hard time aligning the holes, and the Japanese foreman was getting quite agitated with us. He motioned for one of us to get out onto the pole and put the bolt through from the outside. We both shook our heads and waved our hands, indicating that we would not do it. Even though we could not hear him for the thousands of riveters going it was obvious that he was lambasting us something fierce.

He indicated that we were cowards and that he would show us how it was done. When he crawled over the side and got a-straddle of the pole, the pole began to weave and the foreman waved for us to be more careful. The man working with me looked at me and indicated that he wanted to push the pole away from the ship; I shrugged my shoulders and he did give the pole a shove. The foreman began to scream as the pole started to fall. Instead of loosening his grip and sliding down the pole, he grasped it even tighter and gravity pulled him to the underneath side of the pole. He hit on the concrete floor and the pole popped him like a paper bag filled with air. We looked around to see if anyone had seen what took place, but we could see no signs of anyone having done so. The weather was warm and I was working without my jacket on. I had left it hanging down below where our lunch boxes were and next to where the foreman and pole had landed. Japanese workers below had seen the pole hit and several of them rushed over to see. They gathered up all the parts and since my jacket was there handy, they put his remains in it and carried it off to the infirmary. When the day's work was over and we were lined up for the trip back to camp, a guard brought me my jacket, which was covered with blood and intestines and I refused to wear it. He insisted, and I adamantly refused so he began to beat me with his rifle butt. One of the interpreters came over and told me that I should be proud to wear a jacket that had a Japanese on it.

When we returned to camp, I was beaten again for not having a jacket. After *tenko* was completed everyone was dismissed except me and I was beaten some more. They did finally issue me another jacket.

The 29th of April was a red letter day for us, because it was the Emperor of Japan's birthday and we were granted a day of *yasume*, or rest.[6] We had worked continuously ever since we started in December of the previous year. There was much rejoicing for they even permitted us to go

6. The Emperor's birthday, *Tenchō-setsu* ("Heaven-long festival"), was one of Japan's four national holidays.

to bed. Whenever you saw a group of men huddled together and raptly listening to someone speak, you could be sure that they were exchanging their favorite recipes and trying their best to memorize them. Some of the would-be thespians had been practicing to put on a camp show if the opportunity ever arose. The Emperor's birthday seemed to be the right occasion, and it was announced that at so-and-so hour this very evening there would be a musical review with skits, poetry and song. Everyone was welcome and came early in order to get a good seat.

That evening at the appointed hour, the Japanese camp staff and some of the guards were on hand around the crudely erected stage and every man that was able was seated out front in a sometimes eager and some- times dubious state of expectation. The show started and it was surprising the talent that these walking skeletons had. Some had fashioned musical instruments out of odds and ends and they played them fairly well. Now most of the participants were Limeys and when you heard them talk you would have thought that the King's English or at least half of the King's English consisted of some form or tense of the slang word for sexual inter- course. They could speak a sentence that contained fifteen words and ten of them would be some form of this word. Well the show's MC announced that the next thing on the program would be a solo by a well known Limey singer. The band struck up the tune of the "Rosary," and out on the stage walked the boniest man that could possibly be. He was literally a walking skeleton and each and every bone in his body could be seen. He wore a G-string so that his bones would stand out with the greatest effect. When the audience was primed to the right degree of expectancy this skeleton sang out in a surprisingly strong and clear voice, his own version of the "Rosary." "There's fuck-all left of me—of what there used to be" and the rest of his words were drowned out with hilarious laughter. When so much laughter came from the POWs, the Japanese joined in and laughed too, even though they did not understand the words and so did not get the implication.

The day of rest was over entirely too quickly and we had to return to the grueling work in the shipyards. On May the 1st, we got the postcards back to be signed that had been written on 10 March, and they were actually mailed, via the Red Cross, I suppose. On the 24th some bulk supplies, supplied by South Africa, came into camp. There were boots and some food stuff. Also, some individual Red Cross parcels came in and they were issued to us—fifty-one parcels for each fifty-seven men. The chocolate and sugar and everything else in the parcel, for that matter, sent us off in a fit of ecstasy. For a while it was amazing to see the difference that a few extra calories would make in our physical well being.

The harassment and beatings by the guards continued unabated and this afflicted us with our worse torture—the constant, mind bending fear that you would be the next victim. We could not shake this fear. It was with us every waking moment in camp and at work. When your luck finally ran out and then you realized that you had survived another beating, you sort of relaxed a bit, for only as you lay there battered and bleeding did you feel that at least you would not be singled out again right away.

One morning as we were all lined up and awaiting *tenko,* I stuck my head out the door to see how far down the hall the Japanese officers were and Wham! My eyes almost popped out of my head, my brain was sending out all kinds of alarms and SOSs, and I gasped and choked to get air and momentarily passed out from sheer pain. When I had stuck my head out the door, a Japanese guard standing there crashed the butt of his rifle into my Adams apple. I was helped to my feet by roommates and managed to make it through *tenko.* After *tenko* was over, the guard came back and told me he hit me because my jacket collar was unbuttoned.

Eddie Donaho's feet turned black and he was put into isolation with a very ill Englishman. Gangrene had set up in Eddie's feet and he smelled as if he had already been dead for several weeks. When anyone became ill enough to miss work, the Japanese cut their food rations, and this is when they needed food the most.

年月日	品 名	数 量	替	買入金額	支拂金額	借貸	差引残高

June 6, 1943

These Crazy Bastards tried to get me to join the Japanese Army. They got mad as hell when I laughed at them and told them they were doomed. There are millions of fleas.

July 4, 1943

The Yank Medicos leave again — DUTCH M.D. → "Rice paste" (Viusvitch) takes over the sick Bay again the son of a Bitch — all men here swear to kill him.
Go back to work at dock yards

July 5, 1943

Alwilda Naoma Allen — 2 years ago we met

7

GUARD DISCOVERS FOO'S

JAPANESE HERITAGE

June 1943–July 1943

On June 1, 1943, almost one year and three months after we were captured in Java, a Japanese guard realized that my name was Japanese, here in Nagasaki, Japan. This guard, like so many people in Japan, could read something printed in English, but they could not understand when it was read back to them. On this particular evening he was going from one room to another, showing off how he could read the roster, which was posted at the front of each room just inside the door. I was standing by the front table (tables were placed in a row between the bunks) when he came into the room. He called everyone to come close to him, and he motioned to the roster board indicating that he was going to read it to us. As room chief my name was at the top of the roster and when he saw it, his eyes liked to have popped out and he pointed to my name and said: "Fujita! Fujita Nippon no namai!" ("Fujita is a Japanese name!") And then he asked me where Fujita was, and I told him that he had gone to the *benjo*. He said that he would wait and I moved towards the back of the room with my heart in my mouth and shaking like a leaf. I was as close to being scared to death as I will ever come. The guard remained at the front of the room and asked everyone that came into the room, where Fujita was.

Almost everyone in the room was as keyed up as I was,

for they had sweated my being found out, too, and now that the time had come they all stood around with bated breath to see what would happen next. Another man came into the room and the guard asked him where Fujita was and he looked around and saw me, and before anyone could caution him, he pointed to me and said "There he is!" The guard looked surprised and also a little put out with me for having told him that Fujita had gone to the *benjo.* Any other time I would have been beaten up on the spot, but this time he was much too excited over his discovery to think of bashing me about.

He called me back up to the front of the room and looked me up and down, sucking his teeth and muttering something incredulously about Fujita being a POW. He tried to carry on a conversation with me, about me, and finally decided that I really could not speak the language. He would feel of my skin and then put his arm next to mine and compare them, and like the guard at the wash rack, he said "*Somma, Somma.*" He would turn to the other guys in the room and then point to me and then to himself and tell them that we were somma, somma. Finally he could not stand it any longer, that he was the only Japanese to know this so he took off for the guard house. I really became frightened then and felt very strongly that my untimely demise could be forthcoming posthaste! Even though I felt like this, I still felt hope way down deep that I would survive the war in one piece.

In a little while he brought another guard with him to look me over, only to have the lights go out, for it was bedtime and all room lights were turned out at 10:00 P.M. Well, there was no sleep for me this night and Sgts. Heleman and Lucas were trying to comfort me and convince me that maybe they would not kill me after all. I was in such mental anguish that even the bedbugs, fleas, and mosquitos were not bothering me. During the night, each time the guard shift changed, the guards would take turns coming to my room and looking at me, even those who normally patrolled the other side of the camp and those who patrolled outside. It was late when the first guard had discovered my identity and all the officers and office crew had gone home except the aged Camp C.O., who lived above the guardhouse and galley.

The next morning, we had our usual *tenko* and as the officers who took head count were going down the hall from room to room, I was going over in my mind what I would do or how should I react if they made a threatening advance toward me. Should I grab the rifle from the guard and try to take as many of them with me as I could before I went down, or should I play it cool and try to wait for the situation to develop and then play it by ear? I finally decided that the latter was the best and most prudent course to follow, and so that is what I did.

My adrenaline began to overflow and I was fearful that I was about to hyperventilate as the *tenko* crew entered Room 19 next door. Somehow I managed to put on an outwardly calm demeanor as the officers and guards entered my room. I was standing at the front of the room as usual and had to give my usual accounting of my roommates, such as how many were in the hospital, how many sick in the room and how many sick in bed, and then everyone had to count off in Japanese. If the vocal count tallied with the written count and head count, then *tenko* was over and they would proceed to the next room. I thought I was ready for whatever happened, at least I thought that I was. But I had not counted on a normal daily routine *tenko,* which is exactly what took place. I was left stunned as they told us to stand at ease and then went on to the next room.

I was amazed along with everyone else that no mention, whatever, was made about my being half Japanese. I had to pinch myself to make sure that I was not dreaming. After living in almost abject fear for over a year for the arrival of this moment, I could not believe that this is all that there was going to be of it. We had our dab of rice and barley and a half a smelt each for breakfast and then went outside on the parade grounds as usual and formed into our normal work parties, had our *tenko* and then marched off to the shipyards. The whistle blew and the thousands of riveters immediately blocked out other sounds and we were plunged into our own little world of limited vision.

At the lunch break, all the shipyard came to rest while the multitude of workers hurriedly ate whatever they had so that they might finish in time to have a leisurely smoke before the thirty minute break was up. The quiet was almost deafening but soothing and these lunch periods were enjoyed by all.

Today, however, my enjoyment was short-lived, for an interpreter and a guard came up to my crew and told the foreman that Fujita was to re-port back to camp. My heart almost stopped with apprehension and I realized that the unexpected calm exhibited since the guard discovered my Japanese name had been nothing more than the "calm before the storm." The guard and the interpreter escorted me back to camp and it was quite obvious that they were having difficulty subduing their curiosity and ex-citement. As we left the road and entered the camp area, all eyes from the guard house and others standing around were glued on me. I was taken to the camp office and placed in the center of the room in front of several tables that had two or three officers around them. The giant seven foot sergeant-major was hovering about with pencil and paper, ready to jot down anything he was told to.

The aging camp commander was there sitting quietly off to one side chain-smoking. The assembled officers and a few civilians were eyeing me up and down and muttering among themselves. At first, I was very scared and apprehensive, but as I stood there at attention, I consciously tried to put on a very military appearance and soon I began to calm down.

After what seemed to be a very long time the interpreter took a position between me and the seated officers, and as they would ask questions he would relay them to me:

"Is your name Fujita?"

"I am Sgt. Frank Fujita, 20813132, United States Army."

"Fujita is a Japanese name, is it not?"

"It is."

"Then you are Japanese?"

"I am an American citizen."

"Your name and your blood are Japanese."

"I have other blood than Japanese and I am a native-born American."

"Does the American army mistreat you?"

"No."

"Were you mistreated in America?"

"No."

"Was your family mistreated in America?"

"No."

"Do you like America?"

"It is my country and the greatest country on earth."

"Are you not ashamed that you are not on the side of Japan in this war?"

"We are at war and Japan is my enemy."

Questions like these were asked again and again and over and over. They seemed determined to make me say that my family and I were mistreated and they could not believe that we were not.[1]

I was kept in camp, mostly in the office, and was put on display each time that a visiting officer came into camp. The word had spread around the Nagasaki military complex that there was at the Fukuoka #2 POW camp a Japanese who was an American POW. Visiting officers of the different branches of the military and civilians from the area would come out to see this Fujita, and I would be brought out and put on exhibit and questioned again for their benefit.

After two or three unsuccessful days of their trying to get me to become a real Japanese, they evidently decided that if I could speak Japanese I would be more amenable to the idea. I was assigned to be the *toban,* or man servant, to the old camp commander. I had to learn to cook rice and whatever else he wanted to go with it. He must have been a very tolerant and forgiving man for he had several days of some pretty bad cooking until I learned how much water to add to the rice and how to manipulate the charcoal in the hibachi in order to have the rice come out just perfect.

In between meals, I was made to study the Japanese language from a small book called *Japanese in Thirty Hours,* and an English-speaking corporal was assigned to me to be my instructor on how to take care of the "Old Man" and how to learn the Japanese language. I decided right off the bat that to learn Japanese would only lead to even more difficulties than I already had, and so I kept playing stupid and made no progress. It was decided that I might as well be used to get and serve the food for the guards, since they took their meals in the same room that I was using.

1. On a number of occasions during the war, the Japanese government expressed its concern about the treatment of Japanese in enemy countries, especially the approximately 40,000 Japanese citizens interned along with other Japanese-Americans in United States relocation centers. P. Scott Corbett, *Quiet Passages: The Exchange of Civilians between the United States and Japan During the Second World War* (Kent, Ohio: Kent State University Press, 1987), pp. 88, 97–98, et passim.

I would have to go to the galley and get enough food and rice for the guards, usually two or three wooden pails about two gallons in size.

As I would go down the corridor, carrying the pails stacked one on top of another, I would have to peer around them to see where I was going. This also afforded me an excuse not to bow or salute the guards and I relished being able to pass them without having to do so. Most of the guards did not mind since I was carrying their food and my arms were full. A few, however, were very unhappy about it and made no effort to conceal their anger. One even made me set the pails down, bow to him, and then allowed me to go on my way. I complained of this to my tutor who in return reported it to the giant sergeant major and he must have ordered all guards to leave me be while I had my arms full of food trays. This made angry guards even more angry and they would glare at me with obvious hatred as I would pass them with a smug look of satisfaction, which irritated them even more.

My lessons in Japanese were not very productive, and after a week I was just as ignorant of the language as I had been to start with. The corporal was a decent sort of guy and enjoyed talking with me about Texas. After about a week of schooling, I was called back into the front office and put through the usual question-and-answer bit, but this time something new was added:

"Do you enjoy studying the Japanese language?"

"No."

"You should feel honored that we have made this possible for you. Wouldn't you like to be on our side?"

"No."

"Are you ashamed to be a Japanese?"

"I am an American!"

"But you have Japanese blood. Are you ashamed of that?"

"I have seen many things that your soldiers have done that make me ashamed."

"Many unpleasant things sometimes become necessary in a war. We want you to be in our army and we offer you the rank of captain and will provide you with as many women as you like and give you some land of your very own if you will join us. Will you accept this offer?"

"No."

"We are winning the war and you will be in a very good position when the war is over, to be on the winning side."

"Your winning is only temporary. I am already on the winning side, so why should I quit a winner to join a bunch of losers?"

The interpreter was obviously ill at ease having to tell them what I said, and he told me to not be foolhardy. I do not know what he told them, but they came back with:

"But you have already lost the war, you are a prisoner."

"My loss is only temporary and even if it were not, it would have no bearing on the war's outcome. America will win and you will still be the loser."

Some of the officers present were very upset by my words and some heated discussions broke out among them. Finally, order was regained and as questioning resumed I was getting put out with myself for not being able to convince them that I meant "No," and so was determined to squelch this type of interview once and for all.

"We will win this war! Will you not reconsider our offer?"

"Why do you want me in your army? We are enemies and before I was captured I killed five of your soldiers and shot down one of your fighter planes. I only wish I was still fighting!" I had no sooner said this, when the thought struck me that this was probably not the wisest thing I could have told them. All the office crew stopped what they were doing and just stared at me.

The officers that had been unhappy before were now fit to be tied. The interpreter looked as if he would rather be anyplace but here. There was a lot of loud debating and it was obvious to me that some were demanding my head right on the spot. I do not know why things turned out the way they did. Some higher headquarters must have said not to harm me while they were endeavoring to make a real Japanese out of me. Everyone in the office continued to stare and even the sergeant major, who had spent the whole morning trying to get the telephone operator, stopped yelling "*Moshi, Moshi—Moshi, Moshi*"[2] into the phone and turned to see what was

---

2. Equivalent to "Hello, Hello."

coming next. (I was always amazed at the size of this man. When the war first started we were told that all Japanese were little bitty runts but soon after we were captured there was a detachment of Imperial Marines that we came across in Java, who put the lie to this statement, for each one of these marines were between six and seven feet tall. I had never seen so many big men in one group before.)[3]

To my utter surprise I was told to go back to my duties as *toban* and student. If looks would have killed, I would not have made it to the door. Word had spread like wildfire among the guards, all of whom were crippled up war vets, that Fujita had killed five of their countrymen and shot down one of their vaunted Eagles. This certainly did not win any points for me with these guards and I dreaded being cooped up with them in the small dining room. When mealtime did come, they filed in and took their places around the table (the table was about thirty inches by ten feet by twelve inches high, and everyone sat on *tatamis,* or straw mats, that were about eighteen inches above the floor). They glared at me and did a lot of muttering among themselves, but made no hostile movement towards me. This fact convinced me that they had had orders not to molest me.

The guards never ate all that was sent to them, and I was determined that none of it would be returned to the galley, given instead to our officers' room (one meal) and to Room 19, 20 or 21 (rotating them at each meal). All these rooms had Americans in them and they were the only rooms between my kitchen and the camp galley. My machine gunner Eddie Donaho's feet had become much worse and the blackness of gangrene was creeping further up his foot, so I gave the first portions of extra food to him and his English roommate. I believe that this extra food I gave Donaho and the Limey was the main reason that they survived. The Limey had leprosy and I do not know his final fate.

I could only give these leftovers to the rooms if there were no guards in

3. There was no such organization as the "Imperial Marines" within the Japanese armed forces. What Americans usually referred to as "Imperial Marines" were in fact simply Japanese naval ground troops, quite different in organization and function from U.S. Marines.

the corridor. If there was one, I would just amble along very, very slowly until he went into one of the rooms or he became suspicious of my slow movements and ordered me to hurry to the galley while he watched me go. Under this situation there was no way that I could drop off the extra food and there was a lot of bitching and grumbling because I could not come up with a way to get the food to them. There were some who even bitched because the Limeys in my room got to share the laggy (what we called extra food). They said I was an American and that I should only give the laggy to the Americans. These same bitchers did not give a damn if I got beaten or not, just so long as they got some of the laggy. Several times I was caught by one of the guards as I was coming out of one of the rooms carrying the empty food pails. The guard would call me to attention, look into the pails and then ask me where the leftover food was. I would tell him that there was none left over but he knew better and would bash me around a few times before taking me back to the galley.

I would always go to Donaho's isolation room first and then duck into the room whose turn it was to receive the laggy and they would empty the food into other containers and then divide it up after I had left. I could not possibly wait until they could settle their squabbles and divide the laggy. I was not on a set schedule as to when I had to get the pails back to the galley, and since I knew the guards' routine I would try to time my entrance into the corridor just after a guard had made his round. This little bit of extra food that I was able to drop off in the rooms went a long way in helping ease the hunger pangs and malnutrition.

The old camp commander liked to go fishing in the bay which was a few yards from camp, and he would have one of the soldiers row him out in a little dinghy type boat. He liked to catch little smeltlike fish, anywhere from three inches to six inches in length, and then he would have me cook them for him. He liked them cooked whole by dipping them in a soy sauce and sugar mixture and then broiling them over the hot coals in the hibachi. After they had been redipped and toasted about three times they would have a sort of candied, salty-sweet glaze on them. If fishing was good he would allow me to eat one or two of them and surprisingly they were quite good.

One day one of the soldiers was walking along the riprap at water's edge and he spotted and caught a small octopus that weighed about three pounds. He brought it to me and told me to prepare it for the C.O. It was too late in the evening to fix it, so I put it into a pail of water to keep it alive until the next morning. The next morning when I opened the door to my kitchen, there was no octopus in the pail. I looked around the room but he was not to be seen, and I was afraid that one of the guards had come and absconded with this eastern delicacy.

As I was measuring up the old man's rice ration, I noticed that the small four-legged cabinet that I used to keep my supplies and utensils in was moved away from the wall a little. I attempted to push it back in place but it would not push. I pulled it out to see what the problem was and there was the elusive octopus, clinging to the wall behind the cabinet. I got hold of a tentacle to pull him away but found out real quick that it was going to take more than one tentacle to get that dude loose. I was amazed at the tenacity with which the octopus clung to the wall. The harder I would pull the greater the vacuum would be created. Finally the corporal came in for my morning language lesson, and he helped me get the critter loose. I prepared the octopus in the same manner that I fixed the small fish and when I took the meal upstairs to the old man's quarters, he was delighted and offered me some. It was tasty.

The front office was getting very upset because I was not learning the Japanese language. I was supposed to learn in thirty hours what it had taken them two thousand years to learn. They had begun to put pressure on the corporal to do better with his teaching and probably told him that he was incompetent and not qualified for the job. The corporal almost always carried a samurai sword, and it was beautiful work. I had asked him before how come he, being only a corporal, was permitted to carry the sword when others of higher rank were not granted the same privilege, and he told me that because he was from samurai stock he could do this.[4]

The chewing out that he got for my ineptitude caused him to lose face and he became so worked up over my refusal to learn (he knew that I

4. Japanese non-commissioned officers sometimes carried swords, but the corporal was probably either boasting or simply pulling Fujita's leg by attributing his sword to his samurai ancestry.

was deliberately not learning) that he unsheathed his sword and grabbed it with both hands and ordered me to stand up on the *tatami*. He drew back the sword and made a violent pass at my neck with it. I jumped back against the wall and he continued to swing the sword viciously back and forth with all his might. I could feel the breeze from the blade and I thought that this was surely the end of the road for me. This was yet another time that I was to come so close to death but still come out un-scathed. He was in such a rage that he could have easily misjudged his swing and laid my throat open. I seem to have a faint memory of his having nicked my jacket collar. He finally stopped and then sat down in a sort of slump with his head down and I thought for a moment that he was going to cry. I kind of felt sorry for him and in a way I regretted having caused him to lose face, for I liked him and he liked me. Good and con-siderate guards were few and far between. Finally he put his sword back into its sheath, picked up the book *Japanese in Thirty Hours* and left the room. A day or so later I was returned to my old job as *honcho*, or chief of the stagebuilders, at the shipyards.

On July 17, 1943, we heard the darndest racket coming from the bay. There were four big long Viking-like canoes, with about fifty oarsmen in each, and they were having some sort of ceremonial race. There was a drummer in each boat and he would set the pace for the rowers and they would all yell in unison at each drum beat and dip the oars. From across the bay we could hear a multitude of voices cheering the boats on. We were told that the local Chinese held these races annually and this was quite a festive occasion for them.

All during the time that I was being questioned and tutored in camp, not one time was I ever asked where my dad had come from. If they had it might have been an entirely different story. Since this was something that did not develop, it only whetted my longing to find out for sure if I really did have living relatives in Nagasaki, and so I asked the younger *nisei* interpreter if he would endeavor to find out for me.

After I told him that Nagasaki was the very spot from which my dad had left, and that I thought that his people were wealthy farmers or nursery owners, he became excited about it and assured me that he would make a special effort to find out if any of them were still around. As time went on,

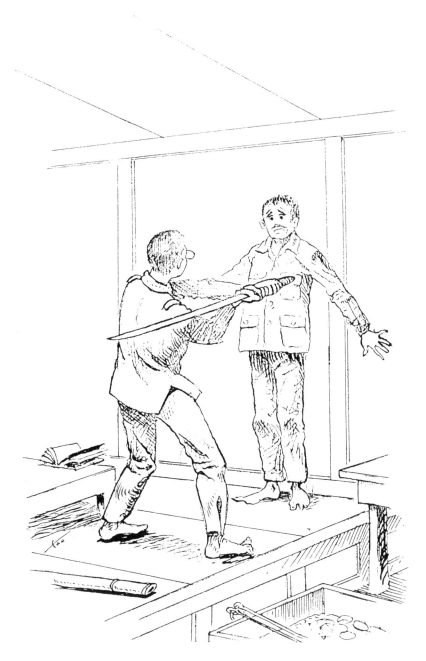

*Pencil drawing by Fujita. "He drew back the sword and made a violent
pass at my neck. I jumped back against the wall as he continued to swing violently,
back and forth."*

he would come to me and was excited that he was getting some local leads. Each time he got a little closer he would get more excited and expected to make contact with the Fujita family at any time. Then he quit coming around me and obviously was trying to avoid me. One day I cornered him and asked him the reason for his current behavior, since he had been so close to finding my relatives, and all of a sudden he could not speak English—as least to me.

It was evident to me that he had indeed found some relative of mine and I surmised that due to the war situation that no personal contact was possible or desired. The Japanese had an entirely different view of Prisoners of War than did the rest of the world, and it would not exactly be a feather in the local Fujita family's cap to have one of their own right here in their own backyard as an enemy POW. Sometime later a basket of fruit was sent into camp for the Americans only. Right away many of my buddies presumed that my kinsmen in Nagasaki had sent them in. They reasoned that under the circumstances they were unable to help me individually but could help me somewhat by helping the one hundred or so Americans in camp. This is not known to be a fact but it makes a good story.

On July 4 the Yank medicos that had come in the previous March were sent out to another camp. We were sorry to see them go because now the Dutch doctor we called "Whitefish" took charge of the hospital again. He was hated by most POWs and some had sworn to kill him if the chance ever came.

年 月 日	品 名	数 量	特	買入金額	支拂金額	借 貸	差引殘高

October 4, 1943.

An Englishman of my room died of intestinal operation. (S. Pickles R.A.F.) That makes four to die in my room. (Deaths here average 5 per day)

October 10, 1943

Was first told I would go to get my head cut-off. I was told by the Jap's that they I was wanted to in Tokyo to draw propaganda cartoons — to leave in 4 or 5 days — I sure don't like the looks of things — domei do! (NO GOOD)

October 20, 1943

I am 22 years old today.

October 28, 1943

The "Chinless Wonder" or "Sgt. Teeth"

8

FOO BEATEN,

DUTCHMEN TORTURED—

July 1943–October 1943

The miserable days dragged on and there was nothing to distinguish one day from the next or the last or the one before that, and there was nothing to cause anyone to think that tomorrow would be different. Morning would come all too soon, and as I would crawl out of bed every cell of my being would cry out for just a little more rest. The effort was excruciatingly painful and I wondered if I would be able to make another day before my body broke down for good. Would I be able to go through another day, consumed with the fear that I would be killed or tortured and maimed for life at the whim of some sadistic guard? Once as I dressed for work I thought that the previous night had been a particularly bad night for fleas and bedbugs, or had it been the night before? I tried to think what day of the week it was. Was it Wednesday? No, it must be Friday. As I pondered this, I realized that I did not know what month it was, and then I became alarmed because I suddenly could not remember the year.

Was this really even me, at this place and at this point in time? Was this horror-filled place with its violence and sickness, its slave labor and death, in fact a reality? Or was it some horrible nightmare from which I would awaken? What about my mother and dad, and Abilene, Texas, and Dora (not her real name) and Abilene High School and the Texas

National Guards? Did they exist? Were they real and had I really, ages and ages ago, been a part of that? Or were these things just figments of my imagination? Were these things visions, conjured up by a feverish mind no longer able to cope with reality, in order to draw my attention away from the facts as they were?

The mind is capable of being our salvation or our destruction, and it has the ability of making things seem other than what they are. The resulting fantasy makes it possible for someone to endure the soul-shattering, mind-destroying experiences of a Japanese POW camp. Dora is one such fantasy that went a long way in preserving my sanity and saving my life. In 1940, my buddy Roy McCullough and I, dressed fit to kill in our straw derbies, loud ties, walking canes and big cigars, had decided to take in the festivities at the "Old Settlers' Reunion" held annually at Buffalo Gap, south of Abilene, and to see if we could find a couple of cuties that might feel they just couldn't possibly make another day without our company. We met two pretty gals from Merkel, Texas, and the one that I went with was Dora. After a number of dates, we were at the Merkel swimming pool. Dora and I were atop the high dive platform and she suddenly said to me, "Foo, don't fall for me because I don't want a romance on my hands." I thought to myself that she was certainly a vain one, and then aloud I assured her that that would never happen. We dated for several months, and had many good times together.

In the hellholes that were Japanese prisoner of war camps, where sanity and life were precariously maintained by hatred, hope and fantasy, my mind conjured up this idyllic love affair between Dora and myself, and when reality became too much for me I would switch my awareness to the fantasy mode and revel with Dora in this utopian wonderland of love and happiness. This fantasy became one of the main straws to which I would cling in an ever widening river of despair.

In the same vein, but to a somewhat lesser degree, was my fantasy about Willie (not her real name), a pretty and pleasant orphan girl that I had met in Haltom City, a suburb of Fort Worth, Texas. I was on weekend pass from Camp Bowie and she was working as a carhop at a drive-in restaurant. I liked her very much and went back to see her every weekend that I could until we shipped out. My feelings towards her were mixed. At times

I had a brotherly sort of feeling, wanting to befriend her and help her and be a brother, and at other times I would fantasize a wonderful relationship with her as I did with Dora—another straw to cling to.

On July 11, Lt. Allen issued E Battery a five yen partial pay per man from the funds that he received from Col. Searle back in "Bicycle Camp."

Word was passed around that our camp was going to be inspected by a team from the International Red Cross who would report back to our government and to the world how we POWs were faring. The camp was put in shipshape and we were told that we would not be restricted on what we said to the inspection team but to just remember that we would be here after they were gone. The threat did not fall on deaf ears. We were certain that any one who saw all these walking skeletons could not help but become aware of the true conditions of this camp. A few of the POWs that were in better condition than the others were presented to the inspection team and when questioned they said that we all were healthy, happy, and well-fed, and that the Japanese were very kind and considerate to us, and this is what the team reported. This added fuel to the fire of dislike that I had already developed for the Red Cross in Java.

We could hardly believe our ears when on the 15th we were told that we could have two days *yasume,* or rest. Not only did we get to rest, but the Japanese, for some unknown reason, issued us one half bottle of beer per man. In addition to my own share I had some given to me and I traded for more and wound up with nine bottles. I got pretty loop legged but sobered up by *tenko* time.

On the second day the Japanese said that three men could write a letter home; two Yanks and one Australian lucked out and Pvt. "Corky" or "Bo" Woodall was one of these. He told me that he did not want to write and that he would trade the chance to me for some laggy or extra food. I had been eating about half of my evening meal at meal time and saving the other half to eat before going to bed. Psychologically, it made me feel like the food was doing me more good that way. I jumped at the trade, for I wanted to take every opportunity to get word back to my folks. I knew how anxious they would be for my safety in the hands of the Japanese.

The weather was very nice and the extra rest had already done wonders for the POWs. I, and many others, were lounging around outside in our

G-strings and watching other POWs play ball. It would be heart-rending to anyone to see these walking skeletons, and many POWs would look at others and then look at themselves and feel sorry for themselves. I did not allow myself this self-pity and instead of feeling sorry for our lot in life or the condition of our fellow POWs, I would stare in fascination at these skeletons and study the bone structure and marvel at how intricately the bones fit together and how the sinews manipulated the whole into any desired configuration. Each bone and sinew and wasted muscle was plainly visible. I was completely awed by this creation when I tried to imagine what man himself would be faced with if he tried to duplicate his own body. It boggled my mind to try and visualize what it would take to duplicate the movements of the mouth and lips alone. Such thoughts were more beneficial to longevity than self-pity.

The two days *yasume* did us a world of good. Our exhausted muscles were refreshed and we had had ample time to pick the "grey backs" and their nits from our clothing and had even managed to kill quite a number of fleas and bedbugs, although it did not really seem to diminish their numbers any. Being able to take our bedding out in the sun and fresh air seemed to give us a new lease on life.

Work at the shipyards resumed with all its miseries and hazards and the merciless driving of the Japanese foremen. Every thing was "*Hayaku! Speedo! Speedo!*" These foremen seemed like prodding puppets doing pantomime in tune with the ear splitting noise of the riveters.

How we fared at both the shipyard and the camp seemed to be tied in directly with how the war was progressing, for or against Japan. Here in the latter part of July, 1943, the war must have had some upsets for them for they became even more harsh in their treatment of the POWs and more relentless in prodding us to greater effort.[1] On my stage-building crew we were accustomed to carrying the staging planks from one ship to another, with one man on either end of the plank, which weighed over 100 pounds

---

1. What might have caused this is not evident. In the spring of 1943, the Japanese suffered a number of reverses in New Guinea and the Solomon Islands and were ejected from the Aleutians. Ronald H. Spector, *Eagle Against the Sun: The American War with Japan* (New York: The Free Press, 1985), pp. 179–82, 225–37.

each. One day, just as I was stepping up to take one end of the plank from the two men who did the lifting, a Jap guard stepped up and with some shoving and jerking he indicated that from this time forward it would be one man—one plank. He pushed me into position in the center of the plank and I was frantically trying to indicate to the guard that it was not possible for one man to carry one of these planks, but he angrily ordered the two lifters to let go of their ends. When they did, my frail 90 plus pound frame buckled under the weight and I went down with the plank on top of me. The guard became very angry and began to jab me with his bayonet and indicated that I should get up quickly and carry the plank to where it was needed. The two lifters raised the plank once again, and once again I was savagely pushed into place in the center of the plank. When I again protested the guard became highly agitated and began forcefully jabbing me with the bayonet and it hurt terribly even though he did not puncture my skin. He assured me in no uncertain terms that if I did not or could not carry the plank that he would run me through with his bayonet. I had already learned in other camps and from firsthand accounts from other POWs, that the Japanese soldier, imbued with the creed of *bushido,* would not hesitate to kill a POW whom he considered not worthy of life to begin with.[2] I have always been amazed at the resilience and capabilities of the human body—how it can withstand unbelievable amounts of torture and starvation and forced labor on a caloric intake far less than inadequate and yet continue to function.

Here was I, a 90-pound weakling, plagued with malnutrition and no fat or strength reserves, performing a completely impossible feat. I feel certain that even now, being healthy and well-fed, I would not be able to carry a 100+ pound plank. When the immediate threat of death was the only alternative to carrying it, my brain was somehow able to draw forth

2. *Bushidō,* literally "the way of the warrior," was the feudal code of conduct that theoretically governed the behavior of the Japanese military. Observed less strictly than in the breach during World War II, it also stressed loyalty and self-sacrifice rather than compassion and mercy. G. B. Sansom, *Japan: A Short Cultural History,* rev. ed. (New York: Appleton-Century Crofts, 1943), pp. 288–89, 348, 495–500; Stanley L. Falk, *Bataan: The March of Death* (New York: W. W. Norton, 1962), pp. 113–14, 191–92, 230–32.

strength that was not there. I walked off with the plank and did so from that time on, as did the other men on my crew.

Ever since my repeated interrogation sessions where I had revealed my war efforts in Java, the crippled-up staff of guards hated me with an intensity that they made no effort to conceal. It was obvious that they would have liked nothing better than a chance to do me in.

Surprised that they had not already mauled me over, I had come to believe that for some reason they had been ordered not to lay a hand on me. As long as the officers and the sergeant major were in camp, the guards were content with harassing me and making me stand at attention for long periods of time and making me bow to them repeatedly. They shoved me around and continuously made threatening gestures at me with their fixed bayonets, which made me feel each time that this was my final hour.

One day in early August, the 6th to be exact, some sort of meeting of the military was held in Nagasaki at which all of our camp officers and the sergeant major were required to attend. With all the wheels gone, the guards that hated me so much decided that now was their golden opportunity to commit physical mayhem on Fujita. There was one guard that was a real nice sort of fellow. His face was terribly disfigured, for somewhere he had become too inquisitive about an American hand grenade. After having pulled the pin, he was practically blown to bits. Being no longer fit for combat he was assigned to our camp as a guard. On this fateful day he found me and tried to tell me that some of the other guards intended to do me bodily harm and that he felt sorry for what was about to happen and wanted me to know that he was not involved.

Before long I heard guards going through camp calling out my name and asking everyone where Fujita was. I was in the carpenter shop talking with Cpl. Cecil Powers when he said to me "Somebody's sure hollering for you." I said, "I know but I'm not going to them. They will have to come to me." And this they did.

Two of the guards found me and pushed and shoved me out to the guard house which sat at the entrance to our camp's main doorway. One of the guards was a particularly mean character and was forever giving the whole camp a hard time. He was a very small, dark-complected, weasel-faced man, and we had nicknamed him "the Jeep." The other guard was

Pencil drawing by Fujita of his beating.

a slightly larger man with a withered arm and hand that he kept tucked behind his back. I do not recall that we had a nickname for him, but he too was forever giving the camp a hard time.

The guardhouse was one end of the building that housed the guards' quarters and dining area, the one that I used when I was the old camp commander's *toban*. The whole end of the building was open and the back wall was about ten feet from this opening. Three rows of benches were lined up in this area and the guards who were on duty sat on these benches. Just inside the room on the right as you enter was a rack that held a number of clubs, about the size of a baseball bat or a little larger. These clubs were for the sole purpose of beating the POWs.

The "Jeep" and his buddy stood me up in front of all the seated guards and began to berate me up one side and down the other and kept talking to the seated guards while making all sort of gestures towards me. Without understanding a word I knew that they were relating to them how I had admitted to killing five of their buddies and helped shoot down one of their Zeros in Java. The more they talked the more they became worked up and finally the "Jeep" ran to the rack of clubs and grabbed the biggest one and came back to me and ordered me to bend over and grab my ankles. He took up a position behind me and drew back the club and hit me across the buttocks with all his strength. While his preparations were going on, I mentally prepared myself for the blow to come. The blow was much harder than I had expected and immediately my entire rear end felt as if it were being seared with a white hot slab of iron. The force of the blow threw my body forward and ole "Withered Arm," who was standing in front of me, brought his leg up with all his might, crashing his knee into my face—smashing my nose and face.

The "Jeep" raised his club again and again he swung with all his strength and the club landed in the same place as before. I could not believe how much that hurt. I felt as if my eardrums had burst and my eyes had popped out of my head and then came the knee from the front, crashing even harder into my face and snapping my head backward, almost breaking my neck. I reeled and staggered sideways and they positioned me back in the same place and drew back again. I thought that I could not possibly take another blow. I kept telling myself, *do not make a sound; whatever happens, do not fall to the ground, do not let these sons-of-bitches think that they have broken your spirit.*

Wham! Wham! Wham! Oh how that did hurt. I did not know that pain could attain such a high degree of intensity. My entire head seemed to explode, my senses spun around and seemed to pulsate in and out, bordering on unconsciousness, and then came the frontal attack. This time the guard kicked me in the chest with his heavy army shoes and at the same time his shin crashed into my already battered face. *Don't fall down. Don't cry out.* Again I staggered away and was placed back in the same position. The "Jeep's" next blow missed the spot and came crashing down at the base of my spine. My God, how that hurt!

If anything, it hurt even worse than the buttocks. The blow to my face did not seem to hurt any more. My face must have become numb. Up went the "Jeep's" club again and I felt sure that I could not withstand another blow. One more and I would go stark raving mad. Wham! This time I could not help it. I let out a long and loud groan that could probably be heard all over camp. Perhaps that is what the "Jeep" was wanting to hear. He moved me into an upright position in front of the other guards and left me standing while he and his cohort took a rest. As I stood there without being hit, my senses began to clear somewhat and I felt certain that I had not fallen to the ground or made a sound other than the groan. I slowly realized that I was still alive and I felt proud that I had taken all that they had dished out and had not asked for mercy. I pulled myself up rigid to attention, threw my chest out and held my head up high. I would show these native Japanese what a Japanese-American was made of. My face was so swollen that my eyes were wedged shut and I could see nothing. A cool breeze was blowing in off the bay and it felt soothing on my throbbing face.

Suddenly I heard some feet shuffle up to me and then I heard the "Jeep's" voice berating me and then his fist crashed into my face, knocking me a step backward. Then he crashed his other fist into my face which also knocked me a step backward, and each time I snapped back to attention and held my head high. Again and again he hit me and each time I was rocked back a step. Finally he quit and "Withered Arm" took over with the same results, with the exception that he could only hit with his good arm and hand and so that side of my face became more mangled than the other.

Several yards away there was a cliff that was being blasted away to increase the area of usable land around the camp site; as the cliff was blasted away, that extended the usable area farther inland, and as the rock was dumped into the bay it accumulated and extended the area further out into the bay. As the two guards took turns bashing me in the face I was gradually worked backward until I reached the cliff face and then they turned me around and beat me all the way back to the guard house. They stood me again in front of the other guards and for the first time I could hear the other guards taking part in the discussion. Blood was gushing out of my face at all points but I was still standing proud and erect, or at least I thought I was. How I managed to keep on my feet during my ordeal I don't know. Someone was watching over me for sure. I had seen too many times in the past that if a POW fell to the ground while he was being beaten then he would also be stomped and bashed with rifle butts, resulting in a far worse beating than he would have received had he not fallen, sometimes resulting in death.

My tormentors, finally tired of beating me, turned me towards the main entrance to the camp and gave me a shove. I walked with what I thought was pride and dignity until I was in the midst of the many POWs who had been watching the whole thing, and then I promptly passed out. I was unable to go to work for my face was swelled to where the features were not recognizable. When I was able to open my eyes I was returned to the shipyard. The beating was after all a blessing, for I was never again harassed by any of the guards at this camp.

On August 8, all POWs were allowed to write a post card home.

On the 25th of August one Yank and two Limey medicos were shipped to another camp and wild rumors had it that many more men would be shipped from this camp very soon. It was being said that those who would be shipped out would be shipped on the basis of job skills. Immediately there were some who felt that anything that would get them out of the hated shipyard would be better than the debilitating existence that we had here. And others, which were probably in the majority, felt that here we knew what we were up against, we had learned how to stay alive within this given set of circumstances and that any move would be into unknown locations with new circumstances and guards which might or might not be better than this place.

Sure enough, the very next day twenty Yanks and Limeys were called to bring all their gear. They had all been motor mechanics and electricians before capture. Cpl. Monroe D. Woodall was one from E Battery that I remember was among this group. No one knew where they were headed, but they were loaded up in trucks and taken out of camp without delay.

One day there was quite a stir at the shipyards at evening *tenko*. Each and every day we had to go through with six *tenkos:* morning *tenko* in the barracks; work party *tenko* before leaving the camp; *tenko* when we arrived at the shipyard when the army turned the POWs over to the navy; day's end *tenko* when the navy turned us back over to the army; evening *tenko* when we returned to camp and before we were dismissed; and the last just before bedtime. It was at the day's end *tenko* that the excitement took place. We were counted and recounted and then counted again and each time the guards became more excited. One man was missing.

It was finally agreed upon between the army and the navy to march the rest of us back to camp while a thorough search of the shipyards would be made to try and locate the missing man. By the time we went through the same type *tenko* back at camp, one of our E Battery men noticed that another of our men, a Pvt. Luz Ortiz, was missing. It turned out that he had crawled into a stack of crates, out of sight, and had fallen asleep. The navy beat him up pretty good before bringing him back to the army, which in turn gave him another severe beating before putting him on half rations for the next forty days. Pvt. Pancho Valdez, another Mexican-American, was called out and soundly scolded for being lazy, and given ten days on half rations.

The long-to-be-remembered month of August was now gone, and as September came in, the weather began to cool down. This brought back memories of the miseries of the last winter and how we never stopped shivering until the weather warmed up in the spring. Without any explanation the Japanese had piles of two inch by two inch wooden bars brought into camp and put them on all windows of the camp.

On the 23rd, eleven Dutchmen broke into the supply house, which contained all the supplies for both the Japanese garrison and the POWS, and absconded with sugar, cookies, cigarettes and beer. It was no problem for the Japanese to find out who the culprits were, for they had drunk all the beer and were so drunk at *tenko* they could not stand steady.

The Japanese had built a number of wooden cells that they used for jail cells. They were too small for a man to stand up in and too short to lie down in and the floors were concrete that stayed wet all the time. The Dutchmen were lined up in front of the guardhouse and all the guards took turns at beating them. They were then put in the jail cells for the night. The next day they were taken back to the guardhouse, half at a time, and beaten with the clubs from the rack inside the guard house. They were beaten with fists and when one would fall to the ground, they would stomp him and kick him.

There was a pile of rocks weighing from five to fifteen pounds each laying near by, and the Japs would get these and stone the men as they writhed on the ground. Hot, near-boiling water was brought out in a coffee pot, and while the man was held down by some guards, another would hold his head back while yet another guard would pour the hot water down his throat. These beatings were more or less continuous. When one guard would tire, another would take his place. By mid-afternoon they were all tired and began bringing pedestrians in from the road that ran along the front of our camp and making them beat on the Dutchmen. That evening the prisoners were returned to the wet jail cells. The weather had now cooled considerably and the men were given no blankets to cover themselves with and were placed two men to a cell that was not large enough for one. They were bloody from head to foot and could make no sound because of the hot water treatment. They were sentenced to five days without food or water. Some of them took pneumonia. I understand that nine of these men died as a result of their ordeal.

The arduous work at the shipyards continued and the beneficial effects of our two *yasumes* had long since worn off and we were bone weary again. We took any and every opportunity to rest or goof off and one of the best places to this was in the *benjo,* or toilet. The *benjo* was an enclosed affair, about ten feet by twenty feet and consisted of one wall being stuccoed, with a slit trench at the bottom. This was used for urination by standing up and facing the wall and for defecation by dropping your pants and squatting over the trench while facing away from the wall.

Someone would always be watching for the approach of a guard and would give the warning in time for someone to leave or pretend that he was relieving himself. The women workers used the same facility and it did not bother them that the POWs were lined up at the urinal. They would come in, drop their *mompies,* aim their buttocks at the wall and by whipping their bare rear ends sideways, they would wedge an opening to the wall and then cut loose from a bent over position. We enjoyed this feminine exposure immensely. The Japs were not completely unaware of our goofing off and they posted a sign warning: "You must not resting in *benjo!* You will be killing to death!"

Some of the POWs in the shipyards would trade items of interest to some of the coolie boys for blow jobs, or to one of the women for sex, down in the bilges or under the ship. I would marvel at how anyone could manage an erection on our diet.

October the 4th, another Englishman in my room, RAF, died from an intestinal operation. He made the fourth man to die in my room, three

September 23, 1943. POW Camp Fukuoka #2, Nagasaki, Japan. Two watercolors by Fujita of Dutchmen being punished for stealing food from the storeroom. They were stoned, beaten with clubs and tortured with boiling water.

Englishmen and one Canadian. On the tenth of the month a sergeant of the guard, who seemed to be all teeth, came around to me and while grinning from ear to ear and showing off all those teeth, said to me "Fujita—Tokyo!" and he would point off in the general direction of Tokyo and then he would say "Fujita—Tokyo" and would draw his finger across his throat, indicating that I would be taken to Tokyo and have my head lopped off. This scared the britches off me and in my own mind I felt that since the Japanese had had no success here in getting me to turn coat that they would send me to Tokyo and try again, and then if I did not join up with them they would behead me.

We had *nisei* interpreters in this camp who, like many, many other *nisei*, were caught in Japan when the war broke out and were forced into the service of Japan even though they were American citizens; in many cases they did not fare much better than we POWs. The oldest one of these was the chief interpreter, a guy by the name of Onishi, from San Diego, California. He came to me and told me to have all my gear packed and be ready to leave. I asked him where I was going and if anyone else was going along. He told me that I was the only one going and that I was being sent to Tokyo and he thought that it might possibly have something to do with propaganda. I thought that he knew that I was going to be executed and was only trying to allay my fears by mentioning the propaganda aspect. I was convinced that "Sgt. Teeth" was correct and the fact that no one besides me was going convinced me of this. I felt that my days on this earth were truly numbered and so I went to the officer's room and called for Lt. Allen and asked to speak with him and Maj. Horrigan, the senior American officer in camp, and then proceeded to tell them what was about to happen and that I felt that the Japanese were going to make one final attempt to get me to join their side or else.

Both officers told me that if it really came to do it or die then by all means I should comply with their wishes. I would not be able to help them with any military secrets and I certainly could not be of any use to my country if I was dead. It might be possible later on to do something that could benefit our war effort.

I told them that in that case they had seen the last of me, for I had no intention of joining up with them. The very idea was repugnant to me.

Since my capture I had felt that my real war with the Japanese started the day I was captured. If they could not sway me, being part Japanese, over to their side, then perhaps they would not be too eager to attempt the same thing with others who were not Japanese. I had to prove to all the POWs I was thrown in with that I was 100 percent American, and meant to thwart the Japanese in any way that I could and still keep my head on my shoulders where it belonged. It now seemed that my success in this was soon to cease.

I was packed and ready to take off at any time but the only thing that happened out of the ordinary was that Sgt. Teeth still came around daily to go through the "Fujita—Tokyo" and throat slashing bit, which only served to increase my level of apprehension. I had my 22nd birthday on the 20th, and mused that that was much too young for life to come to an end.

Finally, on the 28th, the "Chinless Wonder," another nickname that we had for Sgt. Teeth, came and ordered me to get my gear and accompany him. I said my farewells, and deep down I was hoping that at least one of my army buddies would make it back home to tell my folks what was taking place. We went back across the bay to Nagasaki where we spent the night in the railroad station. At 5:15 in the morning we boarded a train and pulled out, going northward. The train followed the beautiful valleys between the picturesque mountains and at 11:30 the same morning we arrived in Yawata.[3]

We detrained and walked up a very steep road for about a mile to another POW camp. News of this Japanese who was an American POW had preceded me and the entire Japanese garrison was out to see this strange freak arrive. By the time we had walked to the camp it was lunch time, and the POWs of this steel mill camp were on break. They too had heard of me and were ganged around to get a good look at me.

Sgt. Teeth was in his glory as he paced back and forth in front of the assembled Japanese, pointing to me and telling them all about me. The Japanese officers came up to me and looked me over thoroughly and were

3. A coastal city near the northern trip of Kyushu and an important steel mill center. The POW camp here was another one in the Fukuoka complex of camps.

saying, "Ah so!" When I got the chance, I asked to see the senior American officer and was taken inside the building to see him. I do not recall his name, if I ever knew it, nor his rank, but I proceeded to tell him my name, rank and serial number and what my unit was and asked him to make a notation of this event so that my final movements could be traced after the war was over. I was given food and tea, and as I ate I saw Cpl. Monroe Woodall, who had recently been sent from our Fukuoka #2 camp, but I was not able to talk with him.

After I had eaten, I was taken back out to the front of the camp where Sgt. Teeth was waiting for me. With him were two very big white men. One was dressed in a Dutch army uniform and walked with a limp and the other, even under these circumstances, was a big, big American. He thought I was Japanese and asked me what the hell I was doing in an American uniform. I had on my homemade shirt with "T" Patch and chevrons. He told me that I very nearly handed him his head back on a plate. I did not remember this. It became obvious that these two were to accompany Sgt. Teeth and me. After we had said "hi" to one another. I told the other guys: "I don't know what y'all have done to get your heads lopped off, but I have never been so glad to have company before in my life." As we four walked back down the mountain, I told them what I felt was going to happen to me, and they each began to go over in their minds all the events that they had lived through so far and tried to remember anything that they might have done that would cause them to be executed.

The Dutchman was Nickolas Schenk from Java, and was an Adjutant in the Netherland East Indies Army. The other guy, Gaylen McCray, was an American merchant marine from Grants Pass, Oregon. He was Chief Engineer on a U.S. Texaco tanker that had been sunk in the Atlantic by a German raider. The Germans picked him out of the ocean and carried him around in the raider for a month or two and then turned him over to the Japanese, who in turn brought him to Japan.

We boarded a train at the Yawata station. Sgt. Teeth had picked up another guard from the Western Army and they had us all together so that they could keep their eyes on us. The train pulled out and again headed north. Mack, as I now called McCray, asked me if the guard could understand any English and when I told him that he could not, he wondered out loud just what our chances would be of escaping. I told him that I had already given that idea a lot of thought and that escaping would be no problem at all; what we would do and where we would go on this densely populated island is where the rub came in. We could study the country closely as we proceeded to Tokyo and remember the best areas for hiding out in case we did, at a later date, decide to take our chances in the mountains.

I told Nick, the Dutchman, and Mack about the propaganda thing that Onishi had mentioned and Nick said that he was a journalist and Mack said that he had extensive knowledge of radio. These two facts made the propaganda thing seem a little more believable except that I had no experience in radio or writing. The Japanese knew of my artistic ability but we could not figure just how an artist would be utilized. As we were pondering this, everything suddenly went dark. We had entered a tunnel. It turned out that this tunnel went underwater from the island of Kyushu to the main island of Honshu.

I asked what sort of camp Yawata was and Mack said that it was a steel mill and that there were 544 men there of several nationalities and that 333 of these were American. In addition to military men there were also civilian war workers from Wake Island, a few more merchant marines and some North China Marines. We had left Yawata at 9:17 and after riding all night we stopped at a station at 5:15 in the morning and were taken to a nearby POW camp. This was a very clean looking camp and the POWs here were mostly officers. Four hundred were British officers, a few were American officers and a few enlisted men. Four of these American officers, a limey corporal, a civilian and an Australian officer, were bunched in with Nick, Mack and I. We all were put on a train at 2:00 P.M. We pulled out, following the coastline of the very beautiful Inland Sea.

The many little islands that dotted this placid sea were covered with pine trees. I was spellbound by the twisted and gnarled shapes of these trees. They looked like something right out of a Walt Disney fantasy land.

In talking to the new men, we found that they were all newspaper men, printers, journalists and another artist. They had no idea what they were being moved for until talking with us. It now seemed a sure thing that we were going to be used in some sort of propaganda thing. We traveled all night again and on this trip two more guards were placed over us and each had a rifle. At 8:15 A.M. on the morning of October 31st we pulled into Tokyo and were put on a truck and taken to Omori POW camp out in Tokyo Bay.

9

CAMP ROUTINES

AT OMORI CAMP AND

BUNKER HILL

October 1943–December 1943

Omori, called the headquarters camp, was mail center for all POW camps under Japanese control.[1] I guessed it to be 60 yards wide by 150 yards long. It was a man-made structure and sitting out in Tokyo Bay about seventy-five or eighty yards from shore. The camp, with eight-foot-high wooden walls, occupied three-fourths of the island and a garden area

1. By the end of the war, there would be approximately 100 POW camps in Japan organized in seven administrative areas, each of which had its own headquarters camp. Altogether they held more than 32,000 Allied prisoners. Omori was the headquarters for camps in the Tokyo area. It was also used as a disciplinary center for "problem" prisoners, who would be sent to Omori for "training." It housed about 600 POWs, most of them British. The POW mail center appears to have been at the nearby Shinagawa camp, at least after the spring of 1943. *Reports of General MacArthur,* 2 vols (Washington, U.S. Government Printing Office, 1966), I Supplement, pp. 102–104; E. Bartlett Kerr, *Surrender and Survival: The Experience of Americans POWs in the Pacific, 1941–1945* (New York: William Morrow, 1985), pp. 180, 189; Alfred A. Weinstein, *Barbed-Wire Surgeon* (New York: Macmillan, 1948), pp. 217, 219.

> also in package. ~~~ U.S. Matches
> comb + mirror – matches, look
> as big a large. Kinshaw
> ...... package.
>
> 12/18/43 I will remember
> today for the rest of my
> life. for I received a
> parcel from home. It
> contained cookies, candies,
> chewing gum, soaps, tooth
> brush, tooth powder, razor,
> razor blades, wash rag,
> towell, handkerchiefs,
> malted, milk, vitamins
> pills, dominoes + prunes.
> It's impossible to say
> how I feel over it.
> It was mailed since
> June 2nd there is a
> possibility of me having
> another one from this
>
> last exchange ship. Some
> mail will be here for
> me by Xmas — I hope.
> The things in my box
> were just what I
> needed. My folks couldn't
> have made a better
> selection of items.
> This is the best thing
> to happen to me in years.
> Also Maj Cousins (Aussy) +
> Capt. Wallis (Inse) were
> moved in with us today
> *12/20/43 36 Div in (TNG) .....
> giving 'em hell in Italy ...
> .... problem
> ...... ranslq

took up the remaining fourth. A wooden bridge connected Omori to the shore.

Our truck took us across the bridge into the camp and we were ordered to unload and fall in to formation in front of the camp office building. The building faced the main gate and blocked the view of the rest of the camp. We were ordered to come to attention by two guards with fixed bayonets and then the camp commander and a Sgt. Watanabe came out of the office and walked directly to me. Watanabe began to berate me loudly and had a very angry look on his face. He would then slap me in the face several times and then repeat the whole thing again. This lasted for about five minutes. I do not know what he was saying but it was very obvious that he had no liking for me.[2]

We were ordered to open our gear and then the guard went through our belongings and thoroughly mussed things up. This completed, Watanabe came back to me and repeated the ranting and slapping bit but with his fists this time. No one else was put through this treatment. We were then ordered to pick up our gear and we were taken around the office into the main camp. Here we were separated and the officers were put into one barracks and the rest of us were put into other barracks. Mack and I were put into barracks #5. All the occupants were Americans except one. As soon as the guard left, all the guys in the barracks ganged around us and began questioning us. In any POW camp, when someone new came in he represented a new camp where maybe some of your buddies were being held and you might be lucky enough to find out some bit of information about them. The questions came fast and furious—Where did we come from and what outfit were we in? What was our nationality? Did we know any news about the war? When I told them that I was from Fukuoka #2 at Nagasaki, one man asked me, "Have you heard of a Japanese down there that is an American POW?" I said "Yeah, that's me! What about him?" The guy would not pursue his questions and so I never knew what it was that he had heard about me. I wondered, if this camp had heard about me, how many other camps had heard also?

I had wondered why there were so many men in camp and found out that at this camp you went out on work details by roster and not everyone at the same time. The food here was, if anything, worse than it was in Nagasaki. I was only too glad when night came. I was exhausted, for I had practically no sleep at all since leaving Nagasaki. After *tenko* I bedded down and never woke up until the next morning.

2. There was general agreement that Watanabe was one of the most sadistic Japanese encountered by POWs anywhere. He was particularly hard on prisoners who were officers, but no one escaped his cruel attention. POWs referred to him as "the Animal," the "Bird" or "Wily Bird," or "Mr. Adam." Kerr, *Surrender and Survival,* p. 180; Weinstein, *Barbed-Wire Surgeon,* pp. 219–24, et passim; Donald Knox, *Death March: The Survivors of Bataan* (New York: Harcourt Brace Jovanovich, 1981), p. 379.

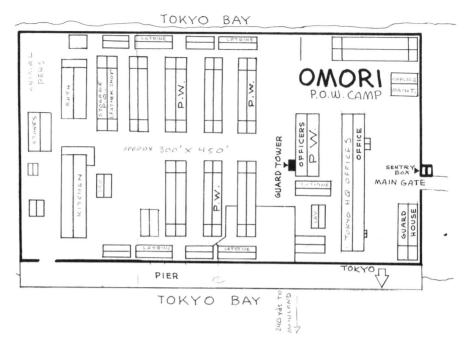

Drawing by Fujita of Omori POW Camp.

The first thing after breakfast and *tenko* the next morning, I was escorted back to the front of the office and Sgt. Watanabe came out and repeated his actions of yesterday. He would yell at me and push me around and then slap me several times. He did this twice again with a club on this first day in camp. I thought that if this was going to be my lot in life at this camp, then I was in for a mighty unpleasant winter. There were interpreters at this camp but they never had one present when he was bashing me around, so I still did not know why he was doing this to me.

The POW who was in charge of sorting out the mail came by and told me that there was a letter for me and as soon as the camp censor went over it he would bring it to me. Boy! I went into orbit over this news and could hardly contain myself. Later that same day I did get my letter and there are not words that can describe my elation. It had been two years since I left home and this was the first word that I had had of my family in that time. My hand shook as I opened the letter and I felt a little anxious. Was my family being mistreated because of my dad's ancestry? How was Dad being treated? Had they all been cast into some relocation camp like most of the Japanese-Americans? As I unfolded the letter and began to read, my fears vanished and this indescribable elation came over me. Mom and my two older sisters were working and my youngest sister was in school. My brother had made first sergeant and all seemed to be going well.

We who had come to Omori on this new project were not put on the work roster and we did nothing but sleep and eat. The food was very little and very bad and the harassment and beatings by the guards were about as bad here as in Nagasaki. After those first four sessions with Watanabe, he had left me alone. On the 10th, ten more men and two officers came in on the "Tokyo Deal," as we began to refer to our position. These men were all musicians and they were brought in from Keijo, Chosen or Korea.

A number of us were interrogated but the interrogation did not make sense for it was conducted in Japanese and none of us knew what it was that they wanted. On the 11th, nineteen of us "Tokyo Deal" men were moved into barracks #6. In camp were some U.S. airmen who had been shot down fairly recently—P-40 pilot, Lt. Col. Pike, who told us that all POWs were advanced one rank, had been shot down over North China and a staff sergeant from a bomber crew which was shot down as recently as last September, who brought us up-to-date on the war situation and also told me that an army buck sergeant was now drawing $72 per month. These two airmen were released from isolation and put into the main camp with the rest of us.

On the 18th six men were brought in from Taiwan and put into our barracks. Among them was T/Sgt. Newton Light and a three-stripe sergeant, John David Provoo. Both Americans, both army and both were taken in the Philippines. They had not been in the barracks long when in came the C.O. and his aide. The C.O. began to chew Provoo out and yelled and spit in his direction and every once in awhile Provoo would say something back to the C.O. in Japanese. All of us in the barracks really perked up at this and wondered just what was going on with this guy who could speak Japanese. After the C.O. left, Mack asked Provoo what that scene was all about, but Provoo moved to the head of his bunk space, did not respond to the question and just sat there with his head down. Later that night the

T/Sgt Light got Mack and me off to one side and told us that Provoo was known as "The Traitor of Corregidor."

He then told us that Provoo had spent time in Japan, studying Japanese and the Shinto religion and was some sort of minor priest in the Shinto sect. He said that when Corregidor surrendered, Provoo donned his Shinto robes and walked out of the tunnel, greeted the Japanese landing force and offered his services. Provoo was put in the Japanese supply section and any American needing or wanting supplies had to go through Provoo to get it. Light then said that an American army captain had gone to Provoo and told him that he wanted something or other for himself and some other officers and that Provoo had refused. The officer became irate and Provoo ordered him out and then the captain threatened that he would have Provoo court-martialed. Light said that the officer was executed and that all GIs on Corregidor thought that Provoo had him shot. Evidently the camp C.O. detested him for turning against his own country.[3]

On the 26th, five men were brought in from Shanghai, China—four civilians and a marine corporal. All were Americans and all were from Wake Island. On December 1, 1943, fourteen of us on the "Tokyo Deal" were ordered to take our gear and load on to a truck out front. I was one of the fourteen but Mack was not, so we had to split up. Mack and the others were to follow later. We had become good friends and I had drawn a portrait of him, which I still have. I would have given it to him had I thought of it. Whatever the "Tokyo Deal" was going to be, it sure must be big to bring this many people from such a big area.

We loaded into the back of the truck along with two guards with fixed bayonets and were driven through the city of Tokyo, the world's third largest city, and taken to the Bunka district, about eight blocks north of the Imperial Palace. We stopped in front of a three-story brick building

3. Accused of a number of treasonable acts, including having helped bring about the execution of Capt. Burton C. Thompson on Corregidor, Provoo was tried in federal court in 1952–1953. He was convicted and sentenced to life imprisonment but was subsequently released on procedural and constitutional grounds. Kerr, *Surrender and Survival*, pp. 73, 298. (see p. 353)

Bunka POW Camp was a pre-war Girls High School. Photo is of the Administration Building from the POW Building. "The arrow pointing to the building on the left is where I hid my diary."

with a drive-through opening on the right side that was now partitioned off. We left the truck and were taken through a doorway in the partition and this opened out onto a large, black-top courtyard or compound that was about 150 feet × 200 feet. Along the right side as we entered was a two-story stucco building that was one room wide, two rooms high and four rooms long.

Beyond that and running the full length across the back of the property was a three-story stucco building; one third of the lower floor was below ground level and was sealed off except two rooms at one end, which were the living quarters for an elderly Japanese couple who were the caretakers of the property and the camp galley. The top two floors consisted of a room on each end and extended eight feet farther out than the large center room, which was separated from them by a stairwell. Each stairwell opened out onto a landing that had steps going down to ground level, facing one another and lacking ten feet of meeting at the center of the building. The center room on the top floor extended out over the steps and was supported by arches. This was to be our home until the war's end. Before the war, this had been a girls' high school. The area is called *Bunka Gakuin Kanda* and we promptly nicknamed it "Bunker Hill."[4]

We were lined up inside the compound and were ordered to stand at attention. Soon, a Jap army officer came out of the front building and addressed us.[5] He said that we were here to put on a radio program and that

4. The *Bunka Gakuin* ("Cultural Institution," but referred to in a pre-war English-language guide book as the "Women's Higher Normal School") was located in central Tokyo's Kanda ward. Closed by authorities, it became the living and working quarters for POWs assigned to radio propaganda work under the Japanese army. This work was kept secret and the *Bunka Gakuin* itself was guarded by armed sentries and publicly identified as a "Technical Research Center." The fourteen men who arrived there on December 1, 1942, were the first contingent from a group of fifty-three Allied prisoners who had been brought to Omori prison camp for use in the radio propaganda project. Masayo Duus, *Tokyo Rose: Orphan of the Pacific* (Tokyo and New York: Kodansha International, 1979), pp. 83–84; Ivan Chapman, *Tokyo Calling: The Charles Cousens Case* (Sydney: Hale & Iremonger, 1990), p. 170; T. Philip Terry, *Terry's Guide to the Japanese Empire* (Boston: Houghton Mifflin, 1933), map of Tokyo following p. 108.

5. This was a Capt. Koimai, one of about 30 Japanese army officers, enlisted guards,

our lives here would be very pleasant and enjoyable if we followed orders and did as we were told. Each one of us would participate and if we did not our lives would not be guaranteed.

Each of us was handed a mimeographed sheet of the daily routine that we would be expected to follow:

07:00	Wake up
07:30	Tenko
08:00	Breakfast
08:40	Work period
11:40	P.T.
12:00	Chow
13:00	Work period
15:00	Recess
18:00	Chow
19:00	Work period
22:00	Taps

The camp faced south and the upper east room was the officers' quarters; the upper west room was quarters for civilians and enlisted men. The large upper center room was to be our recreation room. On the second floor, the east room was the work room, the center room was our dining room. The galley was on the bottom floor behind the caretaker's quarters and the other rooms had the school equipment and supplies stored in them and were sealed. The *benjo* was at ground level at the west end of the building.

The name of this radio program was "The *Hi no Maru* Hour," which translated into "The Circle of the Sun Hour." It was to be a politically-oriented program giving the Japanese point of view, which is to say a propaganda program.[6] The fourteen men brought from Omori for this purpose were:

---

and civilians (including a few American *nisei*) who ran the *Bunka Gakuin* facility and its program. Duus, *Tokyo Rose*, p. 84.

6. *Hi no Maru* was the term used for the Japanese national flag, a red sun centered

Rank:	Name:	Military unit:	Captured at:
1st/Lt.	McNaughton, Jack	Royal British Army	Singapore
2nd/Lt.	Kalbfliesch, Ed Jr.	U.S. Army Reserve	P.I.
Ensign	Henshaw, George	U.S. Navy Reserve	Wake Isl.
Adjutant	Schenk, Nickolas	Dutch E.I. Army	Java
T/Sgt.	Light, Newton	U.S. Army	P.I.
Sgt.	Fujita, Frank	U.S. Army	Java
Sgt.	Provoo, John David	U.S. Army	P.I.
L/Cl.	Parkyns, Kenneth	R.A.A.F.	South Pacific
L/Bdr	Bruce, Donald	Royal British Army	Singapore
Civ	Williams, George	British Civil Service	Gilbert Isl.
Civ	Quillé, Larry	Contract Labor	Wake
Civ	Astarita, Joseph	Contract Labor	Wake
Civ	Shattles, Steve	Contract Labor	Wake
Civ	Streeter, Mark L.	Contract Labor	Wake

The civilians were somewhat disgruntled for they were supposed to be granted officer status. After we had picked out our bed spaces we all

---

on a field of white, symbolizing Japan as "the land of the rising sun." The *Hi no Maru* hour was one of a number of English-language propaganda radio programs beamed by the Japanese to Allied audiences. The programs began in mid-1942, aimed at listeners in Australia, but were broadened to include southeast Asia and in 1943 to target America. American, British, and Australian prisoners, most of whom had previous experience in radio or the entertainment field, were persuaded or forced to participate. The prisoners might simply read statements giving their names, stating that they were well, and sending personal messages to their families; at other times they were made to read propaganda blurbs extolling the Japanese or boasting of Japanese victories. A few cooperated willingly, but most attempted, by the manner in which they read their scripts, to discredit the Japanese message and otherwise render their presentations unbelievable. Prisoners were also required to write material for the programs, but frequently managed to so pervert the essence of their scripts that the Japanese either rejected them or rewrote them drastically. About a dozen American *nisei* women who had been trapped in Japan by the war's outbreak were also involved in some of these radio programs and were collectively dubbed "Tokyo Rose" by listening American servicemen. Lionel Wigmore, *The Japanese Thrust* (Canberra: Australian War Memorial, 1957), pp. 679–81; Chapman, *Tokyo Calling,* pp. 102–11, et passim; Duus, *Tokyo Rose,* pp. 64–85, 158; Kerr, *Surrender and Survival,* pp. 189–90.

roamed around familiarizing ourselves with our new surroundings. The day was very clear and from the recreation room windows we could see Mount Fuji off in the distance. There were guards at the entryway and in the front building, but they never came into our area or quarters. Boy! Was that ever a nice change.

Later in the day a Japanese civilian who could speak English came in and told us that in the morning we would be assigned a topic to write about and that each of us would be issued paper and pencils and that we would have to write an article about it in our own words and if anyone did not write his life would not be guaranteed. We did not have evening *tenko* for the first time since being captured but were told that lights would be turned out every night at ten o'clock.

Nick, the Dutchman, and Joe Astarita were assigned to the galley and all food supplies would be issued to Nick, who was to be the camp cook, and Joe was to be his helper. Between meals they too would have to write on the assigned subject. Nick was up at six the next morning to put our rice on to cook. It was not plain rice, but a mixture of one-third rice and two-thirds barley. He was issued some vegetables to make a soup, and this is what we had to eat every meal, every day, with variations according to what was in season.

The rest of us were awakened at seven and we had to make our beds and fold our five blankets and put them at the head of our bed space and then make a run for the *benjo* for our morning relief, and wash up and comb our hair at the one and only lavatory and mirror located just outside the *benjo* entrance. After two years of captivity we still did not have soap, toothbrush, toothpaste or toilet tissue, and each man had to improvise as best he could. At 7:30 we had to fall in to formation in a hallway that ran between the recreation room and the upstairs windows for *tenko*. The officer of the guard detachment who was our immediate camp commander, Lt. Hamamoto, came over to take head count. He could not speak English. After *tenko,* those who had been unable to get to the lavatory before, were able to do so now.

At 8:00 we went to the dining room for breakfast. We had two rows of tables running lengthwise to the room, and chairs on each side of these. The officers sat at one end and had a table to themselves and the rest of us

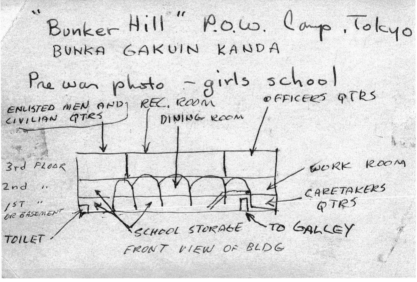

Pre-war photograph of "Bunker Hill" POW Camp, Tokyo, Japan. On the back of the photo Fujita explained the different areas of the school.

sat where ever we pleased. The meal was terrible. The rice was more like raw dough, but the soup wasn't too bad. We really had some bad rice until Nick learned just how much water to put with how much rice. We each had our own bowl and spoon and we each took care of them.

At 8:40 we fell to in the courtyard and an officer from the front office came out with a *nisei* interpreter and told us once again what we were to do and that if we did not "our lives would not be guaranteed," and then asked if anyone felt that he could not cooperate. George Williams, the English civil servant from the Gilbert Islands, stepped forward. The officer turned toward the partition in the gate and yelled something, and two guards came running in with rifles in hand. The officer barked an order and the two soldiers took George by the arms and led him out through the front gate. The officers then asked if anyone else did not wish to cooperate, and when no one stepped forward, we were dismissed.[7]

The interpreter told us all to go to the work room and he followed. A balding Japanese civilian came in with pencils and paper. His name was Domoto and he could speak English.[8] He and all the Japanese civilians who worked in the front office wore western style clothing. He told us what the topic was that we were to write on and how he wanted the subject matter presented. He then told Lt. Kalbfliesch, Sgt. Provoo and a civilian, Steve Shattles, to follow him. They were going to downtown Tokyo, to the radio station, to make a broadcast from a script that would be given them there.

The rest of us sat, pencil and paper in hand, looking at each other and waiting for someone to make the first move. I had already decided that I did not want any part of this propaganda program and intended to play out the role of a clod too dumb to learn anything that I had started in

7. Williams, who is sometimes identified as a New Zealander, told the Japanese that complying with their demands would be treason. He was severely beaten and then transferred to another camp, where he managed to survive the war. Chapman, *Tokyo Calling,* p. 171; Duus, *Tokyo Rose,* p. 84; Kerr, *Surrender and Survival,* p. 189.

8. Kaji Domoto, an American *nisei* and graduate of Amherst, had lived in Japan since 1925 but still liked American jazz. He was friendly to the prisoners and helped them when he could. Chapman, *Tokyo Calling,* pp. 176, 181–82, et passim.

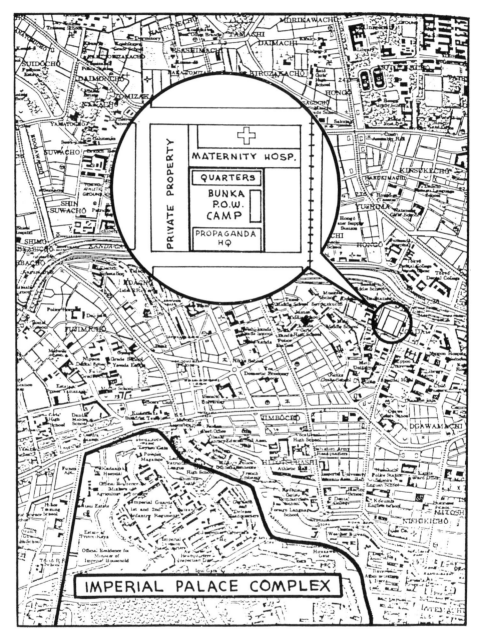

Fujita's map of Tokyo showing the Imperial Palace complex and details of Bunka POW Camp.

Nagasaki when they tried to make me learn the Japanese language. I really turned in a pathetic article.

At 11:40 we were told to knock off and assemble in the courtyard for physical training. We all went out and just milled around, for there was no one to tell us what to do. The weather was cold and there were no fires or heaters of any kind in camp, so we did do a sort of exercise by jumping up and down and slapping our arms to keep warm. At noon we went in for lunch and afterwards we sat around the recreation room and wondered out loud what would be George's fate. Would they really execute him as they threatened? What were the three who went to the radio station having to go through?

We followed the daily routine and about the middle of the afternoon the three were brought back to camp and told to go eat their meals, which had been saved for them, and then report back to the workroom. The Japanese did not stay in the building and came in only to pick up the essays that we had written, and to give us new assignments. So after the three men had eaten, they came back to the work room and told us about the trip to the radio station.

The *nisei* interpreter who had been with the officer this morning was the one that took the three men to town in a taxi. I suppose that he was not really considered an interpreter since several of the Japanese that we had to deal with could speak English. His name was Kazumaru Uno and he spoke just plain American with no accent, and I think that he came from Omaha and was a newsman or correspondent. I never learned how he came to be working with the Japanese.[9] I heard some *nisei* were offered a free trip by the Japanese government to see the homeland of their parents, and were caught there at the outbreak of the war and then were forced into some kind of service for Japan. Perhaps he was one of these. Some were even put into the military.

9. Uno had been in Tokyo since 1939. He was very hard on the prisoners and was particularly efficient in censoring the scripts they were required to write. In September 1944 he was transferred to the Philippines to head a similar radio propaganda project in Manila. Chapman, *Tokyo Calling*, pp. 167–85 passim, 249, 278, 298; Duus, *Tokyo Rose*, pp. 85–86, 200.

Uno had taken them to the radio station, where the *Hi no Maru* Hour's studio was several floors up. They were taken into the studio and each one in turn was given a script and told to read it into the microphone. There were several Japanese in business suits in the control room listening to them read and watching them through the soundproof glass window.

Uno came into the workroom later and introduced himself and told us to call him "Buddy," which he said was his nickname. He told us that each one of us would have to go down and do a reading and therefore they could determine who had the best radio voice.

The first day followed the schedule and as the periods came that offered us a chance to talk with each other and get to know one another, everyone was very cautious in what he said and how he responded to questions put to him. We were all strangers to one another and here we were thrown together in a very unpalatable situation. I was suspicious of everyone here and I kept my eyes and ears open, hoping to learn if any of these men were here of their own free will, and just how they viewed this propaganda program. I wondered about Provoo, whom Light called "The Traitor of Corregidor." Did he have some past skill in radio or writing that caused him to be chosen for this deal or was he a plant, put here by the Japs to analyze each of us and to report to them which of us could be utilized more fully for the Japanese cause? Were any of these men collaborators with the Japanese in their previous camps? What about this guy Streeter? He was the first man to start writing on the assigned topic and he seemed to throw himself into it with unnecessary zeal. Probably some of these men, and maybe all of them, had the same feelings and doubts that I had. I decided I would just have to play it cool until I could find some answers.

Each day someone new would be taken to the *Hoso,* that is what the Japanese called the radio station,[10] to have his radio qualities checked. Provoo was now designated as the MC for the program and Kalbfliesch was to be the commentator. The program was broadcast every day at 1:00 P.M. Tokyo time.[11] Two or three days later, the Japanese told us that George

10. *Hōsō* is short for *Nihon Hōsō Kyoku* (Japan Broadcasting Corporation).

11. It ran for half an hour and consisted of music, POW messages, news discus-

Williams had been shot. (I found out after the war that he had not been shot and had survived the POW camps.)

The front and main building of our compound had been some sort of school, for it contained a very large room that was full of biological specimens of every shape and description. The building was now the headquarters for the Japanese propaganda machine. Many high-ranking military and civilian personalities frequented it.

At the beginning, most of us had misgivings and problems with our consciences about writing anything for an enemy nation, and each had his own battle to fight to cope with the situation. I was already writing such juvenile tripe that it was completely unusable. When I would try to analyze the possible damage to my country that could be done by broadcasting the stuff that I wrote and compared it to the immediate prospect of being shot if I did not write, then I felt that my course of action was excusable. Politics had held no interest for me up to this time, and we had no access to current news that would enable us to write anything meaningful and timely.

The Japanese would take the essays that the group wrote and rewrite portions, inserting some of their own writing in order to bring out their point of view. The finished articles in most cases were so ridiculous that I felt that anyone hearing them over the airways would probably be more inclined to laugh than to take them seriously.

On December 7, two years since Pearl Harbor, the Japanese brought in an aging American missionary by the name of "Mother" Topping to visit with us. It was obvious when she began talking that she had been in Japan so long that she thought as they did. She was going to be on the radio program the next day and wanted to meet the "Bunker Hill" boys beforehand.[12] The weather was very cold and she was wrapped up pretty good, and she had a hand warmer that intrigued me. It was a double-ended muff-

---

sion, and sometimes dramatic or humorous sketches. Duus, *Tokyo Rose,* p. 85; Kerr, *Surrender and Survival,* pp. 189–90.

12. "Mother" Topping is reported to have "tearfully appealed to Americans to stop fighting the Japanese." Duus, *Tokyo Rose,* p. 158.

type thing and she could insert both hands into the ends. When she saw
that I was looking it over she allowed me to take it for a closer look, and
I was surprised that it was almost hot. She did not know how it worked,
but she thought it used charcoal somehow.

The food was insufficient and we complained about it while we were
lined up for morning *tenko*. This upset Lt. Hamamoto and he said for
all who felt that the rations were not enough to step forward. Everyone
stepped forward except Streeter and Light. Hamamoto started at one end
of the line up and gave each one of the complainers a slap in the face.[13]

On the 10th of the month a Maj. Tsuneishi from Imperial Headquarters came into camp and reenforced the threat that our lives would not be
guaranteed if we failed to cooperate.[14] He talked with us for awhile and
asked if we were satisfied with camp conditions. We complained that the
food was of poor quality and insufficient and that we did not have enough
covers to keep warm in the unheated quarters, and that it was hard to
write anything when our hands were so cold we could hardly move them.
He said that we could have more and better food and more blankets as
well as heaters for the building.

The major had with him to do the interpreting Tomatsu Murayama,
an International News Correspondent for the largest newspaper in town,
who had attended American universities and spoke English just like we
Americans did. Both the major and Tommy, as Murayama asked us to
call him, seemed to be real nice guys. Tommy called me "Yagi," which
meant goat, for I was attempting to grow a goatee. Tommy assured us

13. Hamamoto was particularly vicious, often striking prisoners in the face without
cause. On this occasion, he also reportedly drew his sword and warned that future
complaints would be punished by death. Chapman, *Tokyo Calling*, pp. 172–74.

14. As head of the army's "psychological warfare" (i.e., propaganda) program, Maj.
(later Lt. Col.) Shigetsugu Tsuneishi constantly pressured the prisoners to cooperate.
Although he shouted, threatened, intimidated, and on apparently rare occasions struck
them, he could at times be helpful. Tsuneishi later denied mistreating POWs and even
wrote a book (*Recollections of Psychological Warfare*, 1978) about his role. Duus, *Tokyo
Rose*, pp. 65–66, 72–77, 83–86, 157–61; Chapman, *Tokyo Calling*, 103–108, 111, 171,
179–80, 358–59.

that he would see to it that the major did not forget his promise.[15] Both he and the major were as good as their words, and the very next day our food allotment was increased and we received two more blankets per man. I do not know what material the blankets were made of, but they had very little warmth compared to their bulk. Also there were two small coal-burning stoves brought in, one for the workroom and one for the recreation room, (These stoves were never properly installed and never used), and a "Hibachi" for the workroom. The Hibachi, or fire box, was a wooden box lined with sheet metal, filled half full with sand, for burning charcoal. This Hibachi was the only source of heat that we were to have for the duration of the war.

Our bunk area was a platform raised fourteen inches above the floor and topped with a one-inch straw *tatami,* or mat, from one end to the other. I had taken one of the boards loose under my bed space and secreted my diary there, and whenever the opportunity presented itself I would take it out and make my entry or entries. None of the other POWs knew that I kept a diary and I had no intention of letting anyone know. Consequently, at times it might be a week or two before I could get it out to make an entry.

With the two additional blankets we could now sleep quite comfortably. We had learned to make an airtight mummy bag with them, and with the snug fit, what air that was left in it after we crawled in was quickly warmed by body heat.

I was still in the dark as to just how they intended to use an artist on a radio program. I had a sketch pad and a pencil and so I would sit around and make portraits or sketches of some of the other guys. Streeter was one that I sketched.

In order to follow the printed Daily Routine, we all had to go out into the courtyard at 11:40 each morning for physical training. Since I was the only one with experience at leading P.T., I was chosen as the leader.

15. Murayama is reported to have urged better treatment for the prisoners on a number of occasions. Tsuneishi could be a "nice guy" sometimes, but menacing and overbearing otherwise. Duus, *Tokyo Rose,* p. 86, et passim; Chapman, *Tokyo Calling,* pp. 312–13, et passim.

Three days after Maj. Tsuneishi was here, a general from Imperial Head-quarters came to look us over.[16] Evidently, he was satisfied with what he saw, for we never had any feedback from his visit, either good or bad.

December 18, 1943, turned out to be a day that I will long remember, for Ens. Henshaw and myself both received parcels from home. I could not believe it when Uno turned the parcel over to me. I just stared at it for a while, and everyone was eagerly anticipating my opening it. When I did open it my hands were shaking and I was fumbling the process, so great was my excitement. Oh! What nostalgia the contents evoked. As I slowly took out each item a chorus of oohs and ahs rang out as I displayed each item so that each man could see. My mother was certainly intuitive when she packed the box, for it contained: cookies, candies, chewing gum, soap, toothbrush and tooth powder, a razor and razor blades, a wash cloth and towels, handkerchiefs, malted milk, vitamin tablets, dominoes and prunes.

Once again it is impossible to describe my elation. Insofar as I could, I shared the goodies with all the other men. Henshaw took his parcel to the officers' room and opened it in private. Oh! What a joy it was to shave with a new razor blade. I was almost reluctant to discard my old double edged blade, for I had shaved with it for almost two years. Salt was a precious item in every place and camp that I had been to, and so when I bit into one of the Oreo chocolate creme-filled cookies—all I could taste at first was the salt that was in them. Boy! Did I ever give myself a good scrubbing—with soap!

After the excitement of the parcels, two officers were brought into camp to be quartered with us and take their meals with us, but who otherwise would have nothing to do with us or the *Hi no Maru* Hour. We were told that they had a radio program of their own called "The Zero Hour" and had been living downtown in the Dai Ichi Hotel and had been going to

16. This was probably Lt. Gen. Seitaro (or Mikio) Uemura, chief of the Prisoner of War Administration Bureau of the War Ministry who had previously shown an interest in the broadcasting project. Kerr, *Surrender and Survival,* pp. 38, 47; Chapman, *Tokyo Calling,* p. 103; Southwest Pacific Area, Allied Translator and Interpreter Section (ATIS), *Alphabetical List of Japanese Army Officers* (ATIS Publication No. 2, May 1943), p. 609 (copy in U.S. Army Center of Military History).

the radio station from the hotel and back unescorted. They were immediately suspect to me and most of the others, and we had many a discussion trying to figure out just who they were and what their program was. Were they operating of their own free will and accord? One was an Australian infantry major, Charles William Cousens, and the other was an American Infantry Captain, Wallace Ince. As we were introducing ourselves, the major heard that I was from the 36th Division. He told me that the 36th was sure giving the Germans hell in Italy. With the addition of these two, we now had fifteen men in this camp. The major and the captain left camp and returned each day in a taxi, without an escort.[17]

We had now been in "Bunker Hill" a month and I did not know what to think about my situation. After my welcome reception at Omori, I had really feared the worse for my welfare, but after this first month in this camp no mention has ever been made of my being half-Japanese and no demands had been made of my talents. I turned in my usual pathetic

17. Cousens, a former Sydney radio announcer, was captured at Singapore and, under severe pressure and threats, started broadcasting in August 1942. Ince had run "The Voice of Freedom" radio program on Corregidor, where he and a young Filipino member of his staff, Lt. Norman Reyes, were taken prisoner. Both were brought to Tokyo and pressed into service by the persistent Maj. Tsuneishi who, once he had forced their cooperation, treated them reasonably well. In April 1943 Tsuneishi inaugurated a program called "Zero Hour" which relayed reports of major accidents, fires, floods, and other bad news from the United States (picked up from American medium-wave domestic broadcasts) to GIs in the Pacific. Tsuneishi had Reyes open the show with recordings of popular American songs, which he then followed with the disaster reports. "Zero Hour" was so well received by the GIs—who were delighted with the music and not disturbed by the news—that in August Tsuneishi expanded the show, adding Cousens and Ince to its staff. The three did their best to undermine the propaganda aspects of the program and "Zero Hour" became even more popular with its audience. It was expanded again in late November when Iva Toguri, an American *nisei*, was forced to join it.

After the war, Maj. Cousens was charged with treason but acquitted. Iva Toguri, unfairly convicted of being "Tokyo Rose," was fined and imprisoned but eventually pardoned by President Ford.

Chapman, *Tokyo Calling*, and Duus, *Tokyo Rose*, are detailed accounts of Cousens' and Toguri's experiences.

essays, and to my knowledge none had ever been used on the program. The writing assignment was now to try and influence America into accepting a mediated peace.

The group had been cautioned again about not cooperating, and we were told that it was obvious by our essays that we were not entering into the proper spirit of seeking a peaceful solution to the war. Streeter was the only one to really go all out in his effort to write for the Japanese. He had taken to spouting all kinds of anti-American statements. He hated President Roosevelt and his cabinet. He hated all bureaucrats. He called the American flag "a dirty piece of colored rag!" and called all of us other Americans "suckers for being patriotic" and that we were "playing into the hands of Roosevelt and his thugs, who were systematically bankrupting the nation and running up debts that our children and grandchildren would have to pay!" It was obvious that he was a "dyed in the wool" Communist. When I asked him why he was so eager to further the Japanese cause in his lengthy essays, he said "Japan is the only logical leader for the downtrodden and subjugated masses in the Orient, to lead them out of the bondage of colonialism," and that Japan was aware of the true nature of Roosevelt's policies. Therefore we all should help them as much as we could. I called him some bad names, and told him he ought to be hanged for treason.

At least Streeter was one guy in camp that I did not have to wonder where he stood. The others I was always trying to evaluate. Just who could I trust if the need ever arose, and who, when I was around them, did I have to be careful of what I said and how I said it. At this stage, I did not trust anyone in camp.

10

BUNKER HILL BOYS

BROADCAST

December 1943–June 1944

The radio program was not completely devoted to propaganda. A sort of comic soap opera was developed for it by Henshaw and Jack McNaughton. Jack had been an aspiring movie actor in England before the war and had appeared in several movies in "bit parts." He was very enthusiastic about this aspect of the program, as were all the others who would sit exploring all sorts of situations around which they could build an on-going program.

On Christmas Eve, all hands except the galley crew had to go to the *Hoso* and put on a Christmas program. The missionary, Mother Topping, joined us and we had a pretty nice program. This is the first time that I had had to go to the *Hoso*. At the camp, we were loaded into the back of an army truck and had two soldiers with us armed with rifles, but their bayonets were not fixed. I enjoyed the trip to town very much, and I was still fascinated with the grotesque shapes of the pine trees. As we approached the Imperial Palace, we were ordered to face the palace and bow. In the future, this would be required each and every time that we passed the palace.

The galley crew had been issued a special batch of food stuff and told to prepare a good Christmas dinner. We were going to have a Christmas dinner party and some of the

12-18 Cousens + Ince sent to Bunka

1-6-44 Benjo Hancho ~~Wiseman~~ Wiseman - Rickart
1-8-44 Cox ~~Smith~~ - Pearson - ~~Rickard~~ - ~~Oslin~~ came in
3-1 { R.C. Clothes. Jap movie of "Fall of Corregidor"
        (Rickart appeared in it)

3-10 Start working in galley

3-28 { Kalbfleish sent away — used to insure
        cooperation on our part.
      { Changed from "Hino Maru Hour" to "Humanity Calls"

6-17 Installed blackades and armed guards in Hoso.

7-7 { Jimmy - Ramon - Rickart - Smith ⊃ Dodds - Hoblitt
     { Odlin came in

7-8 back to Benjo Hancho

9-7 Dooley came in

11-21 Eat Cat

115
.15
375
115
.125

Lt. Hamamoto
Lt. Otaka
Lt. Taniyama

Tazaki
Ikeda
Ozaki
Murayama
Domoto
Hishikawa
Uno
Morino
Ogishi
Ando,

Loose page Fujita later incorporated in the diary, showing Foo's drawing of a
Japanese officer.

Japanese staff were going to join us: Lt. Hamamoto, Lt. Taniyama, Count Ikeda[1] and "Buddy Uno." Nick had come a long way in his cooking skills and could now do a fairly good job with what he had to work with. The meal consisted of small portions but it was really a banquet compared to the drab meals that were our daily fare. For the dinner we had: shark steak, greens, sweet beans and dumplings, apples, gin and sake, cookies, toast, and oranges.

Count Ikeda, with great ceremony, said that for our Christmas present he was going to give us a piano and an extensive library for our enjoyment. Even though we certainly did enjoy these things, we found that it was not benevolence that prompted him to give them to us. It seems that he was in the Philippine Islands when they were taken by the Japanese forces and that he was in on the looting of the Philippine University. These items that he offered us came from that school and he needed a place to store them until a later date. Whatever the case may be, they certainly were a blessing to us.

The library contained very few novels, but it had books on just about anything else that one could wish to study: religion, history, science, anthropology or philosophy. The piano was used for working out skits to be aired on the program, but we enjoyed it to some extent because one or two of the guys could pick out a few tunes.

Since we had been at this camp, with several men going to the radio station every day, we were able to get all the news. We got a lot of rumors too, and they always sounded better than the real news. Most of the time, we accepted the rumors to be the real news so we were disappointed more than once. Sometimes Uno or one of the others from the front office would bring over a cablegram of legitimate news, especially if they thought that it would dampen our spirits. One day Uno brought over a cablegram and read it to us. It stated that America expected to lose 500,000 men in 90

---

1. Viscount Norizane Ikeda had been a member of the Japanese diplomatic mission in Melbourne, Australia. He later wrote two books about his *Bunka Gakuin* experiences. How he came by the materials from the Philippines, described below by Fujita, is not evident. Ivan Chapman, *Tokyo Calling: The Charles Cousens Case* (Sydney: Hale & Iremonger, 1990), pp. 58, 380.

days, in landings in Europe. He told us outright that the closer America came to Japan the closer we came to death.

It seemed to me as if Uno had been a little extra nice to me and in a way was sort of "buttering me up" to get me to become more active in the program. I had been against the program from the start and had made no bones about it. Uno asked me if there was anything at all that I would like to put on the air. I thought a little and then told him that I would like very much to be able to broadcast a message back to Texas and tell what had happened to my battalion and that I would like to read it myself. He told me that I could and that I could name names and mention dates. Was I ever thrilled at this, for ever since this *Hi no Maru* program started I had been itching for a chance to tell the folks back home everything that had happened to us since we left. I wrote a lengthy article and called it "The Lost Battalion From Texas." In it I told everything that I could remember that we went through, who was left in Java, who was in Camp Changi in Singapore, who came to Japan with me. I told about Bingham and Barnes being killed in the B-17 at Malang. I turned the article over to Uno and reminded him that I wanted to read it over the air myself, because I wanted to make sure that it went over. He edited it and changed where I said that our officers went to Madoera. He said that they went to Australia. Objecting to this did me no good, so I decided that the rest of the message was important and I read it on one of the programs. I was very pleased that I was able to get authentic information back to our loved ones and was only sorry that I did not have any current information to send back. (I learned later that this message was never allowed to go over the airways. Every message that I sent had international response, in the news media back home, except this one.)

Two American Red Cross parcels came in and were divided between the thirteen of us. We each got a can of "corn Willie" or "corned beef." Boy! Was that ever good eating.

I felt so good about broadcasting my "Lost Battalion From Texas" that I fell for the bait again when Uno asked me to write about my "Hopes and Views for 1944." I wrote about this and would read it myself. I went to the *Hoso* with Uno and the other participants on that day's program. Uno took us down to the *Bunka* Tram Station. Riding a Tokyo tram was quite an experience within itself. We were jostled around by the hundreds of commuters just as every one else was. We were standing next to four gigantic men who wore their hair in a big "bun" on the very tops of their heads, and each wore a plain brown kimono and straw sandals. All the people were oohing and ahing, and we thought they were looking at us, but Uno told us that they were admiring these big mountains of flesh, each one as big as four or five of me. They were *Sumo* wrestlers. People would donate part of their food rations to these guys so that they could maintain their great weight.

When we arrived at the proper downtown station, we got off and walked several blocks in the very heart of Tokyo to the *Hoso,* or radio station. At one point as we were waiting at a busy intersection for the traffic light to change, there stood a very nice looking Japanese girl, dressed in Western-style clothes. We were long since used to the Japanese soldiers and civilians we had worked around not being able to speak English, so we were not careful when we were vociferously extolling this young lady's looks and good points and voiced how much we would like to get in her britches. We were all taken aback when the light changed. She turned to us and said, "You men are the vulgarist men I have ever seen!" and stomped off.

The New Year (1944) came in very cold and miserable, and for days I had a bad cold with a touch of the flu. On the sixth I was made Camp Quartermaster, which merely meant that I had to keep track of how much black tea, red pepper and vitamin B_{12} that we had on hand—the only items we could purchase outside camp—and when we were in need of more to take up a collection and order more. Also on this day we had our first snow of the year, and I feared that we were in for another winter without heat.

On the 8th four new men were brought into camp: three Yanks and one Limey. They were:

Major	Williston Cox	USAF	Shot down over New Guinea
2/Lt	Jack Wisener	USAF	Shot down over New Guinea
Cpl	Albert Rickert	USMCR	Wake Island
L/Cpl	Harry Pearson	Royal Army	Singapore

Their addition to this camp made a total of nineteen POWs here.

I had taken to writing poems, mostly for my own pastime, but at times they would use one on the program. A jamboree was put on each Saturday. It was a fun party-type program with a lot of comedy. Each of us would play several parts and sing solos as well as participating in group singing. Boy! It got pretty corny. On one jamboree I read one of my poems and then played the part of the "Boss" on a skit of "Of Mice and Men." On another skit I played a cowhand and sang "Ragtime Cowboy Joe." I was even the M.C. on one jamboree and sang "Blue Eyes."

Some of the men received mail on the 5th, but I was not one of them. I did, however, along with all the others get a new pair of "Go Aheads." These were wooden clogs with one strap across the instep area. We called them this because we could not back up in them. Also, ten Red Cross parcels came in to be split between the nineteen of us. The Japanese decided to start paying us by the month, and I drew fifteen yen and fifty sen. At the pre-war rate of exchange, that had me drawing $3.10 per month as a sergeant. The Geneva Convention states that any nation using POWs for labor must pay them the same pay as their equivalent rank as well as equal food and clothing of their army. Even though Japan subscribed to the Geneva Convention at its inception, they declared early in the war that they would not abide by its rules and they didn't.[2]

The Japanese had us start another program called "The Postman Calls," devoted to playing recorded messages over the air that POWs from all over the "co-prosperity sphere," or Japanese-occupied lands, were permitted to send.[3] I know that many POWs never believed that their messages would be broadcast (before coming to Tokyo, I was among this number), and I was very happy to know that now we would be able to broadcast these messages. Messages from two E Battery men had come through so far— one from Pvt. Bob Stubbs and one from 1st/Lt. Ruben Slone.

The Japanese or "Jeeps," as we nicknamed them, decided to give us all vitamin C shots, and we were very happy to get them. Unfortunately, the

2. See note #1, p. 85–87 in Chap. 4.

3. Like the *Hi no Maru* program, "The Postman Calls" ran for 30 minutes. E. Bartlett Kerr, *Surrender and Survival: The Experience of American POWs in the Pacific, 1941–1945* (New York: William Morrow, 1985), p. 190.

arm of a civilian became infected, swelling to about twice its normal size, and he became feverish. We notified the front office and they took him to one of the hospitals that surrounded us, where they lanced his arm. When he changed bandages the first time, he showed us the incision. It was opened up to the bone, with the bone laid bare for about four inches. They did not sew it back up right away, wanting to wait until the infection cleared up before doing so.

The small building that sat just in front of the caretaker's quarters on the east side of camp was the supply room where the food for both us and the Japanese in the front office, which included the guard detail, was stored. I would view this building day after day, looking into the window and seeing the rice and sugar stacked in there and was determined to get some of it. I found a large nail and made a key that would open the door. I waited until about 1:00 A.M. and sneaked out and went into the supply room. I was very apprehensive because I could see vividly in my mind's eye the eleven Dutchmen at Fukuoka #2 and what happened to them when they broke into the supply room there. I got me some sugar and, after looking out the windows for any sign of life, I went out and locked the door behind me and breathed a big sigh of relief.

One of the guys had managed to get an electric hot plate at the radio station, and he also made himself a key to the supply room. He found that the key he made would also open the large center room in the basement, which was supposed to remain sealed. He would set up his hot plate in that room and cook rice and some stuff he managed to get from the outside through his contact. Mickey and I decided that we, too, must have a hot plate. Mickey Parkyns went to the *Hoso* more than I did, and he secured an outside contact that got us an electrical hot plate element and the ceramic plate for it to fit into, but we had to put it together. We took the cord from an old lamp that was in the downstairs room and finished our hot plate. Then we were able to cook some of the rice from the supply room.

Before long it seemed that half the camp had their own hot plates and outside contacts and were able to get edible items that they would cook on their hot plates. After we got some Red Cross parcels, we all would have a "hey-day" cooking different concoctions. One day all the lights went out. The overloaded circuits had blown the main fuse. This became a frequent occurrence and the "Jeeps" wondered why the fuses started blowing all of a sudden. No one was able to get fuses through their contacts, and so I put a large nail across the fuse contacts, and we agreed among ourselves to limit the number of hot plates operating at any one time. This worked out fine.

Before the war I liked to take my coffee with cream and sugar, but here, where there was none available except in the Red Cross parcels, I decided that to have coffee in this manner would use up three precious items at one time. I was determined to make the parcel go as far as possible and so I learned to drink coffee black.

On the 13th the "Jeeps" suggested that we have a dinner party, using our Red Cross food, and invite them. We grumbled a lot but each one of us donated a little something and Nick fixed up a pretty good meal. Like all our dinner parties, there wasn't much of what we had, but what we had was good.

Lt. Hamamoto now had an assistant—a Warrant Officer—and we considered them both to be a couple of disagreeable bastards. We felt lucky that at this camp we were under the control of the propaganda office and not the military, or "Hamhock" [Hamamoto] would certainly deal us a hard time.[4]

Prisoners of War Mail
Sec Des Prisonniers De Guerre

Tokyo No. 2805 Camp
Date March 24, 1944

Dear Little Mother:

Sending you once again a few lines to comfort you. Write often about the families [sic] health and welfare. I have received one letter and one parcel for which I am truly thankful. Give my regards to friends and

---

4. Despite Fujita's impression, the propaganda programs which he describes, and especially the arrangement at the *Bunka Gakuin*, were very much under the control of the Japanese army. Masayo Duus, *Tokyo Rose: Orphan of the Pacific* (Tokyo and New York: Kodansha International, 1979), pp. 65–66, 83–84; Chapman, *Tokyo Calling*, passim.

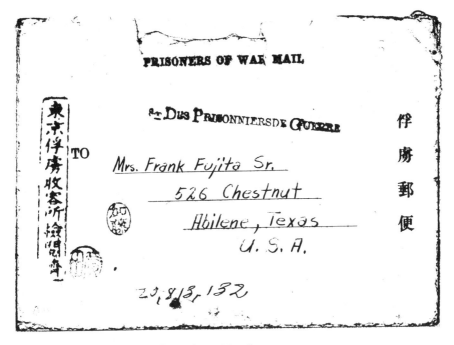

POW letter to Fujita's mother written March 24, 1944.

buddies, also have them write. Keep a firm hand on Patsy and make her study art. I was glad to hear you and Willie know each other. Watch over her and help her as I would. How is [sic] Herbert and my old buddies now? Be sure to keep me posted about Wayne. Have Dad and the girls each to write and to send plenty of photographs. Such things will strengthen my thread of hope for the future. If there has been any change in my rank or pay let me know. How can you draw allotment? For I didn't make one out. On Easter send Dora some flowers from "FOO." Do same for Willie on July 5. Always hope for the best and expect the worst and you can face the future with impunity. Lots of love:

"FOO"
Frank Fujita Jr.

I had written a poem about my Fort Worth girl friend, Willie, and I entitled it "Willie." I went to the *Hoso* and read it myself and I had Beethoven's "Moonlight Sonata" and the "Rosary" played in the background. Two more E Battery men had recordings go over the "Postman Calls" program—Sgt. O. B. Williams and Pvt. Bob Savell.

March 1944. Some American Red Cross clothing and shoes came in and were issued to us. One day Uno told us all to get ready for he was going to take us to the movies. This was very surprising and we wondered what the occasion was and what the movie would be about. We were loaded onto a truck and taken to the theatre, about a mile away. The movie turned out to be a "Jeep" propaganda film and it was about the Philippine campaign. It was a lousy bit of propaganda, but the actual scenes of the bombing of Clark Field, the 31st Infantry under attack and the action against Corregidor and Bataan were really worth seeing.

The 10th marked the second anniversary of my capture on Java. I was also assigned to work in the galley with Nick from 10:00 A.M. to 7:30 P.M. every day. On the 24th we got to send two-page letters home. We had had several snows that month and winter showed no sign of letting up. We kept a one-gallon tea kettle full of black tea on the hibachi in the work room at all times and this sure helped keep us warm, even though it was very demanding on our kidneys.

On the 28th we were formed up in the courtyard and the "Jeeps" had two armed soldiers come in and escort 2nd/Lt. Ed Kalbfliesch out. We were told that he was being removed for not cooperating. We were reminded that our lives would not be guaranteed if we failed to cooperate. We felt that was the end of Ed. I suspected foul play in Ed's being shipped out. He and Maj. Cousens were not on the best of terms and I felt that Cousens had been the one to "finger" Ed. There were hints many times after this by the "Jeeps" about Ed's being taken out and shot in order to throw more fear into the rest of us. Ed, like George Williams before him, was not executed and lived through the war. He still lives in Saint Louis, Mo.[5] Recordings of E Battery men were still going over, but the

5. Kalbfleisch had been writing scripts with hidden messages and then went so far as to change the meaning of a line of script while actually reading it on the *Hi no Maru* program. According to Cousens, it was Sgt. Provoo who revealed these things

guys on the program didn't write down the names so I did not know who they were.

The front office had decided to make a movie theater in their building in order to facilitate chopping up captured American movies and making propaganda films out of them. They brought in one 35-mm movie projector and sound equipment and a good screen. I told them of my experience as a movie projectionist and they were only too glad to have me help set up the equipment. I was in hopes that they would allow me to run some of the movies before they were cut up for the POWs.

April 1944. A photographer was sent into camp to take a lot of pictures of us in all our activities—in groups and as individuals. We were told that we could all have copies of what was taken for our own. The name of our program was changed from "The *Hi no Maru* Hour" to "Humanity Calls."[6] There was no change in the program format consisting of the same corny soap opera and Saturday jamborees. There was never any shortage of propaganda material, for Streeter wrote mountains of poisonous ravings against the United States and Roosevelt and his bureaucrats. He became so vitriolic in what he was writing that the Japanese told him to "cool it." It was so bad that they were ashamed to use it. Others, at times, would write more willingly and in greater volume.

Lt. Hamamoto got married and was assigned to a different post. I cannot say that any of us were sorry to see him leave. We had a stroke of good fortune one day when a delivery cart brought in a very large pail of fresh oysters. They were not intended for us, but the deliveryman had had them on his cart in the sun for so long that he feared they were very near being spoiled and so was given permission to leave them. Man alive! Were they ever good eating. Those of us who liked raw oysters were permitted to eat as many as we liked. For lunch we had fried oysters—all we could eat—

---

to the Japanese. Kalbfleisch was beaten in the face, not fed for a day, and transferred to another camp. Chapman, *Tokyo Calling,* pp. 174–75, 210.

6. The change was made after Maj. Tsuneishi became convinced that the title, *Hi no Maru,* was probably meaningless to American audiences. Duus, *Tokyo Rose,* p. 85; Chapman, *Tokyo Calling,* p. 179.

In April, 1944 a photographer was sent to Bunka POW Camp to record
the prisoners' activities. The men each received ten photographs of their choosing.
These are some of the photographs chosen by Fujita.

   A. *Back row, L to R: Henshaw, McNaughton, Uno, Provoo. Front row, L to R:
Cox, Kalbfliesh, Pearson, Wisener.*

   B. *Back row, L to R: Henshaw, McNaughton (Uno and Provoo with no heads).
Front row, L to R: Cox, Kalbfliesh, Pearson, Wisener.*

   C. *L to R: John Provoo, Kazimura "Buddy" Uno,* nisei *interpreter.*

   D. *L to R: Maj. Cox, Lt. Wisener.*

   E. *Back row, L to R: Henshaw, McNaughton, Kalbfliesh, Provoo. Front row,
L to R: Cox, Rickert, Pearson, Wisener.*

   F. *L to R: Rickert, Ed Kalbfliesh, "Bucky" Henshaw.*

G

H

I

G. *P.T. (physical training) at "Bunker Hill." L to R: Kalbfliesh, Pearson, Parkyns, Light, McNaughton, Bruce, Shattles, Henshaw, Streeter, Fujita (back to camera).*

H. *Playing ball. Foo in foreground. Four men across the center, L to R: Kalbfliesch, Light, Kid, Henshaw. Three men far right back, L to R: Shattles, Bruce, Parkyns.*

I. *Front row, L to R: Bruce, Light, Pearson, Wisener. Middle row, L to R: Rickert, Shattles, Provoo, Kalbfliesh, McNaughton. Top Row, L to R: Parkyns, Astarita, Fujita.*

and at the evening meal we had oyster stew. We had no refrigeration so they would not keep until the next day. The front office ate on them as well, so there were very few to be thrown out.

Almost all the men became ill, probably from overeating and the fact that our systems were not prepared for such rich food. Mama San, the wife of the caretaker, when she found out that we were all sick, came up to our beds and catered to us. She tucked us in and did whatever she could for us. She called us her family and said that when the time came for us to leave she would cry. There is no telling how many classes of girls she had seen come and go from this school. In a way we were just another class to her and Papa San.

Our rice ration was not all rice, but still the five parts of maize to one part of rice. It was almost nauseating, and if it were not for the crushed red pepper that I piled on it with vitamin B_{12} pills for garnish, I could not stomach it. There was always lots left over. It's a wonder that any of us have teeth left, there were so many rocks in it.

Uno brought us two bunny rabbits and said that we could raise our own meat. He also brought some guinea pigs and a pup. We already had a small white dog that we called Whitie. The rabbits and guinea pigs fared pretty good on parings from the vegetables that the galley would get in, and on the leftover *kori*, the "Jeep" name for maize.[7] The pup grew to about twice the size of Whitie, and we called him Brownie. Both dogs were male. When our prospective meat supply, the bunnies, grew up, they also proved to be both male.

The front office had decided to allow Uno to take a few POWs at a time each Sunday on a sightseeing trip in and around Tokyo. In early April, Mr. Hayasaka, who could speak Spanish and English, came over to us and declared that he intended to start a Spanish language radio program and wanted to know if any of us knew any Spanish-speaking POWs. I gave this a lot of thought. Remembering how bad things were and the daily death toll at the Nagasaki shipyards and camp, I became convinced that if

7. Fujita may have misheard or misunderstood this word. The Japanese word for maize is *tōmorokoshi*. The reference here may have been to *koge,* rice or grain that had been burnt or scorched.

I got someone out of that and brought them to this camp their chances of survival would be greatly increased. They would have to take their chances on being able to hold any participation on a radio program to a minimum. I gave Hayasaka the names of two E Battery men—Pfc. Jimmy Martinez and Pvt. Ramon Martinez—same name but no kin.

Mr. Hishikari of the front office furnished the trimmings for another dinner party. There were nine Japanese, all total, who attended. I don't recall any particular reason for this dinner, but we were always happy to get different and better food.

Every time someone had a birthday I made them a special card and everyone in camp signed it, including some of the Japanese. I also made everyone a Christmas card.

Some reports about "Lost Battalion" men came in with the stuff for the "Postman Calls" program. These men had been left in Java when all the others had shipped out. It seems that some of them were in a thirty-six-hour battle with the Japanese landing forces at Buitenzorg, and then were captured at Garoet, Java.[8] In the spring of the year, this camp was a wonderful smelling place, for camellia bushes were planted around three sides of our compound and when they were in bloom their heavy sweet smell filled the air.

On the 7th I got six letters from home: four from Mom, one from Dad and one from my old friend Roy McCullough. One of the letters had photos of the family in it and I hardly recognized my little sister. I was one of the seven that got to go on the city tour this week. Uno took us downtown on the tram and we toured the Ginza area, the most famous shopping area in Tokyo. As we walked down the street window shopping, I was surprised to see a man urinating on the wall. Before the tour was over, I saw others doing the same thing. Uno took us through one of the largest department stores, and except for the signs, one would feel as if he were shopping back home.

8. As part of Blackforce in western Java, the bulk of the 2d Battalion, 131st Field Artillery, had participated in the vain effort to halt the Japanese advance inland after most Dutch forces had withdrawn. Lionel Wigmore, *The Japanese Thrust* (Canberra: Australian War Memorial, 1957), pp. 497–503.

While we were in this store, one of the men had to go to the rest room and so we were taken to this public toilet and we were shocked. Both men and women used the same facility, which consisted of a long row of porcelain stalls with a porcelain trough in the floor. There were no doors on the stalls and everyone watched everyone else use the toilet—those who were waiting in line, that is.

May 1944. Some of the radio audience of Station JOAK, Tokyo, complained to the front office that our soap opera was getting to be "too risque" and so we were told to tone the dialog down and avoid getting too raunchy. Eight American invalid parcels packed for sick bay use came in along with some bulk pipe tobacco and some cigarettes. We had been able to smoke pretty regularly since the Red Cross parcels and bulk stuff had been coming in. I would light up a cigarette and could not help but remember the Nagasaki shipyards when we had no tobacco. As I would carry my stage building components across the yards I always kept my eyes peeled for "snipes," cigarette butts. The POWs would dive down and grab anything that looked like it might be a butt. The Japanese have a cigarette that is half cigarette and the other half is a hollow paper tube. I lost every time I made a grab for what I thought was a butt. It would be one of these tubes or a piece of chalk. When I would think of this, I would contentedly take a long pull from my cigarette and enjoy it to the fullest.

The drain pipe for the whole complex stopped up and I was given a pick and shovel and told to try and unstop it. I worked on this for several days and had quite a hole dug out near the supply room. The toilet situation was getting critical when I finally managed to get the drain to flowing. The front office was so pleased that they let Uno take me to the neighborhood movie. What a bore! A propaganda film, all in Japanese.

One day the "Jeeps" took everyone that wanted to go, boat riding. I did not trust the "Jeeps" enough to go, for I thought how easy it would be to dump us out into the drink and then claim it was an accident. The boating trip came off without a hitch and when the guys returned to camp, they had a wind-up phonograph and a number of classical records that the "Jeeps" had given them. I was very anxious to hear some music and could hardly wait for the phonograph to be set up in our recreation room. Harry

Pearson gave it a good winding and then put on "Ave Maria," by Bach-Gunod, and sung by a German gal, Maria Eggert, who was hitting notes so high that I thought our windows were going to shatter, not to mention my ears. I can't say that this really turned me on. Harry then put on the "Hungarian Rhapsody #2," by Liszt and I thought that this was the most morbid thing that I had ever heard. Before the war's end, though, I was a confirmed lover of classical music.

The proofs of the photos that were taken some time back came in and we were told that we could choose ten apiece for our very own. There were some very good shots and I would have liked to have a copy of each one of them. We all made our choices and returned the proofs. We were told that it would be a while but that we would receive our ten photos eventually.

The daily routine was never static, for moods and feelings and suspicions changed with the news that came in. One day the program would be O.K. with different ones and then something would be said and the whole complexion would change and there would be little "cliques" formed with a lot of whispering and suspicions towards other cliques. Then there would be falling-outs and the cliques would change in makeup. Streeter was, for the most part, not included in any of the cliques, for no one wanted to be identified with him. He denied that he was an American citizen and said that he was a citizen of the world.

Sgt. Provoo played "low key" for the most part. He knew that all in camp had heard of his actions on Corregidor and he was careful not to go too far in his writings and talking so as not to get the group down on him anymore that they already were. He was willing and able to write articles that extolled the virtues of the Japanese and staunchly maintained that they were fulfilling their destiny of becoming the leader of the Orient.

It was obvious that someone in camp was keeping the front office informed on all that went on and all that was said. They always knew what had happened or what was said, almost as soon as it took place or was said. I did not trust anyone in camp and was always careful to not say or do anything that would really get me in serious trouble. Mickey Parkyns and I hit it off together pretty good and we became good friends and shared things like sneaking into the supply room and stealing rice and sugar and breaking into the other sealed rooms. We thought that perhaps the building had been bugged when the "Jeeps" were finding out so many things about us.

In one of the sealed rooms there were a lot of art supplies and pieces of sculpture that past students had done in clay. I found a roll-up projection screen and I thought that it would make a good shirt, so I cut it loose from its tripod and took it with me. I also found a good hard back ledger book that was little used and I took this, too, to transfer my diary into it. I found an old hard baseball whose cover was about to come off and I thought that the string the ball was made of would come in handy for sewing and patching, and I took it as well. I did make me a shirt from the projection screen but I could never get the starch, or whatever, out of it. Every time that I put it on or took it off it sounded like a piece of tin, and when I did wear it it would rub me raw. I washed and washed and soaked and soaked but was never able to soften it up.

One day after we had been sitting around shooting the bull on a rest break, Donald Bruce said that he would like to read us something. After he got everyone's attention he began reading back to us verbatim just what we all had said during the bull session. He had taken it all down in shorthand and we were stunned to find out just how very little contextual wording we had during the course of normal conversation, after we took out all of the curse words and obscenities. Another time I was sitting near Cousens, McNaughton, Cox and Pearson, who had a conversation going, and it suddenly dawned on me that I was only understanding about one or two words out of every five. When I left home I was one of these smart teenagers who thought that what I didn't already know wasn't worth knowing. But here and now it was being brought home to me that there was a hell of a lot that I didn't know and that I could not even understand good English when it was being spoken.

I decided that I was going to do something about my ignorance. We had this fantastic library and I began to read every chance I had. History and philosophy were fascinating and were filled with so many words I did not understand that I spent as much time reading the dictionary as I did the books. As I pursued my studies, I was appalled to find out just how very little I really had known in all those years when I thought that I knew so much. Attaining a little knowledge engenders a thirst for greater knowledge. As I was finding this out about myself, I found at the same time that such was also the case with mankind as he struggled from his humble beginnings to better his lot in life.

After the thousands of years of his trial and error methods, of discarding the unworkable and accumulating the proven, he arrived at the wonderful state of enlightenment—this high plane of civilization—that we had fallen heir to. As I looked around me and saw how cruelly the Japanese treated us captives, how the nations of the world were bent on destroying one another, and how right down to the POW level survival took precedent over compassion, it was disconcerting to realize that our thousands of years of existence had only produced a very fragile and thin veneer of civilized behavior concealing the savage beast within.

I also decided to study the many books that we had on the different religions of the world, and while doing so perhaps I could find a replacement for the concept of God and religion that I had lost in the trenches of Java. I wondered why there were so many different religions, especially when most of them were monotheistic. Even within Christendom itself there seemed to me a confusing array of secular beliefs, all directed at worshiping and achieving oneness with the one true God, yet their methodologies differed greatly one from the other. The members within a single church were far from being unanimous in their beliefs and church doctrine. There was a small book of poetry that I found among the religious books called *When God Laughs,* written by Jack London. One of the poems struck me as being very close to the truth and it went like this:

> As one is, so is his God
> Thus is God—often strangely odd.

Finally I found out how they had intended to use me, an artist, on a radio program. I was supposed to draw pictures of all the types of military equipment that we had been issued at the start of the war. A Japanese civilian artist who specialized in depicting various army and naval battles of the Imperial forces—an excellent artist, I might add—was Chuo Hasegawa. He brought me some artists' drawing pads, sketch pencils and

Japanese artist Chuo Hasegawa, who gave Foo materials to work with in Tokyo, 1944.

water colors. Through Uno he outlined to me just what the front office wanted. I told him that I understood and that I would do my best. I did not have any qualms of conscience about doing this since everything that we were issued was left over from WW I, except our fatigues.

I painted GIs wearing the "tin lids" of WW I and armed with the 1903 version of the .30-caliber Springfield rifles. These weapons, along with the .45-caliber automatic pistol were scattered all over the world. Our 75-mm field guns were WW I French weapons with an American-made split trail. Our canteens, pistol belts, first aid packs and clip holders were all WW I. Our gas masks were WW I and were good for two hours only in tear gas. The front office could not find a great deal of use for my drawings.

Our bedroom was on the top floor at the west end of the building. Outside our windows were trees that towered above our windows. These trees grew on the property next door, which we were told belonged to some Japanese "Blue Blood," a count or something. In any case, these trees were loaded with large golden-colored spiders which wove the most beautiful webs. I could sit and watch these spiders for long periods and never cease to be amazed at the precision with which they worked and the efficiency and speed that was theirs in wrapping a hapless victim that might stray into their web.

"Bunker Hill" was located in an area that had a number of hospitals. There was one on the east side of us and an eight-story maternity hospital immediately behind us. Running along the back of our building was a three-foot-wide walkway, with the building on one side and a four-foot wall on the other, which was to prevent someone from accidentally falling into the delivery and refuse area of the maternity hospital that was two floors below our ground level. During warm weather the nurses would open the windows and we could see into the delivery rooms. All the beds with the stirrups were pointed towards the windows. I suppose this was for maximum lighting for child delivery. We could watch the whole procedure from our walkway. I watched a number of babies brought into this world during my time at this camp. One woman was having a very difficult time of it and she lay strapped to the stirrups with her bottom bared for several hours moaning and sometimes screaming. The nurses would check on her at times and then leave again. I felt so sorry for this lady.

As I watched I would mentally try to help her push. Finally, they came and wheeled her out of the room, and I presumed that they took her to surgery for a caesarean section delivery.

On June 5, the "Jeeps" were going to show one of their propaganda films to proof it and said that any of us who wanted to could go over and watch it. The new movie room was on the same level as our lower floor and looked out upon the courtyard. Most of us went to see it for want of something better to do. I much preferred that to writing until 10:00 P.M. The movie was about half finished when one of the Japanese came in all excited and told us to go back to our quarters and remain quiet. There was a general alert in Tokyo and the sirens were sounding. It turned out that B-29s were bombing Kyushu, the island that Nagasaki is on, and I wondered if E Battery would have a job to go to in the morning. This was very thrilling, for it was the first air raid alarm to be sounded in Tokyo since Doolittle's raid.[9]

9. The Japanese had been aware for some time of the new long-range very heavy American bomber called the B-29 and the development of bases for it in India and China. On the morning of June 5, 1944, in their first combat mission of the war, some 80 B-29s of the U.S. Twentieth Air Force attacked Bangkok, Thailand, from India. There was no raid on Kyushu that day, but that was the rumor reaching the *Bunka Gakuin* POWs and it provided them with what Fujita now recalls as their "first jubilant moment of the war." For the Japanese, however, the Bangkok attack meant that B-29 strikes on Japan itself could soon be expected, and practice air raid alerts in Tokyo that night and the next were evidence of their concern.

The Doolittle raid had taken place on April 18, 1942, when Lt. Col. James Doolittle led 16 medium bombers from the deck of the aircraft carrier *Hornet* in a surprise attack on Tokyo and three other Japanese cities. The bombing did little material damage but seriously raised Japanese concerns about the vulnerability of their homeland. Wesley Frank Craven and James Lea Cate (eds.), *The Army Air Forces in World War II*, 7 vols. (Chicago: University of Chicago Press, 1948–58), I, pp. 438–44, V, 94–96; E. Bartlett Kerr, *Flames Over Tokyo: The U.S. Army Air Forces' Incendiary Campaign Against Japan, 1944–1945* (New York: Donald I. Fine, 1991), pp. 60–61, 103.

11

BOMBING RAIDS,

BENJO HONCHO PLANS

ESCAPE

June 1944–January 1945

June 6, 1944. The long hoped for second front was opened in Europe. The news arrived here in Tokyo at 3:00 P.M. The news caused excitement and a lot of speculation as to success or failure of the landing and what, if any, effect it would have on our situation. I was thrilled beyond words and at the same time felt a great sense of being cheated out of participating in the greatest military undertaking in history. I could just see in my mind's eye the vast armada storming the beaches while thousands and thousands of planes filled the air, raining death and destruction on the German defenders. The earlier news bulletin that had mentioned the expected losses also said that the end of the war in Europe was in sight.

The end of the war in Europe being in sight caused me a good deal of concern for our own well being as POWs of Japan. Uno had already told us that "the closer America came to Japan, the closer we came to death," and that Japan did not intend to leave any POWs alive to present an internal threat in the event that the home islands were invaded. I had no doubts whatever that they meant what they said. I had decided that I was going to escape prior to execution when

年 月 日	品 名	数 量	替	買入金額	支拂金額	借 或 袋	差引殘高

December 23, 1944 ☆

    Air Raid 3: A.M. One B-29 bombed.

December 24, 1944 ☆

    <u>at 5:00 A.M.</u>
Air Raid — One B-29 bombed — Smith
and I make the best sweet thing
that we have tasted outside of
the States it was my reciep for
~~Sonfu~~ "Yaroshi Pie" — all hands go
nuts over it — other dam good reciepes
by my self are "Horio Meat Loaf" and (HURRY UP)
"Snafu Pudding" — by Smith "Hiyaku
Hash", "Welsh no Usangi" and "Pate
Arimasu" — 5 tons of coal came in
  (15)

December 25, 1944 ☆

    Christmas Day — Air Raid at 3:00 A.M. —
several
~~One~~ B 29's bombed — no Tenko this
              Roll Call →

the "hand writing on the wall" indicated that this situation was in the offing.[1]

I had found a map of Japan in the sealed storage room with all the writing in Japanese. I had made me a blown-up map covering Tokyo and all the mountains to the west, including Fujiyama and beyond. I made the map in color and indicated elevation by differing colors. I drew it to scale and located all the towns. The names were written in *Katakana,* one of the forms of Japanese writing.[2] In order to know what these towns were, I had to learn the *Katakana* alphabet. I then put the names on the map in English. I was always very observant of the people who came and went in and out of the propaganda headquarters in the front building. I noticed when a high-ranking general, admiral or cabinet member arrived how the guards and civilians would react. Each one would also have his own flag flying from each fender of the car or taxi. One general, in particular, who came around occasionally, really evoked reaction as if he were the Emperor himself. I copied his flag and made me a set exactly like his.

I also noticed that when a *kempeitai* (Japanese military police) came on the scene, he was treated with the highest degree of respect, or perhaps it was fear. In any case, no one messed around with a *kempeitai*. I also duplicated their arm band and vehicle marking. I had begun to lay back items of food that would not spoil—some sugar cubes for quick energy and a can of potted meat—from Red Cross parcels. I had an extra pair of socks and matches. Once when Ozaki took me out to a neighborhood shop to

1. Fujita's concerns were well founded. POWs elsewhere were told essentially the same thing and there are other indications that an American invasion would precipitate the prisoners' execution. On Palawan Island in the Philippines, for example, Japanese guards killed nearly 150 POWs in order to prevent their rescue by invading American forces. Benis M. Frank and Henry I. Shaw, Jr. *History of U.S. Marine Corps Operations in World War II: Victory and Occupation* (Washington: Hqs, U.S. Marine Corps, 1968) p. 774; E. Bartlett Kerr, *Surrender and Survival: The Experience of American POWs in the Pacific, 1941–1945* (New York: William Morrow, 1985), pp. 212–15, 261.

2. *Katakana* is one of two Japanese syllabaries, or *kana* ("borrowed names"), adopted from Chinese characters. It is used primarily to represent foreign names and words.

get tea I saw a small "hara kiri" knife[3] and told Ozaki that I would like very much to buy it. This scared him a bit and he wanted to know why I wanted it. I told him that I would like to take it home with me after the war. He was afraid of what the front office would do to him if they ever found out about it. He finally allowed me to buy it and I placed it in my private cache in one of the sealed rooms. No one knew of my hiding place or of what I had in mind. I had given some thought to letting someone in on my escape plans, but at this time there was no one that I trusted enough, and besides the war situation was not critical enough.

On the 15th a general alarm was again sounded in Tokyo, but no planes ever came over. The "grapevine" had it that the Mariana Islands was where the action was taking place. The next day another alarm sounded and this time the grapevine said that a glass factory in northern Kyushu had been bombed, killing twenty-four and wounding sixty-five, and that twenty-five U.S. planes had been shot down. This scoop did not sound too plausible. I could not see how a glass plant would be that strategically important and I doubted the plane loss figure. I was, however, elated that our forces were near enough to Japan to use land-based aircraft to bomb Japan with.[4]

On the 17th all hands were required to participate in the 200th broadcast. When we went into the radio building, it was apparent that the air raid warnings had brought about some changes. At the front entrance to the building and at points along the corridors there were sandbag barricades set up, and each one had an armed soldier with fixed bayonet stationed by

3. *Hara kiri* ("belly cutting"), the traditional ceremonial form of Japanese suicide.

4. On June 15, 1944, American amphibious forces began the invasion of the Marianas, barely 1,300 miles from Tokyo and the projected base for B-29 operations against Japan. The same day also saw the initiation of B-29 raids from southern China on southwestern Japan when nearly fifty very heavy bombers of the Twentieth Air Force attacked the Imperial Iron and Steel Works in Yawata, Kyushu. While the raid did relatively little damage, this blow combined with the Marianas invasion greatly increased Japanese fears about the growing danger to their homeland. Philip A. Crowl, *Campaign in the Marianas* (Washington: Office, Chief of Military History, 1960), Chap. 5; Wesley Frank Craven and James Lea Cate (eds.), *The Army Air Forces in World War II*, 7 vols. (Chicago: University of Chicago Press, 1948–58), V, pp. 98–102.

it. There were armed guards in the studio and the control room as well. When we went back to Bunker Hill we found that we were going to have another "dinner party" for the 200th program.

It was obvious that dinner parties were going to be the norm for each 100th broadcast. We did welcome the piddling amount of different foods, but we also had to endure the propaganda speeches made by the attending Japanese. They would tell us how fortunate we were for having the opportunity to work for world peace through our radio program, and how fortunate we were to not be in one of the labor camps.

I was happy indeed not to be in the work camps with the diseases, cruel guards, back-breaking labor, *tenkos* and harassment. I never got into my bed without thinking of those horror-filled nights of bedbugs, fleas and lice. At times even now I lie there and remember the cold, cold winters where food, clothing and bedding were minimal, and how we would start shivering when cold weather would set in and not quit shivering until spring, and how every fiber of my being was sore on account of it.

I felt sure in my own mind that what I was doing in this camp could not possibly have any detrimental effect on my country's war effort. I continued to badmouth the program and anyone that I felt was writing too freely. The front office was aware of this and their treatment of me reflected how they felt. What puzzled me was why they were not more stern or even cruel to me. They had removed George Williams and Lt. Kalbfliesch from camp for doing less than I was doing.

On the 25th some general sent in a case of beer for us to share. We were not told of any reason for this. Also on this date we began taking dysentery shots. We had a pair of scissors and a barber type comb that we used for hair cutting. We would take turns about cutting each others' hair. Before long they all thought that I did the best job of cutting hair so I became the camp barber. Even the camp C.O. came over a time or two for a clip.

We received another dysentery shot on the 1st of July and Maj. Cousens had a heart attack on the third, which was Saturday, and broadcast day. He was taken to hospital in Shinagawa.[5] He made it through O.K.

---

5. Shinagawa, in the southern outskirts of Tokyo, was the site of a hospital for POWs. American and British doctors treated patients under the strict and harsh super-

Our rabbits had grown up and one of them managed to get through the fence into the Count's yard and he never offered to let us have it back. The other one we named Buck, and he gave us all many hours of entertainment. On our break periods or lunch hour we would sit out in the compound and enjoy the fresh air and sunshine. One day we were sitting there when we noticed Buck acting very un-rabbitlike. He was stalking Whitie, who was napping in the sun. Buck was sneaking up on his belly like a cat stalks a bird. He moved very, very slowly and when he was about three feet from Whitie he made a leap and landed right on top of him. In the typical lightning-fast action of a rabbit, he had seduced squealing Whitie, leapt into the air, turned a flip backward and taken off at high speed, with a very irate Whitie one jump behind snapping and growling. Finally, Buck stopped and faced Whitie, and they both stood on their hind feet pawing at each other as if they were boxing. I was really amazed to see a rabbit behave in this manner. This little bit of action became routine and afforded us many laughs.

Brownie, the big pup, came in for his share of harassment too. Buck would stalk him in the same way but instead of trying to make love to him, he would run the last few steps to where Brownie was napping, leap over him and as he went over he would give Brownie a resounding thump on the head with his hind legs. Brownie too was irritated and would chase Buck until he would turn and fight Brownie face to face. This was one of the funniest and most unbelievable things I have ever witnessed.

On the 7th of July, six new Americans were sent into our camp. They were:

---

vision of Japanese medical officers and guards. Conditions were difficult but the prisoner patients probably fared better than they might have at other POW installations. Kerr, *Surrender and Survival*, p. 180; Alfred A. Weinstein, *Barbed-Wire Surgeon* (New York: Macmillan, 1948), pp. 187–217.

Cousens' heart attack apparently occurred at least two weeks before he was finally sent to the hospital. After a month, he returned to the *Bunka Gakuin* but was then transferred to a nearby civilian hospital where he received somewhat better treatment until he again returned to *Bunka* in December. Ivan Chapman, *Tokyo Calling: The Charles Cousens Case* (Sydney: Hale & Iremonger, 1990), pp. 180–97.

Frederick Ferguson Smith (?), Radioman 1st USN, captured at Guam.

Walter Odlin, S/Sgt. US Army, captured in the Philippines.

Fred Hoblitt, Cpl. USMCR, captured in the Philippines.

Jimmy Martinez, Pfc. US Army captured on Java.

Ramon Martinez, Pvt. US Army captured on Java.

Darwin Dodds, Civilian war worker, captured on Wake Island.

The two Martinezs were the E Battery men that I had recommended to Hayasaka, some time back. I greeted them and told them why I had recommended them, and they said that things had changed for the better in Fukuoka #2 since I left there. The food was better and the POWs were allowed to raise a garden. They seemed to be resentful until they began to realize how life would be without the yelling guards, the beatings, no inspections, no shipyards, no bedbugs, fleas or sand crabs, and enough blankets that one could actually keep warm at night.

On the same day that the new men came in, several Japanese carpenters came in and began to build a bathhouse on the West side of the courtyard about half way between our building and the front office. It was going to be a Japanese type bathhouse with a coal-burning fireplace under the tub. The building was only fifteen feet by fifteen feet and a four-foot room running down one side for keeping kindling wood and coal out of the weather. I am sure the others, like myself, had ecstatic visions of what a hot bath would be like.

Before the bathhouse was completed, the front office had become so upset with my poor efforts on the program that they decided to punish me by making me the toilet clean-up man, or the *"Benjo Honcho,"* as I referred to myself. In addition to this, I was to take care of our building and the courtyard and was to be in charge of the bathhouse. When the bathhouse was completed, I had to fill the tub with water and then build the fire.

The coal that they brought in was more shale than coal and it was next to impossible to get a fire started with it. Finally, the bath was ready and everyone was excited and eager to bathe when Otaka, the camp C.O., came strolling out in his robe with a towel around his neck and informed us that he would bathe first. Our officers then decided that they would bathe next, and after them the enlisted men and civilians could bathe. This was not too bad, for we had been thoroughly instructed as to how to take a bath Japanese style. At least in my new position of *Benjo Honcho* I had nothing further to do with writing materials for the radio programs, and this just tickled me pink.

Before I became the *Benjo Honcho,* everyone was supposed to clean up after himself. Even though the *benjo* could stand a lot of improvement, it was, at least, livable. Now that the clean-up was put on me, I think that everyone reverted to "neolithic" toilet habits. For short periods after toilet tissue was issued, the *benjo* was in fairly good shape, but as it began to be used up, the finger came into play more and more. Some men would step outside to the lavatory and wash their fingers off, while others must have descended from the ancient Assyrians, for the walls of the *benjo* looked as if they had cuneiform writing on them.

This "fecal grafitti" infuriated me greatly, and I was forever at war with the nasty finger-writers. I would almost come to blows every day with Shattles, for he would lie in bed at night until he absolutely could not hold his water any longer, then he would leap out of bed and make a mad dash for the latrine. He would have his penis in hand, trying to choke back the flow. All he succeeded in doing was to cut the flow down to a spray, and he sprayed all the way from his bed to the *benjo* and upon reaching that, he just let go and what he had left was splashed on the floor.

Also in July, we had our first obvious incident of homosexual behavior. One of the original Bunker Hill boys was caught giving oral sex to one of the newcomers. One of the civilians and one of the officers had obviously become enamored of each other. The officer would be writing and the civilian, who was employed in a different part of the building, would come running up the stairs, open the door to the workroom and gaze longingly at the officer, who would smile and flutter his eyelids at him. The civilian would then give a deep sigh and return to his own area, only to repeat this performance about every half hour. At night they would sit outside on a bench and hold hands and coo at each other. As far as I know their relationship never went past this stage.

The bombing raids evidently caused the officers to reappraise their participation on the "Humanity Calls" radio program, and they had decided among themselves to petition the Japanese to send the officers to a different camp and leave the enlisted men and civilians to do the programs. One of the Japanese from the front office told us about this, and some very hard feelings cropped up because of it. More than ever, little cliques would form which would talk about the other cliques and would accuse some of willfully cooperating with the Japanese. I was convinced more than ever that there was no one that I could trust with my escape plans.

I had had diarrhea for a month, and had dropped twenty-seven-and-a-half pounds in weight. I was very weak and the stomach cramps were bothersome. I could not help but feel lucky, though, that they were not the mind-boggling cramps that accompany dysentery.

On the 7th of September, an Australian warrant officer, Tim Dooley, was brought in from Bangkok. With him, we now totaled twenty-five men at Bunker Hill.

• • •

E*lectra News* (newspaper)
Electra, Texas
October 10, 1944
FRANK FUJITA GETS MESSAGE FROM SON, FRANK JR.

Frank Fujita, Japanese born, who has lived in the United States for thirty years, and who married an American woman, has two sons in our armies. One, Herbert, well known in Electra, is in France with the 442 Infantry,[6] and the other Frank Jr., is a prisoner of the Japanese. The Fujitas have recently received from Provost Marshal General in Washington the following message from Frank Jr.:

Following enemy propaganda broadcast from Japan has been intercepted: Quote, Dear Mom, is everything and everyone o.k.? Tell Dad I have received his letter and have sent an answer back. Is Pat doing well

---

6. This was the all-*nisei* 442nd Regimental Combat Team that had distinguished itself fighting in Italy and had just joined invading American forces in southern France. Masayo Umezawa Duus, *Unlikely Liberators: The Men of the 100th and 442nd* (Honolulu: University of Hawaii Press, 1987), p. 159.

Photograph taken in 1942 of Cpl. Herbert Lee (Fujita) Elliott, Frank Fujita's brother, who served with the 442nd Regimental Combat Team.

with her music? If, and when I get back I want her to play "Hungarian Rhapsody" number two for me. If you get to send me a Christmas box this year put plenty of pictures of family and friends in it. Incidentally, why don't my friends write? You have no idea how much a few lines from the people we know mean to us. Be sure, Mom, not to destroy any of my drawings for I want them all. I suppose my buddies are officers now. How does Wayne like married life? Tell Mrs. Etheridge I dream of those butterscotch pies of hers. Is Herbert or any of the girls married yet? Give my regards to Willie and all my friends. Until we meet again, I shall remain your loving son (FOO)

Signed Sgt. Frank Fujita Jr.[7]

• • •

October 1944. The theater the front office had been building was finally completed. The Japanese propaganda staff had already tried it out and were satisfied with it. That part of the front office staff that deals with us POWs decided that we could watch the first half of *Gone With the Wind*. Boy! Did we ever enjoy that.

On October 8th I went to the *hoso* and broadcast a message home. We here at this camp were permitted to broadcast a message home each month, and this fact was so frustrating to me, for here I had this great opportunity to send information back home to our families, but I had no information to send.

The 10th marked the 300th broadcast of the radio program, and as usual we had a dinner party with Uno and several others from the front office. The new camp C.O. was a big man and sure liked his sake. We had never had any Japanese guards or officers come over and fraternize with us before, but this officer, Otaka, would get a snoot full of sake and then he would come over and want us to join in with him and have a singsong.

---

7. The War Department normally monitored enemy shortwave broadcasts and provided next-of-kin with information about individual POWs. Many short-wave operators on the West Coast would also pass on such information to prisoners' families. Kerr, *Surrender and Survival*, p. 190.

He would stop every so often and have a drink of sake. He wanted to sing "Auld Lang Syne" and would really boom it out in Japanese. When finished, he would smile real big and declare that that was a real good Japanese song. When we told him that it was a Scottish song, he would puff up and say that anyone could see that it was a Japanese song because it had Japanese words to it. He could not speak English but could understand our motions and insistence that the song was Scottish, and he became quite upset and began to get angry. We then agreed with him that it indeed was a Japanese song. He grinned real big and then wanted to sing another Japanese song, "The Peanut Vendor." On the 20th I had my third birthday in a POW camp, and the other POWs gave me fifty yen for a present. I was twenty-three years old and only wished that I had something to spend the fifty yen on.

Earlier we had been given some baby chicks and they had now grown to the point where one pullet began to lay. One day she began to walk around the courtyard, cackling at the top of her voice. This unusual sound got the attention of not only the POWs, but of some of the front office staff as well, and we all ran out into the courtyard to see if we could locate the egg. One of the POWs found it, and the next day the same ritual took place, with someone else finding the precious egg. The next day I picked the pullet off her nest for that day and gently took her into the kindling room of the bath house and fixed her another nest. Since my job was to take care of the courtyard, I was conveniently near when the cackling started. Everyone in both buildings was sitting on ready, for no sooner than the pullet started to cackle than the doors to both buildings burst open and out rushed the egg hunters. I stepped over, opened the door to the kindling room, let the pullet out and retrieved the egg. I sure got the glares from all concerned. It was unbelievable how good a poached fresh egg could be, even without salt and pepper. That night we got to see the last half of *Gone With the Wind*.

November came in with a bang! The air raid sirens were screaming to high heaven and the atmosphere seemed charged with fear and excitement, too. I was beside myself with excitement and joy and was scanning the sky for planes. This was the first raid on Tokyo, other than Doolittle's, and all of the front office staff and the POWs were out in the courtyard scanning the sky.

Finally four or five B-29s came into view. The ack-ack were firing away but did not seem to reach the altitude that the bombers were flying at. Some Zeros went up but they did not get up that high either.[8] That night I was permitted to run the movie projectors for the POWs and any of the Japanese who wanted to watch. I showed Walt Disney's *Fantasia*. It was the full version and had not been cut up yet to be made into propaganda.

The next few days gave us ample time to speculate on the origin of the bombers. Did they come from China, or did they come from some island to the south? The grapevine finally put their origin as being the Marianas. One thing we knew was that the B-29s were land-based planes, and the very fact that they were able to bomb at all indicated that the American noose was drawing ever tighter around Japan itself, and this was a big morale booster.

On the 5th, the sirens began screaming again and the radios and loud-speakers in the neighborhood were telling the type and number of incoming enemy planes. It sounded like: "*Tobugunka, Kajoho—Tobugunka Kajoho, Binijuku wa, ichi hentai arimasu!*"[9] We became adept at interpreting these broadcasts and therefore we always knew how many flights of B-29s were coming in. On this day there was one flight coming in and

8. What in fact appeared in the skies over Tokyo in the early afternoon of November 1, 1941, was a single American F-13A (modified B-29) photo reconnaissance plane based on Saipan in the Marianas. At 32,000 feet, it was much too high for the few Japanese fighters that managed somewhat belatedly to take off. These fighters were probably Japanese army planes, from one of five bases that ringed Tokyo, rather than the Zero naval fighter. While Zeros would be used in increasing numbers against the B-29s—and Fujita would tend to assume that all Japanese fighters were Zeros—the aerial defense of Tokyo was primarily an army mission. Naval aircraft, more concerned with defending naval bases and shore areas, would be assigned only later to support missions protecting Tokyo. E. Bartlett Kerr, *Flames Over Tokyo: The U.S. Army Air Forces' Incendiary Campaign Against Japan, 1944–1945* (New York: Donald I. Fine, 1991), pp. 61–63, 92–93; Craven and Cate, *Army Air Forces,* V, p. 555.

9. Probably *Tōbugunkan keihō jōhō:* "Eastern District Army Command Alarm Information: One flight of B-29s."

when it came into view we counted twenty bombers. Ack-acks opened up, but did not seem to reach the planes. A few Zeros went up but they did not seem to present any danger. We never heard any explosions, and the B-29s disappeared.[10]

On the night of the 7th two more B-29s came over and all hands ran out to get into our latrine, which was our only shelter. Since the *benjo* was directly beneath our bedroom, any bomb that would get the bedroom would also get the *benjo,* so Sgt. Odlin and myself didn't even bother about getting out of bed for a few planes.

The front office responded to our request for a bomb shelter and said that we could dig a shelter in the lot to the west of our compound. We figured that the raids thus far were only the tip of the iceberg, and so we dug with enthusiasm until we had a shelter that was large enough for all of us. All our work was in vain, as it turned out, for as the raids became more frequent and larger the front office staff used the shelter and we were left with our *benjo.*

The food continued to be a soup, made of whatever vegetables were in season and the ever-present maize. The chickens, guinea pigs, "Ole Buck" and even the dogs seemed to subsist on it much better than we did. One day we were surprised to have fresh shark meat brought into camp. That night we had shark steak, and was it ever good. What was not so good is that there was enough meat for one week, and the galley crew was only allowed to cook the daily allotted portion. We had no icebox and the weather was not cold enough yet for the meat to keep sitting out on the table.

That first day the meat was delicious; the second day it was slightly tainted. The third day it was spoiled and the fourth day it was beginning to rot and to smell to high heaven. We would not eat it and the Japanese would not let us throw it out until the time it was supposed to last us ran

10. On November 5th and again on the 7th, a few F-13 reconnaissance planes photographed aircraft plants and naval and harbor installations in the Tokyo-Kawasaki-Yokohama-Yokosuka area (the western side of Tokyo Bay). Neither Japanese fighters nor heavy anti-aircraft fire were able to interfere. Craven and Cate, *Army Air Forces,* V, 555–56.

out. On the fifth day the meat began to resemble jelly and glowed at night like a watch dial.

On the fifth night Nick went to the galley and immediately began yelling for some of us to come help him catch a cat that had been lured into the galley by the rotting shark meat. Several of us ran down to help and after almost demolishing the galley we finally captured the cat. Nick said if someone would open the door we could throw the cat out. I told them that we were not about to let that fresh meat get away. Someone asked if we would really eat the cat and Mickey Parkyns and I said, "You bet!"

Since I had had a lot of experience in skinning rabbits as a boy back in Oklahoma, I volunteered to skin and butcher the cat if someone else would kill it. That cat was a big old tom and from the size of his accouterments I figured that he would be awfully tough and strong tasting. He had originally been white but in prowling the alleys he had been turned almost black. I took him out to the bathhouse and dressed and washed him down. The meat was pretty and white and looked like skinned rabbit.

Nick had the galley fire banked and it did not take much to get a fire going. We had no salt or seasoning of any kind except the crushed red pepper, and so this is what we put in the pot. We had gotten in some very large leeks, looking like overgrown green onions, for our next day's soup. We took a poll and all agreed that we could sacrifice one blade from the green top to cook in with the cat. By the time we got the cat boiled to perfection the whole camp was on hand—some to claim a portion and most to see if we would actually eat the cat. The meat looked like boiled chicken and compared to the dog in Singapore it looked like a meal fit for a king. I did not hesitate in eating it and slowly most of the others began to try it. Most of the officers abstained.

The cat tasted so good that we built a wooden box trap and the neighborhood cats began to disappear. Once I was skinning a cat in the bathhouse when one of the Japanese from the front office walked in. He was startled, to say the least, and turned and made a hasty retreat. This was at night and most of the staff had gone home. However, the word was put out and the next morning at *tenko* we were told to cease and desist with the cats, for if the neighbors found out about it they would think that we were not fed meat.

We had learned to get into the front building without being caught and systematically explored the building bit by bit until we knew what was in there and where it was located. There were only four of us who made these reconnaissances, Dar Dodds, Fred Smith, Mickey Parkyns and myself. One day, eighty-four Red Cross boxes came in from Vladavostok. Boy! Were we excited. Nothing was said about them, however, and we could not mention them because that would let the whole camp know that we had been going into the front building.

On the 24th Tokyo had its fourth raid, and this time there were around one hundred B-29s. They blasted something in southern Tokyo. This many planes really sent thrills through me and I would inwardly be rooting for them and urging them on. The bombings had no effect on the program, but some hostility was becoming evident among the populace as our group was taken to and from the radio station.[11] One B-29 came over on the 29th and the next day came seventy more. Near midnight on the 30th an incendiary raid was carried out, and we were unable to guess at how many planes were involved. They dropped their wares very near us, and huge fires began to burn a few blocks away.[12]

After almost three years of sowing death and destruction, murders and

11. Twentieth Air Force B-29s bombed Tokyo for the first time on the afternoon of November 24, nearly ninety of the big planes hitting an aircraft factory, docks, and urban areas. Japanese fighter defense, a variety of army and navy aircraft, was strong but ineffective: only one B-29 was lost when a damaged Japanese fighter rammed it; another bomber ditched in the ocean when it ran out of fuel. A few F-13s followed the bombers to photograph damage. The Japanese reacted by announcing that downed B-29 crews would be executed as criminals, and Japanese fighters and bombers on Iwo Jima—halfway between the Marianas and Tokyo—began striking back at the Saipan B-29 base. Ibid., pp. 558–60, 581; Kerr, *Flames Over Tokyo*, pp. 97–102.

12. These dates are slightly off the mark. The second B-29 raid actually came on November 27 against the same targets struck three days earlier. Clouds covered the city, so the sixty B-29s making the attack had to drop their bombs by radar or fly on to hit cities to the west of Tokyo. No attack took place during the day on the 29th, although an F-13 probably overflew the Japanese capital. That night, however, nearly thirty B-29s dropped incendiary bombs on docks and industrial areas—the first incendiary raid on a Japanese city. An F-13 followed up as usual the next day. Craven and Cate, *Army Air Forces*, V, pp. 560–61; Kerr, *Flames Over Tokyo*, pp. 108–10.

atrocities and riding rough shod over vast areas of the far east, the Japanese were now experiencing the "chickens coming home to roost." The war was no longer far off but being dumped in their laps at home. This month of November 1944 brought Tokyo its first air raid and six more days of the same before the month was out.

December 1944. We were elated at the bombing of Tokyo, but did not dare show our elation around the Japanese for fear of stirring up some reactions that would be counter to our best interest. At 2:00 P.M. on the 3rd, thirty B-29s started huge fires in southwest Tokyo.

• • •

E*lectra News* (newspaper)
Electra, Texas
Thursday, December 7, 1944
More than thirty letters and telegrams as well as a phonographic reproduction were received by Mrs. Frank Fujita of 526 Chestnut St. Abilene and Mr. Frank Fujita, proprietor of the Electra Neon Sign Company, following the broadcast of a Christmas greeting by their son, Sgt. Frank Fujita Jr., who is a prisoner of war of the Japanese. Sgt. Fujita is a member of the famous "Lost Battalion" the 131st Field Artillery and was captured by the Japs after the fall of Corregidor. The message was undoubtedly authentic and Sgt. Fujita again, as in previous radio messages, asked for photos of his family, especially his "kid sister, Pat." He ask that greetings be sent to his buddies and their families and he mentioned his brother, Sgt. Herbert Fujita who is with the "Fighting Texas 36th" Division in France.[13]

One soldier in China who picked up the shortwave message which was copied verbatim and transcribed by telegram from the War Department Communications Service, wrote Mr. and Mrs. Fujita. Some of the amateur radio fans who heard the broadcast said the program following Sgt. Fujita's Christmas message was concluded by singing, "Goodnight Mother."

13. Herbert Fujita was still with the 442d RCT, but the all-*nisei* unit had recently been attached to the 36th Division. Duus, *Unlikely Liberators,* p. 196.

● ● ●

December 7, 1944, the third anniversary of Pearl Harbor, was certainly a day to be remembered. Tokyo was hit by four separate TNT raids and three big earthquakes.[14] Around the perimeter of our camp were three tall brick smokestacks. I was more frightened of these during an earthquake than I was of the bombing. When the quakes would start, I would stumble and stagger my way out of the building and go to the center of the court-yard where I could keep my eye on the stacks. It was unbelievable how wide an arc these stacks could swing in without breaking in two. If one did fall, I had no intention of being under it when it hit.

We had one or two air raids almost every day and each time that the sirens sounded the bombers came over Tokyo.[15] Because of the fire danger, the Japanese had us initiate a twenty-four-hour watch which was to be maintained by rotation of personnel. The person who had the watch for the day also had to maintain a daily diary. This was certainly a switch from all the other camps, where any written record was punishable by death. Personal diaries here would still draw the death penalty.

We were issued one Red Cross parcel each, and it was just like "Manna from Heaven." The four of us who had known about the parcels since last month had begun to wonder if the Japanese had taken them for them-selves. There were enough left from the original eighty-four boxes for us to have two more parcels each. On Christmas Eve five tons of coal were brought in for the bathhouse. We were refused permission to use any of it for our heating stoves.

Christmas Day 1944. We did not have to have *tenko* this morning and some slept a little later than usual. The weather was very cold and the warm bed was a good place to be, even if you were not sleeping. The Japanese

---

14. There was no attack on Tokyo on December 7. Four days earlier, however, about seventy B-29s had made another daylight raid on the city. Craven and Cate, *Army Air Forces,* V, p. 561; Kerr, *Flames Over Tokyo,* p. 110.

15. In most cases, these were photo reconnaissance F-13s. As stated above, bombing attacks on Tokyo during this period came on November 24, 27, 29–30 (night raid), and December 3.

Sgt. "Foo" Fujita

Merry
Xmas
1943

"Bunkwa"
Tokyo

All
YOURS

Inside and outside of the Christmas card made by Fujita and signed by the "Bunker Hill" men.

offered to take all who wanted to church and all but four went along. We were told to have a dinner party and so we killed three of our chickens and the Japanese furnished a little beef and veal.

On the 27th, fifty-three B-29s came over and lots of Zeros went up to oppose them. Five of them were shot down, and one of them fell very near our camp. For the first time, one of our B-29s was shot down within our range of vision, and we watched as two parachutes opened up and floated gently to the ground.[16]

For some time now we had been getting a small bun of bread instead of the maize and rice mixture. It was a welcome change, even though at times the bread was beginning to mold. The "Jeeps" had us start weighing every Saturday, and we had to keep a record of the weights, just as we did the daily diary. I had gained four pounds since we had gotten the Red Cross parcels a week before.

The last day of the month became the twenty-first day of raids this month, with up to four raids per day. Mickey and I decided that we would like to have a pot of sweet tea to sip on while we awaited the New Year to come in. We got out our key to the supply house and got some sugar. As we came out and locked the door we saw a shadowy figure steal over to the supply room from the front building. It was Ando, the "Jeep" in charge of the supply room, and he was stealing sugar and rice too.

Almost at the stroke of midnight a single B-29 came over and dropped a very large cannister-type bomb which seemed to burst open directly above our camp and scatter a lot of smaller bombs in every direction. Very quickly fires started in the neighborhood.[17] I was standing out in the courtyard watching the action when something whizzed past my head and hit the blacktop at my feet. I looked down and picked it up. It was a fuse from one of the ack-ack shells that was being fired at the plane.

January 1945. On the 5th we had a light snow and a lone B-29 came

16. Nearly forty B-29s made the attack, dropping a mixture of high explosive and incendiary bombs. Craven and Cate, *Army Air Forces,* V, pp. 564–65; Kerr, *Flames Over Tokyo,* p. 118.

17. B-29s were not in action on December 31st. The fires may have been started by a flare dropped by a reconnaissance plane.

over about 9 P.M., and another lone plane, or sortie came over on the 6th. It was a different story on the 9th, when forty B-29s came over. A lot of Zeros, or Zekes, as we called them, attacked the formation. One Zeke made a pass at a B-29 and set fire to one of its engines. No sooner he had attacked and begun to pull away than he was hit head-on by another Zeke that was attacking the same bomber. They made a terrible explosion. The B-29's engine was belching out a lot of smoke, but before it went out of sight, the fire was out. Altogether, six Zekes went down.[18]

We learned a new phrase from the radio, "*Keikai Keiho*," which turned out to be an alert instead of a warning. When the B-29s were bombing places other than Tokyo, they would give this alert in conjunction with the sirens.[19]

On the 11th, Mr. Domoto brought us some pork from the black market. He was not a bad sort and had brought us some beef and some milk from the black market before. We continued to have alerts and sorties. In view of the stepped-up bombing, I decided that I should choose a buddy to escape with me when the time came. I had studied everyone very closely and tried to analyze each as to how he might act or react under the imagined circumstances that would be encountered if and when my plans were put into effect.

I felt that it would certainly be a boon to have someone along who could speak Japanese. Sgt. Provoo and Cpl. Hoblitt both could speak the language fluently. I did not really consider Provoo because he was excitable and could easily go off the deep end. Then, too, because he had turned against our country I certainly could put no trust in him. Hoblitt too, I felt, was moody and excitable and might tend to be panicky in a tight spot. I liked Mickey very much and he certainly would be a good man to have with me in case we had to defend ourselves. He had enough guts for two

---

18. The planes on January 5th and 6th were probably F-13s. The attack on the 9th was made by seventy-two B-29s but high winds and clouds scattered them all over the Tokyo area and only 18 actually attacked the aircraft factory at which the raid was directed. Craven and Cate, *Army Air Forces*, V, p. 565; Kerr, *Flames Over Tokyo*, pp. 120–21

19. *Keikai keihō:* "precautionary alarm."

men, but for this reason I ruled him out for fear that he would tend to take unnecessary chances.

I finally decided that Maj. Cox was the one that I would like to have with me. I had to pick the right time and way to approach him. I spent some time in feeling him out, for he could certainly throw a kink into my plans if he were not agreeable. After deciding that he was the right man, I had the opportunity to be alone with him and so outlined my plans for escape to him. I told him that when the time arrived that I needed someone to get the camp C.O. to come into the courtyard at night where I would bushwhack him from behind, drag him into the bushes between buildings and put on his uniform, complete with sword. We would then install the general's flags and license plates on a small sedan that was usually parked in front of the main building. I would also put on the *kempeitai* arm band.

In the absence of street lights, I figured that Cox's white skin would not be noticed. I had the route to the mountains practically memorized, and would rely on the *kempeitai* captain's uniform to be sufficient to squelch any would-be questioner. I told Cox of the supplies and rations and knife that I had stashed. He was agreeable to make a try with me because if we had to put the plan into action the war situation would be such that the Japanese would be on the verge of killing all POWs and any chance for escape and survival would be preferred to passive slaughter. Cox agreed that we should not let anyone else in on the plan and that he would start laying aside any supplies that he could. I felt better now that I had someone who would make the escape attempt with me.

On the 18th I went to the *hoso* and broadcast my monthly message home. After the war I found that some of the other "Lost Battalion" mothers had been highly resentful towards my mother for hearing from me so often when they did not hear from their sons or husbands. They indicated, without saying so, that it was due to the fact that I was half Japanese that I was permitted to do this. This is understandable. If they had only known how frustrated I was because I had no news that I could send back. I felt it was better to say nothing about my outfit than to send back erroneous information.

The air raids continued and more areas of Tokyo were set ablaze, and more Zekes were downed.[20] On the 20th we were issued another Red Cross parcel each, or what was left of them. The parcels had been looted and the chocolate bars were missing and the cigarettes too. Several days earlier we had been issued some of the cigarettes in bulk, like maybe 10 cigarettes per man. When they were American cigarettes, it was obvious where they came from.

Almost ever since we had been at this camp we were each issued a bar of face soap, about the size of a motel room bar, every two months and a bar, a little bit larger, of laundry soap every three months. We still had not received our face soap for December 10th and we were out.

On the 29th Hoblitt came to me and said that he knew Cox and I were planning an escape and that he wanted in on it. This stunned me, for I thought that Cox and I had been successful in not arousing suspicion. I immediately wondered, if Hoblitt had guessed, if anyone else had also guessed. I told Hoblitt that he was dreaming, but that it might not be such a bad idea. I wondered if I had miscalculated Cox and that he had let the cat out of the bag.

Hoblitt said that no one else knew. He had become convinced that we planned an escape after having observed our actions and relationship over a period of time. He wasn't certain, but was so sure that he began to relate his opinion that we could not pull it off without someone who could speak Japanese. That is where he would come in. He said that he also could get us a dependable "outside contact" that could help with our get away and arrange hiding if it became necessary. I was very upset that he guessed

20. After the raid of January 9th, B-29s attacked Tokyo only once more that month. On January 27th, about sixty B-29s reached the Japanese capital and were met by an estimated 300 enemy fighters, the heaviest opposition encountered to that time. Clouds and high winds limited bombing effectiveness and the Japanese fighters downed nine B-29s, the highest B-29 loss yet experienced. The bombers destroyed possibly as many as one third of the Japanese planes. This was a serious blow to Japan's fighter defense force and never again did such a large number of fighters contest the skies with attacking B-29s. Kerr, *Flames Over Tokyo,* pp. 128–32; Craven and Cate, *Army Air Forces,* V, p. 568.

so accurately, and Cox and I decided that we had no alternative to taking him in. Since we had access to all the war news through the grapevine, we decided that when it became time to make the break that it would be by unanimous consent.

Smitty and I had both been suffering from dry beriberi for sometime now, and Hayasaka decided that he would give us some vitamin B shots, and he did. After several shots we were doing no better, and we found that he was shooting us with a camphor mixture instead of vitamin B.

In view of the increased bombing of Tokyo, the front office was considering moving us to a new camp in the countryside. I was both pleased and apprehensive with this news. I knew it was just a matter of time before we would be eliminated in the bombing, for, after all, we were only eight or nine blocks north of the Imperial Palace. On one of the raids the previous week, the railroad was bombed, as were a lot of the buildings near the *hoso*.

• • •

Telegram to Mr. and Mrs. Frank Fujita, Sr., from the War Department

Provost Marshal General
Washington, D.C.
January 19, 1945

Following enemy propaganda broadcast from Japan has been intercepted, Quote, Dear Mom and Dad: Hoping that this message finds everyone well and in good spirits. Did you have a big time over the holidays? I expected to get a parcel and some mail from you but did not. The last letter I received from home was written over a year ago and I'm quite eager for some late news concerning family and friends. You have quit mentioning Willie in your letters. Why? Tell the girls that if they marry any draft-dodgers they had better keep them on cold storage when I get back. How is Pat coming with her piano lessons? Please remember to enclose photographs in all your letters. Explain to all my buddies and friends that it is impossible for me to write to each and every one of them but that I send them my best wishes for the New Year. Well I'll say goodbye for this time and good luck to all. Your son, Sgt. Frank Fujita, Unquote. This broadcast supplements all previous reports. Stop.

Provost Marshal General

年月日	品 名	数 量	替	買入金額	支挑金額	借或袋	差引殘高

NOVEMBER

S	M	T	W	T	F	S
			1	2	3	4
5	6	7	8	9	10	11
12	13	14	15	16	17	18
19	20	21	22	23	24	25
26	27	28	29	30		

DECEMBER

S	M	T	W	T	F	S
					1	2
3	4	5	6	7	8	9
10	11	12	13	14	15	16
17	18	19	20	21	22	23
24	25	26	27	28	29	30
31						

AIR RAIDS

☐ ☑ = Movie — (I am projectionist)

= AIR RAID WARNING ONLY

= " " ALERT

or RED square = AIR RAID

= Number of Raids — minor

✚ = Red Cross parcels (refer to Diary)

④ = Number of cigarettes per man, issued

⊠ = Large raid   Ⓝ = loose tobacco issue

☆ = " "   ✝ = Our plane or planes shot down

★ = Major Raid

Page from Fujita's diary showing air raid calendar and key.

12

FIRE BOMBINGS OF TOKYO

February 1945–May 1945

February 1945. The sirens for an alert woke us up at 1:00 A.M. These sirens were a series of short blasts as opposed to the long, undulating wails of the air raid sirens. It began to snow just before daylight and continued for several hours until we received a total of about one and one-half inches. We had never been issued anything to burn in our heating stoves and, as always, the only heat in the camp was in the galley and the small hibachi in the work room. Only those who were actually writing or typing on the program were permitted to be in this room. In my duties as *benjo honcho* and cleanup man for the camp, I would get quite cold and in spite of the rules, I would go in and warm by the glowing charcoal. I was the one who had to start the fire in the morning and also the one who had to take out the ashes.

The camphor shots that Smitty and I were receiving for our dry beriberi were not doing us any good, but Hayasaka came over today and gave us another injection anyway. We were paid for January and since there was nothing other than black tea, crushed red pepper and vitamin B tablets that we could spend the money on, it began to build up. One night we had a poker game going and I wound up with a queen-high straight flush. I raised and was called and raised. This went on several times and all the other players dropped out except Donald Bruce, if I remember correctly. We bet back and forth until I ran out of money and could not call his next raise. Walter Odlin looked at my hand and said for me to go ahead and call and he would put up the money. It seemed that every one in camp was now gathered around Don and me and either giving me money to bet on or putting money into Bruce's pile. Finally, after what seemed to be a very long time, the betting stopped. Probably most of the yen in camp were now piled up on the table in front of us, and everyone was as excited as I was when I laid my cards down and started to reach for the money. The guys backing Donald began to cheer. I don't know what the odds are on this sort of thing happening, but Don laid down a royal flush. I had never seen a royal flush in a game before, and now here was one butting heads with my queen-high straight flush.

Under the circumstances money wasn't all that important. What we usually played for were cigarettes. These were more precious than gold. The cigarettes would become loose with continued handling and tobacco would fall out of them. If you did not win the hand, you had better not reach for the dregs. You would literally take your life in your own hands if cheating entered your mind. Sgt. Odlin did not inhale when he smoked and some of us were forever giving him a hard time about this. He would respond by lighting up a cigarette, taking a pull off of it, looking very smug and then blowing the smoke in our direction without having inhaled it.

The air raids seemed to have come to a stop[1] and I spent many pleasant hours in our recreation room, reading and listening to classical records. Harry Pearson asked if anyone would like to learn to knit. Some of us said that we would and began to try and scrounge up bits of string. I still had most of the baseball core left and I used it. I am sure that it must have been a comical sight to see these men sitting around knitting. Harry knew what he was doing and did a good job of teaching us how to "knit one and purl two." He taught us how to turn a heel and how to finish a toe. The socks that I made looked very good but I could not wear them. I had made my stitches too tight so there was very little stretch. I managed to get them

---

1. After the January 27th attack, Twentieth Air Force B-29s did not return to Tokyo for more than three weeks. E. Bartlett Kerr, *Flames Over Tokyo: The U.S. Army Air Forces' Incendiary Campaign Against Japan, 1944–1945* (New York: Donald I. Fine, 1991), p. 325.

on but when I tried to stand up, my feet felt as if they were in a vise and the more weight I would put on them the tighter they would bind. There was no way that I could wear them.

On the 8th we had the biggest snow that we had had yet—4 inches. This was Saturday, and the "Jeeps" had made a practice of holding a news conference for us each Saturday morning. We considered these our comedy hour, for they were so ridiculous. The *Nippon Times* was a newspaper that was printed in English all through the war, and it would be the usual source of news. We could normally—along with our grapevine—deduce the war situation from the stories of the war that it would print.

There would always be stories that would extol the virtues and daring skills of the dauntless Eagles (Japanese fighter pilots) who would do battle with the Americans. One such story went like this: "After running out of ammunition in a dog fight with an American, one of our vaunted Eagles flew his plane along side the enemy, and with not a thought about his own hunger, he threw his one remaining rice cake so hard at the enemy that his plane was destroyed." Another story in like circumstances: ". . . pulled out his pistol and pointed it at the enemy pilot and forced him to land behind Japanese lines."

The paper would also have a literary column that never failed to give us a laugh, like "Today I saw a butterfly. Yesterday there was an air raid." And then there would be a critical comment like: "This poem by So and So is generally considered to be a masterpiece."

On the 10th the sirens broke their seven-day silence and we had four separate photo reconnaissance flights, beginning at 10:15 A.M. and ending at 11:10 P.M. I also went to the *hoso* and read a poem on the jamboree. On our trip to and from the radio station, I noticed that more and more of the populace were giving us some very sullen looks. Smitty and I were getting camphor shots every other day for our dry beriberi. They still neither helped nor hurt.

Our bathtub had been broken for three weeks and we sure did miss the hot baths. Our bath soap was now two months overdue and laundry soap had been due seven days ago.

We nicknamed the recon plane "Photo Joe." He had been over every day for the last four days. On the 16th, air raids started at 7:00 A.M. and lasted all day. We were very excited, for the grapevine had it that there were three separate task forces off the coast of Japan. This info was at least partially true, for there were dive bombers involved in bombing something over on the west side of town. We could see them quite well from Bunker Hill, and we watched the planes as they dived time and again. I figured that the Bonin Islands were being invaded or softened up for invasion. There were one thousand U.S. planes over Japan that day.[2]

As I have mentioned before, we became quite good at interpreting the air-raid warnings on the radio. Maj. Cousens, Sgt. Provoo and Cpl. Hoblitt could all speak and understand Japanese and through them we learned how to interpret the warnings. The ever-present grapevine would fill us in on information that was not put on the airways.

The front office staff were almost frantic in their urging for more and better articles that could help bring about a mediated peace. I was sure glad that I no longer had an assigned place on the program.

The dry beriberi was pure hell, and as if that were not bad enough I had the "Tokyo Trots" again. The front office had evidently been informed again of my jubilation over the raids and of my frequent forecasts of the downfall of Japan, for they had ordered Hayasaka not to give me any more shots for the beriberi or medication for the diarrhea. They also withheld the mail that had come in for me, but they gave out what little there was to those others who had mail. I had a feeling that when the group was moved to the new camp in the country, I would not be taken along.

On the 16th our ration of five-to-one maize and rice was changed to three parts barley to two parts of rice. This was really good eating compared to the other. There wasn't much left of it to feed the animals. On the

2. On February 16th and 17th, in preparation for the American invasion of Iwo Jima, carrier planes from the Fifth Fleet's Task Force 58 attacked Japanese air facilities in the Tokyo area. Nearly 1,000 planes, primarily fighters, went after airfields on the 16th, while dive bombers hit aircraft factories and shipping in Tokyo Bay on the 17th. The Japanese managed to knock down about 60 American planes, as opposed to U.S. claims of more than 500 Japanese aircraft destroyed. These Japanese losses, even if exaggerated, were another serious blow to their air capabilities. Samuel Eliot Morison, *History of United States Naval Operations in World War II: Victory in the Pacific, 1945* (Boston: Little, Brown, 1960), pp. 20–25.

17th, Tokyo was dive-bombed again almost all day long and there was no opposition from Zeros or ack-ack either. I did not know if the Japanese figured that it was useless to try and ward off the attackers, if their fighter force had been destroyed, or if they were conserving their resources to be used in the forthcoming invasion of the homeland.

"Photo Joe" came over on the 18th and took pictures that must have whetted the appetite of the B-29s, for they started coming over at 2:45 P.M. the next day in what might have been the biggest raid to date. Two B-29s were shot down by Zeros, within our line of sight, and a number of Zeros hit the deck too. We found out that while the raid was going on in Tokyo our proposed new camp was being strafed, so the "Jeeps" decided that they would not move us there.[3] We each were issued a full Red Cross parcel. The good food that they contained certainly helped my beriberi and trots.

While we were watching the bombers blow up Tokyo, we saw five parachutists hit the silk and one of them landed very near us. One of the B-29s broke in half as it went down and the tail gunner kept firing as he fell. I thought then that was sure enough one "Die Hard" GI. I found out later that the guns were fired automatically and electronically and that the gunner was probably one of those who hit the silk.

The station crew brought back some information on some of the men from the "Lost Battalion." A ship that was bringing them to Japan was torpedoed and sunk. Many lives were lost, both Japanese and POWs. Pvt. Mickey Perez was on the other ship but was not killed. He was one of my machine gunners. Other E Battery men on the ship were drowned: Pvts. Edward Wisman and Ace Lawson. Sgt. Leon F. Sparkman of F Battery and several others from the battalion were drowned.

At first I thought that here was some recent news that I could put in my

3. On February 19th, as part of the pre-Iwo Jima support strikes, nearly 120 B-29s bombed Tokyo's port and urban areas. The strafing Fujita heard about had probably occurred on the 16th or 17th, since Task Force 58 left the Tokyo area on the night of the 17th. Wesley Frank Craven and James Lea Cate (eds.), *The Army Air Forces in World War II*, 7 vols. (Chicago: University of Chicago Press, 1948–58), V, 571, pp. 590–91; Morison, *Victory in the Pacific*, p. 25.

monthly message home, but as I had no confirmation of the event or the casualties, I decided that it would be best for all if I did not report it. The ship was supposed to have been sunk on 20 June 1943.[4]

The biggest snow to hit Tokyo in forty years came on the 22nd and it blanketed us with thirteen inches. It was beautiful, but I could not appreciate the beauty to the fullest when I was so cold. We had no raids on the 23rd but we had three on the 24th, morning, noon and night.

On Sunday morning, the 25th, we had two raids fairly early in the morning and then a big one began at 2:00 P.M. while a snow storm was in progress. There were fifteen flights of bombers. There must have been one hundred and fifty bombers plus around five hundred fighter planes.[5]

Huge fires were started and a vast area was burned out starting two blocks from us. Admiral Togo's shrine was destroyed. Some bombs fell inside the Imperial Palace grounds and a few buildings were destroyed. This scared the hell out of the Japanese, while at the same time they became very upset and angry because their Emperor had been threatened. We had to be very cautious in our dealings with them. Each day the raids would add to the agitation of many of the staff in the front office. This, coupled

4. Japanese vessels carrying prisoners of war did not normally bear the special markings required by international law. Consequently, a number of them were inadvertently sunk by American submarines or aircraft. The identity of the ship mentioned here is unknown. E. Bartlett Kerr, *Surrender and Survival: The Experience of American POWs in the Pacific, 1941–1945* (New York: William Morrow, 1985), passim.

5. The air raid alarms sounded in Tokyo on February 24th and early on the 25th were apparently caused by American reconnaissance flights, anticipated raids, or strikes against targets elsewhere. Around noon on February 25, however, Tokyo suffered its largest B-29 attack so far when for an hour and one half more than 170 of the big planes dropped incendiary bombs on about a square mile of the northern part of the city. No fighter escorts accompanied the bombers, since airstrips on Iwo Jima, from which long-range P-51s would later be flown, were not yet operational; planes from Task Force 58 were over central Honshu earlier that morning, but few reached Tokyo. Fortunately for the B-29s, bad weather and confusion kept almost all Japanese fighters on the ground. Kerr, *Flames Over Tokyo,* pp. 138–44; Craven and Cate, *Army Air Forces,* V, pp. 573, 594–95; Morison, *Victory in the Pacific,* p. 57; Ronald Schaffer, *Wings of Judgment: American Bombing in World War II* (New York: Oxford University Press, 1985), pp. 125–26.

with their paranoid fear of the task forces cruising off shore, caused me to be constantly on the alert for any sign that they were on the verge of eliminating the POWs. I remember only too well the threat that "the closer the Americans come to Tokyo, the closer we come to Death." That scenario seemed on the verge of being carried out.

Our water was off for several days after one of the raids and we had to carry water from about two blocks away. An armed guard went with us. After seeing the hateful stares of some of the people in the neighborhood, I was rather glad the guard was along. Not all the neighbors were resentful. In fact, some seemed quite friendly and were always polite. With the possibility of a contaminated water supply, we were all given smallpox vaccinations.

The attitude of the front office toward me had changed again and I was once more getting camphor shots. I never knew how I was going to be treated from day to day. Their attitude toward me ranged from benign tolerance, to ignoring me completely, to hateful and threatening.

On the 27th I went to the *hoso* and recorded a message to be broadcast on March the 1st. The message was to Ruby and Bowen Blankenship (part owners in a Fort Worth lumberyard) and to Charlie (a Chinese who operated the "Blue Star" restaurant there). Bowen was a brother to one of my fellow sergeants, O. T. Blankenship, when I was in First Battalion Headquarters Battery back in Camp Bowie, Texas. On weekends some of us would go to Fort Worth and enjoy the hospitality of Ruby and Bowen and we would always go to the "Blue Star" for Chinese food.

March 1945. One hundred and fifty B-29s raided Tokyo for two and one half hours, on the 4th, with both H.E. (high explosives) and incendiaries. On the next night, fourteen flights raided for two hours and also dropped H.E. and fire bombs.[6] These raids reminded me of the scenes in *Gone With The Wind* where Atlanta was burning. "Photo Joe" was the only plane over on the 8th after two days of no raids. I suppose it took our air units all the next day to evaluate the damage to Tokyo thus far, for again

6. On March 4, nearly 160 B-29s dropped high explosive bombs, but no incendiaries, in a daylight raid on Tokyo. There was no attack on the night of the 5th. Craven and Cate, *Army Air Forces*, V, p. 573; Kerr, *Flames Over Tokyo*, p. 325.

they did not put in an appearance until just past midnight on the 9th, when B-29s started coming over at very low altitudes from around fifteen hundred feet to eight thousand feet, and they dropped nothing but fire bombs. Almost instantly it seemed as if the entire city burst into flames. Fires created other fires and then their up-drafts would join and create monstrous "fire storms" that sent flames thousands of feet into the air. It was awesome.[7]

The day was Saturday and I suppose that the broadcasting business is like the theatre—"The Show Must Go On!" The usual Saturday Jamboree was put on and I went along to participate, mainly to see what Tokyo looked like. Everywhere I looked the city was still burning. The tram system was still operational and we could not see much of the destruction from the tram cars. The cars were not bursting at the seams with people now.

The rails that had been bombed before must have been repaired and the area around the radio station was still intact. The masses of bustling humanity were no longer in evidence and those who were, were solemn and apprehensive, and kept looking fearfully at the skies. The trip to town came off without a hitch, and as we returned to Bunker Hill, smoke seemed to be everywhere. A complete circle of fire was burning around us. The night before when the raid started in Tokyo, Nagoya was being burnt out, also.[8]

So much had been happening. I had a much harder time getting my diary out and making entries without being seen. I got a chance to talk with Maj. Cox and tell him that obviously the time for escape was rapidly approaching, and we agreed that we had better study the moves and actions of the Japanese very closely and be ready to take evasive action.

7. This was the first major incendiary raid against Japan and the most destructive of the entire war. Flying at low altitudes (between 5,000 and 9,000 feet), for more than three hours, 279 B-29s dropped nearly 2,000 tons of incendiaries on northeast Tokyo, destroying one-quarter of the city and killing about 85,000 people. Kerr, *Flames Over Tokyo*, pp. 148–214; Craven and Cate, *Army Air Forces*, V, 614–17.

8. The firebombing of Nagoya took place on the night of March 11–12, the night after the Tokyo raid, in approximately equal strength, but did less damage. Kerr, *Flames Over Tokyo*, pp. 215–16; Craven and Cate, *Army Air Forces*, V, pp. 618–19.

Having to make a run for it in broad daylight would gravely threaten our plan and could have made it impossible to carry out.

"Photo Joe" was back over on the 11th, but probably could not take many pictures because of the smoke. Our grapevine was running wild. Several of the guys had personal outside contacts at the *hoso* and Maj. Cousens and Capt. Ince of the "Zero Hour"[9] had their own contacts. All sources were giving unbelievable statistics on the Saturday raid: There were over 250,000 homes destroyed, more than 50,000 people killed and one million more left homeless, and thousands and thousands of buildings destroyed. There could not be much left of Tokyo. It was just a matter of time and we would be burned out, too. I sort of felt that the Air Force knew where our camp was located. The fact that we were located among some hospitals may also have accounted for our not being bombed.[10]

The destruction and casualty figures were staggering and my mind had difficulty in comprehending them. I tried to figure how many houses would be in a city block. Back in Abilene there would be an average of twelve houses to the block, but here in Tokyo the number would probably be twice that. I would then try to imagine the area that it would take for enough blocks to make up one thousand houses, and then the area it would take for two hundred and fifty thousand homes plus twenty thousand buildings. My mind balked at both the figures and the area.

I tried to feel compassion for these thousands of people who were being consumed in the fires, but at the same time I could not help but think of the monstrous crimes that the Japanese were committing on the prisoners of war and on the native populations wherever they held sway. I could still see, in my mind's eye, the horror pictures that came out of China when the Japanese were massacring thousands—raping, looting and using living human beings for sword and bayonet practice. I could not feel compassion for them.

I tried to feel sorry for them as noncombatants, but could not escape the fact that there are no such things when two nations are locked in

9. See Chapter 9, note 17.

10. American intelligence knew there were POW camps in and around Tokyo, but believed none were in the target area. Kerr, *Flames Over Tokyo*, p. 159.

total war. All the national energies are expended towards the total destruction of the enemy; the farmer enthusiastically grows the food to feed the factory workers and fighting men. The factory workers just as enthusiastically produce the wherewithal the warriors use to annihilate the enemy. The warrior himself is a culmination of the whole process. He is the implementer of the national will. The national government orchestrates the whole show, which operates as a single whole, with the warrior pulling the trigger or dropping the bomb. Everyone is a combatant.

We had had no air raids for a full week and on Sunday the 18th, I had to go out on a truck with Ando and a soldier to get some supplies. This was eight days since the big fire raid and large areas of Tokyo were still burning. The grapevine reported that this raid alone destroyed an area as large as Fort Worth. As we drove through the smoldering ruins it seemed that even that estimate was conservative. It was unbelievable that one hundred and thirty planes, our estimate of how many planes took part in that raid, could wreak so much damage.

The rest of the month went by very quietly except for three times when "Photo Joe" made a run. On the 24th Hoblitt met with Cox and me and said that he had established an outside contact that would work with us when the need arose. Since the Japanese were becoming more and more edgy this bit of news was welcome indeed. Of course the inevitable apprehensions assailed me: Could the contact be trusted now and when the time for escape came? Was he legitimate or was he a plant?

The B-29s had not been sitting idle. While they had left Tokyo alone, they finished destroying Nagoya and wiped out most of Osaka and Kobe.[11] The grapevine said that there was to be some sort of conference in San Francisco to consider the final phases of the war and to offer an ultimatum to Japan. We would sweat that out and see what happened.[12] I sent another message home on the 28th.

---

11. Following the big Tokyo raid, Nagoya, Osaka, and Kobe were all fire-bombed in night attacks and, when stocks of incendiaries were exhausted, Nagoya was hit again with high-explosive bombs. All three cities suffered extensive destruction. Craven and Cate, *Army Air Forces,* V, pp. 619–23; Kerr, *Flames Over Tokyo,* pp. 216–21, 224–25.

12. In response to invitations issued on March 5, 1945, to the original 1942 sig-

• • •

Telegram to Mr. and Mrs. Frank Fujita from the War Department

Provost Marshal General
Washington, D.C.
March 30, 1945
Following enemy propaganda from the Japanese government has been
intercepted, Quote, Hello, Mom and Dad, Spring is almost here and
we boys are eagerly looking forward to the nice warm sunshiny days. I
guess the cactus and BlueBonnets are beginning to bloom back there
about this time. I certainly wish I was there to see. It has been three
and a half years since I left and that is a long time to be away. I suppose
that all my old friends have forgotten me. The last letter that I received
was from you Mom and that was written two years ago. I haven't the
slightest idea of how any of you look now so please enclose photographs in all your future letters. Tell Pat to be sending some, too. Let
me know when all the girls get married. Mom, there is something I
would like you to do for me. Get a large, beautiful bouquet and send
it without return address to Dora. Well I will close and wish you all
the best of health and good luck. Until we meet again, this is your son
Frank. Sgt. Frank Fujita Jr. Unquote. This broadcast supplements all
previous reports. Stop.

Provost Marshal General

• • •

April 2, 1945. "*Keikai Keiho*" started shortly after 1:00 A.M. and warned
that twenty-five flights of bombers were coming. They bombed some-

---

natories of the United Nations Declaration, the UN Conference on International
Organization met in San Francisco from April 25 to June 26, 1945, to draft and sign the
UN Charter. While the conference issued no ultimatum to Japan, it laid the ground-
work for future international cooperation in many areas. Leland M. Goodrich, *The
United Nations,* (New York: Thomas Y. Crowell, 1959), Chap. 2.

thing about fifteen miles west of here and then "Photo Joe" came behind them to document the results. On the 4th, raids started at 1:00 A.M. and lasted for three and one half hours. They were dropping H.E. this time and were knocking out buildings that did not burn during the fire raids. The bombs were falling all over town and some came close enough to us to knock out some of our windows.[13]

The next two days belonged to "Photo Joe," but on the 7th, starting at 10:30 A.M. three large flights of B-29s plus a lot of P-51s began pounding the west side of town again, probably the Nakajima aircraft works and the huge Mitsubishi factories, or at least what was left of them.[14]

We were all out in the courtyard watching the "dog fights" between the P-51s and the Zeros and the front office crew also came out to watch. The atmosphere was such that each plane left a contrail in the sky and you could look up for many minutes after the fights and still see the action that took place. Each time that a fighter plane was shot down, the front office crew would cheer and shout "Banzai!" Then the plane would come spiraling down and when they came close enough where we could see the "fried eggs" on the wings, the office crew would let out a groan. After three Zeros came down within sight, there were no more "Banzais!"

The increased raids and their devastating effects had some far-reaching effects in the Japanese diet. The Koiso Cabinet resigned and a new one was formed by Adm. Suzuki.[15] On the morning of the 12th at 9:15, we

13. More than one hundred B-29s dropped high explosive bombs in the first hours of April 2; nearly seventy did the same on the 4th. Kit C. Carter and Robert Mueller, comps., *The Army Air Forces in World War II: Combat Chronology, 1941–1945* (Washington: Office of Air Force History, 1976), pp. 616–17; Kerr, *Flames Over Tokyo*, pp. 225, 326.

14. Over one hundred B-29s attacking Tokyo aircraft factories were accompanied for the first time by more than ninety P-51 fighter planes. Kerr, *Flames Over Tokyo*, pp. 225–26.

15. A more immediate cause was the American invasion of Okinawa, but the real basis of the resignation was Koiso's failed attempt to gain control of the Japanese military. Robert J. C. Butow, *Japan's Decision to Surrender* (Stanford: Stanford University Press, 1954), pp. 58–60.

were all loaded onto a truck and told that we were going on a picnic in the country near the place we were to have moved to. This at first frightened me, for I was expecting the worsening war situation at any time to drive the Japanese into acts of desperation such as disposing of all POWs. What a wonderful pretext a picnic would be for hauling us all to the country and executing us.

I was wanting very desperately to take my *hara kiri* knife with me in case this did turn into an execution. I would at least try to take some of the Japanese with me. However, I could not get my knife without exposing my hideaway and all that I had in it. Since there was nothing else that I could do, I crawled into the truck and took a position on the outside where I could jump and make a break for it if I had to. As it turned out, we really were taken on a picnic. Oh how the beautiful countryside brought home to me the agonies of confinement. The cherry trees were in full blossom and the birds were singing. The air was crisp and cool and the fresh, sweet smell of the country was truly exhilarating. After driving through the desolation of large sections of Tokyo, this was like entering into some sort of dream world.

We had no sooner arrived at the picnic area when the sirens began to wail and we could see flights of bombers going over Tokyo, dropping their wares, and unopposed fighter planes strafing at will. This area was on a small hill several miles west of town, and we could get a good view of a lot of the city. I was amazed that there was still so much of the city left after all the bombing. Very near were the bombed out aircraft factory and other buildings that must have been the targets for the raids we had been watching.[16] Uno had brought along a camera and he took some pictures of us. We took a picture of Smitty and me holding a canteen cup and a

16. In this attack about one hundred B-29s, escorted by an equal number of Iwo-based P-51s, just about completed destruction of the important Nakajima aircraft factory at Musashino in northwest Tokyo, a prime target since the beginning of the strategic air offensive. Clouds, high winds, and generally bad weather had frustrated many earlier attacks on the plant, but the cumulative effect of repeated bombings now ended production at Musashino. Craven and Cate, *Army Air Forces,* V, pp. 634, 648.

sake bottle. The "Jeeps" had opened a bottle of sake and shared it among all of us. Finally, Uno called for us to load up and head back to camp and we reluctantly complied.

The next day, which was the 13th, Mr. Domoto came over to our building, called us all together, and told us that President Roosevelt had died two days ago.[17] This was a terrible shock to me, for he was not only my beloved Commander-in-Chief but, I felt, one of America's greatest presidents. We Americans tore up one of our black-out curtains and made ourselves black arm bands to wear as a gesture of mourning. Mickey Parkyns joined us in this.

Streeter was in "hog's heaven" with this news and he made fun of us for mourning our president. He went around prancing with glee and spouting off that this was the best thing that could happen for America. I took all this I could stand and then grabbed him by the shirt front and shook him around a bit, and told him that if he did not knock it off that I was going to break his neck.

Just before midnight the sirens began to blow and what was probably our biggest raid yet started. The radios went crazy and we concluded that there were over four hundred bombers in this raid. They bombed from 11:30 to 3:00 the next morning. Again great portions of Tokyo burst into flame and this time they got a little closer to us. The city was burning up to within one block on the north and south sides of us, and three or four blocks on the east and west sides of us. That left us in the middle of a narrow strip of buildings that had not been destroyed.[18]

I took several parts in that day's jamboree and rode in the truck with the others to the *hoso*. Most everything between Bunker Hill and the Imperial Palace had been burned out. Some of the buildings within the palace grounds were gutted. We still had to bow to the palace when we passed it.

17. President Franklin D. Roosevelt died on the afternoon of April 12, 1945, (early April 13 in Tokyo) at Warm Springs, Georgia, of a cerebral hemorrhage. James MacGregor Burns, *Roosevelt: The Soldier of Freedom* (New York: Harcourt Brace Jovanovich, 1970), pp. 599–600.

18. About 330 B-29s firebombed a large area of northwest Tokyo, site of many armament plants, destroying over eleven square miles of the city. Craven and Cate, *Army Air Forces*, V, p. 636.

"Photo Joe" came over at 9:15 A.M. on the 15th and was followed that night by two hundred B-29s. They bombed southern Tokyo for three hours.[19] Once again vast fires broke out and it seemed that the entire southern skyline was on fire. Yesterday's raid had knocked out our water supply again and we were having to carry water from two blocks away. The hydrant that we had to use must have been the only one in service in the neighborhood, for each time we went after water there would be house-wives there, washing rice or vegetables. Our food was getting pretty bad and the portions were getting smaller. Our bread came to us all mouldy and when we would break it apart there was a stringy substance in it, a type of mold. Our vegetables are wilted and at times even rotted. Our face soap and laundry soap were seven months overdue.

Mr. Domoto came back over and brought a letter to Maj. Cox that Streeter had written to one of the staff officers in the front building. Cox was greatly alarmed, and that night he called a meeting of everyone in camp. He read the letter out loud. There was a faction in the front office that wanted to see us eliminated, and the person that Streeter had sent the letter to was one of these. Domoto had intercepted the letter and upon seeing the contents, knew that it would be detrimental to our welfare if it reached its destination as intended.

In the letter to the Japanese, Streeter had stated that of the twenty-five people in this camp, he was the only one who was truly cooperating with the Japanese in their effort to bring about a mediated peace with America. He stated that the rest of us were against the program, that we made fun of it, that we would sabotage the program if we could, and that we all should be killed. The reaction of the group to Streeter's letter was just short of violence. Maj. Cox declared that a "kangaroo court" was now in session and that Streeter would be tried for treason by his peers. He was tried and convicted of lending aid and comfort to an enemy nation dur-

---

19. On the night of April 15–16, some three hundred B-29s firebombed areas along the western shore of Tokyo Bay and burned out about eleven square miles from south-ern Tokyo to Yokohama. Stocks of incendiary bombs were now again exhausted, end-ing firebombing missions against Japan for several weeks. Ibid., p. 636; Kerr, *Flames Over Tokyo*, p. 226.

ing wartime and of promoting the execution of his fellow POWs. There was no sentence set and I became very agitated because of it. I demanded that he be sentenced to death, and that I would volunteer to be the executioner. I was in front of Streeter and livid with rage when I was making this demand and he felt sure that I was going to do him in right there on the spot. Cox said that any such action would probably bring about our own demise.

I felt that Streeter, now that his secretive effort to have us eliminated had been found out and thwarted, would go in person to the Japanese the next day and make his pitch, putting us all in mortal danger, especially me. I decided that if death or worse was going to be our lot because of Streeter that he had to be the one who was eliminated. I brought out my *hara kiri* knife that night. I crawled up in the canopy that ran along the west side of the courtyard behind the bathhouse and over to the front building. There was very little space in the rafter and it was hard to stay there. I was in a spot directly over the entrance to the latrine.

Anyone entering the *benjo* had to pass directly beneath me. I planned to bushwhack Streeter and then throw his body over the back wall and make it look like an accident, if possible. If he put up too much of a struggle I would have to knife him. The night was very cold and after a couple of hours of being terribly miserable I got down, put my knife away and went to bed. Providence was certainly watching over me by seeing that Streeter did not have to go to the restroom that night. I lay in my bed and was quite agitated at the thought of how close I came to being a murderer. I realized that if I were to be killed, it would be on account of my own hot-headedness and not on account of someone else's. Streeter's intercepted letter caused some more soul-searching by all, and bickering broke out as the "pots called the kettles black." Tempers flared and Cpl. Rickert and Steve Shattles fell to and had a bout of fisticuffs. I don't believe that either one of them had ever been in a fight before. They looked like two women trying to fight. Streeter surprised everyone by going to Cox and stating that he did not wish to write for the program any longer, and he asked the Japanese for a bodyguard.

With all the air activity we had not seen a movie, but finally on the 30th we were shown *A Night at the Opera* with the Marx Brothers. This was enjoyed by all and served to cool tempers down for a while at least.

We had not been able to watch any babies being born through the winter because they kept the hospital windows closed. One pretty day I walked around to the back of the building to see if anything was happening at the maternity hospital. I was standing there looking everything over when I noticed that there were nurses at almost every window in the upper floors and they were all giggling, I thought over me. I pulled myself up straight, smoothed my hair down and waved. Nothing happened; not a one waved back, but yet they were still looking and giggling. I figured that there must be something on our roof that was holding their interest so I went up to our bedroom, opened a window and crawled out to see just what was on the roof. There was nothing on the roof and still the nurses were looking out their windows and enjoying it. At last I saw what was holding their attention. There in the upper window of the long building on the east side of the courtyard was one of our men with his pants down, exposing himself to the nurses. He was well-endowed and had his penis in his hand, waving it back and forth while at the same time he was beckoning for the nurses to meet him below. It turned out that this trick had paid off for him, for almost every night he was going over the wall and making out with one or more of the nurses. How he managed this on our diet is beyond me.

May 1945. Boy! Did this month ever come in with good news. Ye Olde Grapevine declared that Germany had been defeated, Hitler had committed suicide and Mussolini had been murdered.[20] There was jubilation in camp over this bit of news. We speculated on how long it would take the U.S. to concentrate its full might against Japan and what would be the probable scenario for the conduct of the war when that happened. Would

---

20. Germany surrendered on May 7, 1945, and all fighting ceased on May 8, which was officially proclaimed V-E Day. Hitler had ended his life with a cyanide capsule on April 30 and Mussolini had been executed by Italian partisans two days earlier. Robert Goralski, *World War II Almanac, 1931–1945* (New York: G. P. Putnam's Sons, 1981), pp. 400–401, 404–405.

our forces try to destroy the country by bombing or would they resort to invasion? Would Russia declare war on Japan?

Even though the end of the war in Europe was cause for jubilation, that very fact caused our situation to become more critical. From all the experience that I had gained since the start of the war and during my incarceration as a POW concerning the Japanese ability to wage war and their deeply ingrained *Samurai* code of *Bushido,* I felt that the Japanese people would have to be annihilated to the last person if invasion should be the choice. We POWs, of course, would be the first casualties. The loss of life on both sides would be unprecedented.

We had had sorties or alarms every day, and on the 8th some bombers and P-51s came over town. We did not see or hear them drop any bombs, but some of the P-51s came directly over Bunker Hill.[21] I sure did want to wave something at them, but some of the front office staff were outside and I didn't dare get them upset.

The radio program for that day's "Humanity Calls" program was scrapped and our crew was ordered to write a special jamboree to celebrate the fall of Germany. We didn't quite know what to think about this celebration for the defeat of their ally—it was very strange indeed. We finally figured that they intended to use this jamboree to show America that they had not really been too enthusiastic about their pact with Germany and perhaps soften some hardline views about Japan. Whatever the motive the gang had a blast putting it on.

I did not participate in the program. It was my day to be air raid warden and keep the daily diary. With the fire raids coming so frequently, whoever had the warden job had to spend his time on the roof during raids in order to extinguish any sparks or firebrands that might land there. We had set a number of buckets of water on the roof for this purpose. Of course, there was nothing that we could do about a burning stick of napalm.

---

21. B-29s were over Honshu a few times during early May, possibly causing alerts in Tokyo but, except for dropping mines in Tokyo Bay on the 5th, the bombers did not again attack the capital city until late in the month. Separate P-51 sweeps during this period were also directed primarily against other targets. Carter and Mueller, *Combat Chronology,* pp. 643–54; Craven and Cate, *Army Air Forces,* V, p. 635.

This was the 9th of May, and one of the three days this month that we had not had "Photo Joe" or an alarm. The unaccustomed quiet added to the festive atmosphere of the day. The "Jeeps" surprised us even more by issuing us a ten pack of Skoki cigarettes and allowing us to watch most of *The Ghost Goes West* and *The Thin Man*.

I did not know what had gotten into the "Jeeps." They issued us another ten packs of cigarettes on the 11th and another one on the 14th I didn't remember ever having this many fags, and I treated myself to smoking a whole cigarette at one sitting. Normally, I would make a cigarette last two days. I would light one up and take three or four drags and then carefully put it out. We did not blow out the first puff that had the sulphur from the match, if we had a match. It's a wonder that we did not all develop serious lung problems. We would smother the cigarette in order not to lose any tobacco. Then when the cigarette got so small that it could not be held with the fingers, we would take a straw and bend it over and clamp the butt in it and smoke it to where there were only three or four strands of tobacco left. We would save these and when we had enough we would roll them into another cigarette.

Streeter's request not to write anymore for the program came to naught, for Cox did not have the authority to excuse him from writing and the "Jeeps" were just not about to lose their best and most prolific source of anti-American diatribe. He not only was still writing, but since his kangaroo courtsmartial he had convinced the front office that he should have his own program staffed with men of his own choosing.

He submitted a list of names of some of his cronies in Shanghai to be brought over to help him with his new program. I assumed that they were just as communistic in their thoughts and leanings as he was. Schenk and Dooley had become very friendly with Streeter and seemed to be in a huddle with him at every opportunity. I hadn't decided if I thought that they were becoming kindred spirits with him or if they felt sorry for him because no one would have anything to do with him.

1945

月 日 年	品　　名	数　量	替	買入金額	支拂金額	借又貸	差引殘高

June 7, 1945 ✶   Thursday
Sortie 11:40 A.M. Fag situation is kind of rugged – one pack of ten about every five or six days – I expect them to cut us completely off one of these days.

June 8, 1945 ✶
2 planes over at 12:00 noon

June 9, 1945 ✶
Sortie about 4:00 P.M. ∃ΓLΨ∩Δ had 3
bottles of tonsil water ⊐JΓ, V∃Γ<< , ∃ΓLΨ +
I drank it then drank burning alcohol from lamp, pretty good buzz. { From biological specimens

June 10, 1945 ✶✶
About 250 B-29's began raiding at 7:00 A.M.
Target airfields a few miles N.W. of here –H.E.
Smitty + I drank the rest of the wood alcohol.
plenty buzz, no bad effects. almost !

June 11, 1945 ✶✶
Sortie at 9:20 A.M. 10 flights around 10: A.M.
V<F□□<□F'V ⊓⊓⊓F⊐∃ today – Today Humanity
Calls + Postmans Calls Consolidated Program

13

NIGHT OF

ETHYL/METHYL

ALCOHOL

May 1945–July 1945

What time Maj. Cousens was in camp he seemed to always be in a huddle with Mr. Domoto. I did not like Cousens. His superior and haughty attitude chapped me no end. Whenever he talked with an enlisted man or a civilian, he made it quite obvious that out of the goodness of his heart he condescended to function below his level in order to talk with them. I never trusted him and Capt. Ince. I was always suspicious of them and their "Zero Hour" radio program.

I never found out what the format of their program was or what their relationship with the Japanese was that permitted them to live freely in the Dai Ichi Hotel and to dress in business suits prior to their coming to Bunker Hill. I could not shake the feeling that Maj. Cousens was a traitor. I had absolutely no proof of this, only my gut feeling. (After the war we met in San Francisco, where we were both called as witnesses in the "Tokyo Rose" trial, and I told him that the OSS or the FBI had my diary and in it I had said that I thought that he was a traitor. This did not seem to upset him and he told me to think nothing of it.) [1]

1. Once Maj. Tsuneishi had coerced Cousens, Ince, and Reyes into participating in Japanese propaganda programs (see p. 207, n.17)

About this time our "flasher" came down with appendicitis and was taken to one of the hospitals for an appendectomy. When he came back he showed us the incision that the Japanese doctor had made. I was surprised at how small the cut was, only about a half inch in length. I had seen scars on friends who had had an appendectomy back in the States and their scars were three and four inches long.

"Flasher" was relieved from any duty for a few days so that he could heal up. On the second day, however, his passion got the best of him and he went over the fence to meet one of the nurses. The fervor of his love efforts broke open his stitches. He was taken back to the hospital the next day to be sewn up again. Another day or two passed and he did the same thing over again. This time, after he was sewn up he decided to stay away from sex until his healing was complete.

Occasionally Mickey or Smitty would take the secret route into the front building and scout around to see if there was anything lying around that we could use. There were a number of cartons that contained four Red Cross individual parcels each and several that contained clothing. These boxes had been there for almost a week, but the "Jeeps" had made no mention of them. Even though we had been getting more cigarettes recently, Smitty and I decided that we would quit smoking until the first of June. Then when we resumed smoking we could smoke a little more frequently than usual.

Streeter's separate program must have been about ready to start, for he was moved out of camp. We were told that he was being taken to another

---

he treated them reasonably well. They were given private rooms, initially at the first class Dai Ichi Hotel and then at the somewhat less fancy Sanno Hotel, wore civilian clothes (although they would have preferred their uniforms), had special ration cards, and were paid the same amount as Japanese officers of equivalent rank (in a surprising adherence to the requirements of the Geneva Convention). They remained, however, under close surveillance and control. The treason trial of Iva Toguri, accused of being "Tokyo Rose," took place during the summer of 1949. All three men testified for the defense. Ivan Chapman, *Tokyo Calling: The Charles Cousens Case* (Sydney: Hale & Iremonger, 1990), pp. 105, 134–35, 145, 151, 172, 324–25, 329–31; Masayo Duus, *Tokyo Rose: Orphan of the Pacific* (Tokyo and New York: Kodansha International, 1979), pp. 72, 75, 97–223.

camp, but Mickey found that he was put into a room in the front building. Ten new POWs were brought in and put with him. They did not come from Hong Kong after all, or at least one of them did not; he came from my old camp Fukuoka #2.

These men were ragged and sick. Two of them died, one just after they arrived here. We were not supposed to know that these men were here and we were not given any opportunity to talk with them. We did manage to speak with them through the ceiling, and Mickey found out from the man from Nagasaki that there was no longer any work at the shipyards there, since they had been destroyed. They were forced to work in the hills. They had been reduced to two meals per day and the food was very bad. The frustration of the guards were taken out in almost continuous beatings.

We were permitted to see the movie *Mr. Smith Goes to Washington* on the 17th, the same night that the new men came into the front building.

Ozaki, one of the *nisei* from the front office, had always been friendly with us and had always helped us in any little way that he could by bringing us items from the outside and slipping us choice news items. He was always fearful for his own hide, and he would tell us how the homeland Japanese would treat them like outcasts and how they had the lowest priority for any rationed food or clothing.

We liked Ozaki and we missed him, for he had been gone for two or three weeks. He had been reassigned to another job somewhere else. On the night of the 19th he came back to camp and told us that Russia had given Japan some sort of ultimatum, and that Gen. Doolittle was vowing that he was going to drop 20,000 tons of TNT on Japan every day until they were destroyed or gave in.[2]

Seven of the new men were moved to another building a block or two from here, and three were left here in the front building with Streeter. All

2. On April 5, 1945, the Soviet Union announced that it would not renew its four-year-old Neutrality Pact with Japan, but indicated that the treaty would remain in effect until its agreed expiration date in April 1946. Robert J. C. Butow, *Japan's Decision to Surrender* (Stanford: Stanford University Press, 1954), pp. 58–59. Lt. Gen. Doolittle was at this time commanding the Eighth Air Force in Europe but would later return to the Pacific. Whether or not he actually made this statement is unclear.

of the time Streeter was in the front building he never knew that we were observing him almost nightly. We never heard him spout any of the anti-government crap to the new men. Perhaps he only did this in the daytime when we could not watch him.

More Red Cross parcels came in to the front. We were never issued what had come in before, and as it turned out, we were not to get any of this batch either. The boxes were opened and used by the "Jeeps" over a period of time.

With all the bombings and the roving task forces off Japan, we decided to have a lottery on the war's end. I chose my birthdate, 20 October. I missed it by over a month.

On May the 20th, an interpreter from the general's camp in Taiwan came into camp with some other visiting Japanese. He went around talking to some of our men, one of which was me. He asked me where I was captured, and when I told him Java he wanted to know if I was one of those Texans that was taken there. I told him that I was, and he told me that he had just been in a camp with some of my officers. He said that Col. Tharp and my captain were both at the general's camp. I was real excited about this, for here was some late news of some of our men that I could send back home.[3]

The interpreter said that he had left Taiwan in February. I thought that you just couldn't get any fresher news than this, and so in my June message home I sent this information along. After the war was over and I met these officers at our first Lost Battalion reunion (29 October 1945) in Wichita Falls, Texas, Col. Tharp jumped me out and said that I had caused him not to receive mail because he was not at the general's camp. I felt very bad about this. Our captain had evidently received his mail, for he was standing there and made no comment.

Smitty and Mickey were almost caught by one of the guards in the front building when they tried to sneak in to talk with Streeter's men. They

---

3. Most of the senior Allied officers were held at two or three camps on Taiwan. In November 1944, however, they were moved to northern Manchuria. E. Bartlett Kerr, *Surrender and Survival: The Experience of American POWs in the Pacific, 1941–1945* (New York: William Morrow, 1985), pp. 169–71, 107–108, 211–12.

made it back to their beds and crawled in just in the nick of time. The officer of the guards came bursting into our building yelling *"Tenko! Tenko!"* We all bailed out of bed and fell in at our normal place for *tenko,* and the guards were standing there with fixed bayonets. The officer counted noses and seemed genuinely surprised that everyone was there. He went down the line and counted us again. Finally, he dismissed us and stormed out of the room with the guards right behind him. This was a close call and there was no telling what the Japanese would have done had they found out that some of the POWs had been prowling through the front building. Then, too, we did not want any of the POWs other than we four to know how to get into the building.

There was still a lot of ill feeling within the group and the general tone of things seemed to indicate that this group would be split up. I really didn't know just exactly why we expected the split or who would be sent where. Several more big boxes of Red Cross parcels came into the front building. We had never received any of the last two shipments and so I thought we would probably not get any of this one.

On the 24th a total of four hundred planes bombed Tokyo for three hours, beginning at 1:30 in the morning. There seemed to be little damage compared to other big raids. We counted fifteen planes shot down, mostly by night fighters. We were unable to tell just what the downed planes were, bombers or night fighters. There were more search lights than I had ever seen before and the ack-acks were back into play again. The night fighters and the Zeros would fly right up into all the ack-ack bursts to attack the bombers. I am sure that a lot of them were shot down by their own guns.[4]

Photo Joe came over at 12:15 and again at 11:45 P.M.

I did not know the reasoning behind it, but all the men at Bunker Hill

---

4. In a major effort to complete the destruction of Tokyo, more than five hundred B-29s fire-bombed the area south of the Imperial Palace and along the western shore of Tokyo Bay. Although Japanese night fighters were relatively ineffective, anti-aircraft fire was heavy and downed a baker's dozen of the bombers. E. Bartlett Kerr, *Flames Over Tokyo: The U.S. Army Air Forces' Incendiary Campaign Against Japan, 1944–1945* (New York: Donald I. Fine, 1991), pp. 233–34; Wesley Frank Craven and James Lea Cate, *The Army Air Forces in World War II,* 7 vols. (Chicago: University of Chicago Press, 1948–58), V, p. 638.

were ordered to write their impressions about the previous day's raid. Photo Joe came over early that morning and again at 12:00 noon. We all sat around, speculating on why we had been ordered to write our impressions of the raid and how they planned on using them, and then at 10:00 P.M. we went to bed as usual. We had no sooner sacked out when the sirens started howling. This was the 25th day of May and at 10:15 P.M. the biggest raid that we had had to date started.

The raid lasted for three hours, and more than five hundred B-29s took part in it. There was more ack-ack than there had been on the last big raid. We saw three planes shot down before we were socked in with smoke. By 11:15 we could hardly see across the courtyard. Our eyes were burning and watering and we were gasping for air. Fire bombs were being dropped, and we thought that surely whatever was left of Tokyo was now going up in smoke. The raid got all of our utilities and when the water was off, the job of *benjo honcho* really became undesirable.[5]

• • •

A *bilene Reporter News*
Abilene, Texas
Dateline May 26, 1945
TOKYO "PRETTY LIVELY" REPORTS
SGT. FRANK FUJITA, JAPANESE PRISONER

5. Finishing the incendiary devastation begun two nights earlier, an almost equal force of B-29s fire-bombed an area even closer to the Imperial Palace, the site of financial, commercial, and government buildings, factories, and private dwellings. The Japanese were better prepared to meet this attack with searchlights, flares, and the heaviest concentration of anti-aircraft fire encountered so far. Twenty-six of the bombers went down, the most B-29s lost on a single raid during the entire war. Destruction was extremely heavy. Strong winds spread the conflagration rapidly, some of the flames even leaping the moat surrounding the palace to burn out large sections of the Imperial complex. An additional seventeen square miles of Tokyo was gutted, bringing to more than fifty-six square miles—over half the city—the area destroyed in the six incendiary attacks since February 25. Kerr, *Flames Over Tokyo,* pp. 234–53; Craven and Cate, *Army Air Forces,* V, pp, 638–39.

One of the most informative messages from a member of the famous Battery E, 131st field artillery, Japanese captives since the fall of Java, has come to the parents of Sgt. Frank Fujita, Abilenian.

A telegram giving the text of his broadcast, heard here last Tuesday, came this morning from the War Department. Hint of the American air raids on Tokyo where he is held was seen in the sergeant's statement, "Everyday life in a POW camp is generally dull and monotonous, but now things are getting pretty lively at times and I may have seen Roy (his friend Roy McCullough who is in the air force stationed in the states) several times from a worm's eye view." He wrote his mother last October he had received a letter from McCullough saying he was in air training.

Fujita told something of the broadcast system, saying "About six weeks have passed since our last message which was personally broadcasted. I hope you heard me. Without mail, it is hard to maintain a monthly schedule of messages, because the same old theme of 'hello,' 'I am well,' 'good bye,' begins to get a little tiresome after a dozen times."

Last broadcast from him was heard in January, and carried a New Years greeting as a clue to the time it was recorded. The sergeant concluded this broadcast with "goodbye and good luck until next month" indicating that would be when he next would be able to communicate.

He sent personal greetings to his friends, Wayne Cranmer and McCullough and asks if the Ben Keiths had any news of their son, a Battery E corporal. "He was my buddy in Java and I last saw him in Singapore."

Fujita said he would like to return a favor and say a few words for Robert Stubbs and Pete Evans but being away from them for a year and a half I don't know how they are.

During the months before Fujita was moved to Tokyo the only news of him came when he was mentioned by other Abilenians.

Even in prison the soldier is making some post war plans. A cartoonist, he declared, "I intend to take a long course in art when I get back."

Since last October two letters have come from him and he has been heard on eight or nine broadcasts.

• • •

On the 28th our utilities were back on and our routine returned to normal, or as normal as it could be under the circumstances. The previous Friday's raid had been the most destructive yet. Vast areas of the business and manufacturing districts were wiped out, as well as some buildings around the Imperial Palace, and a number of people there were killed.

Those areas that effected us seemed to lead a charmed existence, for they never seemed to be destroyed. Our camp and its immediate area were still here. Our radio crew still managed to get to the *hoso* every day, and the radio station JOAK and its immediate surroundings were still intact.

On Monday the 29th after a couple of earlier sorties, about four hundred B-29s and B-24s with some P-51s raided oil refineries and storage tanks to the south of us. The intense black smoke that billowed up blocked the entire southern sky. There were a couple of POW camps in that area and we learned that a number of POWs were killed in this raid.[6]

The days passed with daily flights by Photo Joe and weather planes and the numerous target areas around town for the most part had burned themselves out. The situation had caused some reevaluation of program priorities, and the front office decided to eliminate the "Postman Calls" program as a separate entity and incorporate it into the "Humanity Calls" program.

The obvious uneasiness of the front office staff only fanned the flames of tension that now were waxing hotter and hotter in our own camp. No longer were the participants on the radio as willing or enthusiastic about going to the radio station. Every day those who were to participate in the program were given a mimeographed transcript of the program so that they could follow along and know when they were to get into the act. Through the years that the *Hi no Maru* Hour and the "Humanity Calls"

6. More than 450 B-29s escorted by over one hundred P-51s made a punishing incendiary raid on Yokohama, nearly 20 miles south of Tokyo, burning out about one third of the city. No B-24s participated in this raid. Craven and Cate, *Army Air Forces,* V, pp. 639–40; Kerr, *Flames Over Tokyo,* p. 257.

programs had been on the air, I had been saving the transcripts that I felt might contain something that some or all of us might have to answer for when the war was over, and had them secreted with my dairy in the wall.

We had no option of whether to write or not to write, for the threat that our lives "would not be guaranteed" if we did not was very real and always present. However, some of the writings, I felt, could have been worded differently and could have been produced less willingly. The Japanese would, at times, inject their own verbage into someone's writing, and in that case there was nothing the writer could do except object. In any case I did not intend to reap any sort of punishment from some future board of inquiry because of something that someone else had said.

On the second floor of the front building there was a very large collection of biological specimens. Some were stuffed, some were skeletons and some were pickled. By far the most numerous were the pickled specimens, containing everything from insects to human organs and embryos. Some of these were pickled in formaldehyde and some were pickled in alcohol.

One evening Mickey Parkyns told Freddy Smith, Darwin Dodds and me that he had found three small bottles of alcohol in the former lab and wondered if there was any way that we could determine if the alcohol was ethyl or methyl. It sure would be nice to have a drink. We all immediately surmised that it surely must be wood, or methyl. We went over to our library and dug out the encyclopedia and dictionary and looked it up. Every thing that we could find on methyl alcohol said that it was deadly poisonous when ingested. It seemed that we all had heard that if methyl alcohol were strained through bread that the bread would remove the methyl and the remainder could be drunk. Our actions from that point on could not be described as anything other than stupid. Here we were, four full-grown men, well into our fourth year as prisoners of war and on the brink of the war coming to an end, and we were actually intending to drink this methyl alcohol knowing full well that it might kill us.

After convincing ourselves that bread would do the trick, the problem was now to find a piece of bread. After asking most of the men in camp if they might have any bread stashed back and being told no, we went back to Smitty's room in the long building and were bemoaning the fact that we had no bread. After a while Mickey said that he had not been feeling well that day at noon and had eaten only half of his bread bun. We all immediately began to con him out of the remaining half.

Mickey went back over to his bed space, got the bread, and brought it back to Smitty's room. We took the half bun, pinched out a hole in the center of it, and gave the pinch to Mickey. We then held the bread over a coffee cup and began to pour alcohol from one of the three-ounce bottles. We were licking our chops and mentally sampling the drippings. The bread was very heavy, with a dense texture, and as it began to absorb the alcohol it started swelling. We emptied the entire bottle into the bun, and still none had begun to drip out. We opened another bottle and began to pour that into the thirsty piece of bread. The bun continued to swell. We had poured almost all of this bottle into it before any started to drip out.

Maybe a fifth of the last bottle dripped out. We decided that we would wait until the last bottle dripped through before we divided it up. Finally the last bottle was emptied. When the bun stopped dripping, we threw the bloated bun out the window and thought perhaps Brownie, Whitie, or Buck would eat it.

We divided the drippings four ways and we made a toast to the war's end. Boy! Was that stuff ever rancid. There wasn't any way that we could drink that "as is." Smitty had a stick of pomade, a highly scented wax that the Japanese used for hair dressing, and since it smelled so good he thought that it might flavor the alcohol enough to make it drinkable. We each shaved some of it into our cup, where it was instantly dissolved. It did not improve the taste a great deal but we decided that it was at least drinkable.

We sipped away and laughingly compared the stuff to other really bad drinks that we had run across in the past. Either the potency of the alcohol or the deprived state of our physical conditions caused immediate reaction to the drink. We began giggling like a bunch of kids, and everything that was said seemed to be extraordinarily funny. Soon our drink was gone and Mickey and Smitty decided to slip back into the front building and get some more. When they got there the "Jeep" guard had changed, and the new guard was in a position to block their entrance.

The little that we drank had given us a good enough buzz to make us want some more. Since that was now impossible we had to think of something else. While Smitty was outside he noticed that the piece of bread had not been touched by any of the animals. After discussing this a bit we decided that we would bring the bread inside. The bun was now about twice its original size, and we cut it into four equal pieces. We each took a piece and squeezed the alcohol from it, mixed it with the pomade and drank it. Well, the old saying that I had heard all my life, "The Lord looks after drunks and damn fools" must be true, for at this time we fit both categories. I still find it hard to believe we were that stupid. None of us suffered any ill effects. The alcohol must have been ethyl to begin with or the pomade buffered the methyl, rendering it harmless, or perhaps the old bread tale was true.

On the 10th of June, about 250 bombers dropped H.E. on air fields northwest of here. On the 11th there was more bombing by ten flights of bombers.[7] Streeter's new program started on that day, probably taking the time slot that "The Postman Calls" had. The latter was incorporated into the "Humanity Calls" program. I went to the *hoso* in order to broadcast my own message home. This was the message that I sent the information about Col. Tharp and our captain in. As we were entering the studio, we saw a woman standing in the hallway talking to a man. Parkyns told me that she was Tokyo Rose. At this point in time, I knew almost nothing about Tokyo Rose.[8]

On the 16th a very strange thing happened. A single B-29 came over Tokyo and dropped something that both looked and sounded like a sheet of tin. There was never an explosion, nor was the plane followed by a bomber force. I do not know what it was unless it had something to do with jamming radar. I also received two letters from home, dated

7. About 280 B-29s bombed sites in central Honshu, some near Tokyo but none in the capital city itself, on June 10. There do not appear to have been any raids on June 11. Craven and Cate, *Army Air Forces,* V, p. 651; Kerr, *Flames Over Tokyo,* p. 329; Kit C. Carter and Robert Mueller, comps. *The Army Air Forces in World War II: Combat Chronology* (Washington: Office of Air Force History, 1976), p. 661.

8. There was no single "Tokyo Rose." At least a dozen *nisei* women participated in the propaganda broadcasts including, evidently, the woman mentioned here. Duus, *Tokyo Rose,* p. 158, et passim; Chapman, *Tokyo Calling,* Chaps. 15–26, passim.

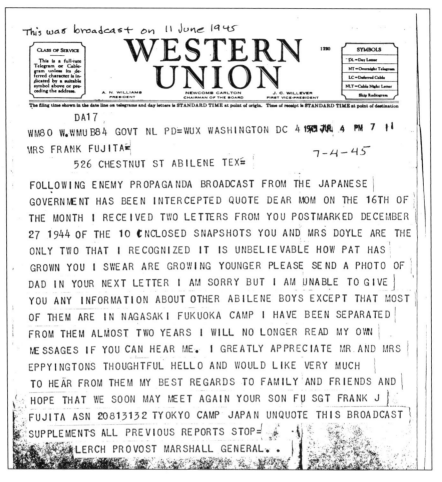

This was broadcast on 11 June 1945

WESTERN UNION

DA17

WM80 W.WMU B84 GOVT NL PD=WUX WASHINGTON DC 4 1945 JUL 4 PM 7 11

MRS FRANK FUJITA=

      526 CHESTNUT ST ABILENE TEX=

7-4-45

FOLLOWING ENEMY PROPAGANDA BROADCAST FROM THE JAPANESE
GOVERNMENT HAS BEEN INTERCEPTED QUOTE DEAR MOM ON THE 16TH OF
THE MONTH I RECEIVED TWO LETTERS FROM YOU POSTMARKED DECEMBER
27 1944 OF THE 10 ENCLOSED SNAPSHOTS YOU AND MRS DOYLE ARE THE
ONLY TWO THAT I RECOGNIZED IT IS UNBELIEVABLE HOW PAT HAS
GROWN YOU I SWEAR ARE GROWING YOUNGER PLEASE SEND A PHOTO OF
DAD IN YOUR NEXT LETTER I AM SORRY BUT I AM UNABLE TO GIVE
YOU ANY INFORMATION ABOUT OTHER ABILENE BOYS EXCEPT THAT MOST
OF THEM ARE IN NAGASAKI FUKUOKA CAMP I HAVE BEEN SEPARATED
FROM THEM ALMOST TWO YEARS I WILL NO LONGER READ MY OWN
MESSAGES IF YOU CAN HEAR ME. I GREATLY APPRECIATE MR AND MRS
EPPYINGTONS THOUGHTFUL HELLO AND WOULD LIKE VERY MUCH
TO HEAR FROM THEM MY BEST REGARDS TO FAMILY AND FRIENDS AND
HOPE THAT WE SOON MAY MEET AGAIN YOUR SON FU SGT FRANK J
FUJITA ASN 20813132 TYOKYO CAMP JAPAN UNQUOTE THIS BROADCAST
SUPPLEMENTS ALL PREVIOUS REPORTS STOP=
LERCH PROVOST MARSHALL GENERAL. .

Telegram received by Mrs. Frank Fujita from Provost Marshall General concerning an intercepted broadcast by Frank Fujita, Jr.

27 December 1944, six months previously. There were ten photos of the family and I was surprised, for I did not recognize my sisters.

On the 17th the "Jeeps" gave us what was left of fifteen personal parcels that they said belonged to dead POWs. They had been looted and the guys that they had been intended for were probably still alive somewhere in the far east. The names had been removed from the parcels. We were given five cigarettes each. Murayama and Go of the front office staff were called to the colors this week. I was working on a colored pencil portrait of Smitty, which looked pretty good. We got to see *The Rains Came* on the 21st.

On the 24th Maj. Cox inaugurated a more or less military routine in camp. This didn't last until the water got hot. Cox was not a favorite person of the Japanese, nor was he liked too well by Maj. Cousens. It was obvious that Cousens did not like the idea of having to answer to someone of his own rank, and an American at that. He obviously complained to Mr. Domoto about it.

The next day immediately after the noon meal, Domoto came over and called a general meeting and all hands had to attend, including the galley crew. Domoto opened the meeting by stating that he was removing Maj. Cox as camp C.O. and was replacing him with Maj. Cousens. With this bit of information the entry in my diary for that day was that "We could now stand by for the shit!"

D.M. (we always referred to Domoto as D.M. among ourselves) then said that Maj. Cousens would answer to him and that the rest of us, regardless of rank or nationality or whether we were military or civilian, would have to obey any orders given by Maj. Cousens. He then called out Sgt. John Provoo, chewed him out royally and accused him of being a double-dealing queer. This was the second time that a Japanese wheel had chewed him out in front of every one. The first time was in Omori camp on the very first day he arrived in Tokyo. In both instances it was obvious that the Japanese detested him.

D.M. then accused Pvt. Jimmy Martinez of being loose mouthed and of talking out of place, and ended the meeting by saying that the Propaganda Branch of the Army would be taking over control of all our broadcasting activities. I had thought all along that the Army was running the show.[9] After the meeting I cornered Maj. Cousens and asked him what was the score on Jim. He said that Jim was supposed to have said something that was detrimental to the group, but did not know what it was. I then went

9. Fujita was right. The army had in effect been running the propaganda broadcasts for some time, despite an earlier organizational structure that theoretically gave the Foreign Ministry and other agencies a voice in setting policy. Duus, *Tokyo Rose,* pp. 65–66, et passim.

to Jim and jumped him out and told him that since he was here because of me, that I was responsible for anything that he might do or say and I damn sure wanted to know what he had said. He assured me that he had never spoken with D.M. or Hayasaka about anything except food. The Spanish radio program had never gotten off the ground floor, so Jim and Ramon both worked in the galley.

Sgt. Provoo's relationship with the Japanese in the front office and at the radio station, too, was suspect to me. For many months he was very sincere in his efforts on the program. He was excitable and worried much about his post-war fate back home. He hated the regimentation of the army, and the military notion that an officer was superior to him was something that he could hardly cope with. He was intelligent, excitable and tended to go off the deep end easily. He was moody and sneaky and was someone that I did not trust. I felt that he would go to the Japanese if he ever found out about my plans for escape.

The physical act of escaping from our camp had never presented a problem. The problem was where to go and what to do once you were outside. The bombings were creating large areas that were denuded of any houses, buildings or vegetation and therefore one would be exposed for long distances if an escape was attempted during daylight hours.

Cousens appointed Capt. Ince to be the camp Adjutant and he in turn took Cpl. Hoblitt as his "dog robber" or flunky. Sgt. Light was designated the camp First Sergeant. We were issued a small amount of loose tobacco. We had started calling the job of fire warden and keeper of the daily diary, "C.Q."

We were issued four cigarettes each on the 4th, and on the 5th we received typhoid shots. Each time that we were to get shots of any kind, I could not help but think how easy it would be for the "Jeeps" to eliminate us with some lethal substance instead. The 5th always brought back memories of my meeting Willie in Fort Worth and the recollection would make me blue and make me think of how barren our existence was without any female contact or influence whatever.

On the 7th, Mr. Otaka from the front office brought us three pounds of butter that he had purchased on the black market. I had never realized that butter tasted so delicious before. There were lots of planes around on the 8th: B-29s, B-24s and P-51s.[10] I had been doing lots of reading and most of it was heavy stuff. One very thick book with small type had kept me occupied for months. It was on the history of man and his world and was entitled *Man's Own Show—Civilization* by George A. Dorsey. This one volume opened my eyes to many areas that I had never even dreamed of before and created in me a lasting thirst for knowledge.

The old wind-up victrola afforded me many hours of pleasant listening. I never tired of hearing Maria Eggert sing "Ave Maria," and Listz's "Hungarian Rhapsody #2" was now one of my favorites, as well as Beethoven's Fifth and Ninth symphonies and his "Moonlight Sonata."

We had a new military man take over the command of the guards, a Maj. Hifumi. He came over today and inspected our quarters and made himself known to us. He did not seem like a bad sort, and we decided if we did not see any more of him than we had of the other guard commanders, then we would see very little of him.

On the 10th we had air raids all day long and three of them were big raids. Something new had been added to these raids. In addition to the bombers there were a lot of P-51s and the first appearance of carrier planes—F4Us, F4Fs, and SBDs. We were sure thrilled at the sight of these planes. They were bombing, strafing and dive bombing the airfield west of town. There must have been over one thousand planes in on the action that day.[11]

Photo Joe was over on the 11th and 12th, and then immediately after midnight on the 13th, one hundred B-29s dropped a lot of heavy stuff on something to the south of town.[12] On the 14th we received our second

10. No bombers were involved, but more than one hundred Iwo-based P-51s attacked targets in areas near, but not in, Tokyo. Carter and Mueller, *Combat Chronology*, p. 672.

11. These planes were from Task Force 38, in position about 150 miles southeast of Tokyo, and were relatively unopposed. Very few P-51s, if any, were in the area. Samuel Eliot Morison, *History of United States Naval Operations in World War II: Victory in the Pacific* (Boston: Little, Brown, 1960), pp. 310–11, 315; Carter and Mueller, *Combat Chronology*, p. 673.

12. On the night of July 12–13, between fifty and sixty B-29s bombed Kawasaki,

shots in the typhoid series and also got seven cigarettes each. For some reason the Japanese had been giving us more cigarettes. We were now averaging about two fags daily. The front office called me over and had me run a movie for them. Their projectionist was not around. I talked to Uno and Mr. Domoto about me running movies for the POWs and it began to look favorable.

On the 14th, Dar Dodds, Mick Parkyns and myself were put on a truck and told that we were going after coal. Our bath had at last been fixed. We went about five miles or more to a coal dump, through what was left of Tokyo. We had seen destruction while going to the radio station and when we were taken out of town on the picnic. We had been taken aback at all the damage we had seen, but there was no way that we could have been prepared to see what we saw on this trip.

The route that the truck took to the coal yard resembled a gigantic graveyard more than the world's third largest city. Every direction that we looked there was nothing as far as the eye could see except iron safes and brick smokestacks of all sizes. It was eerie to see them rise out of the ashes, looking for all the world like headstones, and truly that is exactly what they were, monuments to the hundreds of thousands of people who had perished there and were now a part of the ashes that were piled silently everywhere.

When we arrived at the coal yard, there were still some plants and blast furnaces as well as some other buildings, and right in the middle of the complex, next to a gas plant, was a POW camp. The truck parked on the outside of the fence that surrounded the camp. We were not permitted to talk with the prisoners on the other side. We managed, however, to find out that there were between four and five hundred POWs there and that they were American and English.

We finally got our coal loaded and headed back for Bunker Hill. As we drove back through the ruin and desolation, the smouldering and smoking areas, added to the safes and smoke stacks coming through the ashes, lent an ethereal quality to the vista. As we approached the Bunka district, with

just south of Tokyo. Carter and Mueller, *Combat Chronology*, p. 674; Kerr, *Flames Over Tokyo*, p. 332.

our camp and the hospitals still standing, it looked like an oasis in a desert of ashes.

It seemed that the sirens howled every night, all night long. On the 15th we had three sorties beginning at three in the morning. Three B-29s and two B-24s came over at 9:30 A.M. but did not drop anything that we could see or hear. On the 16th we had three sorties and the one at half past noon dropped leaflets or pamphlets.[13] We did not find out what sort of message they contained. Our noon chow was one bread bun per man and nothing else. They were mildewed and almost inedible. There was a very small amount of *miso,* a fermented soybean paste, mixed with some parched soybeans, and we drew lots to see who would share this. I was one of the four lucky ones to draw out. Cigarettes were now back down to one per day.

We awoke on the 17th to the sirens but there was no raid. There was a light rain falling which continued all day long. Maj. Cox, Lt. Wisener and myself were taken by truck to the new location we were to move to in the country, about two miles from where we had been taken for the picnic. There was one building on the site occupied by a troop of cavalry. This meant that we could not move in as long as they were there. The countryside was beautiful and there were lots of peach orchards. We stopped along the way and were allowed to buy some peaches. They were big and ripe and cost two yen for eight pounds. These same peaches in town would bring fifty or sixty yen for eight pounds on the black market. By the time we got back to camp we were soaked to the skin and were quite miserable.

Just past noon on the 18th a plane came over Tokyo and dropped more leaflets. No sooner had it disappeared than the sirens began again and they blew continuously until 5:00 P.M. There was a task force off Chiba shelling the naval bases at Yokosuka and Futsu, which guarded the entrance to Tokyo bay. We could hear the detonations of the big shells and bombs.[14]

---

13. During this period, B-29s made frequent leaflet drops on many Japanese cities. The leaflets urged Japan to surrender, emphasized the inability of Japanese leaders to protect the people, or warned of imminent raids on specific cities. No B-24s were over Tokyo on July 15 or 16. Kerr, *Flames Over Tokyo,* pp. 265–67; Craven and Cate, *Army Air Forces,* V, pp. 656–67; Carter and Mueller, *Combat Chronology,* pp. 675–76.

14. In mid-July American naval units swept up and down the Pacific spheres of

On the 20th, the downtown railroad station was knocked out with five hundred pounders.[15] On this day I also received six letters from Mom and at long last I heard news of both Willie and Dora. Willie had married and Dora was supposed to write me. After all these long years of using these two as my straws to cling to, to preserve my sanity and my hopes for a future that most of the time did not seem meant for me, these dreams were merging into the real present.

I never received the letter from Dora, but the expectation made the remainder of the war go much easier. After the war, a mutual friend told me that she had been happily married and had a son. Perhaps she never wrote me because she was fearful that that news would be psychologically damaging to me; indeed it probably would have been, even though our whole relationship was a product of my own imagination.

Mom's letters also told me of the death of Vic Cranmer, the father of my lifelong friend Wayne. Wayne and I had met in the first grade in 1927 back in El Reno, Oklahoma. We had spent many days and nights together at each other's homes over the years and Vic was very dear to me.

We had had no big raids in our part of Tokyo for several days but we could hear the massive shelling of Ibaraki.[16] It seemed strange indeed to hear all the detonations and not to hear a lot of planes at the same time. On the 25th there was a big raid on Kawasaki and we had one plane shot down and another was leaving a trail of smoke as he disappeared.[17] I got a chance to write a letter today, also, and I wrote it to Dora. We were

---

Honshu and Hokkaido, bombarding selected targets and also attacking from the air. Air strikes on the 17th against Tokyo were thwarted by bad weather but on the 18th carrier planes made heavy attacks on Yokosuka and other targets at the entrance to Tokyo Bay. That night, also, American cruisers shelled the tip of the Chiba Peninsula. Morison, *Victory in the Pacific*, pp. 310–16.

15. This may have occurred earlier, since no American planes raided Tokyo on July 20th.

16. This is apparently a reference to the night of July 18–19, after which Allied naval units left the Tokyo Bay area. Ibid., pp. 315–16.

17. This was a night attack by seventy-five B-29s. Carter and Mueller, *Combat Chronology*, p. 680.

allowed to send a radio message each month and write a letter about every three months.

On the 26th we were issued ten cigarettes each, and before the day was over we were issued six American Red Cross parcels for twenty-four of us. Streeter and his four men got one parcel. The Japanese kept four for themselves and five were missing out of the original sixteen parcels that we knew had been brought into camp.

Brownie, the pup, died and I skinned him and wanted to tan his hide and make something out of it, but I was unable to get anything to tan it with and so had to dispose of it.

On the 28th there seemed to be a lot of unusual activity going on at the front office, and we could tell by the actions of the Japanese we dealt with that something was in the wind. Finally, the grapevine came through with the information that some sort of peace offer or ultimatum had been offered to Japan and a response was being considered.[18]

On the 30th there were big raids going around the clock, all around Tokyo and it seemed there were a thousand planes or more taking part in the raids.[19] Since none of them came directly over Tokyo, my assessment of Tokyo after our trip for coal that there was nothing left of Tokyo to bomb must have been correct. The month ended with three trips by Photo Joe and no further word about the peace offer.

18. On July 26, 1945, the Allies issued the Potsdam Declaration, calling on Japan to surrender or face "prompt and utter destruction." Japan's statement, two days later, that she would "ignore" the declaration was taken as a rejection by the United States. Butow, *Japan's Decision to Surrender,* pp. 142–49, 243–44.

19. There is no record of any raids in the Tokyo area on July 30. On the 28th, however, nearly 150 Iwo-based P-51s had attacked airfields and other targets in a broad zone around the Japanese capital. Carter and Mueller, *Combat Chronology,* pp. 681–82.

1945

年月日	品	名	数	量	替	買入金額	支拂金額	借或貸	差引殘高

August 11 Saturday ★☆☆☆★★

Two sorties in morning — I think by the end of next month will be blown to hell or on our way home. 11:30 A.M. I just heard some real *Hot dope* and some real *American and Saipan Radio*...

...what if Japan does not kick in by midnight Tokyo and it's near vacinity will be distroyed with Aatomic bombs a 72 hour armistice was declared last night the Japanese have sent terms and are awaiting answers.

Well after almost 4 years our fate is to be decided within the next few hours. We become free men or dead men in two days. If we are to be free we will emerge emaciated, weary fragments of humanity; endowed with nothing but a into a strange world.

Page from Fujita's diary showing both his code and his translation.

14

JAPAN SURRENDERS

August 1945

August. What surely must be the biggest raid yet started at 8:00 P.M. last night and lasted until 3:00 this morning. The air in every direction was filled with the droning of hundreds and hundreds of bombers. They seemed to be everywhere except over Tokyo. All the surrounding areas were being obliterated; Chiba Peninsula, Ibaraki, Izu, Boso and Shikoku were being heavily pounded and Kawasaki, fifteen miles south of us, was bombed from 10:00 P.M. until 3:00 A.M. There were ten POWs killed on the last raid there.[1]

On the 3rd, the radio said that there were large flights of P-51s roaming the area. We could see them off in the distance looking like a swarm of flies. At 12:30 P.M. a lone B-29 came over and dropped leaflets. The AA guns opened up on him, which was unusual, for they had not been firing on a single plane.[2]

1. On the night of August 1–2, about eight hundred B-29s struck targets in north central Honshu and dropped mines in key waterways elsewhere. This was the largest Twentieth Air Force one-day effort of the war, unloading more tonnage than Allied bombers had ever carried on a single mission. In the Tokyo area, Hachioji, to the west, and Kawasaki, immediately south, were heavily attacked. E. Bartlett Kerr, *Flames Over Tokyo: The U.S. Army Air Forces' Incendiary Campaign Against Japan, 1944–1945* (New York: Donald I. Fine, 1991), pp. 267–68; Kit C. Carter and Robert Mueller, comps, *The Army Air Forces in World War II: Combat Chronology, 1941–1945* (Washington: Office of Air Force History, 1976), p. 683.

2. Nearly one hundred Iwo-based P-51s attacked airfields, rail installations, and trains. Carter and Mueller, *Combat Chronology*, p. 684.

Hoblitt came to Maj. Cox and me and said that he did not want to be in on the escape plan any longer. We had had rumors all day long that some sort of action was being taken on the peace offer. Hoblitt did not mention this, but I could not help but wonder if he did not have more news of this rumor than we had. There was nothing that we could do except say O.K. to his wanting out. This was on the 6th and it just might be that he had heard that the world's first atomic bomb had been dropped that very morning on Hiroshima.[3] We did not know of the bomb at this time, but it was obvious that the Japanese were about to go crazy over something.

Smitty and I were cooking some sort of concoction using our Red Cross food, and so were Jim and Ramon Martinez. Most of us would dream up various ways to make the parcels go farther or different concoctions that would enable us to enjoy these goodies more, and we would give these dishes names like "Welsh *No Usagi*" which was "Welch Rabbit," "*Hayaku* Hash" or "Hurry Up Hash" and "*Yoroshii* Pie" or "Good Pie." We were cooking away. We had been using our electric hot plates for so long without being caught that we were a little lax on our watch and Hayasaka walked in on us where we were cooking and caught us "red handed" with the hot plates in use. He raised hell and then confiscated our stoves. Boy, were we lucky that we were not cooking rice that we had stolen from the supply room.

Perhaps the massive bombing had caused the Japanese to become more considerate, for we were getting mail more frequently. I got one more letter and two post cards. The news was that my Dad was doing O.K., my brother was overseas somewhere in ETO, my oldest sister was going to a Nazarene College in Bethany, Oklahoma, and my baby sister was taking

---

3. At 8:15 on the morning of August 6, a single B-29 accompanied by two others as observers dropped an atomic bomb on the western Honshu city of Hiroshima, killing about 80,000 people and destroying more than eighty percent of the city's buildings. Wesley Frank Craven and James Lea Cate, eds., *The Army Air Forces in World War II*, 7 vols. (Chicago: University of Chicago Press, 1948–58), V, pp. 716–22.

One of the other prisoners, Henshaw, claimed to have received the news in confidence from Domoto, while still another, Parkyns, said he had heard it at the *hōsō* on a U.S. military broadcast. Ivan Chapman, *Tokyo Calling: The Charles Cousens Case* (Sydney: Hale & Iremonger, 1990), pp. 192–93.

music and speech. Also there was some sad news; my buddy, Sgt. Donald Heleman, lost two brothers while they were home in Abilene on leave from the service. While riding a motorcycle, they were involved in an accident and were killed. I doubt that Donald ever found this out. He died six days before his camp was liberated.

Strange, is it not, how the cards fall? Some families are hit hard and suffer great losses, while others, in like circumstances, come through virtually unscathed. The pensive old Tent Maker must have been contemplating such things when he wrote:

> Tis but a checkerboard of nights and days
> Where Destiny with men, for pieces plays.
> Hither and Thither he moves, and mates, and slays
> And one by one back in the closet lays.

On Wednesday the 8th, the Japanese were about to come unraveled. We were wondering just what was taking place when Domoto came over and called a meeting of all hands. This was obviously going to be a news briefing like we normally got on Saturday mornings. He was acting very strangely and was quite fidgety and even looked uncomfortable. Finally he began with the usual tripe of "America is a very bad nation. They have no respect for life and are a bunch of murderers." Of course we were accustomed to statements like this in the news briefings, so we sort of nodded that we knew this. What else was new?

He said that this morning one American plane flew over Hiroshima and dropped one bomb. That bomb had completely obliterated the city and had killed 100,000 people. Of course we took this bit of information like we had taken the other items, like one of their vaunted Eagles downing an American plane with a rice ball. We all smiled and someone said that that sure was some sort of bomb alright. Domoto said "This is the truth! This really happened this morning!" When he saw that we did not believe him, he got mad and stomped out of the room and told us to stay right where we were until he came back.

He went over to the front building, and in a little bit he came back carrying a bunch of telegrams and telex forms and passed them out to us.

The blood drained from my face and the hair on my neck stood up, as I read worldwide communications about the Hiroshima atom bomb and its destruction. We all were dumbfounded. I could not imagine how that much awesome power could be contained in one bomb and one plane.

We had been paying very little attention to single planes coming over for quite some time, but you could bet your bottom dollar that we would heed them now. I cornered Maj. Cox at the first opportunity and suggested that the time to head for the hills had come. He said that this new bomb would probably make the Japs "kick in," and that we should hang around just a little longer and see what happened. I reminded him of the threat that "the closer the Americans came to Tokyo, the closer we came to death." He said that he had not forgotten but he felt strongly enough that the bomb would bring about the war's end that it would be unwise to take off just now. Begrudgingly, I agreed. The very next morning, we heard that Russia had declared war on Japan.[4] I had been getting the squirts almost monthly, and today of all times, I came down with them again. The new and fast-breaking events along with my fear of becoming part of the target for the next atom bomb, or of being wiped out by the Japanese, contributed to my malady, and the stomach cramps became so severe that I took to my bed.

On the morning of the 10th, there were all kinds of planes raiding around the area. There were B-29s, B-24s, B-25s, P-51s, dive bombers and torpedo planes.[5] In addition to American planes and task forces roaming at will and systematically destroying everything that had not already been destroyed, I thought the new terrifying atom bombs certainly ought to be enough to cause the Japanese to see "the handwriting on the wall" and to

---

4. On the evening of August 8th, the Soviet Union declared war on Japan effective August 9th. Soviet forces invaded Japanese-held Manchuria at 1 A.M. Tokyo time on the 9th. Robert J. C. Butow, *Japan's Decision to Surrender* (Stanford: Stanford University Press, 1954), pp. 153–54.

5. Twentieth Air Force B-29s and P-51s struck the Tokyo area and fighters and dive bombers from Task Force 38 hit northern Honshu airfields. Okinawa-based B-24s and B-25s, escorted by P-51s, attacked western Honshu and Kyushu. Carter and Mueller, *Combat Chronology*, p. 687; Samuel Eliot Morison, *History of United States Naval Operations in World War II: Victory in the Pacific* (Boston: Little, Brown, 1960), pp. 322–23.

accept the "unconditional surrender" that America was demanding, rather than see their country completely annihilated.

As I lay in my bed doubled up with the stomach cramps, I kept my ears cocked for any unusual sounds of commotion that would indicate that the armed guards from the front building were coming to eliminate us. I had gotten my knife from hiding and was now keeping it in my bedding where it would be easier to get to in a hurry. I had every intention of taking some of them with me when the time came. The entry in my diary for this day was:

August 11 Saturday
Two sorties this morning—I think by the end of next month we'll be blown to Hell or on our way home. 11:30 A.M. I just heard some real [my personal Javanese code here] hot dope! American and Saipan radio warn that if Japan does not kick in by Monday midnight Tokyo and it's near vicinity will be destroyed by atomic bombs. A 72 hour armistice was declared last night. The Japanese have sent terms and are awaiting answers. [end of code][6] Well after almost four years, our fate is to be decided within the next few hours. We become free men or dead men in two days. If we are to be free, we will emerge emaciated, weary fragments of humanity into a strange world; endowed with nothing but a few measly dollars, an unsurpassed knowledge of human nature and such a morbid philosophy on life that it will serve to ostracize us from society, should we put it to use. We will be easy to please and hard to fool. We will be products of 1941 coming into a world five years in advance of us the world of "Buck Rogers."

Most of us will be utterly lost, bewildered and cannot or will not fit into the new way of life and thus become the next genera-

---

6. On August 10th Japan announced its willingness to accept the terms of the Potsdam Declaration if the "prerogatives" of the Emperor would not be prejudiced. B-29 bombing operations against Japan were suspended on the 11th pending resolution of this qualification. The possibility of an atomic bombing of Tokyo was not raised by the United States but instead was a false rumor based on the interrogation of a captured B-29 pilot. Butow, *Japan's Decision to Surrender*, pp. 160, 177–78; Craven and Cate, *Army Air Forces*, V, pp. 699, 730–32.

tion of criminals, human derelicts or philosophers. Yet on the other hand a small percentage of the "Horios" shall fit into society sufficiently enough to enable them to live out their span of life as the bourgeois. And yet a still smaller percentage, in years to come, will join the ranks of America's foremost men; men of medicine, men of ———science and government; men to become world famous in the aesthetic arts,———OR———we shall end our "Horioship," as we would have been better off to have begun it, —in death.

To bring my meandering thoughts to a focus closer to home—What a lash up this has been! This "Humanity Calls" and "Postman Calls" programs and it's 25 duressed (and other wise) prisoners of war captured at Java, P.I., Wake, Guam and Singapore, New Guinea and Rabaul.

One could travel to the ends of the earth and live three lifetimes and never could 25 men such as these be gathered together.

The little group's intelligence ranges from ignorance to genius; we have traitors, confirmed, suspected and potential; education from grammar school to university graduates; erotics, erratic, queers, mental cases, cowards, brave men, good men, no accounts, artists, writers, playwrights, actors, typists, journalists, newsmen, typesetters, farmers, cotton pickers, Americans, English, Australians, Scotch, Dutch, soldiers, sailors, marines, airmen, suck asses, dog robbers, and civilians ——Wow! If that's not a hell of a lash-up to be connected with, I throw in.

U.S. planes had been over all night, singly and in flights of two and three. Sirens, both long and short, blew constantly.

On Sunday the 12th, the grapevine said that Ambassador Grew was in Okinawa and was conferring with a delegation of Japanese. The cessation of hostilities had been arranged and the only thing holding up the formal declaration of peace was the future position of the Emperor.[7]

We were awakened at 5:00 A.M. on the 13th by the sirens, and not

7. Grew was not on Okinawa, but on August 12 the Japanese received the American reply stating that the Emperor's authority would "be subject to" the Allied Supreme Commander. Butow, *Japan's Decision to Surrender*, pp. 191–92.

long afterwards there were shipboard type planes from three different task forces that were circling at will all over the area. They were dive-bombing and strafing communications and transportation and this kept up all day. Some anti-aircraft guns opened up and this was very disappointing, for since there had been no bombs dropped and no ack-ack last Friday and not even a siren yesterday, it made us think that hostilities had ceased, especially with the grapevine story of peace.[8]

Ever since we were told of the Hiroshima bomb, the "Jeeps" had made no effort to prevent the radio crew from talking with people at the *hoso,* and consequently that is where we were getting all the information about what was going on. At 5:15 P.M. a plane came over and dropped more leaflets. Word was out that there was to be an important speech to the Japanese people by the Japanese officials.

I had crawled out of bed earlier in the day to make a final attempt to convince Maj. Cox that we ought to get the hell out of there. He was sweating blood like I was, but still felt certain the Japanese were going to kick in. I told him that I sure hoped that he was right, because now we didn't even have time to get out of the blast area.

We almost literally sweated blood while we watched the hands of the clock as they crept slowly towards midnight. The hour was upon us when Tokyo and its near vicinity was to be destroyed by atomic bombs if the nation had not surrendered. Midnight came and nothing happened. We began to breathe a little easier, and after a sigh of relief we went to bed. At 2:00 A.M. we all bolted out of bed in stark terror, for a single B-29 was passing over. Was this it? Another B-29 came over about daylight and was equally frightening, but again nothing happened and we decided that the war was over.

The daily newspaper that was printed in English ran a front page story that in part said: "Think not of today but look forward to the future, for Japan is a great nation." That made it obvious that they were softening up the population for some devastating news. Today was the last broadcast of the combined "Humanity Calls" and "Postman Calls" program. Martial

8. This was a heavy strike by Task Force 38, aimed at pressuring a Japanese surrender. Morison, *Victory in the Pacific,* pp. 333–34.

law was declared for all Japan at 5:00 P.M. We felt if we could just make it through the next few days without some diehard military group breaking into our camp and slaughtering us, we would be Free. We had rumors that the U.S. Navy was standing by to repatriate or reclaim us POWs.

Smitty was in very poor condition, and the Japs gave him a Red Cross parcel and gave the rest of us four parcels to share. I was hoping it would help me; I had been more or less isolated for the last few days with dysentery. I had had fourteen bowel movements that day along with terrible cramps, lots of blood and mucus, and I was very weak.

August 15, 1945

Today, at noon, for the first time in the two-thousand-year history of Japan, the Emperor spoke directly to the Japanese people, and told them of the country's surrender.

• • •

To Our Good and Loyal Subjects

After pondering deeply the general trends of the world and the actual conditions obtaining in Our Empire today, We have decided to effect a settlement of the present situation by resorting to an extraordinary measure.

We have ordered Our Government to communicate to the Governments of the United States, Great Britain, China and the Soviet Union that Our Empire accepts the provisions of their Joint Declaration.

To strive for the common prosperity and happiness of all nations as well as the security and well-being of Our subjects is the solemn obligation which has been handed down by Our Imperial Ancestors, and which We lay close to heart. Indeed, We declared war on America and Britain out of our sincere desire to ensure Japan's Self-preservation and the stabilization of East Asia, it being far from Our thought either to infringe upon the sovereignty of other nations or to embark upon territorial aggrandizement. But now the war has lasted for nearly four years. Despite the best that has been done by everyone—the gallant fighting of military and naval forces, the diligence and assiduity of Our servants of State and the devoted service of Our one-hundred million people—the war situation has developed not necessarily to Japan's advantage, while the general trends of the world have all turned against her interest. Moreover, the enemy has begun to employ a new and most cruel bomb, the power of which to do damage is indeed incalculable, taking the toll of many innocent lives. Should We continue to fight, it would not only result in an ultimate collapse and obliteration of the Japanese nation, but also it would lead to the total extinction of human civilization. Such being the case, how are We to save the millions of Our subjects; or to atone Ourselves before the hallowed spirits of Our Imperial Ancestors? This is the reason We have ordered the acceptance of the provisions of the Joint Declaration of the Powers.

We cannot but express the deepest sense of regret to our Allied nations of East Asia, who have consistently co-operated with the Empire towards the emancipation of East Asia. The thought of those officers and men as well as others who have fallen in the fields of battle, those who have died at their posts of duty, or those who met with untimely death and all their bereaved families, pains Our Heart night and day. The welfare of the wounded and the war-sufferers, and those who have lost their homes and livelihood, are the object of Our profound solicitude. The hardships and suffering to which Our nation is to be subjected hereafter will certainly be great. We are keenly aware of the inmost feelings of all ye, Our subjects. However, it is according to the dictate of time and fate that We have resolved to pave the way for a grand peace for all the generations to come by enduring the unendurable and suffering what is insufferable.

Having been able to safeguard and maintain the structure of the Imperial State, We are always with ye, Our good and loyal subjects, relying upon your sincerity and integrity. Beware most strictly of any outbursts of emotion which may engender needless complications, or any fraternal contention and strife which may create confusion, lead ye astray and cause ye to lose the confidence of the world. Let the entire nation continue as one family from generation to generation, ever firm in its faith of the imperishableness of its divine land, and mindful of its heavy burden of responsibilities, and the long road before it. Unite your total strength to be devoted to the construction for the future. Cultivate the ways of rectitude; foster nobility of spirit; and work with resolution so as ye may enhance the innate glory of the Imperial state and keep pace with the progress of the world.[9]

● ● ●

August 16, 1945

There was absolutely nothing to do once the broadcasts ended except speculate on the probable sequence of forthcoming events and the progress of any cease-fire or peace negotiations. Now, as had been the case for about a year, Maj. Cousens spent an awful lot of time in huddles with Mr. Domoto. This morning he came back from one of his tete-a-tetes and told us that we all would be called to fall in in the courtyard for an important announcement.

He said that we all should stand at attention and make no show of emotion at whatever was said. He had no sooner told us this when we were ordered to form up in the courtyard. After we were in place, Maj. Hifumi and all the front office staff came out and formed up. The major was out in front of the rest of them, and he began to speak without any formal opening and told us that "the war was over for the time being." He said some more stuff but I was so emotional that I do not recall what else he said.

Wow! This was not a rumor, nor was it the grapevine—this was the real thing! Some of the staff members were on the verge of tears and none of them had looked in our direction. When the major dismissed them, they then turned to us, bowed, and left. Well, I was certainly ready for the navy to come in and take us out of there. We were told that a delegation of Japanese "Big Wigs" had flown to Iwo Jima to meet with the Americans and then would fly to McArthur's headquarters in Manila for finalization of procedural plans.[10]

---

9. Text in Butow, *Japan's Decision to Surrender,* p. 248.

10. Early on August 19, a Japanese military delegation flew to Ie Shima in the Ryukyus aboard two disarmed navy bombers. The group then transferred to an American army transport place and reached Manila late that evening. *Reports of General Mac-*

We heard that the U.S. Navy had entered Tokyo Bay and was patrolling up as far as Yokohama, which was right south of us.[11] Mr. Hayasaka and some of the office staff had left, or as I said in my diary—"gone AWOL!" Maj. Hifumi had also left. The army had been sent home. Mr. Domoto and the soldiers guarding us were still around. D.M. told us to stay where we were, that we would be as safe there as anywhere, and that we would be provided for until arrangements could be made to have us moved to another camp.

Maj. Cox had placed Sgt. Provoo under arrest, and Streeter had been making contact and trying to get in good with us. On the 18th, one B-29 and one B-24 came over Tokyo around noon, and it seemed so strange that there were no sirens, ack-ack or Zeros.[12]

Since we had nothing to do and the movie theater in the front building was not being used, I took Smitty over and taught him how to operate the 35-mm projectors. We then began to run some movies to pass the time away. Most all the POWs came over and sat in on them. On the 19th we ran the *Petrified Forest* and *Adam Had Four Sons,* and on the 20th we ran *The Lives of the Bengal Lancers.*

On the 21st we were rerunning "Adam Had Four Sons" when we were called out and told that tomorrow we would be sent back to Omori Camp out in Tokyo Bay. U.S. occupation troops should be in Tokyo within the next few days. The 22nd came and there was no attempt to move us to Omori. After waiting around all morning and we still not moving, we de-

---

Arthur, 2 vols. (Washington: U.S. Government Printing Office, 1966), I, pp. 447–48, II, p. 746.

11. Units of the American Third Fleet did not enter Tokyo Bay until August 28. Morison, *Victory in the Pacific,* p. 361; Benis M. Frank and Herny I. Shaw, Jr., *History of U.S. Marine Corps Operations in World War II: Victory and Occupation* (Washington: Hqs, U.S. Marine Corps, 1968), p. 484.

12. During this period, American aircraft continued surveillance and weather flights over Japan. While B-24s did not reach Tokyo, a few of the recently arrived new B-32 bombers were over the city on August 17th and 18th. Despite the Japanese surrender, the B-32s came under fighter attack on both days. They took no losses, however, and shot down three of the Japanese. Craven and Cate, *Army Air Forces,* V, pp. 694, 699, 733.

cided to watch some more movies. After we filed over to the front building and took places in the theatre, Smitty and I put on a Russian film that we could not read the title to. The dialogue was all in Russian as well, so we did not care for that too much. We then put on *The Rains Came* and this was enjoyed by all.

After the movies, we were all assembled in the courtyard and told that we would be taken back to Omori the next morning, and that no written material would be permitted out of this camp, including copies of any of the radio programs. We would be searched before boarding the trucks and if anyone did have any written material on them or in their gear, "Their lives would not be guaranteed!"

After the meeting I went over to Smitty's building with my diary and the scripts that I thought we might have to answer for. I had done a series of watercolor anatomy studies, showing the skeletal formation and how all the various muscles and muscle groups were attached to the skeleton. I had put in many hours of work on these and they were really quite good.

I removed a plywood panel from the wainscot of one of the upper rooms and placed all these items in there and then sealed the wall back up again. The next morning we gathered up whatever we were going to take with us and placed it out in the courtyard. We then said our good-byes to Mama San and Papa San, the caretakers. They were genuinely sorry to see us go and each had tears in their eyes. Streeter brought his gear from the other building and piled it down with ours. Immediately, Maj. Cox came out and placed him under arrest.

Now, having arrested Sgt. Provoo and Mr. Streeter, Maj. Cox then assigned Capt. Ince to be the Officer of the Guard, and then assigned Smitty and me as guards until such time as we could turn them over to American authorities.

This was Thursday, 23 August, 1945. About 9:00 A.M. we took our gear through the archway and loaded onto two army trucks. Maj. Cox ordered Smitty and me to "ride shotgun" on Streeter and Provoo until we reached Omori. We rode through what was left of Tokyo, and as we neared the shoreline of the bay area, we were surprised to see that there were still some portions of town that had not been destroyed.

We arrived back at Omori about an hour later and carried our gear across the bridge and into camp. The camp had escaped the bombing raids and so everything was intact. There was a difference, however, and that was in the fact that everyone in camp was out in the courtyard to see us come in. I was leery as to how we might be received, since the POWs here knew that we had been on the propaganda radio program ever since we had left twenty months earlier. It turned out that everything went well and most men were eager to know what Tokyo looked like now and to find out if we had any news that they did not already have.

Maj. Cox informed the senior American officer, Arthur L. Maher, that Sgt. Provoo and Mr. Streeter were under arrest and were to remain so until they could be handed over to Americans. We had been assigned our barracks and then had nothing to do. All work parties at Omori had ceased. I was talking with a couple of guys I had met when I was here before, when some guy came up to me and said that I was wanted in the "Head Shed."

I said "Oh no! The sons of bitches beat the hell out of me for three days the first time I was here!" the guy said, "No, it's not the Japs that want to see you. It's our officers in the POW 'Head Shed' now, and some fly-boy colonel that shot down twenty-six Jap Zeros. They call him Maj. Gregory 'Pappy' Boyington and he is supposed to have been given the Congressional Medal of Honor. He's the one who wants to see you."[13]

I made my way around to the room used by the POW C.O. for his office, wondering what this colonel wanted with me. The door was open and there was an assorted gathering of officers who all seemed to be hanging onto every word that was said by a guy seated at the desk. When I stepped into the room, I saluted and the guy at the desk stood up and saluted me back and said "Come in, Sergeant. I'm Pappy," and we shook hands. "Are you the half-Japanese sergeant that was captured with that bunch of Texans down in Java?" I said "Yes Sir." He then asked me if the

13. A marine officer, Boyington had been shot down and captured near Rabaul, New Britain, early in 1944 and was subsequently awarded the Medal of Honor for his exploits as a fighter pilot and squadron leader. Robert Sherrod, *History of Marine Corps Aviation in World War II,* 2d ed. (San Rafael, Calif.: Presidio Press, 1980), pp. xix–xx, 195, 197. See also Gregory "Pappy" Boyington, *Baa Baa Black Sheep* (New York: G. P. Putnam's Sons, 1958).

Japs had been rough on me for being part Japanese, and when I told him that they had, he said: "By damn I'm glad to meet you! I've heard how they treated you at this camp. Always stand tall and don't ever be ashamed of your heritage."

I returned to my barracks and found out that there were some bomber crews who had been brought into camp recently. I went over to where they were and talked with them. I was congratulating them on their bombing accuracy and telling them how much we appreciated their sparing us at Bunker Hill. They asked me where the camp was located. I told them that it was about nine blocks north of the Imperial Palace and then they informed me that they had not missed us on purpose because they did not know that the camp was there. They knew where some camps were but not ours.

The Japanese issued us cigarettes, toilet tissue, and laundry and bath soap. Before the week was out, they had issued us more soap and tissue than they had issued previously during the entire war.

I was standing outside when someone shouted, "Looks like we're about to be strafed!" A "gull winged" U.S. Navy fighter plane circled low over the bay and made a run directly at the camp. We knew right off it was not a Jap plane, so we all just stood there and watched it come in. The pilot waggled his wing before he got to us and came over not more than two hundred feet above us. He waved as he passed and waggled his wings again as he went away. He made a very wide circle and it looked as if he were going to come back over.

I ran to one of the *benjos* and climbed up onto the roof so that I could get a good look; others were doing the same thing. The fighter came in for another pass and this time he opened his canopy and threw something out. Again he waggled his wings as he disappeared out over the bay. When he came over we all waved and I was going to shout or let out a big yell for joy but no sound would come out. There was a lump in my throat about the size of a grapefruit and the harder I tried to yell the worse it hurt. I was so emotional and elated that I almost burst out in tears. The fighter pilot had tossed out his half empty pack of cigarettes with a note in it which said: "Hang on! It won't be long now!" Soon other types of planes began to come over and they came so low that we could make out their facial features. They were waving and taking pictures. There were F4Us, F4Fs, and SBDs.

It seemed that all the pilots in the fleet wanted a chance to wave at us, and each one of them would drop us something—a candy bar or a pack of cigarettes. (Even now, as I write this some forty-two years after the fact, a big lump comes in my throat and tears to my eyes as I relive the emotions of that time.) The navy got a little more organized with these overflights and began dropping us medicines, food and clothing.

The first drop contained all kinds of pills, mostly vitamins. They were all sugar coated. Everyone made a mad scramble to get some and the officers made everyone put them back and then appointed a team to distribute the pills equally. We opened all of what we got, and started sucking the sugar off the pills until we came to the medicine, and then we would spit them out or swallow them with water. We were eating these things by the handsful.

The next day we were being dropped foodstuff, clothing, toilet articles, razors, toothbrushes and the whole bit. Tables were set up out in the compound, and everything that was dropped was brought to this central point. It was then sorted out according to category, piled onto the tables and issued equally to all men in camp, paying no attention to the size of clothing or shoes. We took what was given us and then some wild trading took place to get something that fit. The cigarettes were especially hot items of trade.

Suddenly, someone yelled, "Here comes a bomber real low!" and ran out to where they could get a good look. It is a very good thing that they did. A B-29 was coming in real low and as he approached camp, he opened his bomb bay doors and dropped a food pack. The food pack consisted of two fifty-five gallon steel drums, tack-welded together and filled with smaller cans of food. This was attached to two large parachutes. When the chutes opened, they did not withstand the shock and broke loose from the drums, which then came tumbling down, end over end, right for our camp. Everyone ran for cover just in time, for when the steel drums hit the ground, the tack-welds broke loose and here came all the little cans of food, shooting out like shrapnel, doing damage to buildings. Another B-29 came over and made a drop. The same thing almost happened again. As soon as someone said that another bomber was coming, we all cleared the barracks, for we did not want to be caught inside when two fifty-five gallon drums full of tin cans came crashing through the roof. A big sign was hastily made on the roof of one of the buildings that said "Drop Outside. Thank You." We were fortunate that one or more barracks were not demolished or that some of us were not killed. We wanted very much to show our appreciation to the planes dropping us food. We cut up one of the parachutes used in the food drops and made a big "Thank You" banner out of it. I drew some cartoons on it and most everyone in camp signed it and we hoped to present it to the aircraft carrier *Shangri-La*. Other parachutes were made into national flags.

These huge B-29 bombers were quite the biggest things that I had ever seen. Coming over us at a very low altitude made them seem even bigger. I remarked to one of the B-29 crewmen in camp that I would like to take a weekend off and go through one of the B-29s. The Japanese Camp Commander and the guards no longer came inside the camp and this was a welcome change, even though it seemed strange. The guards were on duty now more to protect us from any fanatics than to keep us corralled. They made no effort to stop POWs who loaded up with American cigarettes and chocolates and went over the fence and into Tokyo to trade for sex and souvenirs.

During the day, Provoo and Strecter were required to sit on a bench outside and Smitty or I had to stand there and guard them and prevent them from talking with anyone. I was taking my turn at guarding them and Smitty had gone into town. Later, he came back and said that he would take over while I went into town. He said that the Japs sure had some good beer and that I ought to try some.

I put some cigarettes and chocolate into a ditty bag and was just about to go over the fence when someone yelled out that we were about to be blown out of the water. Some torpedo boats were coming across the bay right straight for Omori. I jumped down off the fence and ran across the camp to the other side and crawled up on the fence there. Sure enough,

The Navy pulling "Foo" and others out of Tokyo Bay, August 1945.

there were three or four torpedo boats coming toward us at top speed.[14]

As the PT boats came nearer, someone else said that the U.S. Navy had entered Tokyo Bay, and that these boats were surely from our own U.S. 3rd fleet. I felt that this was the case. I was so excited and so emotional that I just could not wait for the boats to get to us, so I jumped into the bay to swim out to meet them. Two or three others jumped in also and we started swimming out towards the on-coming PT boats, which turned out to be landing craft. I went into the water with my clothes and shoes on. Needless to say, they caused quite a drag. After I had made about forty yards, my strength left me instantaneously, like the air from a punctured balloon. Just that quick, I was completely exhausted. I began to take on water and started to sink.

14. On August 29, Task Group 30.6, organized especially for the emergency evacuation of Allied prisoners in the Tokyo area, entered Tokyo Bay and dropped anchor off Omori. Landing craft (LCVPs) carrying medical and evacuation parties headed for shore to effect the rescue. Frank and Shaw, *Victory and Occupation*, pp. 484, 781–82.

Omori POW Camp, August 1945. Circled is Frank "Foo" Fujita (Photo from the collection of Robert Martindale)

I was completely underwater but somehow managed to get my head up for one more breath. I tried to hold my breath and tilt my head backwards to enable me to stay afloat longer. One of the landing craft was bearing right down on me, and I remember thinking that they did not see me.

I could no longer maintain my floating position and my exhaustion was so complete that I slipped beneath the water again. I was expecting the boat's propellers to chop me to bits. The mind works at such lightning speed, I recall thinking how absolutely stupid I had been to try and swim out and meet the boats. I had ended my own life just at the moment of liberation. A terrible panic filled me, which triggered my survival mechanism—"the flight or fight" syndrome—so enough adrenalin was pumped into my system to enable me to make one last effort to get my head above water.

The next thing I knew, two large hands had me by the head and were pulling me out of the water, and then another sailor helped lay me on the deck of the landing craft. As the other landing craft picked up the rest of the swimmers, I lay on the deck too exhausted to move.

There was a navy commodore in charge of these boats,[15] and there were war correspondents aboard and navy photographers who were taking pictures like mad. The sailors were about as rough and tough a looking bunch as I have ever seen. They wore beards or needed a shave and each one of them carried a sub-machine gun. Looking at them from the deck, they seemed like giants.

As the boats pulled into the Omori docks, the whole camp was crowded at the little island's edge, and from somewhere American, British and Dutch flags appeared and were being wildly waved. One of the photos taken of this scene made all of the world's newspapers. The camp gates to the dock area had been opened and as we touched the docks the sailors jumped out and took up strategic positions with their sub-machine guns cocked and held at the ready.

All the POWs in camp were whooping and yelling as the landing party came ashore and was met by our camp C.O. They no sooner had shaken hands when the Japanese camp commander and his staff came through the camp and walked up to the commodore and demanded to know what he was doing here and stated, "The war is not over yet!"

The commodore told him that the war was over for him and that he was removing all the POWs from Omori immediately, and what was more, he had better be damn sure that all Allied POWs in the Tokyo area were at this very spot tomorrow morning because he was taking them out also.

The really sick and bad off were taken aboard the landing craft first and taken to a hospital ship out in the bay. Then we others were taken, first

15. Commodore Roger W. Simpson. Morison, *Victory in the Pacific,* pp. 358, 361; Frank and Shaw, *Victory and Occupation,* pp. 781–82.

come, first serve. Capt. Ince, Smitty and I, and the two prisoners got on board just after midnight on the morning of 30 August 1945. We were taken to a big white ship that had a big red cross painted on the sides. It was the hospital ship SS *Benevolence*.

We were stripped of all our clothing, given fresh clothes, deloused and then transferred to other ships that were anchored nearby.[16] Before we would submit to the delousing procedure, Capt. Ince demanded to see the ship's officer of the day, or whatever the navy calls them, and wanted to turn Provoo and Streeter over to the navy to be held in the brig until our government decided what to do with them. The ship's officer did not want to accept them and tried to talk Capt. Ince out of jailing them. The captain told him that these men were charged with treason and if he wanted to let them go afterward, he would have to bear full responsibility. He took them.

16. After boarding the *Benevolence*, liberated POWs were given a chance to bathe and change into clean clothes, then given a quick medical checkup and a meal. After that, they were asked about camp conditions and the mistreatment they suffered. Men in poor condition were assigned beds on the hospital ship; the others were transferred to a nearby transport. Frank and Shaw, *Victory and Occupation*, p. 782.

15

OKINAWA, ALABANG,

REUNIONS WITH OLD

FRIENDS, HOME

September 1945

After Capt. Ince got the navy to accept the prisoners Provoo and Streeter, we—the guard detail—went back to where the POWs were being deloused and given new pajamas and went through the procedure too. I had an old khaki army shirt that was well patched and nearly rotted. I had cut the sleeves off in order to make patches for the rest of the shirt. I had hand sewn a small set of Buck Sergeant stripes and a 36th Infantry Division "T" Patch, and had affixed them to this old shirt. I was proud of the shirt and had been saving it through the years for this very occasion—Freedom! I had put it on to leave Omori and thus would be wearing it when I was reclaimed by our troops. It had to come off in the delousing line and was tossed into the common pile of discarded clothing. It sort of hurt me to leave that shirt behind.

After being deloused, the prisoners of war were segregated into groups according to their nationalities and were taken to other ships that were anchored about the bay. I was taken to an APD (navy designation for High Speed Transport or Destroyer Transport) the USS *Gosselin*. Here we were taken down to the mess area and passed in front

Sept. 6. Thurs
Still in Okinawa —
Herb is not here.

Sept 7 Friday
We leave by plane
at 7:00 A.M. or at
least leave Camp.
Left on C-54 10:00 AM
landed at Nichol's Field
at 3:00 P.M. go to
29th Repl Bn. 18 mi. S
of Manila — free everything
got Card from Gordon
Sept 8 Sat
Medically processed

out many forms —
Boy! What a surprise !
Capt Moko + Big Ed
came around tonight

Sept 9. Gave G-2
dope on Streeter + Provoo
Ed came around will
be back Moko
going to Tokyo today
I didn't see Moko before
he left — spent afternoon
with Ed — drew dog
tags + pay book
letter from Mom + one from Dad.

Page from Fujita's replacement diary, after he hid the original diary in the wall of the girl's school.

of some cook stoves. There were sailors there who asked us how we wanted our eggs and bacon cooked and how many. I had crisp bacon and two eggs over easy with toast and jelly, milk and black coffee. Boy! Was that ever good.

After we had been fed, we were loaded again on a motor launch and taken to another transport that was anchored near the biggest ship I had ever seen—the battleship *Missouri*. This transport was the USS *Monitor* and would be my billet until after the peace ceremonies. The ship was spic and span. We were each assigned a bunk which consisted of a piece of canvas stretched on a galvanized pipe frame; these were then fastened to bulkheads, or walls, three deep. I crawled into mine for I was sure ready for some sleep. We had been up all night, and after my near fatal swim I was dog-tired. I thought how luxurious the canvas bunk felt. We had been sleeping on wooden planking covered with a thin straw mat and it was very hard.

I fell asleep almost immediately, but sleep was fitful and of a short duration, with a lot of tossing and turning. Finally, it dawned on me that the tightly stretched canvas bunk was just too soft. I crawled out of my bunk and bedded down on the steel deck. It wasn't long before I was sound asleep and I slept the rest of the night without waking. When I awoke the next morning, most of the other ex-POWs were also down on the deck.

We had nothing to do except eat and sleep. It seemed strange that after dreaming of food and craving food for three and a half years, it now was a matter of indifference to me. When the planes started dropping food to us in Omori, I lost my obsession for food. I felt that from that moment forward, there would always be food available, whatever I wanted, in whatever amount I wanted, and food ceased to be important.

I did, however, take a liking for milk, and I drank it at every meal. Much to my dismay it had a detrimental effect on me; it constipated me to the extent that I had to go to the infirmary and have a corpsman assist me in getting relief.

2 September 1945, Tokyo Bay, Japan

I was still on board the USS *Monitor* and we had been on deck watching all the activity taking place on and around the "Mighty Mo."[1] There had been destroyers pulling alongside and transferring people to the battleship. About 9:00 A.M. we could hear the national anthem being played and then the unconditional surrender was signed. We were getting a blow-by-blow description over the ship's PA system. Peace at last! Then suddenly the whole sky seemed to fill with all kinds of planes flying over the Mighty Mo. There must have been a thousand or more. All American.[2]

1. Nickname for the battleship *Missouri*.

2. The formal Japanese surrender on board the USS *Missouri* was presided over by General of the Army Douglas MacArthur, newly designated Supreme Commander

We "lollygagged" around ship for two more days, fretting and bitching because things were not moving fast enough to suit us on getting started towards home. Finally, on the 4th, we were told to get what gear we had and get into a launch that was alongside. We had been issued fatigues while we were on board and that is the only thing that we had to wear. We got into the launch and were taken to Yokohama, debarked, and then taken to Atsugi Airfield.

I looked around in amazement, for there were yellow people all over the place wearing American uniforms. They were a deep yellow color, and the Japanese looked white compared to them. Also there were yellow women everywhere too, and they were wearing khaki uniforms with American chevrons and officer insignias. I saw very few white people here. Finally, my curiosity got the better of me, and I went up to a yellow first lieutenant and asked him what country he and the others were from. He looked surprised, but said "America, of course." I asked "How did y'all get so yellow?" and he said that they got that way from taking atabrine, an anti-malaria drug. I then asked him if they were now allowed to have female companions and pointed to a female staff sergeant walking by. He laughed and said that they were in the service and called WACs.[3]

I was completely astonished at this information. I don't know why; surely I must have had some inkling of there being women in the armed services. The yellow-colored skin threw me almost as much as the women. It appears that all troops in the Asiatic-Pacific Theatre were required to take a yellow pill, called atabrine, to keep from getting malaria. Its continued use would cause the skin to turn yellow and the longer one used it,

---

for the Allied Powers. In the presence of representatives of all the Allied nations that had fought against Japan, as well as senior American commanders and former prisoners of war, the Japanese delegate signed the surrender document, binding Japan to accept the provisions of the Potsdam Declaration, to surrender Japanese armed forces unconditionally, to free all POWs and civilian internees, and to carry out the orders of the Supreme Commander. The entire ceremony took less than half an hour. *Reports of General MacArthur*, 2 vols. (Washington: U.S. Government Printing Office, 1966), I, pp. 454–58.

3. Women's Army Corps.

the deeper the yellow tint of the skin. You could tell how long someone had been in the theater by what shade of yellow his skin was.

At about 7:30 P.M. a full load of us were put aboard a C-54[4] passenger plane and at 7:50 we took off into the night. We flew for several hours in a southerly direction. The plane was fitted for passengers so the adjustable seats were very comfortable, and I was enjoying the flight. I had managed to get a seat next to a window, and occasionally I would glimpse a ship far below.

As I relaxed, my mind went back in time to my very first flight in 1939 at Abilene. I was in the Texas National Guard then, and a flight of five or six army bombers going across country landed and spent the night there. The Flight Commander contacted our guard unit and wanted several men in uniform to pull guard duty on the bombers overnight.

I was one of the men chosen for this. We were to get a free plane ride in lieu of payment for this duty. The bombers of that era were covered with fabric instead of aluminum; they were painted yellow with blue tail stabilizers. The flap on the vertical stabilizer was painted with alternating horizontal red and white stripes from top to bottom. On the sides of the fuselage and on the wings were blue circles with a white star that had a red dot centered. Mr. Derryberry, the airport manager, took us up in his enclosed plane, and I remember that I was very thrilled.

About 1:00 A.M. thousands and thousands of lights appeared ahead and below. We were coming in to Naha Okinawa, and it looked as if every ship in the entire world was at anchor. In my wildest imagination I could not have come up with this many ships. The night was very black which made the lights look like jewels twinkling on black velvet.

Our pilot brought our huge four-engine plane down and was running downwind, alongside the runway. When he got just past the end of the runway, he flipped the plane around 180° and sat the thing down as smooth as you please. The G force of the abrupt turn probably caused some messed up skivvies. I am sure that that sort of maneuver for a C-54 was not only unorthodox, but very hazardous as well.

4. The military version of the DC-4.

A light rain was falling as we were taken to an army camp outside the city. The whole country looked waterlogged, and there was trash and sheet metal all over the place. A typhoon had hit the island a day or two before, and all this wreckage bore testimony to it. We were put into pyramidal tents, and then told to go to the supply tent and draw new uniforms and chevrons the first thing in the morning.

The whole place was nothing more than a slippery morass. The typhoon had practically drowned the area and it had rained ever since. I drew two sets of new khakis, a raincoat and new combat boots. Occasionally, we could hear far-off gun fire, and were told that there were still pockets of resistance and Jap snipers around the area who had not been pacified.

I was roaming around the area when someone yelled, "Hey, FOO!" and a small group of GIs standing near by turned out to be some men from my Lost Battalion. Two or three were from E Battery: Pvt. David "Bear" Woods and Sgt. David A. Williams. Williams is the one that had yelled at me, and we sort of danced a jig and hugged and whooped and hollered and had a great reunion. Some of the men had looked startled when they saw me, like they had seen a ghost or something. They told me that over a year ago the Japanese had boasted that they had cut my head off, giving my name, rank and unit. With that much information, the POWs hadn't the slightest doubt that they were told the truth.

Sgt. Williams said that he still had the book that I had left with him when I was taken out of Fukuoka #2. I did not remember what it was until he gave it back to me. It was the book I had started in Jaarmarkt, our first POW camp in Java. I had called it "The Lost Battalion From Texas." I had intended it to be a record of our outfit throughout the war. (This book is now located in the "Lost Battalion Museum" in the Wise County Museum at Decatur, Texas.)

Also at this Camp, which was being used as a staging area for "reclaimed prisoners of war," was Lt. Edwin Kalbfliesch and Mr. George Williams, both of whom the Japanese made us believe had been executed for not cooperating on the propaganda programs. There were two men representing different magazines who hit me up to have an exclusive account of my experiences as a half-Japanese soldier fighting the Japanese and then being captured by them and becoming a prisoner of war under them.

They were reluctant to offer a price in the presence of the others, for fear that the others then would up the ante. One of them said that he could not offer me near what *Life* magazine would offer me. The whole idea did not lay well with me since I did not know what the repercussions would be, if any, for my having been on the propaganda programs. I told them that I did not have a story to tell or sell either and that I was not interested in their offer. Then as I walked away from them one said: "I'll bet you take *Life* magazine's offer!"

I walked over to a sort of concession stand that was run by the Red Cross and got a pack of cigarettes. One of the girls who was working the stand was really good-looking and had a figure that just about popped my eyes out. I decided that I sure would like to get with her and so I asked if I could see her after she got off work. She said yes, if I would get three more fellows and it would be fifty dollars each. I was stunned, to say the least, and told her to forget it. I went away wondering if this was a ploy of hers to keep from being harassed by horny GIs or if she was a nymphomaniac. It was hard for me to believe that this pretty young thing was serious.

I went back for another beer, and while I was drinking it, a guy came up to me and introduced himself as a correspondent and representative of *Life*. He said that his magazine was very interested in doing a story on me and that he could make me a good offer. I told him I had already heard about him and I was not interested in any offer and walked off leaving him standing there. These magazine men made me wonder just what it was they had heard about me that was so interesting. I didn't like it.

As I walked away I noticed a group of GIs standing around a machine and they were all eating something that looked like ice cream cones. Sure enough, that is exactly what they were eating, and the machine was making ice cream as they were eating it, instantly. I got a cone of it and it came out of the machine in the form of a rope as long as someone held the lever down. I asked about this, and was told that it was a new machine that made ice cream without all the refrigeration equipment needed normally. It was highly portable and for the first time ice cream could be had in forward areas. This machine was so new and limited that it was not available for civilian use—armed services only.

The rain was coming down at a steady rate, and it was getting dark. A lot of GIs were gathering in front of the big outdoor movie screen and were squatting or sitting in the mud, for there was nothing else to sit on. I got mud on my last set of khakis while watching the movie, and the next morning I went back to the supply tent and drew another set. The Lost Battalion men that I had seen when I first arrived on Okinawa had shipped out the next morning and I sure was ready to move on.

On the morning of the 8th a planeload of us were flown to Manila in the Philippine Islands. As we neared Manila, the co-pilot was pointing out Bataan and Corregidor to us. After arriving in the bombed out city of Manila, we were taken by truck to the 29th Replacement Depot, located at the town of Alabang 18 miles south of Manila. This camp was a receiving station for reclaimed POWs from a good part of the Far East and there were a lot of us here.

There was a huge bulletin board outside the office tent and each time that a new batch of POWs arrived their names, ranks and branch of service were listed. Troops from all over the area would come by if they had friends or loved ones who were known to have been POWs and check the names of the new arrivals.

We were assigned to pyramidal tents and the weather was so hot and humid that the side flaps remained rolled up at all times except during rains in order to catch whatever breeze there might be. Each bed had a mosquito net attached to it, but I do not remember having to use it. The area was sprayed with DDT regularly. There were several flights of POWs coming in daily and there were about a thousand here now.

Here we found out that General of the Army, Douglas MacArthur, had put out an order pertaining to reclaimed prisoners of war of the Japanese, called "Project J." I do not know what all the order said, but we found out that it really was a potent weapon for POWs. For instance, it said that the camp was to maintain a twenty-four hour a day kitchen for the POWs and that if the POW wanted something the kitchen did not have, the kitchen was to get it! No one, absolutely no one, was to give an exPOW a hard time about anything; that if they were issued something and did not want to sign for it, the supply clerk was to sign for it himself. The power that was implied in this "Project J" saved me a court-martial a time or two.

The order given to the kitchen wasn't a very smart idea at all, for there

"Foo" three weeks after liberation, Alabang, Philippines.

were many men who, after having starved for three and one-half years, had no control whatever over their eating. Many of them were getting some severe physical complications and there were even a number of deaths from overeating.

As soon as we were settled in, the group that I came in with was called to go to the administration building for a briefing. There were chairs set up in front of a podium at one end of the building. The rest of the building was filled with tables, with a clerk sitting at each to interview us. We first had to sit in front of the podium and hear some colonel from the Medical Corps talk on how much they did not know about the results of long-term starvation, malnutrition, physical torture and overwork of POWs. They did not know how it would effect us physically or mentally, but the colonel said, "There is one thing that we feel safe in saying, and that is that each of you has a life expectancy of at least ten years less than the average American." Boy! If that wasn't a hell of a thing to tell us.

He told us that we would be given medical checkups, and that if anyone was having a problem of any kind be sure and let them know about it. We also would be interviewed to find out as much as they could about us in hope that it would assist them in locating our records.

After the colonel had finished, we were told to have a seat at one of the tables and the clerk would interview us. The clerk that I got started off by asking my name, rank, serial number and what branch of service. I gave him the answers to all these questions and then he asked what my unit was. I told him, and then he asked where I had been captured. When I told him "Java," he asked again "Where?" I said, "Java, in the Dutch East Indies." He said, "You trying to be funny or something? I don't have any time for playing around. I asked you where you were captured." Again I said, "Java," and he responded by saying we didn't even have any troops in Java.

I said "Damned if that's not a fine howdy do! We go fight a war for our country with a bunch of secondhand stuff, left over from WW I, get captured and spend three and one-half years of being starved, tortured and overworked, and you mean to tell me that the army didn't even know we were there?" He said that he would have to check with headquarters to see if there was an army battalion in Java at the start of the war.

He continued the interview to find out the dates of capture and liberation so he would know how many "hershey bars" (over seas bars) to authorize—one for each six months service in a combat zone. In lieu of any records, he was having to make me out an affidavit of service. He said that by an act of Congress, all POWs were to be promoted one rank.

I took the slip that he gave me and went to the supply room and drew another khaki uniform, three pair of staff sergeant chevrons, three hershey bar bands of seven bars each and three single hash marks.

I went back to my tent to get my other uniforms and take them to have the chevrons and stuff sewed on by a native seamstress in a nearby village. There was another GI having some of his uniforms fixed up. We got to talking and then decided to go to a native beer joint and have a beer or two while we waited for our uniforms. We ordered a beer each and sat down at a table looking out into the street and began to observe the goings-on of a native *kampong,* or village.

A couple of native belles were giving us the eyeball, and so we invited them over and bought them a beer. They could speak English, and over several beers we were finding out all about them. The gals sat down by us and began to sort of snuggle up real close to us. They got prettier with each beer. I hadn't had a girl rub up against me in three and a-half years, and the experience was sure upsetting my composure, to put it mildly. I was on the verge of suggesting that we find a room when the girl who had sat down by me said she was hungry and would I buy her something to eat. I was more than a little perturbed, for the urgency of my yearnings weren't hankering for any delaying tactics. I told her, though, to go ahead and order something.

She asked if she could order a *balut* (Baloot); since I did not know what it was I told her to go ahead. The waiter brought her a whole duck egg, still in the shell. A *balut* is a duck egg in the process of incubation; the egg takes twenty-one days or so to hatch, and one can order a ten-day *balut,* a twenty-day *balut* or whatever number of days the customer finds the egg most satisfying. A *balut* was obviously a delicacy in this village. I thought that it was just a boiled egg, but when she cracked it open, there was an embryonic duckling inside, just about to the hatching stage; she began to eat it, and all my years of pent-up manhood clamoring for expression metamorphosed into near nausea. I paid for the *balut* and left.

I stopped in a liquor store, or the native equivalent of one, and bought a fifth of Philippine whiskey. There seemed to be all the well-known brands of American and Scotch whiskies, or at least the bottles of them. However, it was obvious that the tax seals had been tampered with. There was no telling what the bottles actually contained and I was afraid to buy them. There were daily cases of men going blind, or even dying, from drinking native whiskey. They had American cigarettes done the same way.

I went by and picked up my finished uniforms and went back to camp. I put my uniforms away and offered a drink of the native whiskey to anyone in the tent that wanted it. I had no takers. I took a drink and chased it with water from my canteen and then put the bottle under my bed without trying to hide it. Because of "Project J" we had no inspections or supervision and everyone did as he pleased. Almost every bunk had whiskey and beer under it in plain sight. Our only restriction was that we had to sign in and out when we left camp.

I took off my tie and lay back on my bunk to rest up after my walk to the nearby village. No sooner had I lain down when two captains walked in and the first one yelled "Where's that Mad Dog Spaghet?" That was a nickname that my National Guard buddies had hung on me back in the days when the 36th division was changed from a square to a triangular division, and when we "dressed right" we did so at arms length, with the fingers of our left hand touching the right shoulder of the man to our left. I was so much shorter than the rest of them that their fingers came to my mouth and not my shoulder, and I would bite them; thus the reason for the nick-name.

I sat upright in my bed to see who was calling my name, and there, swaggering in, swinging a fifth of genuine Johnny Walker Red Label scotch whiskey, was Conally "Big Ed" Etheridge. Big Ed had been a high school chum and a fellow sergeant back in our early days in the Texas National Guards. I had visited in his home many times and dearly loved his mother's butterscotch pies. I had mentioned these pies in one of my messages to Mom. The other captain had also been in the National Guard at that time and was a master sergeant in Service Battery of the 131st Field Artillery, and I had known him as "Moko." I jumped up out of bed and Big Ed and I grabbed each other and danced around the tent like a couple of kids and we let out some good ol' Texas yells.

Big Ed said that he had saved the Johnny Walker Red Label whiskey during the entire war just for the day when I got out of the POW camps. He said that he had turned down as much as $500 for it. He said that he had come to the 29th Repo Depo every day since Allied POWs were being brought here to read the bulletin board, watching for my name. He knew I would make it through.

I was called back to the processing center the next day, and we went through all the interrogation again. This time when I was asked where I was captured and I told them Java, the clerk looked through some papers that he had, and this time he said that there had been a small unit of American soldiers in the Dutch East Indies when the war was just starting, but they had all been wiped out. He said that if I was part of that outfit I was supposed to be dead. I told him that if he did not get me out of there and on my way home, that I was going to be the hell raisingest corpse he had ever seen.

The clerk finished making me a temporary service record from various source materials and my affidavit and then made out some orders that authorized me to wear certain medals: the American Defense Medal, American Theater of Operation Medal, Asiatic Pacific/2 Bronze stars, Good Conduct/1 knot, Philippine Defense/1 Bronze star, Bronze Star Medal/ for Valor, and the Presidential Unit Citation/with two bronze cluster, Victory Medal and the Combat Infantry Badge, which was later taken away from me.[5]

I went back to my tent and had a drink or two and then walked around the area to see if anyone that I knew had come into the camp. I passed by the supply tent and the supply sergeant asked me to come in. He wanted to ask me all kinds of questions about POW camps and POW life, and was it true that the Japs had tortured us, starved us and overworked us. He had a bottle of bourbon whiskey when we started talking and we were making "short work" of it.

He asked me if I wanted any kind of weapon to take home and he handed me a .30-caliber carbine and bayonet and said that it would easily fit in my barracks bag and that it would make a good deer rifle back home.

---

5. The Combat Infantry Badge is a special medal awarded only to members of infantry units who have been engaged in combat. Soldiers in other types of units, whether or not they have seen combat, are not eligible. As a field artilleryman, Fujita would not have been entitled to this award. U.S. War Department, Circular 408, 17 October 1944.

The medals Fujita was authorized to wear: "the American Defense Medal, American Theater of Operation Medal, Asiatic Pacific/2 Bronze stars, Good Conduct/1 knot, Philippine Defense/1 Bronze star, Bronze Star Medal/for Valor, and the Presidential Unit Citation/with two bronze cluster, Victory Medal and the Combat Infantry Badge, which was later taken away from me."

About that time, some Japanese POWs came by in single file, each one carrying a piece of wood one inch by four inch by fifteen foot on his shoulder; they were sauntering along at a snail's pace and the sight infuriated me. I had instant visions of the one-hundred-plus pound planks that I had to carry in the Nagasaki ship yards, and the bayonets that were jabbed into me to make me go faster.

I told the supply sergeant about this, and then told him that I would show him how they would make us bow down to them. The next Jap POW who came by, I went outside the tent and yelled *"Kura!"* at him. That is a word used by the Japanese to get your attention.[6] Then as he stopped and looked in my direction, I gave him their sign to "come here." (This sign is identical to the hand signal that we use to tell someone to back off or get away. I learned this the hard way on a work party early in the war. A "Jeep" guard gave me this same sign after getting my attention. I thought he meant for me to back off and so I did. He started yelling *"Motogoi,"*[7] and making this sign vigorously. I backed off faster and he chased me down and bashed me several times with his rifle butt, and then tried to explain that he wanted me to come to him.)

I then yelled *"Motogoi!"* to the "Jeep" and he came running over to me with a big grin which instantly disappeared when I told him to *"Kiostuke!"* (come to attention). He looked startled and then, when I yelled it again and tried to look fierce, he snapped to attention. I then told him *"Keirei!"* which meant to bow; he did a very stiff, slight bow and then I yelled it again rather nasty-like and then he bowed way down. I said *"Yush!"*[8] and motioned him to go on.

The supply sergeant enjoyed this immensely and so did a lot of our guys who were lining up nearby for evening chow. However, a second lieutenant came running over and started chewing me out, telling me that he had witnessed the whole episode. According to him, I had disobeyed an order that stated anyone who bothered a Japanese POW would be committing

6. Actually, *kora,* "Hey, you!"
7. Probably *motte-koi,* "bring," or *kochi koi,* "come here."
8. Short for *yoroshii,* "fine" or "all right."

a court-martial offense, and he intended to throw the book at me with an immediate court-martial.

All the guys from the chow line had now crowded around the lieutenant and me. They were ex-POWs and fresh out of the Jap POW camps. They were pushing right up to the lieutenant and one guy got right in his face and told him that if he even looked like he was going to court-martial the sergeant that his ass wouldn't last until the water got hot. Everyone was bad-mouthing him and called him a USO commando[9] and such. He worked his way out of the mob and beat a hasty retreat. I never saw that lieutenant again.

I was given a perfunctory medical exam and asked if I had any medical complaints. I did not want to say anything that would delay my starting for home so I never launched a complaint. Every time I had been through debriefing, I was always asked if I had kept a diary and did I have any information that would or could be used against Japanese officers or soldiers for war crimes purposes. I wanted very much to have my diary that was secreted in a wall back in Tokyo, but I was afraid if I told the army about it, I would have to be taken back to Tokyo in order to show them where it was located. There would be no telling when I would be able to go home, so I never mentioned it.

The army was still trying to get enough data on me to send me home, and in the meantime I had more medical briefings. Other ex-POWs whose records were processed sufficiently were being shipped or flown back to the States. There were a lot of military egos crushed in the process, for "Project J" men had priority and even colonels were "bumped" off flights to make room for more POWs. Finally, after seventeen days of raising hell to go home, I had my orders cut and was put aboard the U.S. Army Transport *Admiral Hughes*. With a name like that it must have been a navy transport.

It was at 5:00 P.M. on September 24, 1945, when I went aboard. The ship filled quite rapidly with American, British and Canadian ex-POWs

---

9. The United Service Organizations, a civilian agency endorsed by the government, ran clubs and other recreational and entertainment facilities for enlisted members of the armed forces.

and the balance of the space was filled with all sorts of military personnel going back to the States to be processed out of the service. Most of these people had not been in a war zone long enough to have more than two or three hershey bars each. After we had been assigned our bunk spaces and had stowed our gear, I went topside to become familiar with the ship.

While strolling the decks, I passed a group of GIs and one of them pointed to my six hershey bars and then told the others, "That sergeant done took out citizenship papers over there." We were not assigned any duties on the ship; however, there were some who volunteered for different duties to help pass the time away. I spent most of my time as I had on the old *Republic* coming over, hanging on the rails watching flying fish and porpoises.

As will always happen when a bunch of GIs get together with time on their hands, poker games and crap games broke out around the ship. Evidently there were a lot of guys who had had some sort of lucrative operation going on besides fighting the war, for these games were being played for big bucks. The winner of one game was a colored GI, and his take was upwards of twenty thousand dollars.

When the game was over, he had money crammed in every pocket and his shirt was stuffed full. He began to back away from the crowd, which the big stakes had attracted, and it was obvious that he was very uneasy with that much money on him. He backed away, keeping a wary eye on everyone in front and back of him, and disappeared into the ship. This soldier was never seen again on the ship and someone suggested that somebody had "waylaid" him, taken his winnings and then fed him to the fish. Who knows?

The trip home seemed to take forever, and I had ample time to reflect on everything. I wondered where Provoo and Streeter were at this moment and what sort of future they faced. I wondered too, why I had never been asked anything about the propaganda radio programs. I could not believe that our country could just let that drop without even asking something about it, but that is exactly what happened.

After an eternity of sailing, we were pulled into the Strait of Juan de Fuca, between the Olympic Peninsula and Vancouver Island, British Columbia, Canada, and then on to its capital city Victoria. Sirens and whistles and car horns were blowing from the city and there were hundreds and hundreds of boats and ships of every description. They were blowing foghorns and whistles, ringing bells, waving flags, and many of the tugs and larger boats were squirting streams of water high in the air with high pressure hoses. The British and Canadian ex-POWs were off-loaded, during all this hoopla, onto a ship that had pulled up alongside to take them.

After dropping off those POWs, our ship entered the Puget Sound and went down to Seattle, Washington. In contrast to the welcome the Canadian and British got, we were greeted with silence. Not a bell, not a whistle, no welcoming committee—nothing.

16

TACOMA TO TEXAS

September 1945–February 1946

We were transferred to a ferry boat, taken to Tacoma and disembarked there. It had been three years, eleven months and eighteen days since I had left the good old U.S.A. I bent down and kissed the ground, as did many others. We were entered into Madigan General Hospital, on the main base of Ft. Lewis, and assigned to wards. We kept our gear under our beds and there were closets to hang our uniforms in.

Here too, because of "Project J," we were left alone and were not restricted in movement except to sign in and out. There was a bulletin board that kept us posted on anything that pertained to us or that might be of interest to us, the daily menu and the theater schedule. Any time one of us was scheduled for some sort of medical or physical examination, that information was also posted. Departing train schedules were there too. Anyone who had been cleared for discharge from the hospital could select which train best suited him.

We acted here like we had in the Philippines. We just put our beer or whiskey under our beds and had a drink whenever we wanted. We had a jewel of a nurse and she considered all of us heroes. She would spend most of her tour of duty in our ward talking to us. We were all quite fond of her. There was a cashier's window down the hall from us where we could draw a partial pay, which seemed to frustrate the cashier no end. There was no way, from our temporary service records, for her to tell if we had as much money

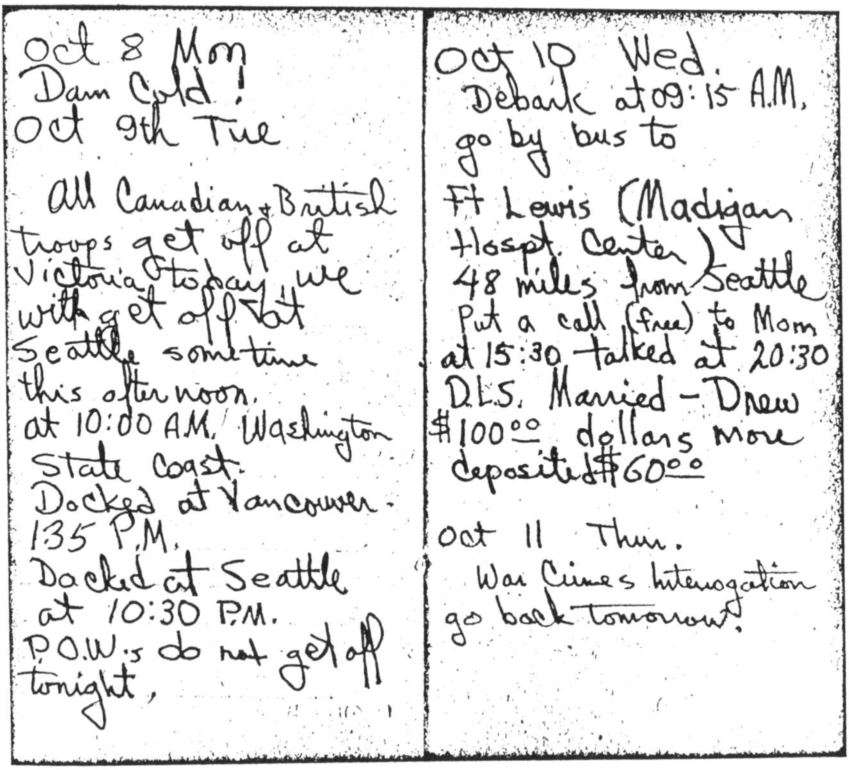

Oct 8 Mon
Dam Cold!
Oct 9th Tue

All Canadian & British
troops get off at
Victoria today we
with get off at
Seattle sometime
this afternoon.
at 10:00 AM. Washington
State Coast.
Docked at Vancouver.
135 P.M.
Docked at Seattle
at 10:30 P.M.
P.O.W.s do not get off
tonight,

Oct 10 Wed.
Debark at 09:15 A.M.
go by bus to
Ft Lewis (Madigan
Hospt. Center)
48 miles from Seattle
Put a call (free) to Mom
at 15:30 talked at 20:30
D.L.S. Married - Drew
$100.00 dollars more
deposited $60.00

Oct 11 Thur.
War Crimes Interogation
go back tomorrow!

coming as we wanted to draw out. I went to her and drew three hundred dollars.

Pvts. Jim and Ramon Martinez of my E Battery had come over on the same ship with me and were here in the same hospital ward with me. Along towards the middle of one evening, when there was no likelihood of any further exams or processing, Jim and I and two other ex-POWs decided to go into Seattle to do some shopping and have a night on the town.

We stopped in a bar and had a drink and then I told them that I was going to find a jewelry store to buy a good watch and that I would be back in a little while. I found a Longine-Whitnauer watch that I liked and paid one hundred dollars for it. I did a little more shopping and bought an aluminum cigarette case and a Ronson lighter.

I decided I wanted another drink and went into a bar to get it. The bar was pretty well filled with sailors and GIs and a scattering of civilians. I "bellied up to the bar" and ordered an Old-Fashioned. I was sipping away and enjoying it when something happened that I will never forget. Sitting behind me at a table were two highly dressed women who looked as if they had just stepped out of the latest fashion catalog. These women were talking about their careers and one of them said, loud enough for us to hear, "If the war had lasted another six months I could have had my home and business paid for."

This made me instantly and violently mad and I turned around with the intention of smashing my fist into her face but another ex-POW beat me to her. He hit her so hard in the face that her fur flew off and she went sliding across the floor, out cold.

This upset me terribly, not the woman's face being bashed in, but the sentiment that she had expressed. I looked around at the other civilians and from then on I wondered how many more of them looked upon the war as an opportunity for personal enrichment, reaping huge benefits at the expense of their fellow countrymen dying on the far-flung battlefields of the world. This did terrible things to me psychologically, to think that I had undergone the years of torture and mind-boggling pain, of starvation, and abject fear, and that there were people such as this woman wanting the war to continue until they had become even richer.

I left this bar and stopped off in another. As I walked up to the bar, a man dressed in a civilian suit came rushing over to me and said, "From the looks of all those medals and stripes and overseas bars, you must be one the those prisoners of war who came in yesterday." I told him that I was and he said that he was very proud to meet a POW and he would consider it an honor if I would let him buy me a drink. All the while he was shaking my hand and patting me on the back. I said that I appreciated that and would have a drink with him.

It turned out that this "true blue" American had slipped me a "Mickey Finn" and took my money and my new watch. About 3:00 A.M. I found myself wallowing in the floor of a jail cell, trying to rally my senses. The cell was full of drunks, both civilians and GIs. Finally I managed to get to my feet. I was quite dizzy and my head felt as if it would burst at any moment.

There were SPs and MPs[1] (navy and army police) milling about the place, as well as civilian cops. I got the attention of one of the MPs and he came over and let me out of the cell. He figured that I must be one the returned ex-POWs. I asked if they had taken my watch and billfold, and they told me that they had been missing when they picked me up. When I told them that I was a returned ex-POW and was out of Madigan General Hospital, they took me and a couple more GIs back to Fort Lewis and dropped me off at the hospital.

I lay around all morning trying to get myself back together, and by the middle of the afternoon I was feeling pretty good. The same guys I had gone out with the day before were wanting to go out again, and so I told them to hang on long enough for me to draw some more money. I went to the cashier and wanted to draw three hundred dollars more. She couldn't believe that I had gone through the other three hundred so fast. She gave me the money and said that she sure hoped I had enough back pay coming to cover these withdrawals.

The four of us took a couple of bottles of whiskey with us and started walking down the street. We would take turns having a drink as we passed the bottles from one to another. We were in Class A uniforms and we looked very impressive with all the medals, stripes and hershey bars. One of us was a buck sergeant, one was a technical sergeant and two of us were staff sergeants. We came to a large permanent concrete barracks with a big sign out on the front lawn which declared that these Women's Army Corps barracks were "Off Limits" to all male personnel.

We decided that we wanted to see what a WAC barracks looked like and went up to the front door and walked in. The halls were empty and so we went into a room marked Orderly Room. There was a young girl wearing corporal stripes sitting behind the desk. When she looked up and saw four male GIs walk in the door, she was startled, to say the least. She jumped up and ran to another door and called the first sergeant out.

The "First Shirt" was a lean and mean brunette and she glared at us and

1. Shore Patrol and Military Police.

Foo and Jimmy Martinez at Seattle, Washington, with one of the WACs from Ft. Lewis.

said, "What the hell you guys think you're doing coming in here? Didn't you see the 'Off Limits' sign?" About that time a WAC came down the stairs. She saw us and let out a big yell, "There's men in the barracks! There's men in the barracks!" In less time than it takes to tell it, there were women in various stages of attire appearing from everywhere.

The first sergeant ordered the clerk to call the MPs just as a very, very buxom blonde in a captain's uniform came around the corner to see what the ruckus was about. She looked at us and said "My God! High point men!" and then told the clerk not to call the MPs. The first sergeant was having a fit until the captain told her to cool it. The captain was the C.O.

She turned to us and wanted to know what we were doing here. I offered her a drink and told her that we were POWs, fresh back from three and a half years in Jap prisoner of war camps and we wanted a detail to accompany us to Seattle. She said, as she looked up the stairs at all the congregated women, "Did you girls hear that?" They said yes and then she wanted to know if any of them were interested. It seemed that every one of them said yes.

The captain said, "If I wasn't engaged to be married, I'd go with you myself. I'll tell you what I'll do, I'll call these girls off from the roster and you guys can take your pick. I'll give a pass to those you choose." She was as good as her word and she ordered the first sergeant to get the roster and start calling out the names. The ones we chose received their passes and we met them at the bus stop at the agreed upon hour and headed to Seattle.

The Martinezs had shipped out, as had everyone else that I had come in with. I had turned down two trains already because I wanted to be routed home through San Francisco. My lifelong friend from El Reno, Oklahoma, Wayne Cranmer, was in the marines and stationed in Camp Pendleton. I was told that I might never get routed from Tacoma to San Francisco, so I told them that I would take the next train to Texas.

I was put in charge of a draft of twenty ex-POWs who were all heading to Texas for discharge. We got on a train and had a Pullman sleeper car to ourselves. We had some time to kill while we waited for departure time and we spent it at a nearby concession stand drinking beer. It seems that there was one thing that almost all returning POWs had in common and that was a love for alcohol, or was it the effects of alcohol?

We boarded the train and long before we got to the first stop we were wishing we had brought something to drink. We asked the porter if there was anything to drink on the train and he said that there was not, but that there was a liquor store about two blocks from the depot at the next stop. He said that the train would not be there for more than a few minutes, so if we wanted to make a purchase we would have to be mighty fast.

Six of the men decided to make a run for the whiskey stop when we got there and we all chipped in some money for the purchase. When the train pulled up to a stop, the porter told them where to go and again cautioned them that the train would leave in about ten minutes. The six men bailed out and took off on a high lope for the "Likker" store. Two men made it back with two bottles each, but the other four didn't quite make it.

The loss of these men gave me four extra meal tickets and four empty bunks. I took turns about giving the extra meal tickets out to the remaining men. By the time we reached the next stop, we were out of drinks again. Some of the guys jumped off to get more and the same thing happened again. I lost two or three more men.

It was almost unbelievable how crowded the train was. We would sometimes walk through it just to break the monotony, and were really shocked at the mass of humanity piled into these coach cars. The seats were overloaded and the aisles were crammed with people so that it was almost impossible to get through. There was a young woman sitting in the aisle floor. She was pregnant and had another small child sitting by her. I felt sorry for her and told her she could come into my coach, for I now had about eight empty seats and bunks. She was so thankful that she was in tears.

About fifteen minutes later, the conductor came in and talked very nasty to her and told her that she could not ride there. I jumped the conductor out and told him that I was in charge of this car and I was the one that had brought her in here. He acted real hateful and said that the War Department would not allow civilians to ride in a troop car.

I lost some more men at other stops and the meal tickets were sure stacking up on me. I gave them out to any of the men who wanted them. We were sure eating "high on the hog." The conductor came in, bringing with him six or eight inductees who were heading for some training center, and he began to point out where they could ride. I went up to him and asked him what the hell he thought he was doing. He said that he was bedding these draftees down in this car. I told him, "You old fart! You're not bedding them or anyone else down in this car. I am in charge of this car and you get out and take the draftees with you!" If he had not been such a horse's ass about the pregnant woman, I might have let him put these guys in my car. He left mumbling something about reporting me to some higher headquarters somewhere.

By the time we pulled into "Cow Town," Fort Worth, Texas, my draft of twenty men had dwindled to six. We were going to have to lay over for about an hour or more before the train for San Antonio and Fort Sam Houston would leave. Most of the guys said that they would roam around the area until train time and they left. I went to a bar across the street from the depot and two men went with me. We sat there on the bar stools and had a beer or two and two "ladies of the night" came up and began putting the make on us.

The temptation was obviously too much for my friends and they said that they would try them out and be right back. I warned them that they had less than thirty minutes before the train left. They didn't make it back, and I reported in to Fort Sam with twenty meal tickets and not one man.

By the time I got settled in at Fort Sam Houston, my new service record was there waiting for me and it was marked with a great big "Project J." I was run through the processing center, given a quick medical checkup which included issuing a lot of vitamins, and then given a 90 day TDY—temporary duty—at home. I called Mom and told her I was coming home by bus and what time the bus was supposed to be in Abilene. It was un-believable how many people could get on a bus. I had to stand up most of the way and the bus stopped at every little wide spot in the road. It was way up in the night when it finally pulled into Abilene.

Since I was already standing, I was one of the first off the bus. I walked into the bus station, looked at all the people in the waiting room, and walked past my mother and baby sister without recognizing them. My mom must have been drowsy, or the sight of me froze her into immobility, for I was two or three people past her before she came into action. She let out a whoop that could be heard for blocks and grabbed me from the rear. It still took a few seconds for me to realize that this was my mom. I didn't know my little sister at all.

We hugged and laughed and cried and kissed. Mom had told the other people who were waiting in the bus station that her son was coming home from three and a half years in Japanese prisoners of war camps, and it seemed that everyone in the station had joined in on the homecoming. It was a happy moment and it sure was good to be back home.

It turned out that I arrived home just in time for the first Lost Battalion

Foo and his parents, Frank Fujita, Sr., and Pearl Fujita at the Lost Battalion Reunion.

Reunion, planned for the coming weekend in Wichita Falls, Texas. This was in October 1945.

Although the Lost Battalion was a name given to the 2d Battalion, 131st Field Artillery, 36th Infantry Division, the survivors of the heavy cruiser USS *Houston* (CA30), the ship that was reported sunk so many times by the Japanese that she became known as "The Galloping Ghost of the Java Coast," also participated in the weekend festivities.

The Battalion, less E Battery, had been captured in early March, 1942 and put into prison compounds with survivors of the *Houston*, which had been sunk in the Java sea battle a week or so earlier. The survivors of the two units went through the rest of the war, working and dying side by side. To this day the survivors are united with an unbreakable bond and hold an annual reunion each August as the Lost Battalion Association.

This first annual reunion had nice weather and most of the planned activities were held outdoors. My mother and father both attended with me even though they had divorced about a year earlier. Those of us who were able marched through the streets of the city amid wild cheers and confetti from the locals. Those who were unable to walk, rode in cars. Afterwards we had a barbecue in a local park. The weather was just a little bit hotter than the highly seasoned meat. We had a couple of speeches and then Governor Coke Stevenson proclaimed the day to be Lost Battalion Day.

All the Battalion had not returned in time for the Wichita Falls reunion so another one was scheduled in Abilene about a month later. All the Abilene men had returned by then, as had almost all the others, and a good time was had by all.

Most of the Abilene men bought big cars, and not to be outdone, I bought a sleek four-door twelve-cylindered Lincoln. Most of us ran around together and went off on what amounted to a ninety-day party, which was indistinguishable from a ninety-day drunk. We all went to the same places but no one would ride with anyone else, so we went through town as a high speed convoy. We partied around the clock. Some of us averaged drinking a fifth of whiskey a day.

Abilene had hoped and prayed to get us back for three and a half years, and now that we were back they wondered what they were going to do with us. The newspapers and radios proclaimed us to be heroes. One thing for certain was that the Lost Battalion was well known in Texas. The local drug stores, our prewar source of prescription whiskey, no longer sold liquor. We were obliged to purchase it from one of the twenty or so local bootleggers at twelve dollars a fifth, or make a run to San Angelo or Fort Worth and bring back our own.

Anyone in uniform who had lots of ribbons, medals and stripes had no problem getting a date. Besides the local belles, there were three local colleges that had bevies of available beauties, and then, too, the bell captains of the local hotels maintained a stable of call girls. I was eating one meal every three days and this, coupled with the excessive drinking and carousing, didn't do my health any good. By the time my ninety-day TDY was over, I had lost almost as much weight as I had in the prison camps. I had gingivitis, acute Vincent's angina and an ulcerated throat that was so bad I could hardly swallow water.

I went back to Fort Sam and reported to the infirmary for immediate treatment. The doctor called in a dentist, who took one looked into my mouth and said, "My God! A perfect set of teeth." He ran out of the room and began hollering down the hall for the other dentists to come have a look. I had all my teeth and had never had a filling. The dentists were taking turns looking at my teeth. In addition to the terrible pain I was feeling, I was also getting lockjaw from holding my mouth open so long.

The dentist eventually got around to giving me two aspirins and a codeine tablet, and soon I was literally feeling no pain. I was treated and then entered into Brooks General Hospital. I was put into a ward filled with ex-POWs some of whom were in E Battery: Pvts. Jim and Ramon Martinez and Cpl. Cecil Powers. This hospital certainly was not like Madigan General. Here they kept our uniforms locked up so that we were unable to get to them.

I was being administered several thousand units of penicillin orally, every hour on the hour, and really big doses by injection every two hours around the clock. The nurses would awaken me for the shots at night, and they were so gentle that I never felt the needle. I asked them not to wake me up each time but they said that it was regulations.

A couple of days later I was feeling much better and asked for a pass to town. I got the pass and went to the clothing room and got my Class A uniform, took it to my bunk area and put it on. As I was leaving the ward a "Bird Colonel" wearing a 36th Division "T" patch on his left shoulder noticed me with my "T" patch on my right shoulder and wearing seven hershey bars and Asiatic-Pacific ribbons.

Army regulations stated that the shoulder patch of the unit that I was now assigned to should be worn on my left shoulder and the outfit that I had been in combat with should be worn on my right. I was wearing the 4th Army patch on my left shoulder and the 36th Division on my right. The colonel ordered me to remove the 36th patch or the Pacific ribbons and seven overseas bars from my uniform before I left the ward. I asked him why and he told me in no uncertain terms that the 36th Division was never in the Pacific, had not earned seven overseas bars, had no APO (Asiatic Pacific Theater of Operations) ribbons whatever, let alone three Presidential Unit Citations and that I should waste no time in removing one or the other from my uniform.

I told the colonel, "No, sir. I'll not do either one." Boy! Did he get mad. He said, "Sergeant, do you realize who you are talking to? I am giving you a direct order to do as I said!" He was acting like such a horse's ass that everyone in the ward was sitting up taking note. One of the doctors and several nurses were also watching. I told him, "Colonel, before you start throwing your weight around, you had better find out what the hell you are talking about." He was really mad now and said that he would have me arrested immediately and then court-martialed. The doctor got his attention, took him aside and said something to him that I could not over hear. The colonel's face turned white and then a beet red as he turned around to me, cleared his throat and said, "Carry on, Sergeant."

Since there were a lot of Lost Battalion men coming through the hospital, the doctor knew that we were from the 36th Division and had been three and one half years as POWs in the Pacific.

There was a chaplain who would come through the ward. He just couldn't seem to hear enough about the POW experience. He would make the rounds and listen to anyone who would talk to him. Seeing him reminded me of a saying that came out of WW I. "There are no Atheists in a foxhole." I suddenly realized that at no time, under any condition, had I seen or heard a man pray or evoke God's name except in cussing.

I remember once back in Room 20 at Fukuoka #2, an Englishman had torn a page from the soldiers' pocket New Testament to use in rolling a cigarette. The page had to do with the genealogy of Jesus Christ and the guy was really making a joke of reading who begat who and this infuriated me very much. I told him to knock it off, that to make fun of the Bible was to make fun of my mother, who was very religious, and I wasn't standing still for that.

As I lay in my hospital bed pondering the vagaries of life and all the experiences that had befallen me, I wondered if there was a predetermined scenario composed for each of us that we blindly followed like some automaton. Each turn in life's road had its own experiences and each experience had its own results and effects on us. As we travel life's road we seem to have, at times, minimal or nonexistent control over which turn we take. The effects of the experiences thrust upon us from making the turn, can be either destructive or beneficial. The results of the turn that took me through the prisoner of war experience could not be assessed at that time as to which category they would belong.

One evening I was talking with Jim Martinez when a first lieutenant came in looking for me. It was Jack Wisener, one of the Bunker Hill boys from the Tokyo radio programs. We shook hands and were genuinely glad to see each other. He told us that he had just bought a Chevrolet convertible and wanted to take us for a ride. The time was around 8:30 in the evening, and we could not draw our uniforms due to the lateness of the hour. We were required to be back in the ward by 10 P.M. when we were out on pass.

The lieutenant had had a few drinks and was feeling pretty good. He said that we did not need the uniforms anyhow and for us to follow him. We went out into the parking lot and got into his convertible. He suggested that the first thing we should do was to get us a bottle. We agreed and away we went to find a liquor store in some out-of-the-way place. We found one and went in to make our selection. The store operator saw that we were in Army hospital pajamas and probably thought that we were escapees from the Nut Ward. He grabbed the phone and said that if we did not get out of there immediately he would call the MPs.

We explained to him that we all were ex-POWs and that we had just met again for the first time since we were liberated and just wanted to have a few drinks to wash down the memories of three and a half years of Jap beatings and starvation. He said that he had read about POWs being brought to Fort Sam and he thought our Lost Battalion were all heroes for sure. We said that he wanted to give us each a fifth of whiskey, which he did—a fifth of Old Guggenheimer each. We thanked him and left.

The lieutenant was taking us for a fast ride through town when a traffic light turned red on us. He said, "Open the glove compartment and hand me that pistol that I just bought." We handed it to him and he shot at the traffic light but failed to hit it. We continued to drive around, passing a bottle back and forth, and each time that we were caught by a red light we would take turns at trying to shoot it out. I don't remember us ever hitting one and it was a wonder that we didn't all wind up in the "clink."

My mouth and throat had cleared up and I was given another sixty-day leave from the hospital. Once again this amounted to one prolonged party. This time some of the other ex-POWs were telling me of the wonderful time that they had had at Miami Beach, or Hot Springs, Arkansas, at the Army's expense. I knew nothing about this and it turned out that all returning ex-POWs could take their families or their parents to one of these vacation meccas for a two-week stay at the government's expense.

When my leave was up, I returned to Fort Sam and was assigned to a special barracks. This was to be my quarters until I could be processed out of the Army for the convenience of the government. On the lower floor, this barracks had a day room with a pool table, a radio, a record player, a sofa and some easy chairs. I asked at the orderly room when I could take my two weeks all-expense paid vacation to Miami Beach and they said, "Aren't you staying in the special barracks?" I said that I was and they replied that that barracks was luxurious and staying in it was considered the same thing as two weeks in Miami beach or Hot Springs. What a ridiculous statement. I missed out on that one.

I was told to report to a certain building to begin processing to get out of the Army. There were a hundred or more GIs massed around the entrance and they were all sweating out how many points they could come up with to hopefully qualify for discharge from the Army. As I walked up to the crowd, a GI sitting on the railing of the entranceway saw me and declared very loudly, "There comes a Sergeant that's got enough points to discharge all of us!"

The processing and last minute physical took several hours. The paper work for my discharge had already been completed and as I was about to sign it, they asked if I had any medical complaints. If so, this was my last opportunity to have them entered in my records. I told them that I was having lots of pain in my lower back from the severe beating I received in Nagasaki. I was told that, in that case, I had to go back and have this last minute physical. I started not to launch this complaint because it would slow me down more in getting my discharge, but I did, and, as it

THE WHITE HOUSE
WASHINGTON

TO MEMBERS OF UNITED STATES ARMED FORCES BEING
REPATRIATED IN OCTOBER 1945:

It gives me special pleasure to welcome you
back to your native shores, and to express, on behalf of the people of the United States, the joy we
feel at your deliverance from the hands of the enemy.
It is a source of profound satisfaction that our efforts to accomplish your return have been successful.

You have fought valiantly in foreign lands
and have suffered greatly. As your Commander in
Chief, I take pride in your past achievements and
express the thanks of a grateful Nation for your
services in combat and your steadfastness while a
prisoner of war.

May God grant each of you happiness and an
early return to health.

Harry Truman

Letter from Harry S. Truman.

turned out, it was a good thing that I did, for it led to my future Veterans Administration compensation for physical disability.

The physical didn't take too long and then I signed the last of the paper work, took my discharge and my "ruptured duck," the gold pin that indicated I was discharged,[2] climbed into my Lincoln and headed for home as a civilian. The date was the twelfth of February, 1946—four years, three months and eight days after having been mobilized.

• • •

The White House to Sergeant Frank Fujita, Jr .20,813,132

The White House
Washington, D.C.
October 12, 1945
TO MEMBERS OF UNITED STATES ARMED FORCES
BEING REPATRIATED IN OCTOBER 1945:

It gives me special pleasure to welcome you back to your native shores, and to express, on behalf of the people of the United States, the joy that we feel at your deliverance from the hands of the enemy. It is a source of profound satisfaction that our efforts to accomplish your return have been successful.

You have fought valiantly in foreign lands and have suffered greatly. As your Commander in Chief, I take pride in your past achievements and express the thanks of a grateful Nation for your services in combat and your steadfastness while a prisoner of war.

May God grant each of you happiness and an early return to health.

Signed: Harry S. Truman

2. The discharge pin was a representation of an eagle in a circle, but was universally if irreverently referred to as the "ruptured duck."

17

EPILOGUE

My diary was kept all through the war in little pocket note-books and on scraps of paper that I kept sewed into my clothing and gear. In all the Japanese labor camps it was a death penalty to keep a diary, and I had more than one narrow escape during unannounced inspections. One note-book diary was found by a guard on a surprise inspection for knives. The one-track mind of the guard saved me. He was looking for knives and it did not dawn on him that the diary was also banned.

At war's end we were also told that no diaries or writ-ten materials could be taken from the propaganda camp of *Bunka Gakuin Kanda,* or Bunker Hill, as we referred to it. Fearing for my life now that the war was ending, I did not have the guts to take this last chance to get the diary out. In this camp I had transferred the information into a larger hardbacked ledger book, and I nailed this up in a wall of one of the camp buildings, hoping that some day the opportu-nity would present itself for me to retrieve it.

I was asked over and over during debriefing and process-ing, both in the Philippines and in the States, if I had kept a diary and I withheld the information, fearing that to do so would only embroil me in war crimes and treason inquiries that would indefinitely delay my returning home. About one year after my return home, I was thinking of the hazards that I faced by keeping the diary and I wanted it back very badly.

The only way that I could think of to get it back was to tell the government about it. I wrote the government (the War Department, I think) and told them of the diary and said that if they would promise, in writing, to give it back to me after they had finished with it, that I would tell them where it was. They said that they would and so I sent them a detailed letter describing the area of Tokyo that the District of Kanda was in, described the buildings and the panel in the wall behind which I had secreted the diary. They were not considerate enough to inform me that they had retrieved the diary. About five years later I was wanting the diary back more than ever, and on 12 December 1950 I wrote to the Federal Bureau of Investigation in Washington, D.C., and asked for my diary back. I received the following reply.

Federal Bureau of Investigation
United States Department of Justice
422 Federal Office Building
San Francisco 2, California
December 21, 1950

Sgt. Frank Fujita, Jr.
Post Office Box 1306
Vernon, Texas

Dear Sir:
Reference your letter 12/12/50.

There is enclosed herewith the diary mentioned in your letter. I regret that there has been a delay in returning it to you. As you were in-formed by the Agents who secured the diary from you, there exists the possibility that it might be of value to the U.S. Government in the forthcoming Provoo trial. The postponement of this trial has made it difficult to determine if and when your diary would be needed. It now appears, however, that it will not be needed for that trial.

I should like to express my appreciation to you for the use of the diary and also for your offer of assistance to the Bureau in the Provoo trial.

Very truly yours,
Harry M. Kimball Special Agent in Charge

• • •

Article from a New York newspaper:

News of the Week in Review, *The New York Times*
New York, New York
October 23, 1955
Of all the cases of collaboration with the enemy during WW II, the
most extraordinary was that of John David Provoo. A former bank
clerk, Buddhist, and student of Japanese, Provoo went on trial in 1952
on a charge of treason. Witnesses assembled from all over the world told
how Provoo, then an Army sergeant, had shaved his head and donned
the robes of a Buddhist priest after the fall of Corregidor in 1942, and
offered his services to the Japanese. They claimed he had served as an
informer and had been directly responsible for the death of at least one
American officer. The trial lasted 15 weeks and was said to have cost the
government more than $1,000,000. It ended in a conviction of treason
and a sentence of life imprisonment for Provoo.

On appeal, however, the conviction was thrown out on grounds
that Provoo should have been tried in Maryland instead of New York,
and that the trial judge had erred in permitting the testimony about
Provoo's alleged homosexuality. The government obtained a new indictment, but last March a federal court dismissed it. The court ruled
that Provoo, who had already spent five years in prison without bail,
had been denied his rights, under the sixth amendment, to a speedy and
public trial. In handing down the decision, the court was apparently
influenced by the belief that the error in venue in the original trial had
been the result of a deliberate attempt by the Government to try the
case in a district it believed would be more favorable for a conviction.
The Government appealed the decision to the Supreme Court.

Last week the Supreme Court wrote finis to the Provoo case. It upheld the lower court's dismissal of the indictment, thus ending any
chance of prosecution of a case Government attorneys had described as
"one of the most important treason cases in U.S. history."

• • •

There have never been any newspaper items brought to my attention of any charges ever having been levied against Streeter by the Government on any charge. The FBI solicited a statement from me about him and I feel sure that they also took statements from other POWs of the *Bunka Gakuin Kanda* camp about him. I cannot imagine him not being taken to task for all the treasonable (I think) things he uttered over the Japanese airways during wartime.

• • •

Editorial from the *Washington Post* newspaper

The Washington Post
Washington, D.C.
March 28, 1946

The most distasteful of all war jobs, the detention upon mere suspicion and without trial of approximately 120,000 persons of Japanese ancestry, two-thirds of them citizens of the United States, has now been liquidated. It was a job made necessary through the decision early in 1942 of Gen. John L. DeWitt to exclude all Japanese-Americans from the Western defense command, of which he was at that time the commander. His exclusion order has since been validated by the Supreme Court on the grounds of military necessity. For our part, however, we hold still to the opinion we have expressed on a number of occasions that the exclusion was altogether unnecessary, that it was prompted more by blind racial prejudice than by military considerations and that the Supreme Court's validation of it amounted, as Mr. Justice Murphy charged in a dissenting opinion, to a "legalization of racism." The treatment accorded this helpless minority remains a smudge upon our national honor and a threat to elementary freedom.

Once the exclusion error was committed, guardianship of the uprooted Japanese-Americans became a Federal responsibility. They had to be kept in detention centers until they could be relocated in parts of

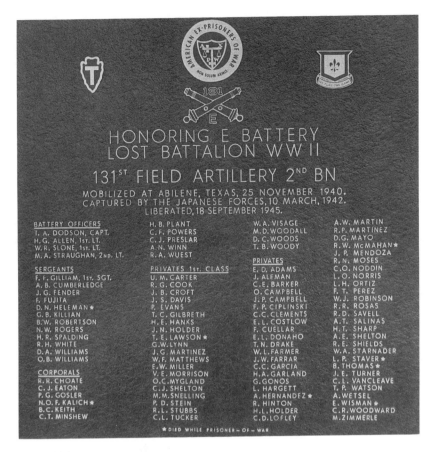

E Battery, Lost Battalion marker.

the country other than the West Coast. The burden of discharging this unhappy obligation was given to an emergency agency, the War Relocation Authority, headed at first by Milton Eisenhower, later and through most of its existence by Dillon S. Myer. It performed its task with humanity, with efficiency and with a conscientious sense of trusteeship towards the evacuees which made some amends for the terrible hardship inflicted upon them. All the men associated in this undertaking, and in particular Mr. Myer, who fought valiantly and pertinaciously against prejudice for the rights of these unfortunates in his charge, can take pride in a difficult job exceedingly well done.

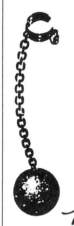

THE LOST BATTALION
— *LIFE TIME MEMBERSHIP* —
THIS IS TO CERTIFY THAT

_____

of_____was an
American Prisoner of War of the Japanese and
as such is entitled to full membership in THE
LOST BATTALION CLUB.
   He is again authorized to wear the ball and
chain, emblem, from the dawn of history, of
servitude and slavery. It shall be worn now,
however, on the lapel as a constant reminder
of FREEDOM!
   Issued in Wichita Falls, Texas, August 16,
1946.
*Bluecher S Tharp*___President

A Lost Battalion membership card.

When at last the army rescinded its exclusion order, about 57,500 evacuees moved back to their former homes in the West Coast States. But about 51,800 settled eastward in new homes. Perhaps the dispersal will have some benefits in better integration of the Japanese-American into the American society. The loyalty of those left here has been meticulously scrutinized. Out of the whole number in the relocation centers, some 3,000, including quite innocent family members, were transferred to internment camps administered by the Department of Justice; and about 4,700 persons were voluntarily repatriated to Japan—many of them, no doubt, because the treatment they received here convinced them they had no hope of leading free lives in America. It seems to us that we owe those who remain generous help in getting reestablished and restitution for their property losses.[1]

---

1. Forty-two years later, finally, Congress passed the Civil Liberties Act of 1988 (PL 100-383), acknowledging the fundamental injustice done to Japanese-Americans during World War II, apologizing to them on behalf of the people of the United States, and authorizing the payment of $20,000 to each Japanese-American (or statutory heirs) who had been detained in an internment camp.

• • •

Federal Court
Lawton, Oklahoma
August 28, 1954
Today my father, Frank Fujita, Sr., who came to the United States from
Japan in 1914, some 40 years ago, became an American Citizen under the
1952 Immigration and Naturalization Act. It was our proudest moment.

• • •

In December of 1948, after a failed marriage and a number of disillu-
sionments with civilian life and the Veterans Administration intent to
eliminate my 100 percent disability rating, I reenlisted in the army. I was
having an awful lot of physical problems, the worse of which affected my
lower back due to the severe beating that I received in Nagasaki. I decided
that if I was going to fall apart I might as well do it in the army, so I
waived my 100 percent and went back in the army.

While in the army I volunteered for service in ETO (European Theater
of Operation) and like in a WW II cartoon, they thought I meant the
Eastern Tip of Okinawa, and I came out on orders for the Pacific. As I
was going up the gang-plank on the ship, my name was called out over
the PA system. I answered and was told to come back down and when I
did I was handed a subpoena from the Federal Court in San Francisco,
ordering me to appear as a witness on behalf of Tokyo Rose. I knew nothing that would either help or hurt her case but I was able to miss out on
another Far East assignment. A number of the other Bunker Hill boys
were also subpoenaed, including two Australians—Maj. "Bill" Cousens
and Mickey Parkyns. Maj. William Cousens was tried for treason by the
Australian Government. He was acquitted but was stripped of all military
rank and pay.

The army released me to the court, which paid me $5 per diem, and I
went back to Camp Stoneman to draw my regular pay each month. I had
two sisters married to sailors living in Alameda and I stayed with them
and also in the YMCA. Mickey and I had a great time making all the bars

in San Francisco and we even were granted time by the defense lawyer, Wayne Collins,[2] to hitchhike back to Texas.[3]

Contrary to the impression that my story might have left, I never became an alcoholic. It took me many years to overcome my wartime experiences to where I could function normally. I make no apologies for my actions during or after wartime hostilities. I am bursting with pride to be an American, and I enjoy to the fullest the blessings it offers. I am comfortable with knowing that I have paid my dues to be called an American and I stand ready to defend my America if that ever again becomes necessary.

"God bless America!"
Frank "Foo" Fujita

2. A San Francisco attorney, Collins was not only Iva Toguri's lawyer in the "Tokyo Rose" trial, but also represented Japanese-Americans in many of their efforts to gain redress from the U.S. Government. Masayo Duus, *Tokyo Rose: Orphan of the Pacific* (Tokyo and New York: Kodansha International, 1979), passim.

3. Released from the army in order to help support his parents, Fujita was called to active duty once more as a reservist during the Korean War. He then resumed civilian life and eventually carved out a career as an illustrator for the Air Force. He finally retired on a disability, the aftereffects of his mistreatment as a POW. He is still hampered with back problems resulting from the terrible beating he received in Nagasaki, and has had one knee replacement and now needs another, additional reminders of the brutal Nagasaki shipyards. These disabilities, however, have not prevented Fujita and his wife from travelling in their motorhome to just about every state in the Union.

U.S. seal handcarved by Frank "Foo" Fujita at Ft. Sill, Oklahoma circa
1954–55. (U.S. Army Photograph)

INDEX

ABDA Command, 61, 62n
Abilene High School, 169
Abilene Reporter News, 11–12, 79, 111–12, 132–33, 282
Abilene, Texas, 33–34, 59, 102, 112, 132–33, 169, 170, 265, 282, 299, 321, 342, 344
Adam Had Four Sons, 307
Admiral Hughes (US Army Transport), 332
Alabang, Philippines, 324, 325
Alameda, California, 357
Aleutian Islands, 172
Allen, Hollis, 75, 79, 82, 83, 84, 87, 95, 96, 106, 107, 115, 121, 123, 171, 182
Allied Far East Command, 70
Amboina (island), 70n
American Red Cross, 214, 215, 216, 218, 224, 233, 246, 248, 250, 253, 261, 278, 280, 281, 295, 298, 304, 323
Ando (Japanese soldier), 250, 266
Anzio, Italy, xv
Arafura Sea, 52
Army Air Corps, 24
Army Air Forces, 62
Astarita, Joseph, 196, 197, 221
"Auld Lang Syne," 242
Australia, 48–51, 100, 196, 212
"Ave Maria," 225, 291

B Battery, 27
B-17 (Flying Fortress), 57, 63, 67, 69
B-24, 284, 291, 293, 300, 307

B-29, xi, xiv, xvii, 230, 234, 243, 244, 246, 247, 248, 250, 251, 253n, 261, 262n, 263, 264, 266, 268, 269n, 270–71, 274n, 281n, 282, 284, 287n, 291, 293, 294n, 297, 298n, 300n, 301, 307, 311, 312
B-32, 307n
Bali (island), 52, 53, 67n, 69, 70n
Bandoeng, Java, 85n
Bangkok, Thailand, 230, 239
Bantam Bay, Java, 73
Barnes, Don H., 63, 212
Bataan, Philippines, 218, 324
Batavia, Java, 70, 108
Battle of Soerabaja, 76
Battle of the Java Sea, 71n, 73, 87n
Beethoven's Fifth Symphony, 291
Beethoven's Ninth Symphony, 291
Benjo Honcho, 237–38
Bicycle Camp. *See* POW camps
Bingham, Jack E., 63, 212
Blackburn, A. S., 71n, 85n, 108n
Blackforce (Australian-British unit), 71n, 73n, 87n, 223n
Blankenship, Bowen, 263
Blankenship, O. T., 263
Blankenship, Ruby, 263
"Blue Eyes," 214
"Blue Star" restaurant, 263
Boso, Japan, 297
Boise (cruiser), 51, 52
Bonin Islands, 260
Boone, Goel, xviii
Borneo (island), 70n, 109n, 113

Boyington, Gregory ("Pappy"), 309
Brett, George H., 52n
Brisbane, Australia, ix, xiii, xvi
British Civil Service, 196
Brooks General Hospital (San
    Antonio, Texas), 345
"Brownie" (dog), 222, 236, 244,
    295
Brownwood, Texas, 18, 23
Bruce, Donald, 196, 221, 226,
    257–58
"Buck" (rabbit), 236, 244
Buitenzorg, Java, 223
"Bull" (Japanese sergeant), 124
Bunka district (Tokyo, Japan), 192
Bunka Gakuin Kanda. See POW
    camps
Bunka POW Camp. See POW
    camps
Bunka Tram Station, 212
"Bunker Hill" boys, 203, 238, 249,
    347, 357
Burma, 109n, 110, 122
Burma-Thailand railway, 109

C-54, 321
Camp Barkeley (Abilene, Texas), 23,
    26, 33
Camp Bowie (Brownwood, Texas),
    23, 25, 26, 34, 63, 81, 170, 263
Camp Fukuoka #2. See POW camps
Camp Pendleton (California), 340
Camp Roberts (California), 41
Camp Stoneman, 357
Camp Wolters (Mineral Wells,
    Texas), 24
Cape York, Australia, 51
Catawba American Indian, 9
Celebes (island), 70n

Cement, Oklahoma, 9
Ceplinski, Frank, 96
Changi military base (Singapore),
    113, 116, 120
Changi Prison. See POW camps
Chiba Peninsula (Japan), 294n, 297
Chickasha, Oklahoma, 9
China, 64, 124, 234, 243, 247, 265
Choate, Rufus, 95
Choctaw Nation, Indian Territory, 9
"Christian Marine House," 83, 87
Civil Liberties Act of 1988, 356n
Civilian Conservation Corps, 18n
Clark Field (Philippines), 57, 218
Clavell, James, 122
Collins, Wayne, 358
Corregidor, Philippines, 218, 225,
    247, 324, 353
Cousens, Charles William, 207, 218,
    226, 235–36, 260, 265, 277, 289,
    290, 306, 357
Cox, Williston, 213, 220, 226, 252–
    54, 264, 266, 271, 272, 275, 289,
    293, 298, 300, 303, 307, 308, 309
Cranmer, Vic, 294
Cranmer, Wayne, 217, 241, 283, 294,
    340
Cumberlidge, Ike, 79, 82, 103

D Battery, 109, 214
Dai Ichi Hotel (Tokyo, Japan), 206,
    277, 278n
Dai Nichi Maru (ship), 110
Darwin, Australia, 70
Davis, L. W., 80, 81
DC-4, 321n
Derryberry, Mr., 321
DeWitt, John L., 354
Dodds, Darwin, 237, 246, 285, 292

"Dog robbers" (soldier servants), 116

Domoto, Kaji, 199, 251, 270, 271, 277, 289, 290, 292, 298n, 299, 306, 307

Donaho, Eddie, 68, 76, 77, 78, 96, 142, 153, 162, 163

Dooley, Tim, 239, 275

Doolittle, James, 230, 242, 279

"Dora" (substitute name), 169–71, 217, 267, 294

Dorsey, George A., 291

Douglass, Griff, 122

Doyle, Mrs., 288

Dunn, Ben ("Dynamite Dunn"), 41

Dutch East Indies Army, 196

Dutch East Indies, ix, 52n, 62, 70, 85

E Battery. *See* 36th Infantry Division

Eagles. *See* Japanese fighter pilots

East China Sea, 124

Eggert, Maria, 225, 291

Eighth Air Force, 279n

Eisenhower, Milton S., 125, 355

El Reno, Oklahoma, 7, 9, 11, 13, 16, 17, 20, 82, 294, 340

Electra Neon Sign Company, 247

Electra News, 239, 247

Electra, Texas, 239, 247

Elliott, Ella (grandmother), 6

Elliott, Herbert Lee. *See* Fujita, Herbert Lee

Elliott, Ida Pearl (mother). *See* Fujita, Ida Pearl Elliott

England, Mr., 14

Eppington, Mr., 288

Eppington, Mrs., 288

Eretenwetan, Java, 73

Etheridge, Mrs., 241

Etheridge, Conally ("Big Ed," "Moko"), 328

Eubank, Eugene L., 57–58, 70–71

Evans, Pete, 96, 97, 131, 283

F Battery, 63, 66, 71, 137, 261

F-13A, 243n, 244n, 246n, 248n, 251n

F4F, 291, 311

F4U, 291, 311

Fantasia, 243

Federal Bureau of Investigation, 352

Fender, Joe, 133

Fifth Column, 61

Fifth Fleet Task Force Fifty-eight, 260n, 261n, 262n

56th Division, 73

"Fighting Texas" division. *See* 36th Infantry Division

Fiji Islands, xvi, 48

"Fish Paste" (Dutch doctor), 142

Flores (island), 52

Ford, Gerald R., 207

Ford, Mr., 14

Fort Lewis (Washington), 335, 338, 339

Fort Mason (California), 35

Fort McDowell (California), 36, 37

Fort Sam Houston (San Antonio, Texas), 342, 345, 347, 348

Fort Sill (Oklahoma), 9, 359

Fort Worth Star Telegram, 104–05

Fort Worth, Texas, 7, 170, 341

48th Division, 73, 76n

45th Infantry Division, 23, 33

442d Regimental Combat Team, 239n, 240, 247

4th Army, 345

France, 239

French Indo-China, 123

Fujita, Frank, artwork, viii, 12, 38, 43, 60, 72, 99, 130, 146, 166, 175, 181, 210, 249, 359; birth, xiii, 9; childhood, 9–11; crossing the equator, 45–46; diary entries, 2, 32, 38, 56, 86, 90–91, 114, 136, 154, 168, 188, 210, 232, 256, 276, 296, 318, 336; ESP experiences, 116; first imprisoned (Jaarmarkt), 95; Japanese heritage discovered, 155–67; maps drawn, 32, 74, 76, 190, 200; medals won, 329, 330; nicknames, 204, 328; offers diary to government, 352; personal phonetic alphabet, 86, 99; photographs, 4, 6, 25, 127, 220, 221, 313, 314, 325, 339, 343; return to Texas, 340; return to US, 334; staff cartoonist, 13

Fujita, Frank, Sr., xiii, 3, 6–9, 12, 16–18, 89n, 111, 133, 191, 217, 223, 239, 247, 254, 267, 298, 343, 356

Fujita, Freda Mae (Rita) (sister), 6, 81, 111, 191

Fujita, Herbert Lee (brother), 6, 11, 81, 191, 217, 239, 240, 247, 298

Fujita, Ida Pearl Elliott (mother), xiii, xv, 6–9, 12, 54–55, 80, 82, 133, 191, 216–17, 223, 239, 241, 247, 254, 267, 288, 294, 342, 343

Fujita, Naomi (sister), 6, 79–82, 111, 191, 298

Fujita, Patricia Ruth (sister), 6, 81, 111, 191, 217, 239–41, 247, 254, 267, 288, 298, 342

Fujita, Tsuneji (father). See Fujita, Frank, Sr.

Fukuoka. See POW camps

Fung, Eddie, 71

Futsu, Japan, 293

"Galloping Ghost of the Java Coast." See USS Houston

Garland, Hugh ("Judy"), 41, 68, 76, 78, 96

Geneva Convention, 85n, 87n, 103, 106n, 214, 278

Geronimo, 9

Ghost Goes West, 275

Gilbert Islands, 196, 199

Ginza (Tokyo, Japan), 223

"go aheads" (shoes), 142

Go (Japanese office staff), 288

Goenoengsari Golf Club (Soerabaja, Java), 74

Gone With the Wind, 241, 242, 263

"Goodnight Mother," 247

Grew, Ambassador, 302

Guam, 64, 144, 237, 302

Gulf of Carpenteria, 52

Hachioji, Japan, 297n

Hague Convention (1907), 85n

Haltom City, Texas, 170

Hamamoto, Lt. ("Hamhock"), 197, 204, 211, 216, 219

Hasegawa, Chuo, 227–29

Hatheral, A. M., 144

Hayasaka, Mr., 222–23, 237, 254, 257, 290, 298, 307

Headquarters Battery, 26th Field Artillery Brigade, 50, 59

Headquarters, 1st Battalion, 263

Heleman, Donald, 123, 134, 137, 146, 156, 299

Henshaw, George ("Bucky"), 196, 206, 209, 220, 221, 298n

"*Hi no Maru* Hour" (The Circle of the Sun Hour), 195, 196, 202, 206, 212, 214n, 218, 219, 238, 274, 284, 287, 302
Hifumi, Maj., 291, 306, 307
Hiroshima, Japan, xviii, 298, 299, 300, 303
Hishikari, Mr., 223
Hitler, Adolf, 20, 273
HMAS *Perth*, 48, 73, 109
HMS *Bloemfontein*, 42, 51, 52, 123
Hoblitt, Fred, 237, 251, 253, 260, 266, 298
Holder, Joe, 67
Hong Kong, 64, 279
Honolulu, Hawaii, 42
Honshu, Japan, 185, 262, 287n, 294n, 297n, 298, 300n
"Hopes and Views for 1944," 212
Hornet (carrier), 230
Horrigan, Maj., 182
Hoso. See Nihon Hoso Kyoku
"Humanity Calls." *See Hi no Maru*
"Humming Birds," 33, 34
"Hungarian Rhapsody #2," 225, 241, 291

Ibaraki, Japan, 294, 297
Ie Shima (island), 306n
Ikeda, Norizane, 211
Immigration and Naturalization Act of 1952, 357
Imperial Headquarters (Tokyo, Japan), 204, 206
Imperial Iron and Steel Works (Yawata, Kyushu, Japan), 234n
"Imperial Marines," 162
Imperial Palace (Tokyo, Japan), 192, 200, 209, 254, 262, 270, 281, 282, 284, 310

Ince, Wallace, 207, 265, 277, 290, 308, 316, 317
Italy, 239
Iwo Jima (island), 246n, 260n, 261n, 262, 269, 291, 295, 297, 306
Izu, Japan, 297

Jaarmarkt, 95–107, 322
Japan, 109, 122, 125
Japanese-Americans, 124–25, 358n
Japanese Broadcasting Corporation. *See Nihon Hoso Kyoku*
Japanese fighter pilots (Eagles), 259, 299
Japanese government, 103
Japanese surrender, 304–06
Jaroet, Java, 223
Java, ix, x, xi, xiv, xvi, xvii, 57–84, 102, 149, 196, 212, 218, 223, 227, 237, 280, 283, 302, 309, 329, 343
Javanese alphabet, 86, 90–91, 98–99
"Jeeps" (Japanese), 214, 216, 218, 224, 226, 230, 250, 258, 261, 270, 275, 278, 280, 286, 288, 290, 303, 326, 331
JOAK radio (Tokyo, Japan), 224, 284
Johnson, Earl, 133
Johnson, Mrs. Earl, 133
Joint Declaration of the Powers, 305

Kalbfliesch, Edwin, 196, 199, 202, 218–19, 220, 221, 235, 322
Kamakura Maru (ship), 123
Kanda, Tokyo, 352
Katakana (Japanese writing), 233
Kawasaki, Japan, 291n, 294, 297
Keijo, Korea, 191

Keith, Ben C., Jr., 62, 83, 84, 87, 89–93, 96, 106, 107, 123, 133, 283

Keith, Ben C., Sr., 133, 283

Keith, Mrs. Ben C., Sr., 133

Kid (POW), 221

Killian, George, 79, 103

Kimball, Harry M., 352

King Rat (novel), 122

Kobe, Japan, 266

Koimai, Capt., 194

Koiso Cabinet (Japanese government), 268

Korea, 125, 191

Korean War, 358n

Koyagi Shima, Japan, 125

Kragan, Java, 73

Krueger, Walter, 28n

Kutsu Nashi (crew), 141–42

Kyushu, Japan, 125, 183n, 185, 230, 234, 300n

Lake Charles, Louisiana, 30–31

Lawson, Ace, 261

Lawton, Oklahoma, xiii, 9

Le Triumphant (cruiserette), 48

"Let's Slap the Jap Off the Map," 80

Life magazine, 323

Light, Newton, 191–92, 196, 202, 204, 221, 290

Lives of the Bengal Lancers, 307

Lombok (island), 52

Lombok Strait, 52

London, Jack, 227

Lost Battalion, xi, xv, 36, 103, 104, 223, 247, 252, 261, 280, 322, 324, 343, 344, 346, 347, 355, 356; article, 212; Association, 343; Book, 322; Club, 356; Day, 344; Museum (Decatur, Texas), 103; Reunion, 342–44

Louisiana War Maneuvers, 105

Lucas, Herb, 137, 146, 156

Lumpkin, "Bo" ("Corky"), 59, 70, 121

MacArthur, Douglas, 49n, 306, 319n, 324

McCray, Gaylen ("Mack"), 184–85, 189, 192

McCullough, Roy, 15, 24, 170, 223, 283

McMullen, Jim, 105

McNaughton, Jack, 196, 209, 220, 221, 226

Madigan General Hospital (Washington), 335, 338, 345

Madoera (island), 53, 212

Maher, Arthur L., 309

Malang, Java, 54, 62, 64, 65, 69, 212

Malaya, 113, 117

Malkin, R. A., 144

Mama San, 222, 308

Man's Own Show—Civilization, 291

Manchuria, China, 280n, 300n

Manila, Philippines, 306, 324

Marblehead (cruiser), 51, 52

Mariana Islands, 234, 243, 246

Martinez, Jimmy, 223, 237, 289–90, 298, 314, 336, 339, 340, 345, 346

Martinez, Ramon, 223, 237, 290, 298, 314, 336, 340, 345

Marx Brothers, 273

Melville Island, 52

Merak, Java, 73

Merkel, Texas, 170

Meyer, Dillon S., 125n

"Mighty Mo." *See* USS *Missouri*

Mitsubishi factories (Tokyo, Japan), 268

Monkey Fur Tobacco, 138–39

"Moonlight Sonata," 218, 291
Moses, Ronald, 41, 122
Mount Fujiyama, 197, 233
Mr. Smith Goes to Washington, 279
Murayama, Tomatsu, 204–05, 288
Murphy, Frank, 354
Muruyama, Masao, 85n
Musashino, Tokyo, 269n
Mussolini, Benito, 273
Myer, Dillon S., 355

Nagasaki, Japan, xiii, xiv, xvi, xviii, 3, 5, 125, 139, 157, 174, 183, 189, 191, 201, 222, 224, 230, 331, 348, 357, 358n
Nagoya, Japan, 264, 266
Nakajima aircraft works (Tokyo, Japan), 268, 269
Nazarene College (Bethany, Oklahoma), 298
Netherlands East Indies Army, 184
Netherlands East Indies. *See* Dutch East Indies
Neutrality Pact (Soviet Union-Japan), 279
New Guinea, 51, 172n, 213, 302
New York Times, 353
Night at the Opera, 273
Nihon Hoso Kyoku (Japan Broadcasting Corporation), 202, 209, 212, 215, 217, 241, 252, 254, 259, 263, 265, 287
19th Bomb Group, 57, 62, 70
Nippon Times (Japan), 259
Nisei, 139, 182, 196, 199, 201, 207, 220, 279, 287
"No Shoe" crew, 141–42
North China Marines, 185
North China, 191

Odlin, Walter, 237, 244, 257, 258
Of Mice and Men, 214
Okinawa (island), 268n, 300n, 302, 321, 324
Oklahoma National Guard, 28
"Old Man," 159–67
"Old Settlers' Reunion" (Buffalo Gap, Texas), 170
Olympic Peninsula (Washington), 333
Omori Camp. *See* POW camps
141st Infantry, 24
131st Field Artillery. *See* 36th Infantry Division
132d Field Artillery, 34
133d Field Artillery, 34
Onishi, Mr. (*nisei*), 182
Ortiz, Luz, 103, 179
Osaka, Japan, 266
Otaka (camp C.O.), 237, 241–42, 290
Ozaki (*nisei*), 233–34, 279

P-40, 67
P-51, 262n, 268, 269n, 274, 284, 291, 295n, 297n, 300
Palawan Island, 233n
Papa San, 222, 308
Parkyns, Kenneth ("Mickey"), 196, 215, 221, 225, 245, 246, 250, 251, 270, 278, 279, 280, 285–86, 287, 292, 298n, 357
Patton, George S., 29
"Peanut Vendor," 242
Pearl Harbor, Hawaii, ix, xvi, 47, 125, 203, 248
Pearson, Harry, 213, 220, 221, 224–25, 226, 258, 314
Perez, Mickey, 76, 261
Petrified Forest, 307

Philippine Islands, ix, xiii, xvi, 36, 123, 196, 211, 302, 335, 237, 351
Philippine University, 211
"Photo Joe" reconnaissance aircraft, 259, 261, 263, 265, 266, 268, 271, 275, 281, 282, 284, 291, 295
Pike, Lt. Col., 191
Plant, Howard, 83, 119, 131, 148
"Plum," 31, 33–55, 57
Port Darwin, Australia, 52
"Postman Calls" (radio program), 214, 218, 223, 284, 287, 302, 303
Potsdam Declaration, 295n, 301n, 320n
POW Camps; Bicycle Camp (Batavia, Indonesia), 108–10, 149, 171; *Bunka Gakuin Kanda* ("Bunker Hill"), xiv, 60, 193, 194, 198, 200, 207, 209–30, 216n, 235, 236, 239, 260, 264, 270, 274, 277, 281, 292, 310, 351, 354; Camp Fukuoka #2 (Nagasaki, Japan), xiv, 117, 125–35, 183, 184, 189, 215, 237, 279, 288, 322, 346; Changi Prison (Singapore), 116, 122n, 149, 212; Omori Camp (Tokyo Bay, Japan), xiv, xviii, 1, 3, 5, 186, 187–208, 289, 307, 308, 309, 312, 313, 314, 315, 317; Shinagawa Camp (Tokyo, Japan), 187, 235; Tokyo No. 2805 Camp, 216
Powers, Cecil, 148, 174, 345
"Project J," 324, 328, 332, 335, 342
Provoo, John David, 191–92, 196, 199, 202, 218–19, 220, 221, 225, 251, 260, 289, 290, 307, 308, 309, 312, 316, 317, 333, 352, 353
Puget Sound, 334

Quellé, Larry, 196, 314

R.A.A.F., 196
Rabaul, New Britain, 302, 309
radio programs. *See Hi no Maru Hour*, The Postman Calls, Zero Hour
Rafalovitch, Danny, 120–21
"Ragtime Cowboy Joe," 214
Rains Came, 289, 308
reconnaissance aircraft. *See* "Photo Joe"
Red Cross, 117, 134, 152–53, 171
Reyes, Norman, 207n, 277
Rickert, Albert, 213, 220, 221, 272
Robertson, Warren, 75, 96
Robinson, Willie, 103
Rock Island Rail Road, 7, 17
Rogers, Novle, 76
Roosevelt, Franklin D., 124, 143n, 208, 219, 270
"Rosary," 218
Royal Air Force, 61; mascot, 122–23
Royal Army, 213
Royal British Army, 196
Russia. *See* Soviet Union
Ryukyu Islands, 124, 306

Saipan (island), 243, 246, 301
Sakakida, Richard, x
Salerno, Italy, xv
Salvation Army, 106
San Antonio, Texas, 22, 342, 345
San Francisco, California, 35, 37, 266, 277, 340, 357
Sanno Hotel (Tokyo, Japan), 278
Savell, Bob, 218
SBD (dive bomber), 291, 311
Schenk, Nickolas, 184–85, 196, 197, 211, 218, 245, 275, 314

Scullyville, Arkansas, 9
Searle, Albert C., 51, 62, 85n, 108–09, 149, 171
Seattle, Washington, 334, 336, 339, 340
2d Army, 27, 33
Service Battery, 328
"Sgt. Teeth" ("Chinless Wonder"), 182
Shanghai, China, 192
Shattles, Steve, 196, 199, 221, 238, 272
Shaw, H. T., 131
Sheppard Field (Wichita Falls, Texas), 81
Shikoku, Japan, 297
Shingawa Camp. *See* POW camps
Shinagawa, Tokyo, 235
Shinto religion, 192
Sikh Indians, 116
Simpson, Roger W., xviin, 315n
Singapore, xiv, 64, 70n, 109, 113, 118, 123, 149, 196, 207, 213, 283, 302
Singosari Airfield (Malang, Java), 54, 57, 58n, 62, 63n, 66n, 70, 71, 75, 107
Sitwell, H. D. W., 85n
61st Field Artillery, 34
Slone, Golda, 133
Slone, Ruben, 133, 214
Smith, Frederick Ferguson, 3, 237, 246, 254, 257, 259, 269, 278, 280, 285, 286, 289, 298, 304, 307, 308, 312, 314, 316
Soerabaja, Java, viii, 52–55, 57, 71, 72, 76n, 82, 87, 96
Solomon Islands, 172n
South China Sea, 113, 123
South Pacific, 196

Soviet Union, 279, 300, 304
Spalding, Henry, 75, 96
Sparkman, Leon F., 66, 261
Steamships, SS *Admiral Halstead*, 42; SS *Benevolence*, 316; SS *Coast Farmer*, 42; SS *Holbrook* (*General Holbrook*), 42, 51n, 52n; SS *Liberty*, 52; SS *Meigs*, 42
"Stage Builders" (crew #8), 146
Stevenson, Coke, 344
Strait of Juan de Fuca, 333
Streeter, Mark L., 196, 202, 204, 208, 219, 221, 225, 270, 271, 272, 275, 278, 279–80, 287, 295, 307, 308, 309, 312, 316, 317, 333, 354
Stubbs, Mrs. S. S., 133
Stubbs, Robert L., 132, 133, 214, 283
Stubbs, S. S., 133
Sumatra (island), 70n, 109n, 113
Sumba (island), 52
Sumbawa (island), 52
Sunda Straits, 73, 85
Suva, Fiji Islands, 48
Suzuki, Admiral, 268
Syrett, Victor, 144

Tacoma, Washington, 335, 340
Taipei, Formosa 124
Taiwan, 191, 280
Taniyama, Lt., 211
Task Force Thirty-eight, 291n, 300n, 303n
Task Group 30.6, 313n
"Taskforce South Pacific," 46
Tencho-setsu (Heaven-long festival), 151–52
ter Poorten, Hein, 85n
Texas National Guard, ix, xiii, xv, 15–16, 23, 107, 169–70, 321, 328

Thailand, 110
Tharp, Blucher S., 51, 109n, 122, 280, 287
Thin Man, 275
3d Army, 27, 28, 33
Third Fleet, 307n, 313
38th Division, 73
31st Infantry, 218
36th Infantry Division (T Patch) 131st Field Artillery, 2d Battalion, E Battery, xiii, xiv, xv, 16, 20, 24, 26, 28, 33, 34, 36, 39, 41, 50, 52, 71, 73, 81, 87, 96, 100, 101, 102, 104, 107, 108, 109, 110, 116, 123, 129, 149, 171, 178, 179, 218, 223, 230, 237, 247, 261, 283, 317, 322, 328, 336, 343, 345, 346
Thompson, Burton C., 192n
Thursday Island, 51
Timor (island), 52, 70n
Timor Sea, 52
Togo, Admiral, 262
Toguri, Iva, 207n, 278n, 358n
Toko Oen Restaurant (Malang, Java), 64
Tokyo Bay, 187, 313
"Tokyo Deal," 191, 192
Tokyo No. 2805 Camp. *See* POW camps
Tokyo Rose, 196, 207, 277, 287, 357, 358
Tokyo, Japan, xvii, 1, 186, 207, 214, 223, 230, 231, 234, 242, 243, 244, 246, 247, 248, 252, 253, 254, 257, 260–75, 281, 282, 283, 287, 289, 291, 292, 295, 297, 300, 301, 307, 308, 309, 312, 315, 332, 352
Topping, "Mother," 203–04, 209
Torres Strait, 51, 52
Truman, Harry S., 349, 350

Tsuneishi, Shigetsugu, 204–06, 207n, 219n, 277
Turner, Jack, 133
Twentieth Air Force, 230n, 234n, 246n, 258n, 297n, 300n
21st Air Flotilla, 63n
29th Replacement Depot, 324
29th Repo Depot, 329
26th Field Artillery Brigade, 31, 33–55

Uemura, Seitaro, 206
United Nations, 267n
United Service Organizations. *See* USO
Uno, Kazumaru ("Buddy"), 201–02, 206, 211–13, 218, 220, 222, 223, 224, 229, 231, 241, 270, 292
US Air Force, 213
US Army Reserve, 196
US Asiatic Fleet, 47n
US Marine Corps Reserves, 213
US Navy Reserve, 196
USNT *Chaumont*, 42, 48
USO, 332
United States Steamships, USS *Gosselin*, 1, 317; USS *Houston*, 51, 73, 87n, 109, 110, 120, 122, 343; USS *Missouri*, 318, 319n; USS *Monitor*, 318, 319; USS *Niagara*, ix, 42; USS *Pensacola*, ix, 42, 48; USS *Republic*, 36, 38, 42, 44, 47, 48, 333

Valdez, Pancho, 179
Vancouver Island, British Columbia, Canada, 333
Victoria, British Columbia, Canada, 333

Vladavostok, Soviet Union, 246
"Voice of Freedom," 207n

WACs, 320, 338–40
Wake Island, 64, 185, 192, 196, 213,
    237, 302
Walker, Fred L., 28n
War Crimes trials, xviii, 352, 353,
    357–58
War Department, 19n, 103–04,
    134–35, 352
War Relocation Authority, 124, 355
Warm Springs, Georgia, 270n
Washington Post, 354
Washington, D. C., 239, 254, 267
Watanabe, Sgt. ("the Ani-
    mal," "Bird," "Wily Bird,"
    "Mr. Adam"), 188–91
Watson, Thomas, 133
Wavell, Archibald P., 61
When God Laughs, 227
White, Roger, 75, 131
"Whitie," 222, 236, 244
Wichita Falls, Texas, 343
Williams, David A., 103, 322

Williams, George, 196, 199, 201,
    202–03, 218, 235, 322
Williams, O. B., 96, 218
"Willie" (substitute name), 170, 217,
    241, 254, 290, 294
Wisener, Jack, 213, 220, 221, 293,
    347
Wisman, Edward, 261
WOG Tobacco, 138
Wolf, Ernest, 93–94, 106
Women's Army Corps. *See* WACs
Woodall, Monroe D. ("Bo,"
    "Corky"), 115, 171, 178, 184
Woods, David ("Bear"), 322
Woolworth, F. W., Co., 79–81

Yawata, Japan, 183, 184, 185, 234
Yokohama, Japan, 271, 284n, 307
Yokosuka, Japan, 293

"Zero Hour" radio program, 206,
    207n, 277
Zeros ("Zekes"), 67, 69, 70, 175,
    243, 244, 250, 251, 253, 261, 268,
    281, 307, 309